Recruitment

Science and Practice

Recruitment

Science and Practice

JAMES A. BREAUGH

University of Missouri-St. Louis

Kent Series in

HUMAN RESOURCE MANAGEMENT

Series Consulting Editor: Richard W. Beatty
Institute of Management and Labor Relations at Rutgers University

PWS-KENT Publishing Company
BOSTON

PWS-KENT
Publishing Company

20 Park Plaza
Boston, Massachusetts 02116

Editor: Rolf A. Janke
Assistant Editor: Marnie Pommett
Production Editor: S. London
Interior/Cover Designer: Julie Gecha
Interior Illustrator: Lisa Sparks
Compositor: Graphic Composition, Inc.
Manufacturing Coordinator: Lisa Flanagan
Text Printer/Binder: Courier/West
Cover Printer: New England Book Components, Inc.

PWS-KENT Publishing Company is a division of Wadsworth, Inc.

Printed in the United States of America.

1 2 3 4 5 6 7 8 9—96 95 94 93 92

Library of Congress Cataloging-in-Publication Data
Breaugh, James A.
   Recruitment Science and Practice/James A. Breaugh.
      p. cm.—(Kent human resource management series)
   Includes bibliographical references and index.
   ISBN 0-534-91943-X
   1. Employees—Recruiting.   I. Title.   II. Series.
   HF5549.5.R44B695   1992   91–41265
   658.3'111—dc20   CIP

To Gail, Mark, and Laura—
My Three Best Friends

Series Preface

It is with considerable pride that we offer an expanded Kent Human Resource Management Series from PWS-KENT Publishing Company. The original four books on federal regulation, human resource costing, compensation, and performance appraisal were a great success, as evidenced by both academic and trade sales. We thank you for your support of this series.

The first revision of the series offered significant updating and expansion of the four original texts. We added three new books to the series, in benefits, recruitment, and human resource information systems. We are currently developing a new series entry in human resource planning, and plan to add titles in areas such as executive development, human resource strategy, and collective bargaining.

As organizations face the new composition created by global markets, deregulation, and advancing technology, they are beginning to "resize," and they are looking at human resources as a source of competitive advantage. Preparing to gain, sustain, or regain competitive advantage raises concerns over the fact that human resources are indeed an organization's most expensive and least well-managed resource. Certainly, organizations have designed and engineered systems that include specific planning and control methods and tools for material resources, financial resources, information systems, and time management. The new competition, however, recognizes the need for better utilization of human resources. Ultimately, this series is designed to have an impact on the practice of human resources in the contemporary economic environment. Implementing these approaches to solving human resource problems will be the ultimate proof of its success.

Many people have helped in the development of this important series. I would like to thank Rolf Janke, Kathleen Tibbetts, and Marnie Pommett for their enthusiastic support of the continued revision.

Richard W. Beatty

Preface

Twenty years ago, the topic of employee recruitment received relatively little attention in either the academic or the practitioner literatures. Today, both bodies of literature are filled with articles that address recruitment-related topics (the use of realistic job previews, job advertising, the choice of recruiters, the importance of the timing of recruitment actions, job candidate decision making, and so on). Twenty years ago, most organizations viewed recruiting employees as a simple, straightforward personnel department activity. Today, organizations realize that, if done improperly, recruitment actions can result in lawsuits, the loss of government contracts, harm to their public image, and an inability to fill positions with qualified employees. Stated more directly, over the past two decades organizations have come to appreciate how the attainment of their strategic business objectives can be influenced by the way they recruit employees. As a result of this realization, line managers and even executives have become increasingly involved in recruitment campaigns. And, although the recognition of recruitment as an important human resource activity has increased dramatically over the past twenty years, predicted labor shortages in the next decade make it likely that recruitment will become even more important. Simply stated, if an organization is unable to recruit a sufficient number of qualified job candidates, it will be unable to compete with other organizations that *are* able to recruit effectively.

This book is intended for practitioners, researchers, and students who have an interest in the topic of recruitment. In terms of the practitioner, this book is based on the assumption that in order to make intelligent recruitment decisions—how to word a job advertisement, at which colleges to recruit, etc.—an individual with recruitment responsibilities must understand the perspective of a job candidate. Furthermore, this individual must be knowledgeable concerning such government regulations as Title VII, Executive Order 11246, tort claims of fraud, and others that apply to recruitment. This text provides a practitioner with numerous examples of the recruitment actions, both good and bad, of real organizations. This text should also be of interest to the researcher. In addition to reviewing the current state of knowledge on several recruitment topics, issues meriting future research are highlighted and suggestions for improving on traditional research strategies are offered. For students, the topic of employee recruitment should be of particular interest because in all likelihood they will be job hunting in the not too distant future. The material covered in this text may help them as they interact with organizations in trying to locate a position that is "right" for them.

In closing, I would like to acknowledge the contributions of three groups of people. At PWS-KENT Publishing Company, the efforts and particularly the patience of Rolf Janke, Kathleen Tibbetts, S. London, and Marnie Pommett deserve recognition. I could not have asked for a more supportive group as I struggled to complete this text. I also want to recognize those colleagues who provided expert advice on this text. The constructive comments of Robert Bretz of Cornell University, Eugene Buccini of Western Connecticut State University, Susan Taylor of the University of Maryland, Sara Rynes of the University of Iowa, and Thomas Lee of the University of Washington were most helpful. Jean Caldwell, here at the University of Missouri-St. Louis, provided excellent editorial advice. Finally, I want to thank my family, who in their own unique ways contributed to this book. My wife, Gail, read numerous iterations of each chapter and let me know when jargon had displaced clarity. More important, she provided the inspiration to keep going. And if it weren't for my children, Mark and Laura, this book would have been finished several months sooner. I want to thank them for constantly reminding me that life is too short to let work drive out the enjoyment of watching your children grow up.

James A. Breaugh
St. Louis

Contents

1

An Overview of
Employee Recruitment

Our greatest resource is our people.[1]

Whether you are interested in creating a first-rate symphony orchestra or a skilled surgical team, a Super Bowl contender or a top-notch sales force, a superior university faculty or a conscientious airplane maintenance crew, it all starts with quality people. After years of glossing over the importance of the "people factor" as a primary determinant of organizational success, employers are finally recognizing the value of employees as a crucial resource, as reflected in the quote above.

There are many indications that increased importance is being attached to the human component of an organization. For example, many organizations now refer to employee-oriented activities as "human resource" (HR) activities rather than as "personnel" functions. Another manifestation of this growing recognition that the human element is essential for organizational functioning is the shift of many traditional "personnel" functions out of the personnel (human resources) department. In many organizations, what once were viewed as traditional personnel department activities (career development, for instance) now are seen as part of a line manager's job. In addition, at AT&T and many other companies, managers from human resources departments are now directly involved in what once were considered exclusively line management responsibilities (e.g., the development of strategic business plans). This new importance being attached to human resource management (HRM) activities is also reflected in recent changes in the graduate curricula of many prestigious M.B.A. programs. For example, Harvard Business School has created an entire course that deals with employee-oriented issues from the perspective of a line manager—a course, it should be noted, that is not merely offered, but is required of all students.[2] Another example of the significance being attached to human resources today is the fact that in many organizations individuals are required to have graduate degrees in the human resource area before they will be considered for positions in the HR department. One final indicator of the growing importance with which employers have come to view the HR function is the fact that the salaries paid to HR professionals have increased substantially in recent years. For example, according to Bennett (1990), between 1985 and 1990 the average compensation of personnel managers increased faster than the compensation of fifteen other positions that were examined, including those of CEO, plant manager, systems analyst, and market research manager.

Although there are several reasons (e.g., changing work force demographics) for the recent attention being given to human resource issues by organizations,[3] most experts agree that a fundamental cause of this increased attention is the growing awareness of the "bottom line" consequences of such HRM decisions as establishing a "pay for performance" system. Not only have HRM decisions been linked to differences in employee absenteeism, turnover, performance, and morale, but these HRM outcomes have been converted into concrete financial consequences for the organization (Cascio, 1991). Schuler and Jackson (1987, p. 217) have done perhaps the best job of summarizing the current view of HRM activities: "Certainly, the success or failure of a firm is not likely to turn entirely on its human resource management practices, but the HRM practices are likely to be critical."

Of the several HRM topics that have received increased attention in recent years, the topic of employee recruitment may have received the greatest increase. Only recently have researchers and practitioners begun to focus on several important recruitment issues. The *Handbook of Industrial and Organizational Psychology* (Dunnette) is a good example of the growth in researcher attention. In the first edition of this handbook (1976), the topic of employee recruitment received less than one page of coverage. In the second edition (1991), an entire chapter is devoted to recruitment-related issues. A good example of increased practitioner interest in recruitment is the initiation of a new publication, *Recruitment Today*, that publishes reports of organizational applications of various recruitment practices.

RECRUITMENT: A WORKING DEFINITION

Historically, writers have viewed recruitment and selection as distinct events (e.g., Hawk, 1967). Recruitment, which traditionally has been viewed as preceding selection, was the process of generating applicants for job openings; selection was the process of choosing from the pool of job applicants. Thus, placing a job advertisement in a local newspaper was a recruitment activity; deciding which job candidates to hire by means of an ability test was a selection activity.

In recent years, however, researchers have begun to question the accuracy and the usefulness of this traditional distinction between recruitment and selection. Today, many researchers no longer view recruitment and selection simply as one-way processes in which an organization tries to attract and subsequently to select individuals. Rather, most experts currently view both recruitment and selection as complex, two-way processes that affect each other. Thus, not only do employers try to look attractive to prospective job candidates, but job candidates also try to look attractive to employers. Similarly, not only does an organization select from a pool of job candidates, but these candidates also decide whether they will work for the organization. As an example of how recruitment and selection can interact, consider a company that uses an intentionally stress-producing interview for screening job applicants. While the interview may help the company choose a person who can effectively handle a stressful job, the same interview may "turn off" an applicant whom the employer ultimately wants to hire.

The following quotations convey a sense of the rationale for viewing recruitment and selection as complex, interdependent processes. "On close examination . . . the distinction between recruiting (attracting applicants) and selection (choosing among applicants) becomes tenuous. Selection, or at least self-selection, goes on during recruiting, and recruiting goes on during the evaluation process" (Schwab, 1982, p. 103). "Many activities conducted prior to extending a job offer might appropriately be viewed as *either* recruitment or selection procedures, depending on how they are used in a particular situation" (Boudreau and Rynes, 1985, pp. 354–355). "Many managers have their organizations spend large amounts of money on recruitment to attract the kind of people they want to hire. This attraction process is, of course, not independent of the selection process, since what goes on during selection influences the attractiveness of the organization. For example, there is evidence that the way in which the selection interview is conducted directly influences the probability that a person will take a job" (Nadler, Hackman, and Lawler, 1979, p. 131).

As will become apparent from the coverage of several recruitment topics in this text, this author agrees that it is generally inaccurate and unwise to treat recruitment and selection as distinct and independent processes. In particular, it will be shown that viewing recruitment in a narrow manner (that is, as simply the process an organization uses to create an applicant pool) can cause one to overlook several crucial issues, such as how unprofessional treatment by a recruiter may be viewed by a job applicant as symptomatic of the way the organization treats its employees, thus resulting in a high-quality applicant rejecting a job offer. Therefore, in this text recruitment will be broadly defined and the coverage of recruitment topics will include not only a consideration of the perspective of the organization, but also a consideration of the applicant's viewpoint. In addition, the treatment of recruitment in this text recognizes that recruitment activities do not always precede the administration of selection devices. Based on this perspective, the following definition of recruitment is offered. Although this definition may seem ambiguous, this lack of specificity is necessary. As various aspects of the recruitment process are covered in detail in later chapters, exactly what is meant by recruitment will become clearer.

> **Employee recruitment** involves those organizational activities that (1) influence the number and/or the types of applicants who apply for a position and/or (2) affect whether a job offer is accepted.

HOW RECRUITING AFFECTS AND IS AFFECTED BY OTHER HRM ACTIVITIES

A key reason that the topic of employee recruitment has attracted so much attention recently is that there is an increasing awareness of the close interdependence between recruitment activities and other HRM activities (Phillips, 1987). For example, the way an organization recruits can affect both the number and the quality of the candidates who are attracted to it. Obviously, the effectiveness of an employer's selection system will be influenced by the number and the quality of the applicants available for screening. For instance, if an organization recruits a large number of applicants, it is more likely to be able to select a sufficient number of qualified individuals to fill vacant positions. However, screening a large number of applicants can be both costly and time consuming. Therefore, the goal of the recruitment process should not be simply to attract a large number of applicants, but rather to attract a sufficient number of high-quality candidates (that is, candidates who possess the personal attributes the organization sees as necessary for doing the job).

Not only does the way an organization recruits influence its selection process, but its recruiting strategy can also influence its training function and its compensation system. For instance, if an employer is able to attract job candidates who are highly skilled, the need for training will be diminished. However, recruiting high-caliber applicants involves potential costs as well as benefits. In order to attract high-quality individuals, an organization most likely will need to offer a higher level of compensation than if less-qualified applicants were being pursued.

An organization's recruitment strategy can also influence employee relations and progress toward affirmative action goals. Concerning employee relations, numerous recruitment policies, such as the use of realistic job previews, can influence employee satisfaction. In terms of affirmative action goals, certain common recruiting practices (the use of employee referrals, nepotism policies, etc.) can substantially limit the number of minorities who are considered for job openings (Schlei and Grossman, 1989).

However, it is not simply the case that recruitment activities affect other HRM activities. These other HRM activities also influence how employee recruitment is conducted. For example, if a large percentage of applicants fail to score at acceptable levels on selection devices, an organization may need to reconsider the applicant population from which it recruits. An employer also may modify the way it recruits if it discovers that the high-caliber but perhaps overqualified employees it has been recruiting and hiring are quitting their jobs during their first year because they lack challenging assignments and are bored.

One key organizational activity that can influence recruitment is public relations. An organization's image—its visibility level and whether its reputation is positive—can have a major influence on the number and type of job candidates who apply for positions (Schwab, 1982). For example, being listed in *The 100 Best Companies to Work for in America* (Levering, Moskowitz, and Katz, 1984) or at the top of *Fortune* magazine's annual list of "America's Most Admired Companies" should have an extremely positive effect on the number of unsolicited applications an organization receives. In contrast, one can imagine the detrimental effect on recruitment that being found guilty of dumping hazardous waste could have.

In summary, the way an organization goes about recruiting employees both affects and is affected by its other human resource activities. Therefore, in order to maximize the value of its recruitment activities, it is essential that an employer carefully integrate its recruitment strategy with its other HRM practices and, more generally, with its strategic business plan (Butler, Ferris, and Napier, 1991). Unfortunately, as will be amply documented in this text, recruitment actions are frequently not mutually aligned with other organizational objectives.

COMMON RECRUITING MISTAKES: THREE EXAMPLES

Although organizations are becoming increasingly aware that their recruitment activities can affect both other HRM activities and applicant behavior (e.g., whether a person accepts a job offer), employers still make costly recruiting mistakes. Following are three vignettes that illustrate some common recruiting mistakes.

Vignette 1: Jack Karnell's Recruitment Ad

On February 15, 1991, Jack Karnell, manager of human resources for a printing company located in Buffalo, placed an advertisement for a "Personnel Specialist" position in the Sunday edition of the local newspaper. The advertisement stated that to be considered for the position a person should possess a college degree with considerable course work in the personnel field. In addition, it noted that work experience in the personnel field was desirable. Interested individuals were asked to apply by mail.

Within two weeks, Jack had received over 125 responses to his ad. While he was initially pleased by this overwhelming response, after reviewing just a few résumés his reaction quickly changed. Jack estimated that it would take at least twenty minutes to carefully review each résumé. Thus, he was looking at more than forty hours of work. In addition to the time he might spend reviewing résumés, Jack also became aware (as a result of complaints from his secretary) of the enormous volume of paperwork involved in processing this number of applications.

Not wanting to spend the better part of a week reviewing résumés, Jack attempted to devise a strategy for streamlining the process. He decided to have his secretary sort through the résumés and forward to him only those from individuals who had both course work in personnel and who had worked in a personnel position. Jack felt he could then go through the résumés of these "semifinalists" and choose three to six individuals to interview. This sorting process proved to be a frustrating experience for Jack's secretary. In a number of cases, his secretary had difficulty determining whether a candidate had work experience in the personnel area. For other applicants, it was difficult to tell whether certain college courses really had a personnel orientation. The end result of this sorting process was forty-eight semifinalists. To further reduce this list of "live" candidates, Jack decided to screen on the bases of college grade point average (3.0 or higher), college major (business), and the candidate's apparent familiarity with statistics and computer packages. This process also proved to be frustrating. Many of the applicants did not list college grade point average or major. Furthermore, most résumés mentioned familiarity with statistics and computer packages in only the most general terms.

Finally, fed up with the amount of effort this screening process was taking, Jack subjectively picked five candidates to interview. After interviewing these individuals, Jack felt three were totally unqualified for the job, one was marginal, and one looked pretty good. Fortunately, the best candidate accepted the job offer. However, in looking back on the process, Jack estimated he had spent over thirty-five hours on filling this position. Jack knew his secretary also had spent dozens of hours sorting résumés, answering phone calls from applicants, scheduling interviews, and so on.

Clearly, filling this position had been a disaster. But rather than try to forget it, Jack decided to learn from it. Thinking back on the process, he realized that many of his problems stemmed from the job advertisement he had placed. Jack had written the personnel specialist advertisement in less than twenty minutes and had created the ad by simply modifying one used by another company for a position comparable to the one he was trying to fill. Reflecting on the events that had transpired, Jack realized that a few minor changes in the advertisement could have drastically reduced the amount of time spent filling the position. He realized that he should have been more careful in specifying minimum job qualifications in the ad. For example, if he had stated just three essential applicant qualifications (i.e., personnel department experience, a degree in business from a four-year college, and a grade point average of 3.0 or better), only seventeen individuals should have applied instead of 125 (some persons may apply even though they do not have the necessary qualifications). Jack also realized that he should have requested from each applicant an official college transcript and a written statement that described the person's work experience in the personnel field, which would have helped him judge the relevance of a person's experience and evaluate the applicant's writing ability (an important aspect of the personnel specialist's position). In sum, Jack realized that if he had thought more carefully about the personnel specialist job and the wording of the job advertisement, he would have saved dozens of hours of labor, the numerous costs associated with processing applications, and the ill will that can be created by rejecting so many applicants.

Vignette 2: Word-of-Mouth Recruiting

Joan Adams is the assistant plant manager for a small bottling plant in New Mexico. As part of her job, she is responsible for overseeing all personnel-related activities, although much of the actual work is done by clerical employees under her direction. The 1980s were difficult times for this plant. Because its equipment was outdated, plant operations were inefficient compared to newer plants, and thus it had difficulty competing against more modern facilities. In 1989, the owner of the bottling plant sold out to a large soft-drink producer, who completely modernized the plant shortly after the acquisition. Almost overnight, the entire operation changed. For the past fifteen years the size of the plant's work force had been gradually declining. All of a sudden, there were more than 120 new jobs to be filled, and Joan was responsible for deciding how to staff these positions. When jobs had needed to be filled in the past, the plant had relied on its current employees to spread the word and refer appropriate candidates for the open positions. Although it had been several years since the plant had hired anyone, the previous use of employee referrals seemed to Joan to have been effective. She thus decided to rely on word-of-mouth recruiting once again.

Jobs at the plant were among the highest paying in the area, so Joan was not surprised when the available positions were quickly filled. With that task accomplished, Joan gave little thought to the use of employee referrals to staff the new positions until an Equal Employment Opportunity Commission (EEOC) investigator contacted her in early 1990. The investigator was following up on a complaint filed by three Hispanic women who claimed that, because of the "secretive" manner in which the plant had filled the positions, they had not heard about the job openings in time to be considered for them. The women charged that the plant had intentionally chosen not to publicize the openings in order to reduce the number of women and Hispanics who applied. Thus, they claimed that the plant had illegally discriminated against them because of their sex and their Hispanic origin.

The EEOC investigator asked Joan to respond to the charge in writing and to report the percentage of the plant's employees who were women and/or Hispanic. Joan realized she had a problem before she looked at the specific numbers, and the actual percentages heightened her concern. Only 5 percent of the plant's hourly workers were women, all of whom were in low-paying clerical positions. Only 3 percent of the work force was Hispanic and they were all in custodial positions. Moreover, Joan discovered that, of the individuals who had been hired to fill the 120 new jobs, no women and only two Hispanics had been hired.

Although Joan did not believe that the plant had intentionally discriminated against women and Hispanics in its most recent hiring efforts, she knew that the numbers painted a stark picture. Given that the population of the area surrounding the plant was 27 percent Hispanic, the plant's work force was clearly imbalanced. After much investigation, Joan concluded that what had happened was logical, obvious—and possibly illegal. Simply stated, the great majority of the employees who were asked to refer individuals were male non-minorities. Not surprisingly, for the most part, they referred individuals of a similar background, that is, white males. Although she was not an expert in the legal aspects of personnel matters, Joan knew she had a major problem. After consulting with attorneys from corporate headquarters, she was fairly certain that her reliance on employee word-of-mouth recruiting would turn out to be quite costly for her and for the organization.

Eventually, after two months of intense negotiating with the EEOC, a conciliation agreement was signed.[4] While admitting no guilt, Joan's plant agreed to develop and implement an affirmative action program in which 40 percent of future openings for hourly plant personnel would be filled by women and/or Hispanics until the plant's hourly work force reflected the demographic composition of the surrounding area. These "to be hired" women and Hispanics would be given seniority equivalent to that of the white males hired during the recent period. In addition, monetary compensation of $12,500 was agreed to for each of the plaintiffs.

Although Joan felt that her plant may have been able to successfully defend itself against the claims of sex and national origin discrimination, she also understood why the suit was settled. The soft-drink manufacturer was concerned about receiving negative publicity in the southwestern United States (in fact, a Hispanic civil rights advocacy group had threatened the company with a boycott of its products).

Looking back on these events, Joan felt somewhat bitter. She had not intended to exclude Hispanics or women from consideration for the new jobs. Rather, because she lacked training in the personnel field, she had inadvertently chosen to use a recruitment method that made it difficult for Hispanics and women to hear about the open positions. Although Joan did not feel it was fair to blame her for this recruitment fiasco, since the plant had previously used employee referrals without difficulty, she was certain that the company did hold her responsible. Not only had Joan's use of employee referrals been expensive in a monetary sense, but it had also raised doubts in the public's mind about the company's commitment to hiring minorities.

Vignette 3: The Naive Recruit

In January 1990, George Signori graduated from the University of Rhode Island with a bachelor's degree in sociology. Looking back on his college career, George had a number of regrets. He regretted not having taken his first two years of college more seriously. His lack of commitment to his school work during his freshman and sophomore years had had a drastic effect on his overall grade point average of 2.49. He also regretted his choice of a major. If he had it to do over, George would choose business or computer science as a major rather than sociology.

George was convinced that his GPA, his major, and the fact that he graduated in January (a time when fewer company recruiters visited campus) all contributed to his difficulty in finding a good job during his last semester. In fact, because George anticipated difficulty in finding employment, he had applied to a few M.B.A. programs. Because his GPA for his last two years was 3.22 and he had an outstanding score on the Graduate Management Admissions Test (top 15 percent), George had been accepted into the M.B.A. program of a reputable university in the Boston area.

However, just as George was about to complete the enrollment paperwork for the M.B.A. program, he received an interesting job offer from a small computer software firm. The company was ten years old and had experienced tremendous growth over the years. George was offered a position that involved selling computer software to hospitals, health maintenance organizations, public clinics, and pharmacies in Maine, New Hampshire, and Vermont. George had attracted little interest from the other companies to which he had applied, and he was flattered by the attention he received from this computer firm. Among the things George liked about the company were its informal atmosphere, its history of growth, the quality of its products, and the fact that he could stay in New England. George was not sure how to evaluate the pay he was to receive. For his first four months, he would receive a salary of $2,150 per month. After four months, his pay would be based on sales. Although George would have preferred a more secure income, the quality of the products he would be selling and the data he was given on the commissions received by other salespersons gave him confidence that he could make a good living. Furthermore, although George was not looking for a career in sales, he accepted the job with this firm because of the potential for upward mobility that a position with such a growing and dynamic firm offered.

Unfortunately, over the next seven months George became increasingly disillusioned with the company. He found he was not very good at selling the computer software products the company offered. He came to feel that his sales quotas, upon which his commission was based, and other performance criteria, such as the number of sales calls per week, were unfair. A key cause of this sense of unfairness was that George was being held to the same standards used for sales personnel with less rural territories. In comparison to salespersons in most of New England, George had to spend considerably more time driving to meet with potential customers.

However, what really bothered George was the way his company made promotion decisions. Although he was not aware of it at the time he was hired, George had come to discover that only individuals with M.B.A. degrees were considered for promotion to management positions. While many of the individuals in sales positions were able to work on their M.B.A. degrees at night, George realized this would be next to impossible for him because of the amount of traveling his territory required. Given his unhappiness, in late July George contacted the university that had accepted him into its M.B.A. program to see if he could still enroll for the fall semester. He quickly received word that he could. After weighing the alternatives, George decided his future would look much brighter if he had an M.B.A. degree. In early August he notified his supervisor he would be leaving. Not surprisingly, his supervisor was angry. His boss estimated that, all things considered (the training he had received, his salary for four months, his relocation expenses, and so on), he had cost the company over $18,500.

Looking back on his seven months with the company, George was amazed at how his outlook had changed. He had gone from being filled with enthusiasm and a sense of purpose to feeling mistreated and pessimistic. George was uncertain whether he had been naive or the company had deceived him, but he *was* certain that both he and the company wished he had never gone to work for them.

Although it may appear that the events depicted in these three vignettes are uncommon occurrences, such is not the case. For example, Wein (1990) reported that a small job advertisement placed in a Southwestern newspaper by a *Fortune* 200 company resulted in 2,500 résumés being received. Throughout the remainder of this text, examples of the experiences of organizations and job candidates will be provided to demonstrate how employers and individuals regularly make costly mistakes during the recruitment process. Fortunately, by becoming familiar with the multitude of issues that can affect the recruitment process, both organizations and job candidates can avoid, or at least minimize, problems such as those portrayed in these vignettes.

THREE QUESTIONABLE ASSUMPTIONS ABOUT RECRUITMENT

Although to some extent each chapter in this text deals with mistakes made in recruiting, at this point it is useful to briefly discuss three common but questionable assumptions made by many organizations that can result in a variety of human resource management problems.

1. An organization should try to attract job candidates with outstanding credentials.
2. An organization should attempt to develop a large pool of applicants from which to select.
3. An organization should attempt to look as attractive as possible to job candidates.

At first glance, the logic underlying each of these assumptions appears sound. For example, since quality employees are essential for an employer's success, shouldn't an organization try to attract the best possible job candidates? And wouldn't increasing the size of the applicant pool increase the likelihood of an employer being able to select quality candidates? Furthermore, since quality applicants may be attractive to numerous companies, shouldn't an organization try to look as attractive as possible in order to increase its chances of a candidate accepting its job offer?

Although initially each of these three common assumptions may seem reasonable, each is based on an overly simplistic view of the recruitment process. Unfortunately, as will become apparent from the discussion of numerous recruitment topics in this text, adopting such a simplistic view of the recruitment process can lead to significant problems. For example, concerning the first assumption, while it may seem reasonable to try to attract high-quality job candidates, it is shortsighted for an organization to focus exclusively on applicant quality. In most cases, an employer not only wants to attract high-quality applicants, but also wants to attract applicants who are likely to remain in their jobs for a reasonable period of time. However, compared to candidates with less outstanding qualifications, individuals with exceptional talent may become more easily bored with their jobs and may also have an easier time finding another job (Mobley, 1982). In addition, in order to compete successfully with other organizations for outstanding candidates, an employer generally will have to pay premium salaries. The difference between the salaries needed to attract outstanding versus competent candidates is not always made up for by the differences in their respective performances.

Similarly, the second common assumption is also too simplistic. There are substantial direct costs in generating a large applicant pool. In addition, as reflected in the first vignette ("Jack Karnell's Recruitment Ad"), many of the individuals in a large applicant pool may be unqualified for the open job. Furthermore, the larger the applicant pool, the more candidates there will be who will not be offered positions. Given that each rejected applicant is a potential source of a discrimination lawsuit, the larger the applicant pool, the greater the chance of a lawsuit being filed.

The third recruitment assumption is also dubious. Putting too much emphasis on looking attractive to job candidates can lead to exaggeration or outright deception during the recruitment process. A common outcome of an employer exaggerating the attractiveness of its job openings is that applicants take positions only to find that their expectations were substantially inflated (Dunnette, Arvey, and Banas, 1973). As portrayed in the third vignette ("The Naive Recruit"), applicants with inflated job expectations often become quickly disillusioned and frequently leave the organization within the first few months (Wanous and Colella, 1989).

RECRUITING EMPLOYEES: CONFLICTING GOALS

In place of the overly simplistic goal of attracting a large number of outstanding candidates, it is important that an organization view recruiting as a complex process involving compromise among numerous competing goals, which may include (1) attracting high-quality applicants, (2) recruiting candidates who eventually will be promotable, (3) attracting individuals who will remain with the organization for a reasonable period of time, (4) conducting a recruitment process that is legally sound, (5) fulfilling affirmative action obligations, (6) filling positions quickly, (7) minimizing recruitment costs, (8) adhering to requirements that applicants live within fixed geographic boundaries, and (9) complying with organizational policies such as an antinepotism policy or a requirement of church membership by a church-owned corporation. Although it would be unusual to have to consider all of these recruitment objectives in filling a particular position, it also would be uncommon not to have to balance at least several of these objectives.[5] For example, a residency requirement may make it difficult for a city to fill certain jobs quickly and with minimum expense.

In considering the recruiting objectives just described, it is apparent that not only are these objectives often incompatible, but different people in an organization may attach different weights to their relative importance. For example, in recruiting for hourly production jobs, a company's contract compliance officer may emphasize the hiring of minorities in order to meet affirmative action objectives. In contrast, officials from the union that represents these production workers may want to give preference to the children of current employees, many of whom are likely to be non-minorities. Alternatively, the plant manager may be interested in minimizing training costs and may therefore favor the rehiring of former employees who apply for jobs. Such differences in perspective can result in conflict and may necessitate compromises in establishing recruitment objectives.

ORGANIZATIONAL RECRUITMENT: SELECTED STATISTICS AND COMPANY PRACTICES

So far in this chapter, few statistics on recruiting have been cited and few examples of what specific companies are doing to help themselves recruit employees have been presented. To provide a sense of the importance of the ways in which recruitment is conducted and of the number of recent recruitment-related innovations, a few selected statistics and examples of company practices are provided in this section.

Concerning the different ways in which organizations try to recruit employees, a survey reported in *Personnel Journal* (Magnus, 1987) identified the top three sources of "professional hires" (e.g., engineers, chemists) to be employee referrals, newspaper advertising, and employment agencies. According to the same survey, the top three sources of management personnel were employee referrals, executive search firms, and newspaper advertising. With one exception, the results of two other surveys on organizational recruitment practices (Bureau of National Affairs, 1988; Blocklyn, 1988) were quite similar to those reported by Magnus (1987). The only exception was that the latter two surveys also cited the use of educational institutions (e.g., college placement offices) as a common source of job candidates.

The Cost of Recruiting Employees

In terms of the actual costs of various recruitment activities, precise information is difficult to gather. It appears that most organizations do not systematically collect data on the costs of various recruitment procedures (Rynes and Boudreau, 1986). For example, Miner (1979) found that fewer than 20 percent of the employers he surveyed were able to provide even basic recruitment cost data. Despite the absence of cost information, it is generally agreed that recruitment activities such as job advertising are expensive. For example, in their paper reporting the results of a survey of the college recruitment practices of *Fortune* 1,000 corporations, Rynes and Boudreau (1986) estimated that the average cost of recruiting a college student was at least $2,000. Taylor and Bergmann (1987) cited research suggesting that recruitment costs equal one-third of the new hire's annual salary. It has been estimated that the cost of recruiting for high-tech positions such as electrical engineers may be more than $5,000 per individual hired (Edwards, 1986). In summary, even if the cost figures reported above are viewed as rough estimates, there is no doubt that organizations spend huge sums on recruiting.

Innovative Organizational Actions to Facilitate Recruitment

One of the reasons that recruitment activities are often quite expensive is that for a variety of positions qualified individuals are scarce. Although such labor shortages are due to several factors (e.g., deficiencies in the skills possessed by high school graduates), the end result is that employers must now expend considerable time and effort in staffing numerous types of jobs. For example, United Research Consultants reported that, in filling its job vacancies, "every 100 résumés produce three telephone interviews or 'screens,' every three screens produce one initial in-person interview, and every six or seven first in-person interviews produce one hire" (Braham, 1988, p. 32). According to these figures, United Research Consultants would need to attract approximately 1,000 résumés in order to fill two positions. Another example of the difficulty a company can have in filling jobs is offered by Lewis (1985). He reported consulting for a company operating in the Middle East that in one year had managed to fill only one of the 125 job openings it had. The experience of Aetna Life & Casualty provides a particularly striking example of the worsening labor market for companies. In 1985, Aetna had 4.5 applicants for every entry-level clerical position; in 1988, it had only 1.8 applicants (Bennett, 1989a).

Given the relative scarcity of qualified individuals for a variety of jobs, some employers have begun intensive training programs in an attempt to teach basic skills to newly hired individuals (Blocklyn, 1988). For example, Aetna has developed an intensive six-month training program to help prepare individuals from the inner city for employment. This program, which costs between $7,000 and $10,000 per individual, not only teaches basic academic skills such as grammar, it also provides individuals with information about how to dress, how to act at work, and how to cope with personal problems.

Another approach to filling job openings that is being used increasingly involves an organization using its current employees to recruit qualified employee prospects. In order to motivate current employees to do so, many employers now pay bonuses to individuals who refer candidates who are subsequently hired. For example, McDonnell Douglas Astronautics Company instituted an employee referral recruitment program that awarded a bonus of $1,000 to an employee for each candidate whom he or she referred and who was eventually hired. In addition, for certain job classifications, an additional $500 bonus was paid to the employee if the new employee remained with the company for one year (Martin, 1987).

In some cases, rather than paying an incentive to current employees for referring job candidates, organizations have geared recruitment incentives to relatives of the recruit or to the recruit himself or herself. For example, some A&P food stores in the worker-tight Northeast offer $50 in free groceries to shoppers who coax their children to work for the chain (Feinstein, 1988). (It should be noted that such recruiting incentives are not generally given in groceries.) "In Boston's tight labor market, Shawmut Bank offers a $1,000 signing bonus for secretarial jobs" (Feinstein, 1987a).

Although organizations have used a variety of approaches for coping with labor shortages, probably the most common approach has been to try to make the open position more desirable to prospective employees. Obviously, one way to do this is by offering a high level of financial remuneration. However, in attempting to attract job applicants to these difficult-to-fill positions, employers have used a variety of other creative approaches. For example, in attempting to attract scarce health care professionals and to retain those currently employed, hospitals have begun to offer flexible work hours. "About 90% of 200 nurses at Children's Hospital at Stanford, Calif., work anything but a 40-hour week. Some work a portion of the year with certain months off; others set their own schedules, working 16 to 40 hours a week. One contracts to work nine months a year, then spends three months as a cruise-ship nurse" (Trost, 1987a).

Another way in which employers have attempted to attract and retain employees is by providing child care facilities for employees' children (Peterson and Massengill, 1988).

Although organizations may be interested in filling most jobs on a permanent basis, it is becoming increasingly common for them to fill certain positions, such as those that are particularly susceptible to a business downturn, on a temporary basis (Nye, 1988). In particular, the use of "employee leasing" (in which a company pays a fee to an outside agency for providing workers on a temporary basis) has dramatically increased in recent years. For example, it is estimated that in 1982 there were 5,000 individuals leased to organizations in the United States; in 1987, there were approximately 310,000 leased employees (McCarthy, 1988a). Contracting with a leasing company for temporary employees has potential advantages for both the employer and the individual. For example, the Chicago Chop House Restaurant reports "it saves up to $36,000 a year and avoids payroll, insurance, and tax hassles by turning to Heatherton Leasing Ltd. for 65 workers. The staffers are happier, too, because they get better benefits than the restaurant can provide, owner Henry Norton says" (Feinstein, 1987b). Another benefit of employee leasing is that, if there are layoffs, there is less impact on the morale of remaining employees when the staff cuts involve only temporary employees. However, the use of temporary employees does not always involve lower-level jobs and does not always require a formal leasing agreement with an employee leasing firm. Recently a number of law firms have begun to directly hire attorneys on a temporary basis (Cohen, 1988). According to this report, approximately 25 percent of the attorneys working on a temporary basis are young mothers who want to keep practicing law so that they can more easily return to the full-time work force when their children are older.

Although many other creative recruitment-related strategies could be discussed (spouse relocation programs, for example), the point has been made. Although in the past employers have often paid little attention to the way in which they recruited and what they offered recruits, this is no longer true today. Today, recruitment activities are being planned and scrutinized more carefully than ever before.

GOALS OF THIS TEXT

This text addresses recruitment topics from the point of view of both the researcher and the practitioner. In covering recruitment topics, four themes will be emphasized. The first theme is that recruitment decisions should be scientifically based. The second is that recruitment activities should be legally sound. The third theme has to do with pragmatism: Given that employers have limited resources to allocate to recruitment, they must get maximum value from their investment. The fourth major theme concerns the need for future research. Although we have learned a good deal about how to recruit effectively in the past decade, there is much we still do not know. Throughout the text, recruitment issues that merit future research will be highlighted.

In order to address these four themes, recruitment topics will be covered both descriptively and prescriptively. That is, in this text, there will be considerable coverage of how organizations typically recruit employees. Describing traditional practice is not sufficient, however, because common practice frequently does not parallel what research has shown to be optimal practice. Thus, the text will also offer prescriptive suggestions on how various recruitment activities should be conducted. The basis for such prescriptive comments will be empirical and theoretical research when available. Where research is lacking, suggestions for improving recruiting may still be offered.

This prescriptive perspective will stress the importance of an employer being proactive rather than reactive in managing its recruitment activities. Proactive management refers to an operating style that reflects an employer trying both to anticipate potential recruitment-related problems and opportunities and to manage these problems and opportunities effectively. An example of such proactive management would be a company that, on hearing that a nearby company will be downsizing, realizes that this may present an opportunity to hire a number of persons with skills it needs. The company makes contact with the downsizing company and is able to hire several of its employees before other employers recognize that this opportunity to acquire skilled personnel is available. By adopting a proactive management style, an organization generally can avoid, or at least minimize, potential problems and can take advantage of potential recruitment opportunities. In sum, the essence of proactive recruitment is an employer taking active steps to stay attuned to the various factors (such as applicant perceptions of the organization as a place to work) that can affect its recruitment operations, and, as a result of this sensitivity, actively managing these factors for the organization's benefit.

In contrast, as used in this text, reactive management refers to a tendency of an employer to rely on its traditional recruitment approach until problems have reached a certain threshold (e.g., its inability to recruit minorities has resulted in the suspension of a government contract) and opportunities have been clearly manifested (e.g., the company that is downsizing contacts your organization along with several others about recruiting its employees). This distinction between proactive and reactive recruitment is an important one. By being proactive (keeping up with recruitment research, checking job advertisements for wording that may be discriminatory, and so on), an organization is more likely to use scientifically based recruitment methods, comply with government regulations, and get maximum value from the resources it expends on employee recruitment.

Finally, given that recruitment is a two-way process in that job applicants also decide which organizations are most attractive to them, the perspective of the job applicant also will be considered in covering some of the recruitment topics.[6] Only by understanding how recruits make job-choice decisions can an organization maximize its recruitment efforts.

In summary, this text should be of value to researchers, to practitioners, and to students who are interested in learning more about the exciting developments occurring in the recruitment area. As will become apparent from reading this text, one can view the topic of recruitment either with optimism, pessimism, or a mixture of both. In terms of optimism, we have made tremendous strides in our understanding of recruitment processes as well as in the sophistication of recruitment practice in the past ten to fifteen years. In terms of pessimism, there is still much we do not know about recruitment processes, and the recruitment actions of some organizations are deplorable. Overall, the tone of this text is optimistic. Although there is much work ahead for both researchers and practitioners, in terms of both science and practice, the work on recruitment has never been more sophisticated.

NOTES

1. Thomas Murrin, President, Public Systems Co., Westinghouse Electric Corp., as quoted in Fombrum, Tichy, and Devanna (1984), p. 391.

2. Beer, Spector, Lawrence, Mills, and Walton (1985, p. ix): "In response to a developing consensus among our alumni and faculty that there is a need in many corporations for better management of human resources, the Harvard Business School (HBS) launched a new required course in Human Resource Management (HRM) in 1981."

3. Beer et al. (1985) provide a detailed discussion of these reasons.

4. Although it was by no means certain that a court would find the plant guilty of employment discrimination, the corporate attorneys, in an effort to minimize the damage to the plant's reputation, determined that it would be unwise to risk such a finding.

5. This list of potentially competing recruitment goals is not all-inclusive.

6. Given the number of books on career-related issues, this text will cover the applicant's perspective in less detail than the organization's perspective.

2

Employee Recruitment: A Framework

In covering the topic of employee recruitment, writers often have treated it as a relatively simple human resource activity. After all, how difficult can it be to place a job advertisement or to recruit on a college campus? However, from the material presented in Chapter 1, the reader should appreciate the dangers inherent in such a simplistic view of the recruitment process. By failing to consider the complexities involved in recruiting job candidates, an employer can get into all kinds of trouble.

Having provided an introduction to the employee recruitment process in Chapter 1, Chapter 2 provides a framework upon which the remainder of this text will build. In particular, this chapter highlights how important it is that an organization make deliberate and informed decisions at each stage of the recruitment process rather than simply follow its past recruitment traditions or blindly mimic what other employers are doing. In order to make prudent decisions, an organization's recruitment activities must be thoroughly integrated with its strategic business plans (Rynes and Barber, 1990). The nature of this integration will be a central focus of this chapter. However, before the interaction of strategic business planning and employee recruitment is addressed, the importance of recruitment should be placed in context.

PLACING RECRUITMENT IN PERSPECTIVE

Although this text emphasizes the important role that a well-designed recruitment strategy can play in contributing to an organization's success, the significance of this role should not be exaggerated. Recruitment is not a panacea that can quickly remedy such things as poor business planning, obsolete production technology, a selection system that lacks validity, or a poorly conceived compensation system. For instance, although a well-conducted recruitment process may result in a job candidate forming a favorable first impression of a potential employer, this initial impression can be undermined or destroyed if the specific position under consideration has several particularly negative features (e.g., a noncompetitive salary or an incompetent prospective boss).

However, the fact that a well-designed recruitment program will not compensate for an unattractive job situation does *not* mean that what goes on during the recruitment process is unimportant. If an organization conducts a poor recruitment campaign, potential job candidates may never become aware that a job vacancy exists because they never saw a job advertisement, they may find out about an opening after they have made other career choices, or they may remove themselves from the job search process before specific information about a prospective position can be presented because they heard a disorganized presentation at a job fair or they lost interest. Furthermore, in those situations in which comparable organizations are trying to fill similar positions, the treatment that job candidates receive during the recruitment process may have a substantial effect on the job-choice decisions they make.

An article by Feinstein (1989a) provides a good example of the way in which a poorly designed recruitment mechanism may restrict organizational productivity (in this case, recruitment literature that limits the ability of employers to hire first-rate job candidates). According to the results of a survey reported in this article, college seniors gave the recruiting literature that they received from companies "generally low grades." For example, only 4 percent of the seniors felt that recruitment brochures provided adequate job descriptions. More surprisingly, 12 percent of the brochures were seen as "condescending or offensive, with hints of sexism or racism." Summing up the results of this survey, Maury Hanigan, president of the consulting firm that conducted it, concluded that "some recruiters may never get a chance to talk with good candidates because of things said, or unsaid, in the recruiting literature."

AN OVERVIEW OF THE STRATEGIC BUSINESS PLANNING PROCESS

Although organizations differ in the relative sophistication of their strategic business planning, the importance of this planning process for an organization's survival and effectiveness appears to be universally recognized.[1] A strategic business plan "provides a long-term vision for the organization. It specifies the organization's reason for existing, its strategic objectives, and its operational strategies" (Dunham and Pierce, 1989, p. 278). A key factor in the strategic business planning process is a careful consideration of the environment in which the organization operates. Such an environmental scan should typically address three external factors: legal regulations that can constrain the organization's activities, the business environment in which the employer operates, and the labor market from which the organization will draw needed personnel.[2]

Exhibit 2.1, on page 23, shows that when the information gained from the environmental scan is integrated with an organization's basic philosophy,[3] the employer is able to conduct a careful assessment of its relative organizational strengths and weaknesses. Based on this assessment, the organization is able to develop strategic business objectives, which are the end product of the strategic planning process.[4] These strategic objectives can, in turn, be used to structure the operational planning process. The operational planning process involves the development of specific plans for the attainment of the strategic business objectives. In contrast to the strategic planning process, the operational planning process tends to focus on a shorter time period and be more concerned with specific actions the organizations should take.[5]

The Impact of Operational Objectives on Human Resource Planning

Not surprisingly, accomplishing the operational objectives that are derived from the organization's strategic business plan often involves the acquisition of new staff and/or the movement of current personnel. For example, if an employer decides to increase the size of its current business, it will generally need to recruit additional employees. In other cases, an organization's strategic business plan may call not for growth, but rather for a change in business emphasis. For instance, a company may decide to scale back one area of business while increasing the size of another area. While this type of strategic plan may not require a net increase in the number of individuals the company employs, it may call for a shift in the location of staff (e.g., a 10 percent reduction in the number of staff in each of two business units and a 20 percent increase in a third unit). Given such a circumstance, an employer may be able to choose whether to terminate some employees and hire others or to transfer appropriately skilled individuals between business units.

In reality, the preceding examples present a simplified view of the personnel decisions that can be necessitated by an organization's opera-

Exhibit 2.1 A simplified model of external and internal factors that influence recruitment

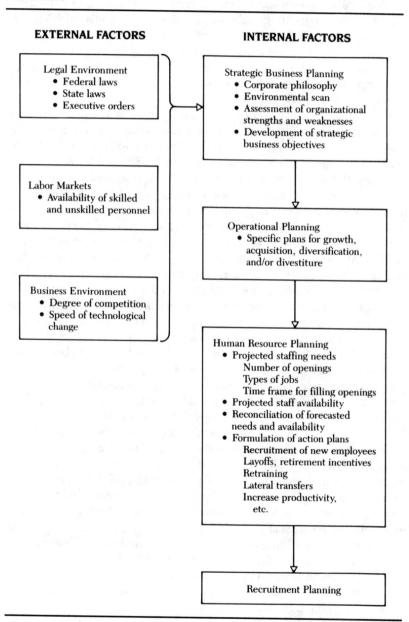

tional objectives. In most cases, in order to make sound decisions about staffing levels, a systematic human resource planning process is needed.[6] Human resource planning enables an employer to systematically "(1) analyze business plans to establish future human resource requirements, (2) estimate future human resource availabilities, (3) reconcile requirements and availabilities, and (4) formulate action plans that will, if properly implemented, contribute to the achievement of business plans" (Heneman et al., 1989, p. 204).

The first human resource planning function is projecting staffing needs. To accomplish this, an organization must be able to estimate, for one or more future points in time, the types of positions it will need to staff and the number and type of individuals it will need in each of these positions. It is sometimes possible to use complex statistical techniques in estimating future human resource requirements, but most employers have relied on the intuitive judgment of managers. For example, if the senior executives of a hospital decide to close a wing of the facility and thus eliminate 16 percent of its beds, they may simply estimate that the number of hospital employees will need to be reduced by a roughly equivalent percentage. Management judgment is also generally relied on in deciding the point(s) in time (say, three and five years into the future) for which forecasts will be made and in determining whether forecasts are to be made for all or only some of the positions in the organization.

In addition to projecting staffing needs, the human resource planning process also requires that an organization estimate the number of employees who will be available for each of the positions at the point or points in time under consideration. In making such predictions, those involved must consider both the organization's current labor force and its external labor market. There are several steps involved in making an accurate forecast of human resource availability for a given position. First, an accurate count must be made of the number of employees in the position at the start of the planning period. Next, anticipated losses from this employee group during the course of the planning period must be considered. Among the common causes of staff losses are retirements, transfers, voluntary turnover, terminations, and promotions. Following this, an employer must forecast staff gains during the planning period as a result of such factors as lateral transfers, promotions, demotions, and normal hiring from outside the organization. Incorporating information about current staffing levels with predicted staff losses and gains enables an organization to develop an estimate of staff availability for a given position at some future point in time.[7]

In estimating the effects on staff availability of such things as losses due to retirement and gains due to promotion, it is important that those who make these estimates be as fully informed as possible about the organization's internal and external environment (Heneman et al., 1989). For example, in forecasting losses due to voluntary turnover and retirement, giving considerable weight to past rates of turnover and retirement would be wise only if the organization's internal and external environments are predicted to remain relatively stable over the planning period. On the other hand, if an employer is about to introduce an attractive early retirement incentive or to begin offering salaries well below those of its competitors, basing staff availability forecasts on historical data would be unsound. In evaluating its external environment, an organization must be especially sensitive to possible changes in labor market conditions during the planning period. For example, a lower unemployment rate may make it easier for people to leave the organization and more difficult for the employer to recruit new employees.

Once information concerning projected staffing needs and availability has been gathered, it should be systematically analyzed to determine projected discrepancies and the reasons underlying such discrepancies. For some positions, an employer may discover that an employee shortage is predicted, for others, a surplus of employees may be predicted.

If an organization discovers a sizable discrepancy between its projected personnel needs and personnel availability for a given position,[8] it may be able to gain insight into possible actions it could take by studying the various factors (turnover rates, increased staffing needs, etc.) that entered into its forecasts. For example, if an organization forecasts a shortage of twenty employees in a given position four years from now, it could try to reduce the number of people leaving the position (by, say, improving working conditions to lessen voluntary turnover), or attempt to increase the flow of individuals into the job (by encouraging job retraining and offering lateral transfers), or, in some cases, both. The organization could also try to reduce the number of individuals it will require in the future by relying more heavily on automation, improving the productivity of its current work force, and so on.

By carefully considering the relative influence of each factor that affects staff availability, an organization might determine that only a small number of factors are expected to have much impact. Once these factors are identified, the organization is better able to formulate a sound action plan for reducing or eliminating the forecasted discrepancy. For example, a company may determine that, for a given position, no one is projected to transfer out, a few employees are expected to voluntarily or involuntarily leave the organization, only one person is expected to get promoted, but several employees are expected to retire. In this case, the company might focus on recruiting new employees and/or convincing people not to retire. Exhibit 2.1 lists several action plans that could be undertaken as part of a human resource plan. Given the focus of this book, only those strategies that are relevant to recruitment will be addressed in any detail in the remainder of this text.

PepsiCo provides a good example of a company putting into practice the concepts discussed in this section. According to Milkovich and Boudreau (1991), PepsiCo has forecast its staffing needs through the year 2000, based on its business plans for its three major businesses (Pepsi-Cola, Frito-Lay, and Pizza Hut). PepsiCo plans to almost double the number of its employees in its restaurant line (from 158,000 in 1990 to 308,000 in 2000) and maintain its present employment levels in its beverage (23,000 employees) and snack lines (27,000 employees). By integrating projected turnover rates (15 percent in beverages and snacks and 150 percent in restaurants) with growth rates, PepsiCo has concluded that it must hire almost 3.7 million people in the 1990s if it is to achieve its business plans. However, PepsiCo's analysis also shows that during the time when it will need to increase its work force by 72 percent, the U.S. labor force will grow by only 13 percent. Thus, PepsiCo will need to attract more than its share of new employees. To fill these projected staffing needs, PepsiCo is considering a variety of actions, including day care and part-time jobs, in order to make itself more attractive as an employer to individuals who might not otherwise consider working there.

Integrating Human Resource Information into the Strategic Planning Process

Given the central role that an organization's employees play in determining its success, one might expect that input from those involved in the human resource management function would play a key part in the development of a company's strategic business plans. However, this has not always been the case (Rothwell and Kazanas, 1989). This absence of input from those with particular expertise in the human resource domain is surprising because the importance of HR information to the success of a company's business plans has been well documented (Fombrum, Tichy, and Devanna, 1984). For example, if a company is considering opening a new production facility, such a decision may only make good business sense if the facility can be located in an area that has a large labor pool from which to recruit and in which wages tend to be modest. As concrete evidence of the increasing corporate awareness of the importance of the human resource function, Fombrum et al. (1984) noted that several progressive companies such as General Electric now require that a human resource section be included in their strategic plans. In fact, according to these authors, at IBM a personnel manager must sign off on a business unit's plan before it can go forward.

In summary, although the model in Exhibit 2.1 accurately represents the way in which planning proceeds in many organizations (i.e., a lack of human resource input into the strategic business planning process), there is evidence that this tendency is changing (Butler, Ferris, and Napier, 1991). For at least some organizations, this model would be more accurate if there were a feedback arrow from the human resource planning function to the strategic planning function.

The Importance of Employee Recruitment to Successful Business Planning

While there are several reasons for the growing attention being given to the human resource management function as part of the strategic business planning process,[9] arguably the most important reason is an increasing awareness of potential labor shortages and their effects on a company's ability to grow, to diversify, or even to survive. To get a sense of the seriousness of the pending labor shortages, consider that it is estimated that the growth of the U.S. work force will slump to 1 percent per year in the 1990s, compared with a growth rate of 2.9 percent in the 1970s (Bennett, 1989b). It is predicted that in the near future organizations will find it more difficult to staff jobs ranging from the executive level to the entry level.[10] In fact, in some areas of the country, labor shortages are already affecting business decisions. For example, Harmonium Moving and Storage of Boston was reported to have passed up the chance to acquire another moving company because it feared it could not recruit a sufficient number of employees to staff both enterprises (Gupta and Tannenbaum, 1989). Given the increasing scarcity of labor, the need for an organization to consider its ability to recruit new employees as it develops business plans is obvious.

In considering recruitment issues, one should not make the mistake of automatically thinking about large organizations recruiting entry-level employees. The need for the integration of human resource information with plans for business expansion is particularly acute for smaller firms, which often find it harder to recruit employees (Gupta and Tannenbaum, 1989). Moreover, as Schuler and Jackson (1987) have emphasized, there is a crucial connection between a company's future business plans and its decision whether or not to recruit executives from outside the organization.

To recapitulate, although not all organizations have integrated the human resource function into their strategic business planning process, it appears that an increasing number of organizations will do so in the future. By involving those who possess HRM expertise in the strategic business planning process, an organization should be able to develop more realistic business plans.[11]

DETERMINING A RECRUITMENT PHILOSOPHY: A FUNDAMENTAL ISSUE

Exhibit 2.2 presents a simplified model of the four major phases—recruitment planning, recruitment strategy development, recruitment activities, and the evaluation of recruitment procedures—of the employee recruitment process. In this model, the development of a recruitment philosophy and the screening/selecting of employees by an organization are *not* treated as formal steps in the recruitment process. The rationale for not treating activities related to the screening/selecting of employees as a component of the recruitment process is based primarily on convention. That is, although it is recognized that those involved in recruiting employees also may be asked to screen out clearly unqualified job candidates, traditionally writers have not treated such screening as a recruitment function.

There are a number of reasons why the development of a recruitment philosophy is not portrayed in Exhibit 2.2 as a major step in the recruitment process, the most important of these being the fact that, in comparison to the decisions and actions that comprise the four major recruitment phases noted above, an organization's recruitment philosophy tends to encompass a wide range of considerations and be somewhat stable. Although making a distinction between recruitment philosophy and the four recruitment phases may seem unnecessary, after each of these topics is discussed in more detail in the sections that follow, this distinction should be clearer.

Internal versus External Recruitment: Pros and Cons

In attempting to fill vacant positions that are above the entry level, a fundamental decision must be made as to whether to recruit internally or externally.[12] As will become apparent shortly, the decision an organization

Exhibit 2.2   A simplified model of the recruitment process

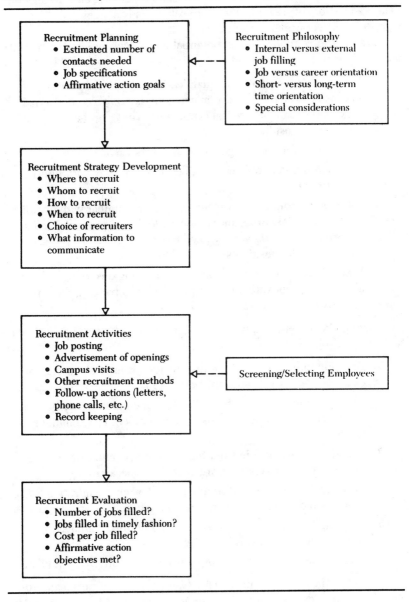

makes will affect several aspects of recruitment planning and strategy development. Not surprisingly, there are relative advantages and disadvantages to both recruitment orientations.

Among the commonly cited potential advantages of internal recruitment over external recruitment are:

1. It is easier to evaluate the qualifications of internal candidates because considerably more information is available on internal candidates than on external candidates. Thus, better hiring decisions may result.

2. Internal recruitment is generally less expensive.

3. Job openings generally can be filled more quickly with internal recruitment.

4. Internal job candidates are generally more familiar with organizational policies, procedures, norms, logistics, products, and key decision makers; thus, they need less transition time to become effective in the position(s) being filled.

5. If positions are filled internally by promoting deserving individuals, this can motivate other employees by convincing them that hard work is rewarded.[13]

Among the potential advantages of an external recruiting orientation are:

1. Bringing individuals in from the outside (from competitors, for example) can expose an organization to new ideas or innovations.

2. By recruiting external job candidates, an employer may be able to reduce the need for expensive development and training activities.

3. Bringing a candidate in from the outside may eliminate the need to upset a well-functioning organizational hierarchy.

4. Recruiting candidates externally may allow an organization to progress more rapidly toward meeting affirmative action goals.

5. Bringing in outsiders can signal to current organizational members that the business is changing.

6. On some occasions, there simply is no viable internal candidate.

Although these lists of potential advantages are by no means complete, they provide a sense of the number of issues that an organization must consider in deciding whether to adopt a philosophy of internal or external recruitment. However, in order to more fully appreciate the importance of the issues involved in developing a recruitment philosophy, a couple of themes that underlie some of the advantages raised above need to be further explored.

In filling positions above the entry level, it is generally accepted that the majority of organizations rely heavily on an internal recruitment approach.[14] In explaining why General Electric adheres to a strong internal recruitment philosophy, Senior Vice President Ted LeVino cited the high cost of recruiting externally, the negative impact on the morale of current managers of bringing in outsiders, and the need for continuity and stability in the managerial ranks. LeVino believes internal recruitment is particularly important in filling executive-level positions: "The top echelon needs to have intimate familiarity with the company in order to run it well and that familiarity comes only from experience" (Fombrum et al., 1984, p. 186). Some other organizations noted for having strong internal promotion policies are United Parcel Service and IBM (Sonnenfeld, Peiperl, and Kotter, 1988).

Although under many circumstances an internal recruitment policy may be beneficial, it is essential that such a policy be congruent with the employer's business strategy and with the environment in which it operates. Otherwise, an employer may end up with a situation similar to that described by a business executive interviewed by Kotter (1988): "We have an excellent group of senior executives for running a highly regulated business. Unfortunately, we no longer have a highly regulated business" (p. 74).

A particular danger of a strong internal recruitment system is managerial inbreeding. For example, Falvey (1987) cites a U.S. corporation that faced an erosion of profits in one product line due to the entry of a foreign competitor into its market. In attempting to deal with this competitor, the organization chose the same strategy it had relied on fifteen years earlier in successfully meeting the challenge of another foreign competitor. Unfortunately, this time the circumstances were different and the U.S. company was forced into layoffs, plant closings, and ultimately the sale of what was left of its product line. In explaining how the U.S. company could rely on an outdated business strategy, Falvey notes that everyone involved in making the decision had been with the company fifteen years earlier when the original decision had been made.

Other research has indicated that the example reported by Falvey may not be an anomaly. A study conducted by the Hay Group Incorporated, in conjunction with the University of Michigan and the Strategic Planning Institute, suggests that Falvey's example may, indeed, have relevance for other organizations. According to Schuler and Jackson (1987), the Hay study found "that when a business is pursuing a growth strategy it needs top managers who are likely to abandon the status quo and adapt their strategies and goals to the marketplace. According to the study, insiders are slow to recognize the onset of decline and tend to persevere in strategies that are no longer effective; so, top managers need to be recruited from outside" (p. 207).

Although a strong promotion-from-within policy can lead to inbreeding, in many organizations the lack of diversity of views is enhanced because companies frequently have established traditional areas of business (such as finance and engineering, for example) from which most, if not all, top managers come. Falvey (1987) has been extremely critical of the managers that result from such a system of intense inbreeding, suggesting that they "look alike," "they dress alike," and "unfortunately, they think alike."[15]

As a way to protect against the lack of diversity of views that can result from such inbreeding, some organizations appear to be becoming more open to the recruitment of external job candidates for middle- and upper-level positions. For example, Lawrence and Dyer (1983) cite how AT&T has been recruiting nontraditional specialists from other companies and appointing them to key positions as a means of trying to keep up with the technological complexity of its business environment.[16] Fombrum et al. (1984) note how Chase Manhattan Bank brought in a manager from IBM to stimulate a more aggressive growth strategy in its trust department. In a similar vein, Schuler and Jackson (1987) relate how recruiting outsiders (including its current president) as members of its senior management team has been instrumental in transforming Stroh Brewing Company from a small, family-run brewery in Detroit to the third-largest U.S. brewer.

In summary, it appears that a strong case can be made for most organizations adopting a recruitment philosophy that aims for a mixture of internal and external job candidates. Although some writers have gone so far as to recommend a specific recruitment mix (including Falvey (1987), who recommends that between 20 percent and 30 percent of all openings be filled by outsiders to ensure a diversity of viewpoints), it appears more prudent to recommend that the appropriate mixture of internal and external candidates be based on a careful consideration of the relative advantages of each approach vis-à-vis the environment in which the organization operates (Olian and Rynes, 1984).

Internal versus External Recruitment: Other Factors to Consider

In addition to the factors discussed in the preceding section, there are a number of other important factors that an organization should consider in deciding what type of recruitment philosophy to adopt (i.e., internal, external, or a mixture).[17] Of primary importance, obviously, is whether an organization that chooses to rely on external recruitment would be able to attract a sufficient number of external job candidates when the need arises. Although some organizations have in the past been able to rely on external recruitment of job candidates to fill jobs above the entry level, it appears that in the near future this may become increasingly difficult, especially if the vacant positions require somewhat specialized job competencies.[18]

Even if they could fill job vacancies externally, many employers (e.g., IBM) prefer to rely on their internal labor pools in filling vacant positions. Although there are exceptions, an organization that has a strong internal recruitment philosophy typically views prospective employees in a different way than an employer that relies heavily on external recruitment. For example, in hiring for entry-level positions, an employer that stresses filling jobs internally tends to view applicants in terms of a career (i.e., long-term potential), whereas an organization that emphasizes external recruitment generally focuses on applicants only in terms of the position under consideration. In addition, because it does not want to be forced to recruit externally to fill higher-level positions, an internally oriented organization tends to have a longer planning horizon and to put more resources into employee development activities.

Merck & Company, which in 1987 received *Fortune*'s award as "America's Most-Admired Corporation" for the second consecutive year, provides a good example of these manifestations of an internal recruitment philosophy.[19] As stated by E. Jeffrey Stoll, Merck's director of corporate personnel relations, "Our objective is to sell Merck as a career opportunity." Given this promotion-from-within philosophy, Stoll says that Merck has a five- to ten-year strategic plan for human resources and provides a variety of training and development opportunities for its employees.

In order to provide a sense of why an employer must reflect carefully on these issues (e.g., an emphasis on filling a job vs. hiring for a career with the organization), the words of an executive in Kotter's (1988) study are instructive: "Part of our problem is that our college recruiting efforts are inadequate. First of all, we hire people based on technical competence or potential in some specific area (e.g., accounting, MIS, market research, product engineering) with little or no emphasis on future managerial or leadership potential. This gets us people who can do entry-level jobs well, but not enough folks with long-term potential. And when you talk to our middle-level managers about this, they essentially say, 'Give me a break. My job is to make my quarterly plan or budget. It is someone else's job to worry about that other stuff'" (p. 72). In contrast to such a short-sighted recruitment orientation, Edison W. Spencer, chairman of the board at Honeywell, Inc., reports that in the 1970s the company's executives and managers were already thinking about "What kind of people are we going to need in the 1980s and the 1990s to manage this business?" (Fombrum et al., 1984, p. 450).

In summary, in deciding how to go about filling positions, an employer should carefully weigh the relative advantages of relying on any particular recruitment philosophy. In some cases, it may make sense to rely heavily on external recruitment in filling positions (e.g., a small company that cannot afford the developmental activities a promotion-from-within philosophy may require. In other cases, a strong internal recruitment strategy may be prudent (e.g., a large company that wants to inculcate in all its employees a particular set of corporate values). Finally, for some organizations, a strategy that combines both approaches to recruitment may be the best one. For example, Alan Lafley, executive vice president of human resources at Chase Manhattan Bank, described the bank's staffing strategy as one that places "development emphasis on the competencies we cannot recruit for effectively and attempt to recruit for those competencies which others develop particularly well" (Fombrum et al., 1984, p. 79).

RECRUITMENT PLANNING

Although an organization can move directly from the human resource planning stage to recruitment planning (see Exhibit 2.1), the advantages of a careful consideration of one's recruitment philosophy as an intervening stage should be evident from the preceding discussion (see Exhibit 2.2). Nevertheless, regardless of whether careful consideration is given to one's recruitment philosophy, at some point the organization must translate the general information that resulted from the human resource planning process (number of likely vacancies, information about the general nature of these openings, and so on) into a set of specific recruitment objectives. This translation process is referred to as recruitment planning.

The Importance of Clear and Relevant Job Specifications

Before an organization initiates any recruitment activities, it should undertake a recruitment planning process that addresses at least two key issues: the basic job specifications for the position to be filled and approximately how many contacts will need to be made to fill all vacancies. Entire books have addressed the development of job specifications, so this topic will be addressed here only briefly and as it relates to employee recruitment.[20]

If an organization is to develop an effective recruitment strategy, it is imperative that those involved in recruiting have a clear understanding of the knowledge, skills, abilities, experience, credentials or certification, and/or personal characteristics such as race or sex[21] that are required in order for an individual to be considered for a job vacancy. This kind of information can be important for such basic recruitment decisions as determining what information to communicate in a job advertisement and deciding where to look for employees, as well as for choosing which of the résumés submitted by applicants should be passed along to a hiring manager. Although the importance of having such job qualification information is widely recognized, this information is not always made available to those who are primarily responsible for recruitment.[22] In future chapters, the importance of specific information concerning job requirements will be discussed in more detail.

The Estimated Number of Contacts Needed

In attempting to fill job vacancies, organizations typically find that some job candidates are unqualified while others ultimately lose interest in the positions for which they applied.[23] Thus, with rare exceptions, an employer will need more employee prospects than it has positions to fill. Given this fact, in planning recruitment activities to fill a specific position, an employer should estimate the number of job candidates needed. Failure to accurately predict the ratio of the number of applicants to the number of hires can result in problems for the organization. For example, if an employer underestimates the number of applicants who must be recruited, it may end up not being able to fill all of its job openings in the time frame desired, or it may be forced to hire individuals who are seen as less than fully qualified for the vacant positions. On the other hand, if the organization overestimates the number of applicants needed, it will waste both time and money in recruiting more candidates than would have been required.

Although forecasting how many job applicants will be needed to fill a given position is an imprecise process, certain actions (studying past recruitment campaigns the organization has conducted for the position, investigating the experiences of other organizations in their attempts to fill similar positions, and so on)[24] should allow useful estimates to be derived. Even if they are not precise, these estimates are likely to result in more efficient recruitment than if no systematic planning process is undertaken. The most common approach for determining the number of applicants needed is an analysis of so-called yield ratios (Hawk, 1967). Yield ratios reflect the relationship between the number of individuals at one step of the recruitment process and the number of people who will move on to the next step.

To clarify matters, consider the hypothetical recruitment flow that is portrayed in Exhibit 2.3. The first stage of the recruitment process is the submission of résumés by candidates prior to the company's campus visits. Of the 2,000 students who submitted résumés, the company selected 500 (a yield ratio of 25 percent) for on-campus interviews. However, only 450 of the students who were invited for interviews accepted the offers. Thus, the yield ratio for this step was 90 percent and the cumulative yield ratio was 22.5 percent (i.e., 450/2,000). From this example, the relative ease with which yield ratios can be computed should be evident. Having

Exhibit 2.3 Recruiting yield ratios based on visits to thirty campuses

	Yield Ratio At This Stage	*Cumulative Yield Ratio*
2,000 students submit résumés to company for prescreening prior to campus visits	—	—
500 students invited for campus interviews	25.0%	25.0%
450 students interviewed	90.0%	22.5%
200 students invited for interviews at the company	44.4%	10.0%
180 individuals interviewed	90.0%	9.0%
100 students invited for second interview	55.6%	5.0%
80 students interviewed for second time	80.0%	4.0%
60 job offers made	75.0%	3.0%
30 job offers accepted	50.0%	1.5%
28 employees begin work (2 individuals renege on job acceptances)	93.3%	1.4%

computed such ratios, an employer can use them as a basis for making predictions about the number of applications it will need to fill a given number of positions in the following year[25] or to decide how it should modify its recruitment strategy in future recruitment campaigns. For example, data such as those reported in Exhibit 2.3 might lead a company to use a different recruitment method, recruit at different types of college campuses, or reword the notice sent to the campus placement offices so that job requirements are more clearly delineated in the hope that fewer unqualified applicants will submit résumés.

In summary, yield ratios can help an organization estimate the number of applicants it will need to contact. However, these yield ratios should be viewed with caution. They can change from year to year due to such things as changes in the labor market and the relative competitiveness of the salaries that the hiring organization offers. Still, even when circumstances do change, yield ratios based on prior recruitment campaigns may serve as a useful starting point for estimating future yield ratios.

RECRUITMENT STRATEGY DEVELOPMENT

Important Conceptual Distinctions in Developing a Recruitment Strategy

Before discussing specific decisions such as where to recruit and how to recruit that must be made in developing a recruitment strategy, it is important that we briefly address some conceptual distinctions that can have important ramifications for making strategy decisions.[26] In beginning to develop a recruitment strategy for filling a given position, it is useful to consider six categories or groupings into which prospective employees can be placed: labor force population, applicant population, applicant pool, selectees, acceptees, and new employees. The broadest of these categories is the labor force population. As defined by Boudreau and Rynes (1985), the labor force population "is the hypothetical population of individuals that would be available for selection using all possible recruitment strategies" (p. 355).

Given practical constraints, organizations obviously do not use all possible recruitment strategies to reach all possible job candidates. Instead, organizations typically focus on a particular segment of the labor force (e.g., graduates of accredited four-year universities) and use only a few recruitment approaches (e.g., job notices posted in university career placement offices). The subset of the labor force population that is theoretically available to an organization for selection purposes when a particular recruitment approach is used is referred to as the applicant population. One of the reasons for making a distinction between the labor force population and the applicant population is that these two populations may differ in significant ways. For example, the use of a particular recruitment approach (say, employee referrals) may limit an employer to an applicant population in which minorities are underrepresented relative to their representation in the labor force population.

It is also important to distinguish between an applicant population and an applicant pool. An applicant pool consists of all individuals in the applicant population who actually are screened by the organization, such as the 2,000 students in Exhibit 2.3 who submitted résumés. As noted by Boudreau and Rynes (1985), although researchers have often assumed that the applicant pool represents a random sample of the applicant population, this appears not to be the case. For example, an employer's hypothetical applicant population might be all university accounting majors. However, if the organization has a reputation for paying poorly compared to its competitors, its actual applicant pool may not include most accounting majors who are in the top 10 percent of their classes. As will be discussed in more detail in a later chapter that addresses legal constraints on recruitment, this distinction can be particularly important if minorities and/or women in the applicant population tend not to pursue jobs (i.e., become part of the applicant pool) because of an employer's reputation or actions vis-à-vis members of protected classes.

A fourth important category to distinguish is that of selectees. This term refers to the group of applicants who actually receive job offers from an organization. In the example presented in Exhibit 2.3, of the 2,000 members of the applicant pool, sixty individuals received job offers.[27] Acceptees and new employees are the final two categories that merit differentiation. As used here, acceptees are those individuals who accept job offers and new employees are the acceptees who actually go to work for the organization. Although authors frequently do not distinguish between acceptees and new employees, it is well established that not all individuals who accept job offers actually report for work (Ivancevich and Donnelly, 1971). This distinction between acceptees and new employees is particularly important in the context of recruitment strategy development because recruitment actions have been shown to affect the percentage of acceptees who renege on job acceptances.

In summary, in beginning the recruitment process, an organization generally has a large labor force population from which it theoretically could recruit. However, various organizational decisions such as what recruitment methods to use and how stringent to make job requirements gradually narrow the number of potential candidates until ultimately only a few individuals may report for work. Although organizations have often ignored how the decisions they make can affect this winnowing process, throughout the remainder of this chapter and in subsequent chapters the importance of considering this filtering process will be highlighted.

Six Basic Considerations in Developing a Recruitment Strategy

Once an organization has completed the recruitment planning process, it should have a clear idea of how many and what types of recruits it requires. Given this basic information, an employer next needs to develop a strategy for recruiting the required number and types of job candidates. In terms of developing such a strategy, as succinctly stated by Robert Armstrong, manager of professional staffing at DuPont Company, "there is no best way to recruit new employees."[28] Instead, Armstrong maintains that an organization must develop "well-thought-out, long-term programs" for recruiting candidates to meet its human resource requirements. In developing a well-thought-out recruitment strategy, there are six key considerations: where to recruit, whom to recruit, how to recruit, when to recruit, who does the recruiting, and what information to communicate to recruits. In this section, each of these considerations will be addressed briefly; in later chapters each will be explored more fully. In providing an overview of these six topics, the emphasis will be placed on the external recruitment of prospective employees for entry-level positions.

Where to Recruit Job Candidates

A fundamental consideration in developing a recruitment strategy is deciding on the geographic area in which to recruit job candidates. In order to reduce recruitment costs, employers typically limit the scope of their recruitment efforts to a geographic area that is likely to yield a sufficient number of job candidates for their purposes. Not surprisingly, the size of this geographic region is generally a function of the type of position being filled and the organization's location. In terms of the type of position being filled, research has shown that employers generally seek clerical and blue-collar workers locally. In contrast, they traditionally seek managerial and professional employees nationally or regionally, and recruit employees with technical expertise regionally or locally.[29] Difficulties in filling certain technical and professional positions have caused some organizations to rely increasingly on recruiting internationally for certain positions.

In addition to the type of job opening, another influence on the geographic scope of an organization's recruitment efforts is where the job is located. Geographic location can affect recruitment in two important ways: labor supply and relative applicant interest. Geographic areas often differ considerably in terms of labor supply, that is, the number of qualified job candidates. For example, a firm that is located in suburban Boston and that needs computer specialists may be able to recruit a sufficient number of qualified individuals from the many universities located in the Boston metropolitan area. In contrast, a comparable firm located in Portland, Oregon, may need to recruit in a much larger geographic area in order to locate a sufficient number of qualified job candidates. With regard to the influence on applicant interest of the geographic location in which jobs are situated, clearly some locales are generally perceived as being much more desirable than others. Thus, an organization that is located in a desirable location may be able to recruit in a much more limited geographic area than a firm with a less desirable location.

Unfortunately, there is relatively little data for an organization to draw on in deciding where to recruit. In some cases, an employer may be able to use its own past recruitment experiences in making decisions. For example, if in the past an organization has placed job advertisements in newspapers in several major cities, it can examine the applicant yield from each newspaper advertisement. From such a study, a company located in Baton Rouge may discover that ads placed in newspapers in Southern cities yield a much greater level of interest than ads placed in Midwestern newspapers. In other cases, an organization may be able to make sound recruitment judgments by staying abreast of the employment trends in other areas of the country. For example, during the late 1970s several companies in the Southwestern United States successfully recruited in Midwestern states that were suffering from the economic recession in the auto industry.

Whom to Recruit

Earlier in this chapter, a number of philosophical issues underlying the adoption of a basic recruitment orientation (internal, external, or a mixture of both) were addressed. In order to translate its recruitment philosophy into a concrete recruitment strategy for filling a given job opening, an organization should make a conscious decision about what specific groups to target. The failure of an organization to systematically determine from which group or groups it will try to recruit can lead to wasted recruitment efforts (for example, placing advertisements in more outlets than is necessary). Among the various segments of the labor market that an organization can draw on as sources of external recruits are students (individuals attending high school, vocational school, or college), former employees (individuals who have retired or are now with other employers), the hard-core unemployed, members of protected groups (minorities), members of a particular religion (more will be said about the appropriateness of this strategy in a later chapter on legal issues), the handicapped, homemakers attempting to re-enter the work force, retirees, individuals referred through a union hiring hall, and/or persons currently working for other organizations (competitors). Although less commonly discussed, one can also segment an organization's internal labor force into different sources of recruits. For example, for a given job opening, an organization could decide to fill a position by promoting someone. Alternatively, the employer may decide that it would consider filling the position via a lateral transfer or a demotion.

As was noted earlier, in attempting to fill entry-level positions, companies are increasingly targeting labor market segments that have been relatively ignored in the past, such as the urban poor and the handicapped. For example, Pizza Hut of New Jersey has begun to staff some of its stores with youths from high-unemployment urban areas by using a van pool system.[30] The reasons for tapping new recruiting sources is summed up succinctly by Madelyn Jennings, senior vice president of personnel for Gannett Co.: "We are looking a lot harder in places that we haven't focused our attention on: the disabled, retired, older workers. . . . It has nothing to do with altruism or concern about society. It has to do with survival."[31]

In summary, a key step in developing a recruitment strategy is the determination of what source(s) of job candidates the organization wishes to inform of job vacancies. Many of the relative advantages and disadvantages of the various sources of recruits are obvious, as in targeting members of protected groups to reduce affirmative action pressure (the pros and cons of various sources will be discussed in detail later in the text). In selecting a source of recruits, an organization's choice should be consistent with its recruitment philosophy whenever possible, although there may be cases where inconsistency is necessary. For example, in attempting to fill a given position, an employer that has a strong internal recruitment orientation may be unable to find an internal candidate with the appropriate level of qualifications.

How to Recruit

Once an employer has decided from what source or sources it will recruit, it next needs to decide how it will attempt to reach the prospective employees in the given labor market segment(s). Among the recruitment methods[32] that are commonly used for attracting the attention of potential job candidates are advertising, employee referral, recruiting at schools, employment agencies, executive search firms, special events, job posting, and direct applications. Each of these methods and many others will be discussed later in this text, so only a brief overview will be provided in this chapter.

Advertising. According to a survey of organizational recruiting practices by the Bureau of National Affairs (BNA),[33] newspaper advertisements are one of the most common methods of informing potential candidates of job vacancies and are used in filling a wide range of jobs. In addition to newspaper ads, advertisements placed in professional magazines and technical journals are also commonly used for publicizing job openings that require somewhat specialized expertise. As the competition to fill certain types of positions has increased, organizations also have begun to experiment with less traditional types of advertising. For example, recent articles have documented the increasing use of radio, television, and direct mail campaigns in advertising job opportunities.

Employee referrals. In addition to advertising, employers also commonly rely on referrals made by current employees as a source of qualified job candidates. Some organizations offer cash incentives for referring persons who are eventually hired (Lockheed Missiles & Space Company's "Referralot" program is an example), while other employers offer no tangible incentive to employees. Although employee referral programs have several positive attributes in that they are generally an inexpensive and quick way to fill vacant positions, as was portrayed in one of the vignettes in Chapter 1, such programs frequently result in minorities and women being underrepresented in the applicant pool.

Recruiting at schools. According to BNA's 1988 survey, in attempting to fill certain types of office/clerical positions, employers have relied heavily on recruiting at local high schools, trade schools, and vocational institutes. The same survey showed that in recruiting for white-collar positions, organizations frequently recruited at colleges and universities. There are several steps that an employer can take to improve the yield from such school visits. Of particular value can be an examination of its past recruitment experience at an institution. Such an analysis may make an employer aware that few job candidates have resulted from a given school or that those candidates who were recruited tended not to be effective employees.

Employment agencies. An organization can also use public and private employment agencies in attempting to fill vacancies. Most public employment agencies are operated under the auspices of the United States Training and Employment Service (USTES). For the most part, public employment offices serve as a source for recruiting clerical and blue-collar employees. Private agencies not only can provide candidates for lower-level jobs, but can also be a source of lower- and middle-level management candidates. In contrast to most public agencies, which provide referrals at no cost to the employer, private agencies generally charge the employer if any of the individuals they refer are hired. Since both public and private agencies typically have a backlog of individuals seeking employment, they can usually supply an employer with a list of job candidates quickly. In addition, both types of agencies generally do at least some minimal level of screening of the candidates they refer.

Executive search firms. As the name suggests, executive search firms are geared toward providing employers with upper-level managers. Individuals generally do not contact an executive search firm; rather, executive search firms initiate contact with executives who may be persuaded to leave their current positions. Given the nature of the positions to be filled and the type of individual being sought (executive-level, currently employed), the work of an executive search firm is both labor-intensive and highly confidential. Thus, in comparison to many of the other recruitment methods mentioned in this section, executive search firms can be quite expensive.

Special event recruiting. Although not as commonly used as the preceding recruitment methods, recently organizations have begun to experiment with special event recruiting as a way to fill positions. Among the activities that employers have used are job fairs, career days, and open houses. Although the specifics of these activities will be saved for a later chapter, two facts should be noted here. First, special event recruiting can be effective for publicizing the organization as a place of employment (as distinct from filling a given position). Second, a number of organizations have found special event recruiting to be an effective method of stimulating interest from groups of people who may otherwise be difficult to attract. For example, during times when the aviation industry was booming, aerospace companies such as Boeing used job fairs to make contact with aeronautical engineers employed at other firms.

Direct applications/Applicant-initiated recruitment. No matter what the type of position, organizations have always relied heavily on direct applications from job seekers as a means of filling job openings. In some cases, job seekers apply in person to the organization; in others, they mail unsolicited résumés in hopes of locating suitable positions. An obvious advantage of direct applications is that they involve very little expense on the part of the employer. In addition, some research has suggested that those who submit unsolicited applications often make above-average employees (e.g., Breaugh, 1981). Although unsolicited applications may seem a burden when no job vacancies exist, given their beneficial features, most organizations should welcome such applications. To generate a consistent flow of direct applications, an organization's visibility and reputation are crucial—it is not enough to be known; an employer also must have a positive image. Several specific ways in which an organization can improve both its visibility and its reputation will be discussed throughout the remainder of this text.

Job posting. For the most part, this overview of recruitment methods has focused on stimulating interest from external job candidates. This is not meant to suggest that employers do not use formal methods for recruiting internal candidates, however. In fact, many organizations advertise job openings internally before turning to external recruitment methods.

When to Recruit

As can be seen in Exhibit 2.1, in projecting staffing needs the human resource planning process should establish a time frame for filling job openings. In terms of developing a recruitment strategy, a key issue is when to start recruiting so that positions are filled in a timely manner. If an organization procrastinates in beginning the recruitment process, it may find that it is unable to fill openings with qualified individuals by the date desired (Rynes, 1991). Thus, the organization may be forced to choose between leaving positions vacant or hiring applicants who are less than fully qualified. On the other hand, if an employer begins the recruitment process too early, it may find that it has to hire job candidates before they are actually needed or that desirable candidates are lost because of the long delay in making hiring decisions.

In attempting to make informed decisions about when to begin the recruitment process, a careful analysis of prior recruitment experiences can be useful. By examining the average time that elapsed between major decision points in filling a position in the past (known as time-lapse data), an organization may be able to derive a reasonable estimate of how much time it should allow for filling a similar position in the future.[34] For example, from a review of historical recruitment data, an employer may discover that the average time between notifying its current employees of a job opening and having a sufficient number of employee referrals is fourteen days. Such data may also show that on average interviews can be scheduled within seven days of a candidate being referred. Finally, an organization may determine that in the past it took an average of twenty-one days after a job offer was made for it to be accepted and for an individual to report to work. By adding up the average amount of time between each stage of the recruitment process, an organization can get a sense of how far in advance of the projected hiring date it should begin recruitment activities.[35]

In addition to being concerned about when to begin recruiting, an organization also should pay attention to the timing of various actions during the recruitment process. A recent statement by a General Mills executive reflects the importance that some organizations attach to timely recruitment follow-up actions: "When we find someone we really want, we work hard to close the sale. For example, if we meet such people at one of our informal wine and cheese gatherings, we'll immediately send a follow-up letter and invite them to Minneapolis. When they are here, we'll make sure they have lunch with a recent graduate of their school or someone from their home town. We will then make them an offer at the end of the day—no 'We'll get back to you in a few weeks' stuff. Then, if they don't accept immediately, we might fly them and their spouses back to corporate headquarters to see the community and meet the chairman. In between, there will be all the appropriate follow-up letters and calls" (Kotter, 1988, p. 86).

Who Should Do the Recruiting

Compared to several of the recruitment topics addressed in this chapter, a considerable amount of research has focused on the effects of the type of person who does the recruiting. Among the variables that have been examined are the influence of the recruiter's personal characteristics (race, age, etc.), position in the organization (line versus staff), and behavior (openness, friendliness, and so on) in the recruitment interview. In general, research has not shown recruiter characteristics to have a major impact on the perceptions or actions of job candidates (Rynes, 1991).

The failure of empirical research to document the importance of recruiter effects is somewhat surprising in that many sophisticated companies believe who does the recruiting can make a big difference.[36] For example, rather than using traditional personnel department recruiters,

Hewlett-Packard goes to the considerable expense, in terms of both time and money, of sending out small teams of engineers and managers to recruit people with whom they will work (Fombrum et al., 1984). Hewlett-Packard believes that such an approach "allows the applicant to get a sense of fit with the culture he or she may have an opportunity to join so that a conscious decision can be made as to whether it would be comfortable for them" (p. 224). As described earlier, General Mills also believes that recruiter characteristics can make a difference. In recruiting it tries to make sure a candidate has contact with someone from his or her home town or who is a recent graduate of the candidate's university. In his study of the practices of U.S. corporations, Kotter (1988) found that, in contrast to the norm of having human resource professionals be primarily responsible for recruitment, the top-rated firms gave primary responsibility to line management. For example, Kotter found that at First Boston the managing director spends half his time on recruiting and that the chairman of the board at General Mills actually visited college campuses. Kotter also reported that senior management at Merck, including the CEO, devote considerable time to recruiting.

This section is intended only to provide an overview of some of the major issues that should be considered in developing a sound recruitment strategy. Some of the possible explanations for the apparent contradiction between research findings on recruiter characteristics and actual practice will be saved for later in this text. However, a few basic issues that should be considered in making a rational decision about who should be involved in recruitment merit consideration at this point.

Since a key function of a recruiter is to provide a job candidate with information relevant to making a job-choice decision, it should be obvious that those involved in recruiting should be quite knowledgeable concerning both the job under consideration and the organization as a whole. However, it is not enough that the recruiter be knowledgeable; the recruiter must also be able to communicate the information effectively. Thus, it is widely accepted that interpersonal skills are important for a recruiter (Lord, 1989).

Beyond interpersonal skills, it is important that the recruiter be seen as a credible information source. For example, the same information about work group climate may be seen as much more credible if it comes from a prospective co-worker rather than from a representative from the human resources department. If, as some experts have suggested, applicants view a recruiter as a signal of unknown organizational attributes (for example, if a recruiter makes remarks that are sexist in tone, the applicant, correctly or incorrectly, may perceive the organization as insensitive to such matters), the importance of a company carefully selecting and training recruiters should be apparent.[37] Clearly, an employer wants to use recruiters who make a good first impression on prospective candidates. In line with making a good first impression, the use of executives has several potential advantages, as summed up in the following statement by an executive in Kotter's study (1988): "Our current senior management is in the best position to know how many and what kind of people will be needed to run the business in the future; they understand where our business strategy is taking us better than anyone. They also are better able to spot the kind of quality minds and interpersonal abilities we want in young people; in a sense, it takes one to know one. And they are in a much better position to sell the company than are lower-level managers or personnel staff" (p. 85).

What Information to Communicate to Recruits

The sixth factor that should be considered in developing a recruitment strategy for filling a specific position is what information the organization should communicate to prospective employees. By carefully considering the amount and the type of information it wants to convey, those involved in recruiting should be able to improve the quality of the job advertisements they draft, the recruitment literature they develop, the job fair presentations they give, and the recruitment interviews they conduct.

In terms of the information to communicate, at least four important issues merit consideration: what topics to cover, how much information to provide on each topic, to what extent the recruitment information communicated should be custom-tailored to the position being filled, and whether the information conveyed should present a realistic as opposed to a flattering view of the job vacancy. Each of these issues will be addressed in detail in a later chapter; at this point it suffices to say that many organizations do not appear to have seriously reflected on these issues in developing a recruitment strategy. For example, in a study that examined the recruitment literature used by companies (Stantial et al., 1979), it was found that information on many of the factors that were rated as being of greatest importance by prospective recruits, such as details of and requisite qualifications for the entry-level position, were seen as lacking or poorly presented in the actual recruitment literature.

Although we will discuss what information to communicate later in the text, an obvious yet often overlooked issue should be noted here. In preparing recruitment-related communications (job advertisements, recruitment brochures, etc.), most organizations are aware of the importance of using language that is at the appropriate level of difficulty for those being recruited. However, with the exception of some employers in the Southwestern United States that regularly recruit Hispanics, many organizations seem unaware of the fact that English is not the primary language of many potential job candidates, especially for lower-level jobs. For example, consider the case of Quaker Fabric Corp. of Fall River, Massachusetts (Gupta and Tannebaum, 1989). Given the labor shortages in the Northeast, Quaker Fabric was having difficulty hiring new employees. Research showed that 80 percent of Quaker's employees spoke Portuguese and 50 percent spoke *only* Portuguese. Based on this fact, with the help of a consultant Quaker designed recruitment posters and brochures in both English and Portuguese. These posters were part of an employee referral program that subsequently resulted in the hiring of 185 employees in a three-month period. From this example, the importance of employers being sensitive to language issues should be evident.

RECRUITMENT ACTIVITIES

As portrayed in Exhibit 2.2, ideally once an employer has developed its recruitment strategy, the conduct of the actual recruitment activities should be somewhat straightforward.[38] For example, on becoming aware of impending job openings (as when an employee requisition is received from the hiring department), those responsible for recruitment might place job advertisements in appropriate outlets, contact college placement offices to schedule campus visits, update recruitment literature, circulate information about the job openings internally throughout the organization, and/or review procedures for handling paperwork relevant to the applicant flow.[39]

Given the various federal and state regulations that can affect the recruitment process, before any specific actions are taken it is generally wise for those responsible for recruitment to contact the department within the organization that is responsible for compliance with government regulations. This step should lessen the likelihood that a recruitment activity will violate existing laws or fail to comply with executive orders. If a job opening is subject to a collective bargaining agreement, those coordinating the recruitment effort also need to determine whether the union should be notified of the vacancy. Such notification can be important if the employer has formally agreed to use the union as a referral source for potential job applicants.

A key recruitment activity that is sometimes undervalued is the day-to-day monitoring of events. For example, as applications and/or résumés are received, they should be logged in at a central office. The use of a central location enables an organization to keep track of each applicant's status more easily. As decisions are made concerning a person's job candidacy, the individual's file should be immediately updated. In addition to keeping an up-to-date record on each job applicant, it is also important to respond to each candidate in a timely and professional manner. For example, following a campus interview, the organization may want to send the candidate a short personal letter. Another important day-to-day recruitment activity is the coordination of on-site visits by job candidates. Those involved in the corporate recruitment function may be responsible for coordinating candidate transportation, hotel arrangements, meals, entertainment, and the actual schedule of interviews.

In summary, if an organization has carefully developed a recruitment strategy, actually carrying out the recruitment activities should generally be a straightforward process. However, as will become apparent in later chapters, even with careful planning things can go astray.

RECRUITMENT EVALUATION

Given that recruiting employees can be an expensive activity, it is somewhat surprising that most organizations do not formally evaluate their recruitment efforts (Rynes and Boudreau, 1986).[40] For example, most employers do not keep track of who their most effective recruiters are, nor do they evaluate the relative costs of different recruitment methods. Despite the lack of formal evaluation information, there is at least some evidence that higher-level managers do not believe that their organizations do a very good job of recruiting employees (Kotter, 1988).

To get a sense of the complexity involved in evaluating an organization's recruitment activities, consider the simple case of a hypothetical company that used only two different recruitment methods—newspaper ads and visits to local college campuses—for filling sales trainee positions. Probably the most basic question the company would be interested in answering is whether it filled the trainee positions. However, to more thoroughly evaluate its recruitment efforts, the company might also want answers to some of the following questions that compare the use of newspaper ads and college recruitment: Did one method yield the majority of the candidates hired? What was the relative cost per hire of each of the methods? Did one or both of the methods help us in terms of meeting affirmative action goals? How well did the employees hired via each approach work out in terms of subsequent performance and job longevity? In attempting to do a better job of college recruiting in the future, the hypothetical company might be interested in even more information. For example, in considering whether it should change the way it recruits, the employer would likely want to know: Were some recruiters more effective than others in yielding college hires? Was our college recruitment litera- ture perceived favorably by students? Did some colleges yield more and better job candidates than others? Should we begin visiting colleges ear- lier next year? Is there any way to work with the colleges we visit to have them prescreen candidates for us?

From this brief discussion, it is apparent that an examination of past recruitment experiences can provide a wealth of information on which to base future recruitment decisions. More specifically, it should be evident that if an employer gathers appropriate data it should be able to intelli- gently address each of the six considerations discussed under the heading of recruitment strategy development. In contrast, without such evalua- tion information, an organization may never become aware that some of its recruitment-related activities are not worth the time and money in- vested.

Allstate Insurance Company provides an example of the importance of examining recruitment practices (Halcrow, 1989a). In comparing the results of using newspaper ads and a direct mail campaign, Allstate dis- covered that a series of newspaper ads it placed in several local papers in 1988 resulted in no one being hired. In contrast, a single direct mail effort that year led to more than 500 calls and twenty people being hired. Given such different yields from these two recruitment methods, it should not be surprising that Allstate was very pleased with its experimental use of a direct mail campaign.

In summary, only by rigorously evaluating its past recruitment efforts can an employer hope to develop a scientifically sound, legally defensible, and cost-effective approach to recruitment. As will be discussed in more detail in Chapter 13, systematically evaluating all aspects of the recruit- ment process can be a complex undertaking.

SUMMARY

This chapter was designed to show the importance of integrating recruit- ment with an organization's strategic business planning process and to in- troduce a model of the recruitment process. Although the information in this chapter will be expanded on in the remainder of this text, the cursory treatment provided here gives a sense of the complexity involved in making recruitment decisions. Given such factors as government regulations, shrinking labor supplies, and increasing global competition, it should be apparent that organizations can no longer afford to treat employee recruitment as a relatively unimportant, nonscientific human resource activity. Instead, as was documented by the numerous examples of how "blue-chip" companies such as Hewlett-Packard recruit, organizations must treat employee recruitment as a crucial process that will either contribute to or detract from the accomplishment of their strategic management objectives.

NOTES

1. Extensive coverage of the topic of strategic business planning is beyond the scope of this text. For more information, interested readers are referred to recent issues of the *Strategic Management Journal* and to Butler, Ferris, and Napier's *Strategy and Human Resources Management* (1991).

2. A discussion of how the external business environment (for example, the degree of business competition) and certain aspects of the legal environment (such as antitrust regulations) can affect business planning is beyond the scope of this text. Legal environment issues (affirmative action planning, Title VII of the Civil Rights Act of 1964, etc.) that relate specifically to employee recruitment will be discussed in a later chapter in this text.

3. Although the term *corporate philosophy* and similar terms such as *organizational mission* have been used in various ways, fundamentally they refer to a shared sense of the organization's basic reason for existence. Obviously, the degree to which a corporate philosophy is formalized and shared will differ across organizations.

4. Although different authors make differing distinctions between the types of planning that can occur (e.g., corporate versus business planning) and the types of planning objectives that can be set (e.g., business versus operational objectives), for the purposes of this text, a simplified treatment of these topics will suffice. As used in this text, strategic business objectives refer to "statements of definable and measurable accomplishments that, when realized, fulfill an organization's mission statement" (Dunham and Pierce, 1989, p. 280).

5. Readers who are interested in a more detailed treatment of the differences between strategic business objectives and operational objectives should refer to Dunham and Pierce (1989) or other similar texts. However, a simple example that conveys some of the differences may be helpful. Some of the strategic objectives that a university would state in its five-year plan might include improving the quality of the student body, improving the financial state of the institution, and expanding academic program offerings. To move toward accomplishing these strategic objectives, the university might establish such operational objectives as increasing the number of academic scholarships by 15 percent in each of the next two years, increasing external financial support from alumni next year by 22 percent, and establishing new graduate programs in accounting and computer science within the next two years. As will become apparent from the coverage of the topics of human resource planning and recruitment planning, this university's strategic and operational objectives

have clear human resource management implications (recruiting more employees to work in the development office, recruiting additional faculty to staff new graduate programs, and so on).

6. The topic of human resource planning is quite complex. Given space constraints, the coverage in this section is focused on those issues that are particularly relevant to the topic of employee recruitment. Readers who are interested in in-depth coverage of the topic of human resource planning should refer to *Human Resource Planning*, a journal dedicated to this subject.

7. Clearly the accuracy of predictions concerning human resource needs and availability depends on the accuracy of the various assumptions that are made. However, an organization will generally make better decisions even if forecast estimates are imprecise than if it gives no consideration at all to forecasting human resource requirements and availability.

8. Given the imprecision involved in making forecasts about human resource requirements and availabilities, an organization may ignore slight numerical discrepancies. Decisions concerning how big a discrepancy must be to merit attention are generally made on a case-by-case basis.

9. Lawler (1988) provides a good discussion of the factors that help those with HRM expertise contribute to the strategic planning process.

10. See Bacas (1988).

11. As an example of how seriously some organizations are beginning to view the recruitment of employees, Bennett (1989b) notes that some organizations regard recruitment as a confidential matter of business strategy. For example, he cites a spokesperson from Amoco Corp. who refused to discuss the company's recruitment efforts because ". . . we see it as proprietary and competitive information" (p. A4).

12. In fact, although organizations rarely consider the possibility of filling entry-level job openings internally, lateral transfers and demotions are internal recruitment methods that can be used to fill such positions.

13. In contrast, an organization can destroy employee motivation if individuals are perceived as getting promoted because of factors that are irrelevant to job performance (e.g., "office politics").

14. See Campbell et al. (1970), Schuler and Jackson (1987), Falvey (1987), and Fombrum et al. (1984).

15. Falvey (1987) is not totally against a philosophy of internal managerial recruitment. Instead, he argues for a recruitment philosophy that aims for a mixture of viewpoints.

16. Fombrum et al. (1984) discuss how bringing in outsiders can also be valuable as a signal to current organizational members that "things are changing." For example, they cite how AT&T brought in senior-level managers from IBM and Procter & Gamble to lead its business sectors when it announced its new "marketing orientation."

17. The author recognizes that organizations may actually have different recruitment orientations for different types of jobs (e.g., managerial versus technical). However, in order to simplify the discussion, the presentation will not address such subtleties.

18. Although Fombrum et al. (1984) refer to organizations that "take the position they will go out and hire the appropriate people from the competition, if necessary, when needed" (p. 45), more recently many organizations have found such a strategy to be ineffective (see Bacas, 1988).

19. For more detail on Merck & Co., the reader should refer to an article by Lawrence (1989).

20. Gatewood and Feild (1990) provide an excellent treatment of the development of job specifications for employee selection purposes.

21. A discussion of the legitimacy of such personal characteristics as job specifications will be addressed in later chapters that directly address legal issues and affirmative action recruiting.

22. In an article that addresses the issue of job requirements in the context of recruitment decision making, Acuff (1982) discusses instances in which a lack of information about job qualification requirements resulted in the use of vague and ultimately ineffective job advertisements. He also cites cases in which artificial, unstated job requirements subjected organizations to potential legal liability.

23. In this text, the terms *prospective employee, job candidate,* and *applicant* will be used interchangeably. Although all three terms are appropriate for most recruitment situations, technically the term *applicant* may not be appropriate for a situation in which the organization directly contacts a person to inquire about his or her interest in a position.

24. Getting access to so-called yield ratio data from other organizations is not easy. In some cases, such information can be gained through personal contacts with other members of a professional organization to which one belongs. Such information is also sometimes reported in practitioner-oriented journals. For example, Bargerstock (1989a) reported yield ratio data for filling an internal management position at a midwestern hospital.

25. For example, if only twenty-one vacancies are forecast for this position next year, the organization might decide to visit fewer campuses.

26. This section draws heavily on the work of Boudreau and Rynes (1985).

27. According to Boudreau and Rynes (1985), "selectees are the group of applicants actually hired" (p. 356). Although this definition served their purpose, in discussing recruitment strategy development it is useful to make a distinction between those who are selected by the organization (i.e., receive job offers) and those who actually start work.

28. Bureau of National Affairs (1984), p. 3.

29. See Heneman, Schwab, Fossum, and Dyer (1989) and Lord (1989) for more detail on issues related to the geographic scope of recruitment.

30. See Tannenbaum (1988).

31. Bennett (1989a), p. A4.

32. In the recruitment literature, the terms *recruitment method* and *recruitment source* sometimes are used interchangeably and sometimes are used to refer to different concepts. For example, Mondy, Noe, and Edwards (1987) use the term *recruitment source* to refer to the targeted labor market segment (e.g., college students) and the term *recruitment method* to refer to the specific means by which an organization attempts to recruit employees (e.g., employee referral). In some cases, it seems unnecessary to distinguish the terms. For example, if an organization recruits through a college placement office, this suggests both a labor market segment and a recruitment method. In other cases, the method used and the labor market segment should be distinguished.

33. This section draws heavily on the results of a survey by the Bureau of National Affairs (1988).

34. Obviously, to compute time-lapse data, an employer must have recorded data on the time intervals between decision points for its past recruitment efforts.

35. Although time-lapse data can be a good source of information to use in developing a recruitment strategy, this information should be used carefully. For example, a user of time-lapse data should be aware that, if conditions that previously affected the speed with which recruiting progressed have changed, then the time estimates derived from past recruitment experiences should be adjusted accordingly.

36. Rynes (1991) suggests a number of reasons why the empirical literature on recruiter characteristics may have underestimated their true influence on applicant decision making. Her comments will be discussed later in the text.

37. A large-scale survey by Rynes and Boudreau (1986) found that most recruiters who visit college campuses had received little or no training.

38. Because this section is only intended to provide an overview of day-to-day recruitment activities, it is written primarily in terms of the actions taken by those in a human resource department with responsibility for recruitment. In some organizations, line managers may be responsible for some of the actions discussed in this section.

39. Specific information on what applicant data should be kept and the advantages and disadvantages of computerizing such data will be discussed in detail in Chapter 13.

40. Although the complexities of rigorously evaluating one's recruitment operation will be saved for Chapter 13, a few basic issues merit consideration in this section.

3

Organizational Recruitment: The Job Candidate's Perspective

Dad: Mark, son, have you given any thought to the sort of job you want when you graduate?

Mark: Oh sure. I don't know what field it'll be in, but I know that it will have to be creative—a position of responsibility, but not one that restricts personal freedom. It must pay fairly well; . . . the atmosphere, relaxed, informal; my colleagues, interesting, mellow, and not too concerned with a structured working situation.

Dad: In short, you have no intention of getting a job.

Mark: I didn't say that.

(Doonesbury by Gary Trudeau, 1973)

In considering most recruitment-related decisions (When should a recruitment campaign begin? Who should be used as recruiters?), it is natural to approach them from an organization's perspective (By what date would the company like the positions to be filled? Who is available next week for a recruiting trip to the University of Utah?). However, as will become apparent from the material presented in this and in the next chapter, the quality of an organization's recruitment-related decisions generally will be substantially improved if the perspective of potential job applicants is also considered. For example, in deciding on whom to send to a campus as recruiters, an employer should consider the perspective of the students being recruited. For example, engineering students may be more impressed if recent engineering graduates from their universities, rather than individuals from the personnel department, are used as recruiters.

Because an awareness of the applicant's perspective can improve the quality of an employer's recruitment decisions, the next two chapters will provide an overview of several important recruitment-related topics from this viewpoint. Bear in mind, however, that space limitations preclude a comprehensive discussion of all of the important issues, and the treatment of the topics that are examined will be necessarily brief.[1]

HOW APPLICANTS VIEW THE RECRUITMENT PROCESS: FOUR VIGNETTES

Before reviewing research that has addressed recruitment-related issues from the job candidate's perspective, four vignettes are presented that highlight the job-hunting experiences of four individuals. These vignettes portray the multitude of factors that must be considered in order to understand an individual's job-choice decision-making process.

Lori Springer: Nursing Student

Lori Springer will graduate in three weeks with a bachelor of science degree in nursing from a university in Southern California. Based on her conversations with other students, Lori believes that job hunting was remarkably easy for her. Reflecting on why she experienced so little stress while many of her fellow students were close to traumatized by job hunting, Lori has decided that several factors explain their different experiences.

A major factor is that, compared to many undergraduate majors, it is quite easy for a nursing graduate to find a good position. In Southern California, most hospitals, medical clinics, and doctors' offices have great difficulty in filling nursing vacancies. This nursing shortage has forced health care institutions to compete aggressively for nurses. To attract nurses, most hospitals have raised salaries substantially, introduced more regular work schedules, and instituted "signing bonuses." For Lori, the nursing shortage meant that all three of the hospitals with which she chose to interview quickly made her attractive job offers.

A second factor that Lori believes made her job hunting go smoothly was the considerable information she had about the hospitals she was considering and her own awareness of her personal goals. Lori has thought about what she wanted in her first job since the beginning of her junior year. From her field experience during her training, Lori knew that she would enjoy a job as a staff nurse in a hospital. However, based on discussions with several alumnae from her nursing program, who warned her of burn-out, lack of career advancement, and salary compression, Lori was not sure she wanted a career as a staff nurse. Given her understanding of what a nursing professor did, Lori thought that she would like to eventually teach nursing. She knew that to do this she would need at least a master's and maybe a Ph.D. degree.

With her wish to attend graduate school in mind as she investigated hospitals during her senior year, Lori paid particular attention to whether they offered tuition reimbursement for employees and regular work hours, and she quickly eliminated any hospital that did not offer both. Because of her interest in teaching, Lori also decided it would be best to work at a research-oriented hospital. Thus, she decided to apply only to hospitals that were affiliated with medical schools. Based on her research, which included calls to hospitals, conversations with alumnae working at various local hospitals, and talks with nursing faculty, Lori determined that only three hospitals met her three major criteria. Because she received offers from all three hospitals, she was in the enviable position of being able to select among them.

Because all three hospitals met her major criteria and offered very similar starting salaries, Lori's decision came down to less-important factors. Ultimately, she selected the hospital she did because it offered the largest signing bonus and because three of her classmates had accepted positions there, which helped her confirm that she had made the right job choice. A final reason that Lori feels so comfortable with her job choice is her knowledge that, if this job does not work out, she could quickly find an equivalent position.

Mark Smith: Human Resource Management Major

Mark Smith is graduating in five weeks with a degree in business from a university located in Houston and has been trying to find a job in the human resource management (HRM) field. So far, he has sent résumés to over fifty companies and although he knew the HRM job market was tight, he is still surprised by how difficult it has been to find a job. With graduation fast approaching and having interviewed with only two companies, today, April 16, Mark accepted his only job offer. While Mark is satisfied with the offer, in looking back on the past semester he wishes things had gone more smoothly.

The first company Mark interviewed with was a large business-equipment manufacturer. Mark had been excited by the prospect of working for this organization because a job with this company would have meant a high starting salary and talented colleagues. His first interview was on campus in mid-January. One month later, he went through a series of interviews at the company's corporate headquarters in Denver, where he would have had to relocate if he had gone to work for the company.

Although Mark initially had a strong desire to work for this company, his desire gradually diminished. One reason for his losing interest is the way he has been treated since he interviewed in Denver. Mark's perception is that since he visited Denver the business equipment manufacturer has shown little interest in him. For example, after his visit to Denver, Mark wrote a letter expressing his interest in a job with the company. Two weeks later, Mark wrote a second letter asking if he could supply the company with any additional information and inquiring when the company anticipated filling the position. Ten days after he sent this letter, Mark received a letter from someone he had never met in the human resource department informing him that the company anticipated filling the position within three to six weeks. The letter was impersonal and struck Mark as being a form letter. After he received this letter, over four weeks passed with no word from the company.

The second organization Mark interviewed with was a construction company located in Houston. Although it was not as glamorous as the business-equipment company, there were many things Mark liked about this firm. First, in contrast to the Denver organization, the people at the construction company seemed truly interested in him. He received warm personal letters after his campus interview in early March and after his visit to company headquarters in late March. These letters were followed by personal telephone calls from the campus interviewer and from the person who would be Mark's supervisor if he were to go to work for the construction company. A second factor to which Mark came to give considerable weight was being able to stay in Houston, where he would be close to his family and friends. Mark also felt that a job with this smaller company would enable him to work in several personnel areas, whereas with the business-equipment company he would have to specialize in one area. While Mark knew that the salary he would receive from the construction firm would be less than the one he could expect from the business-equipment company, some of this difference would be made up for by Houston's cheaper cost of living.

On April 5, Mark received a job offer from the construction company and was given two weeks to make a decision. Given this time constraint, yesterday (April 15) Mark called the business equipment firm to inform them he had received a job offer and needed to make a decision shortly. He was told that the company was still interested in him but would not be able to let him know whether he would receive a job offer for at least two more weeks. After this conversation, Mark had real doubts whether the interest expressed in him was genuine. In fact, he suspected that the company had already made an offer to someone else and was waiting to hear if it would be accepted.

In today's mail, Mark received a letter from a Houston-based chemical company to which he had sent a résumé. The letter stated that he would be contacted shortly to set up an interview. Although Mark thinks highly of this company, he realizes that there is no way he could receive a job offer from them before he had to let the construction company know of his decision. Thus, Mark had to decide whether to accept a job with the construction company or give up his only firm job offer for the possibility of an offer from the business-equipment company, the chemical firm, or some other organization that has yet to contact him. After mulling things over for most of the day, Mark decided to go with the certain offer from a company that seems to really want him. It was not an easy decision. Mark knows a number of people at the chemical company, and they all think it is a great place to work. From what he knows about the chemical company, Mark would prefer to work there rather than at the construction company, but considering the difficulty he had in getting one job offer, Mark is not willing to give up this firm offer for the chance of a better one.

Jerome Katz: Senior Chemist

Dr. Jerome Katz is a senior chemist in the consumer products division of a large corporation. Jerry has been with this corporation since he received his Ph.D. in 1962 and has been very happy with his position—he has a good salary, works on interesting projects, and until recently felt secure in his job. Reflecting on his career, Jerry realized he had never thought about leaving his organization.

Recently, however, several factors have caused Jerry to start thinking about leaving. It all began nine months ago when his company began a study of its product lines for the purpose of developing a strategic business plan. When the study was completed, his company announced that it intended to divest itself of several product lines that were not projected to generate reasonable profits in the next decade. Jerry came to realize the consequences of this strategic plan two months ago when two product lines were sold. Although a severance package was offered to those employees who were not offered jobs with the companies that had acquired these product lines, Jerry realized that this package did nothing to ease the pain that many of those who had lost jobs were experiencing.

Seeing colleagues lose their jobs started Jerry thinking about whether the division in which he worked might be sold and, if so, whether he would lose his job. Despite considerable effort, Jerry has been unable to get formal word on the prospects for his division. In terms of his own job security, Jerry is uncertain whether he would be able to transfer to another division within his company if the consumer products division were sold. However, given his age and his salary, he feels that, if another company were to buy his division, he would likely lose his job.

Although Jerry has always had tremendous company loyalty, these recent events have made him start to question the wisdom of this loyalty. For example, Jerry's organization discourages the publication of research. Thus, although during his career he has conducted several studies that would have been publishable, Jerry has not published a single article since he got his doctorate. Because he was also discouraged from presenting papers at professional meetings, Jerry has rarely attended such meetings. After taking a careful look at his résumé, Jerry realized that his lack of publications and presentations, his age, and his salary would make it difficult for him to find a comparable position if he lost his job. Furthermore, because his wife has a law practice in Chicago and he refuses to have a commuter marriage, Jerry feels that he is tied to the Chicago area. Given these facts, Jerry had become preoccupied by the thought of losing his job.

Although he is concerned about losing his job, Jerry had taken no action to facilitate job hunting if he were to lose his job—that is, until he received a phone call three weeks ago from Jack Kelley, an old graduate school friend who works for a chemical company in Milwaukee and who had heard rumors about the unstable job situation at Jerry's company. Unbeknown to Jerry, Jack had been able to follow Jerry's career over the years. For example, four years ago, Jack had hired a chemist who formerly worked with Jerry and last week he interviewed a chemist who currently reports to Jerry. Both of these individuals spoke highly of Jerry.

Jack's company had an opening for someone of Jerry's experience, and Jack had contacted Jerry to inquire about his interest in the position. Jerry was flattered by the call. He was quite candid with Jack about his job situation and said he was interested in looking into the job opening if it could be done confidentially. Within the next ten days, Jerry visited the company twice for a series of interviews and was extremely impressed by the people he met. At the end of his second visit, Jerry received a job offer. The new job involved similar duties to those he currently had. The salary offered was 10 percent less than he was currently making, but given his wife's income, this lower salary was not a major problem. The new job would also encourage Jerry to publish his research, something he thought he would enjoy. In addition, it was only thirty-five miles from his house in the northern Chicago suburbs to the company headquarters outside Milwaukee.

Once he received a firm job offer, Jerry told his supervisor and asked her what she could tell him regarding his future status with the company. His boss was unable to provide any information. In order to make the right decision, Jerry tried to consider all the advantages and disadvantages of taking the new position. He researched the Milwaukee chemical company as thoroughly as he knew how. For example, he talked at length with the chemist who had left Jerry's current employer and gone to work for the Milwaukee firm and he investigated the Milwaukee company using various materials available in the public library. However, despite the abundance of information he gathered, job security kept dominating his thoughts. Having seen the difficulty encountered by chemists in their fifties in finding jobs, Jerry did not want to go through that experience. Thus, since his current employer could not guarantee him a position, he decided to accept the job offer.

Edith Marble: Retiree

Edith Marble is a 64-year-old widow who, prior to her retirement twenty-two months ago, was a data entry operator for an insurance company. Twelve months ago, her former employer contacted Edith to see if she had an interest in a new program it had established involving retired employees returning to work on an "as needed" basis. When she was contacted last year, Edith had no interest in the program. She and her husband were enjoying their retirement. However, since the death of her husband from a heart attack six months ago, Edith has found that her retirement is filled with many idle hours. Thus, when she was contacted again last week concerning her interest in the program, she said she would think seriously about it.

In thinking about the program, Edith felt it fit her needs almost perfectly. The most important factor was the social environment at the company. She always enjoyed the people with whom she had worked and they had frequently socialized after work. Edith thought that by returning to work she would fill many lonely hours. Another thing that Edith liked about this program was that she would have considerable control over her work schedule, which meant that she could decline to work whenever she had out-of-town visitors (such as her grandchildren). The third major reason she liked the program was the lack of risk involved. Edith knew most of the people with whom she would be working and she knew what the job entailed. If for some reason returning to work did not go as expected, she could simply return once again to being a full-time retiree. After considering her employer's offer for two days, Edith agreed to become part of this retiree program.

AN ANALYSIS OF THE FOUR VIGNETTES

Although these vignettes did not go into great detail, even these abbreviated descriptions provide a sense of the multitude of factors that are involved in understanding the perspective of an applicant during the recruitment process. In the remainder of this chapter and in the rest of this book, several of the themes that have been presented in these vignettes will be discussed and expanded upon as various organizational recruitment decisions are examined. Exhibit 3.1 provides a summary of the recruitment situations faced by the individuals portrayed in the vignettes. While a detailed examination of similarities and differences is unnecessary, a brief discussion of a few of the themes reflected in these vignettes is instructive.

The Job Candidate's Perception

During the recruitment process, an applicant forms various impressions about the organizations for which the person is considering working. These perceptions, accurate or inaccurate, can influence such applicant decisions as whether to sign up for a campus interview, send a résumé to a company, and/or accept a job offer. In the vignettes, there were several examples of perceptions influencing job-choice decisions. For example, Mark Smith's perception that the business-equipment manufacturer was not genuinely interested in him clearly entered into his decision to accept the offer from the construction company. Similarly, Jerry Katz's perception of job insecurity had a major influence on his decision to change jobs.

While the fact that applicants' perceptions influence their job-choice decisions is not very surprising, it is important to point out that in the two examples cited these perceptions may have been inaccurate. Conceivably, the impersonal treatment Mark Smith received from the business-equipment manufacturer was not the result of a lack of interest in him, but rather was due to a temporary business crisis (the unexpected death

EXHIBIT 3.1   Similarities and differences in the recruitment situations portrayed in the four vignettes

Recruitment Factors	L. Springer, Nurse	M. Smith, HRM Student	J. Katz, Chemist	E. Marble, Retiree
Easy to get a job	Yes	No	No	No
Easy to undo a bad job-choice decision	Yes	No	No	Yes
Number of job offers	Several	One	One	One
Self-insight[a]	Yes	?	?	Yes
Job vs. career orientation[b]	Job	Career	Career	Job
Need to relocate	No	Maybe	No	No
Substantial salary difference among job offers	No	—	Yes	—
Applicant- vs. employer-initiated recruitment	Applicant	Applicant	Employer	Employer
Applicant feels well treated by organization(s) doing the recruiting	Yes	Mixed	Yes	Yes
Able to evaluate job prospects simultaneously	Yes	No	Yes	Yes

Note: This table is intended only as a summary device. Some themes raised in the vignettes are not listed. For example, Lori Springer and Edith Marble had more insight into what the organizations they accepted jobs with were like than did Mark Smith and Jerry Katz.

[a]Self-insight refers to the degree to which the job candidate has a good understanding of what he or she desires in a job and/or career.

[b]Job vs. career orientation refers to whether the individual is primarily interested in the particular job he or she will hold or has more of a career orientation (i.e., a focus on long-term job prospects with the organization).

of a key employee, perhaps) that caused company personnel to ignore his letters. In fact, Mark may have been the Denver company's first choice to fill the HRM position. Jerry Katz's job-choice decision may also have been affected by inaccurate perceptions. Jerry's company may have decided not to sell the consumer products division in which he worked. However, because his company did not want to announce which divisions it intended to sell, it was not able to inform Jerry that his job was secure. Although Jerry might still have resigned even if he knew his job was secure, this likelihood would certainly have been considerably less than when he perceived his job was in danger.

In both of the cases cited (and in numerous other instances that will be cited throughout this text), a key reason for inaccurate perceptions is the failure of organizations to focus on events from the perspective of a job candidate. If they had, the business-equipment manufacturer might have notified Mark Smith of the business crisis that had occurred and thus explained the treatment he received and the delay in making a hiring decision. Similarly, although Jerry Katz's company may not have been able to inform him that it did not intend to sell his division, the company might have been able to inform him that he would have a job with another division in the company if his division was sold.

Not only do an individual's perceptions affect whether that person continues to pursue employment with an organization, since such perceptions often are shared with other prospective employees, they can influence whether other individuals pursue job opportunities with an organization. For example, although Mark Smith may have accepted the job with the construction company even if he had been informed of why the business-equipment manufacturer was slow to fill the position, he likely would have spoken about the Denver company in much different terms had he known why he was treated as he was. Because applicants frequently share their impressions of employers with others, those involved in recruitment activities must be constantly aware that the way they treat any individual can have repercussions for the recruitment of other candidates.

Differences in What the Four Individuals Valued

From the vignettes, it is apparent that Lori, Mark, Jerry, and Edith differed in a number of ways. For example, they differed in terms of what they were looking for in a position. Lori Springer was most concerned with finding a job that provided regular hours, tuition reimbursement, and a medical school affiliation. Given his perception of the job market, Mark Smith seemed most concerned with simply getting a job in the human resource management field. Jerry Katz sought job security. Finally, Edith Marble was looking for a way to fill the hours in her day and for social interaction.

Not only did these individuals differ in terms of the major factors they sought in a position, they also differed in terms of their career orientation and their degree of self-insight. For example, while Lori Springer was not thinking about a long-term relationship (i.e, a career) with the hospital she selected, Jerry Katz was very concerned about his long-term job prospects. In terms of self-insight, both Lori Springer and Edith Marble had thought a good deal about what they wanted from a job while Mark Smith and, to some extent, Jerry Katz appeared to have less insight into what they wanted. One reflection of this lack of self-insight is the fact that both Mark and Jerry were still thinking about what was really important to them in a position after each had made a job choice. For example, early in the job search process Mark seemed taken with the prospects of a high salary, talented colleagues, and the prestige that working for the Denver company would mean, but he appears to have gradually discounted the value of these job attributes during the course of his search.

External Factors That Influence Applicants

Although several external factors (i.e., factors largely outside the control of the job candidate) can influence an applicant's job search and job choice, three factors—the labor market, the degree of certainty one has about the existence of particular job attributes, and the ability to evaluate job opportunities simultaneously—are particularly important. Each of these factors appears to have had a major impact on one or more of the job-choice decisions portrayed in the vignettes.

With regard to labor market conditions, an applicant's perception of the relevant labor market (that is, the number of jobs in the person's field compared to the number of qualified individuals) can affect the person's perception of how easily a job can be found and may also affect the person's perception of how easily a bad job choice can be undone by finding another job. Thus, since Lori Springer perceived that nurses in Southern California are in extremely high demand, she entered into the job search process expecting to find a job that can satisfy her major needs and anticipating that hospitals would be trying to sell her on going to work for them. Given her confidence about finding a good job, Lori only applied to three hospitals. In contrast, Mark Smith perceived that the job market was tight for college graduates seeking a position in the HRM field. Given this perception, one would expect someone in Mark's position to contact several organizations (Mark contacted over fifty companies), to anticipate that he might not find a job he really liked, and to expect that he would have to sell himself to prospective employers.

Another factor that can influence the decision process of a job applicant is the degree to which the person can be certain that a position offers specific attributes. For example, Lori Springer was certain that the job she accepted offered tuition reimbursement and regular hours. Edith

Marble felt confident that going back to work would help satisfy her desire for social interaction. In contrast, although Jerry Katz felt that, in comparison to his former position, his new job offered greater security and more freedom to publish his research, he cannot be certain of this. Conceivably, he could find his new position eliminated within the year or discover that his ability to publish findings was exaggerated by those recruiting him.

Not only are applicants sometimes uncertain about the existence of particular job attributes, they are also sometimes uncertain about whether a job offer will be forthcoming. For example, Mark Smith had to decide whether to accept a job offer without having another firm offer to compare it with. Mark could only guess whether he would eventually get an offer from the Denver company, the chemical company, or some other company he had contacted. In contrast to the uncertainty about job prospects that Mark experienced, since Lori had three firm job offers at the same time, she was able to compare their relative advantages and disadvantages in making a job-choice decision. By comparing the experiences of Lori and Mark, one can see that making a job-choice decision can be quite different when one has simultaneous job offers rather than merely the prospect of other offers.

One of the reasons that so much space has been given to presenting and analyzing these vignettes is to provide a sense of the numerous factors that need to be considered to understand recruitment from the perspective of a job candidate. In the remainder of this chapter and in the next chapter, research relevant to many of the themes raised in these vignettes will be reviewed.

AN OVERVIEW OF THE JOB SEARCH PROCESS

In examining the recruitment process from the perspective of a job candidate,[2] it is useful to differentiate three types of activities: job search, job investigation, and job evaluation. Job search activities (reading help-wanted advertisements, sending out résumés, and so on) are directed toward locating job openings (Does City X hire statistical analysts? Does it have any open positions?). Job investigation involves gathering information on job opportunities that may exist (How much does City X pay statistical analysts? What is it like to work in a civil service system?). Job evaluation involves making decisions about the attractiveness of a job opportunity. Job evaluation includes both the values attached to various job attributes by a job seeker (e.g., How much is the opportunity for promotion valued?) and the type of decision process used by a person for determining the overall attractiveness of a possible job (e.g., Is a job offer compared to other job offers or against the applicant's conception of the ideal job?).

In examining job search, job investigation, and job evaluation, emphasis will be given to issues that are of particular importance for an organization that is developing a recruitment strategy.[3,4] The relevance of the information presented here and in the next chapter will become more apparent as this information is built on in later chapters dealing with specific recruitment activities (e.g., recruitment advertising).

Although for discussion purposes job search, job investigation, and job evaluation (which is covered in Chapter 4) are presented as being distinct activities, in practice it is sometimes difficult to distinguish among them. One reason for this is because they may all occur simultaneously. For example, a person may meet with a neighbor to inquire whether the neighbor's employer has openings for secretaries who lack word processing skills (job search). During their meeting, the job seeker may discover (job investigation) that, while the neighbor's employer does hire secretaries lacking these skills, such secretaries are paid poorly until they have mastered the employer's word processing package. Having received this information, the job seeker may ponder (job evaluation) whether he or she values the opportunity to acquire word processing skills at a company's expense through on-the-job training and whether he or she is willing to accept low pay until the word processing package is mastered.

Sources Used to Locate Job Opportunities

Although a person can find out about job opportunities from a number of "formal" information sources (an employment agency, a school placement office, and so on) that employers commonly use for publicizing job openings, research has found that many individuals locate positions without using such formal sources.[5] For example, one of the most commonly used sources of information about job openings is informal word-of-mouth recruitment by friends or acquaintances who work for an organization. Research has also shown that individuals frequently learn about job openings as a result of their own initiative. That is, although an individual does not know that a job opening exists, the person applies directly to an organization (in person or via the mail) in case one does. In addition to word-of-mouth and so-called self-initiated recruitment, not surprisingly, another common source of information about job opportunities is "Help Wanted" newspaper advertisements.

Researchers (e.g., Caldwell and Spivey, 1983; Swaroff, Barclay, and Bass, 1985) have also studied what outcomes are associated with the use of various recruitment methods.[6] For example, several studies (see Wanous and Colella, 1989) have shown that recruits who are referred by employees of the company have greater job longevity than recruits who heard about job openings from newspaper ads. The relationships that have been found between recruitment methods and job outcomes will be discussed in Chapter 12, which addresses the pros and cons of various recruitment methods from the perspective of an organization.

Although considerable research data are available on the approaches used by job seekers to locate positions and the outcomes associated with the use of these methods, very few researchers have investigated what factors cause applicants to use various job search methods. In addition, relatively little research has examined what factors affect the intensity with which job seekers pursue employment opportunities (Schwab et al., 1987).

Factors Affecting Job Search Intensity and the Choice of Job Search Methods

Not surprisingly, most of the research that has investigated the effects of job search intensity has found that individuals who were more persistent in seeking out employment opportunities were more likely to find employment. Among the intensity-related job search measures that have been found to be associated with obtaining employment are not procrastinating before beginning a job search (e.g., Dyer, 1973), the total number of employers contacted (e.g., Dyer, 1973), the number of hours spent per week looking for work (e.g., Barron and Mellow, 1981), and the number of job search actions such as looking in the newspaper for openings, telephoning a prospective employer, and so on, that are undertaken (e.g., Kanfer and Hulin, 1985).

In terms of why people vary in their job search intensity, Schwab et al. (1987) suggest that the two primary determinants are financial need and the individual's personality. Regarding the effect of financial need on search intensity, Schwab et al. cite several studies that link the level of unemployment benefits being received (hypothesized to be an inverse proxy for financial need) and the duration of these benefits to various search intensity measures. For example, Barron and Gilley (1979) found a negative association between the number of hours individuals spent each week searching for employment and the level of unemployment compensation they were receiving.

In terms of a job seeker's personality as an influence on the intensity of job search behavior, only a limited range of personality variables have been examined and only a few studies have been conducted. However, studies have shown that a job seeker's sense of self-esteem or self-efficacy is related to the intensity of one's job search.[7] For example, Kanfer and Hulin (1985) found that self-confidence about job search behaviors (e.g., being able to follow up successfully on job leads) was related to job search behaviors (filling out job applications, looking in the newspaper for openings, etc.) and ultimately to job search success. Ellis and Taylor (1983) examined whether two types of self-esteem—global and job search related—of graduating business students were related to job search variables. As predicted, they found that students with low self-esteem spent less time using a number of formal recruitment sources (e.g., newspaper ads) for finding a job.[8]

While there is little research on factors that affect job search intensity, even less is known about why job hunters use the job search strategies they do.[9] Among the factors that are thought to underlie the use of different search strategies are differences in such job seeker characteristics as motivation, personality, and access to and familiarity with various job search methods. While some of the explanations offered for the use of different search strategies are obvious (for example, college students are more likely to utilize a college placement office than persons who are not college students), some of the other explanations are less obvious. For example, Breaugh and Mann (1984) speculate that certain approaches to finding a job (e.g., self-initiated recruitment) take greater effort on the part of an applicant than other approaches (e.g., responding to radio advertisements).

Although there has been some speculation about why particular job search approaches are used by job seekers, little research has addressed this topic. One study that did investigate the reasons underlying the choice of job search methods was conducted by Ellis and Taylor (1983). These researchers predicted that, in comparison to high self-esteem job seekers, persons who were low in self-esteem would tend to rely on well-established sources of information about job openings (employment agencies, newspapers, and so on) since those sources require relatively little social skill. They also predicted that those with low self-esteem would be less likely than high self-esteem individuals to use sources requiring initiative (such as direct application) and strong social skills (such as contacts from friends and acquaintances). As expected, Ellis and Taylor found that low self-esteem individuals did rely more heavily on formal sources of information about job openings. However, they did not find any relationship between self-esteem and the use of informal sources.

In summary, although we know that individuals use a variety of sources for finding out about job opportunities, the explanations offered for why various job search strategies are used are based more on logic than on empirical data. Despite the lack of data on why particular sources are used, organizations can still make use of the knowledge that many job seekers rely heavily on word-of-mouth recruitment and self-initiated efforts in locating jobs. While an in-depth discussion of the implications of recruitment source utilization is saved for a later chapter, one conclusion that can be drawn from this knowledge about source utilization is that it is important that an organization be highly visible to potential job seekers. By taking steps to increase its visibility (running image advertisements on television, participating in career days, and so on), an organization should be able to increase both the number of direct applications it receives and the diversity of its applicant pool.

From the perspective of a job seeker, what is known about the recruitment methods used by employers is also valuable. For example, Dzubow (1985) found that, of the employers who responded to his survey, over 60 percent filled at least half of their job openings without advertising. Given this fact, it is obvious that a person who passively waits for employers to publicize job openings will miss out on job opportunities. Therefore, in order to maximize one's chances of being aware of job opportunities, a person should actively pursue information about job openings. For example, knowing that many positions are filled through word-of-mouth recruitment, a job seeker should publicize the fact that he or she is looking for a job.

AN OVERVIEW OF JOB INVESTIGATION ACTIVITIES

As with the discussion of job search activities, this examination of job investigation activities is intended only as an overview. In this section, particular attention will be focused on actions that a job seeker can take to increase his or her chances of getting a job that meets his or her needs.

Investigating Organizations and the Jobs They May Offer

Although it was not stated explicitly in the previous section on job search activities, it may be assumed that a job seeker does not want just any job. Rather, a person wants a position that offers particular attributes (a certain salary, working in one's chosen field, etc.). While some of the attributes that a job candidate may desire may be directly linked to the job itself (for example, the job of hospital physician generally involves considerable autonomy), as Schwab et al. (1987) noted, one does not simply accept a job. Rather, in accepting a job offer, one also agrees to become a member of a work group and of an organization. Given this fact, in order to have a better understanding of job applicant decision making, job, work group, and organizational attributes must be considered. For example, in terms of work group attributes, a job seeker may want a supervisor who delegates freely and co-workers who are collegial. In terms of organizational attributes, a job seeker may desire an employer that is recognized as a "blue chip" company and that has a reputation for being socially responsible.

While, as noted by Kotter et al. (1978), it is probably impossible for a job candidate to find out everything he or she wants to know about a position with a particular organization without actually working in the position for several months, numerous sources are available to help a job candidate increase his or her knowledge concerning a job with a particular organization. Kotter et al. categorized these information sources as being of three basic types: published documents, knowledgeable people, and direct observation.[10]

Published Documents

There are several different types of published documents that provide information about organizations. For example, directories such as the *Thomas Register of American Manufacturers* and the *Directory of Department Stores* provide basic information—number of employees, basic products, sales information, etc.—on thousands of companies. To get a sense of the future prospects of particular industries, one can turn to numerous valuable resources, including the U.S. Department of Commerce's *U.S. Industrial Outlook* and *Standard and Poor's Industrial Surveys*.

Although the sources cited above contain much valuable information (for example, a person who is interested in applying to large department stores would be able to compile a list of names and addresses to which to send résumés), most job seekers want considerably more information than these sources provide. Fortunately, several other published sources are available. For example, in order to get an idea of how an employer wishes to portray itself to the public, a person can request information directly from the organization (the company's annual report, copies of the company's magazine or newsletter, transcripts of interviews granted by the CEO, etc.).

In most cases, however, a job seeker wants a more objective view of an organization than its own publications will provide. If a job seeker has access to a good library, he or she should be able to locate information on many employers without a great deal of effort. Wilkens (1988) has developed a series of steps that can be followed in investigating an organization. To locate recent articles on companies, indexes such as the *Business Periodicals Index, The Wall Street Journal Index,* and others may be useful. Many libraries now have access to national computerized reference services that allow an individual to quickly scan thousands of listings and print out a listing of relevant articles on a given company. For smaller companies (especially those operating in only one city), a person may have to refer to local publications. For example, in most large cities there are local business-oriented newspapers (e.g., *The St. Louis Business Journal*) that regularly print articles on local companies.

In addition to newspaper and magazine articles, there are also a few books (including Levering, Moskowitz, and Katz, 1984 and Zeitz and Dusky, 1988) that provide information on the relative strengths and weaknesses of large companies. While such books typically focus on a few general characteristics of the companies that were investigated (pay and benefits, corporate culture, etc.), the information in these sources can help a person compare one organization against another on a number of key dimensions.

People

Although a person can learn a good deal about an organization through various published documents,[11] another useful source of information is people who are familiar with the prospective employer, such as current and former employees. As in using published information, the job seeker should consider the relative credibility of the individuals involved. A job seeker would want to talk to people who have expertise and can supply useful and detailed information about important aspects of a job. In addition, these people must be trustworthy so that the job seeker can be confident that what is said about a position and/or an organization is accurate.

Making contact with current employees will occur automatically if one is invited for an interview. During the interview process, the job seeker usually has the opportunity to ask questions of his or her potential supervisor, and sometimes is also able to talk to prospective co-workers. While it is clearly important to converse with one's prospective supervisor, a job candidate should also do everything possible to talk to potential peers as well.[12] One's prospective co-workers not only may have considerable expertise about what a job actually entails, but also are viewed by most job candidates as a trustworthy source of information (Fisher, Ilgen, and Hoyer, 1979).

While valuable information can be gathered about a prospective employer during an interview visit, a person should usually gather as much information as possible prior to the interview, if for no other reason than to help decide whether to accept the interview invitation. Although it is not always easy to make contact with individuals who are knowledgeable about a potential employer before the interviewing process, there are a number of ways in which a job candidate can locate such persons. For example, the job seeker can ask other people such as friends or neighbors whether they know of anyone who is a current or former employee of the organization. Job seekers who have attended college may be able to make use of their college's alumni office to locate alumni who now work for a particular employer. If a job seeker is able to meet with someone who works or has worked for the organization, he or she should ask for the names of others who may also be able to provide information about the organization. By talking with several persons who are knowledgeable about a given employer, a job seeker should be able to get a better idea of what working for that employer is like (Kotter et al., 1978).

Direct Observation

In addition to researching published documents and speaking with knowledgeable people, Kotter et al. (1978) point out that a job seeker may also be able to gather valuable information about an employer by direct observation during a visit to the organization. For example, a person may observe that, while an organization stresses its egalitarian climate in its public relations releases, it has reserved parking spaces for executives and an executive dining room. Or, an individual may observe that there are no women or minorities employed in white-collar jobs, even though the company has repeatedly emphasized its commitment to affirmative action. For a student, an internship can provide an excellent opportunity to observe first-hand what an organization is like.

Self-Assessment: Investigating What One Wants and What One Offers

As has been noted by several authors (e.g., Herriot, 1984), a job seeker must have self-insight in order to sensibly evaluate job opportunities. Self-insight is an individual's awareness of his or her values, interests, attitudes, life-style preferences, abilities, and qualifications. While a discussion of what is meant by each of these terms is not necessary for our purposes (see Greenhaus, 1987 and Kotter et al., 1978), it is important to draw one distinction.

In conducting a "self-exploration" (Stumpf, Austin, and Hartman, 1984), it is important for an individual to realize not only that he or she wants certain things from an organization (such as challenging assignments), but also that an organization wants certain things from him or her (such as prior selling experience). This distinction is stressed because it is natural for a job seeker to focus on his or her wants and give little attention to what he or she offers. The excerpt from the Doonesbury cartoon at the beginning of this chapter is a humorous example of a potential job seeker's preoccupation with his own desires, but the cartoon also reflects the disillusionment that can result when a person neglects to consider what desirable characteristics he or she offers a potential employer. Although in the cartoon this disillusionment is felt by the job seeker's father rather than by the job seeker himself, in the real world a person's failure to consider what he or she offers a potential employer can result in misdirected effort, wasted time and money, and an ultimately unsuccessful job search.

Self-Assessment of One's Wants/Desires

One commonly used method for gaining self-insight[13] is the use of self-report instruments. For example, value inventories (see Allport, Vernon, and Lindsey's *Study of Values*) and interest inventories (such as the *Strong-Campbell Interest Inventory*) are often used to provide quantitative scores on the different values or interests a person may have. Generally, such self-report measures allow a person (often with the help of a trained counselor) to compare his or her scores against group norms. For example, the *Strong-Campbell Interest Inventory* provides a respondent with information on his or her interests (i.e., likes and dislikes) in twenty-three different areas and shows the similarity of the respondent's interests to those of individuals in more than 100 different occupations. This normative information allows a person to determine in what occupations he or she is most likely to find people who share his or her interests.

In addition to structured instruments, there are a number of less formal methods that can provide useful self-assessment information. One approach is to write out a detailed description of what one's ideal job would entail. Self-insight can also be gained by describing peak experiences, both high points and low points, that one has had during one's life and then reflecting on what made these experiences so memorable (see Kotter et al., 1978).

In summary, there are a number of actions that a job seeker can take to develop a better sense of what he or she wants from a job, an organization, and a career. Some of these actions involve nothing more than commitment of time and effort to analyze one's needs and determine what type of position will satisfy these needs. Other self-assessment procedures involve the use of others, such as career counselors.

Self-Assessment of What One Offers an Employer

As was noted earlier, in conducting a self-assessment the focus should be both on what one wants in a position and on what one offers to a prospective employer. Simply stated, the more value an employer attaches to what a job candidate offers, the greater the likelihood that the person will receive a job offer. In general, an employer will value characteristics that the employer associates with effective job performance. Moreover, the value attached to a characteristic will be enhanced if most job seekers lack the desired attribute (fluency in Japanese, for example). In attempting to assess one's value to an employer, it should be obvious that, while such personal characteristics as intelligence and reliability may be sought by most employers, the value of other characteristics (say, a knowledge of Fortran) may be job-specific. Thus, in assessing one's chances of landing a particular job with a particular employer, one should focus on the specific requirements of that job.

In screening job applicants, an employer generally tries to assess a person's motivation and ability by considering such things as the person's grade point average, academic major, scholastic awards, professional certification, prior work experience, standardized test scores, performance in a simulated work situation, letters of reference, and performance in an interview. Clearly, an applicant has a better chance of receiving an offer if the indicators used by an employer suggest that the applicant will do well in a job than if the indicators suggest a lower expectation for job performance.[14]

While indicators of ability and motivation affect a job candidate's attractiveness to a potential employer, other factors can also influence a person's job prospects. For example, affirmative action pressure can cause some organizations to place considerable weight on a job candidate's race and sex. If an employer has an antinepotism policy, a job candidate's family background may affect his or her job prospects. For certain jobs that require close and frequent interaction with the public, an employer may give preference to an applicant who has existing connections in the community.

Given that such factors can affect a candidate's job prospects, the question becomes: How can a job seeker assess his or her attractiveness to potential employers? Evaluating how appealing one is to an employer is not easy, but certain actions such as a candid review of one's academic record should provide an individual with a better sense of how attractive he or she may be. For example, for many white-collar positions, a student with a low grade point average, irrelevant work experience, and no academic honors will be less marketable than a student with a high grade point average, relevant prior work experience, and a merit-based scholarship. For jobs that require prior work experience, organizations often attach considerable importance to one's work history (e.g., Has the person frequently changed jobs or remained with one organization?). By conducting a careful and honest self-examination, a job candidate should be able to get a sense of how attractive he or she is likely to be to a prospective employer.

Although careful self-study can generally help a person develop a reasonably accurate picture of how attractive a job candidate he or she is, an individual may be able to improve his or her self-insight by seeking the opinion of other people. For example, after discussing her academic record with an accounting professor, a job candidate may decide not to send a résumé to a particular public accounting firm because her GPA does not meet the firm's minimum standard. In a similar vein, a neighbor may instruct a job seeker not to bother submitting an application to his company because the job candidate lacks relevant job experience.

Investigating Jobs, Organizations, and Oneself: A Summary

In this section, it has been suggested that a person can maximize his or her chances of making an intelligent job search by investigating thoroughly what a given position entails, what he or she wants from a position, and what he or she offers to a prospective employer. Of course, such investigation does not guarantee that a desirable job will be located—if a job seeker expects an ideal job, he or she may search forever. But these actions should result in a wealth of useful information upon which a job seeker may base a job search.[15] More specifically, an investigation of what a position in a given organization offers and what one wants in a position should help the job seeker determine whether there is a good fit between the position under consideration and his or her wants. If there is a good fit, a careful examination of what one has to offer a prospective employer should enable the job seeker to better estimate how likely he or she is to receive a job offer.

In addition to providing a job seeker with valuable information for making job-choice decisions, acquiring information about a position with an organization and about what he or she offers a potential employer may increase the likelihood that the candidate will receive a job offer. For example, by including detailed information about an employer in a letter accompanying one's résumé, a person may impress the organization with his or her seriousness about the company. Similarly, a careful self-examination may enable an individual to convince an interviewer of his or her special talent or skill. Although there is little research that has tested whether possessing detailed knowledge about an employer or about one's own abilities results in a job candidate being rated as more attractive by potential employers, a study by Stumpf et al. (1984) is suggestive. These researchers were able to demonstrate that graduate business students who had spent considerable time on "self-exploration" and "environmental" exploration (e.g., jobs, organizations) received significantly higher interview ratings from campus recruiters and were more likely to receive a subsequent job offer.

SUMMARY

A theme running throughout this text is that a good understanding of the perspective of job candidates is necessary for devising an effective employee recruitment strategy. In order to provide a sense of the diversity of the recruitment experiences that different job seekers can go through, four short vignettes were presented in this chapter. Following these vignettes, several issues related to the job search and job investigation processes were examined. Chapter 4 and later chapters will examine in detail how an employer can utilize this information on job search and job investigation.

NOTES

1. For the reader who seeks more in-depth and expansive coverage of the applicant's perspective, there are several excellent sources available, including Greenhaus (1987); Herriot (1984); and Schwab, Rynes, and Aldag (1987).

2. This section draws heavily on the excellent analysis of Schwab, Rynes, and Aldag (1987).

3. Although the terms *job search*, *job investigation*, and *job evaluation* are used in this text, generally the focus is actually on both the *job* and the *organization*. For example, in evaluating a job offer, a job candidate will consider both job attributes (skills utilized,

travel required, etc.) and organizational attributes (company growth projections, prestige attached to working for the employer, etc.).

4. Readers who are interested in more detailed coverage of job search, job investigation, and job evaluation activities should refer to Schwab et al. (1987), Greenhaus (1987), Wanous and Colella (1989), and Kotter et al. (1978).

5. *The Monthly Labor Review* periodically publishes data on sources used by various types of workers for locating jobs.

6. Research in the recruitment area sometimes can be a bit confusing because of the way the terms *recruitment method* and *recruitment source* have been used. Some authors have used the term *recruitment method* to refer to the means an organization uses to recruit employees (employment agencies, for example) and the term *recruitment source* to refer to the labor market segment (e.g., college students) that is tapped or reached by a particular method. Other researchers, however, have used these terms interchangeably. To simplify the presentation of material, in this text the term *recruitment source* will sometimes be used in a way that encompasses the method used. Where the terms *source* and *method* should be distinguished for purposes of clarity, both terms will be used. When one looks at the job search process from a job candidate's perspective, terminology can get even more confusing. For example, technically speaking, a job candidate uses job search methods, not recruitment methods.

7. Although there is a subtle difference between "self-esteem" and "self-efficacy" as used by some authors (Bandura, 1986), for the purposes of this section the terms will be used interchangeably.

8. Not all of Ellis and Taylor's (1983) self-esteem predictions were confirmed.

9. The reader should be aware that in most studies the way researchers determined job search strategies (sometimes referred to as recruitment source) was simply by asking job applicants. Thus, it is possible that some individuals actually hear about an opening from one source but report using another source.

10. This section draws heavily on works by Greenhaus (1987), Kotter et al. (1978), and London and Stumpf (1982).

11. Not only does this information help a job seeker make decisions about the relative desirability of various organizations, having detailed knowledge of the organization is also likely to impress corporate interviewers.

12. Organizations are generally willing to schedule meeting time with co-workers if it is requested. If an organization refuses to let a job candidate meet with his or her prospective co-workers, this may suggest a certain organizational operating style.

13. There are a number of excellent books that provide detailed treatment of how a job seeker can develop self-insight into what he or she wants from a job, career, and/or organization (see, for example, Kotter et al., 1978). This section is intended to provide only a selective overview of some of the methods that may be useful in acquiring self-insight.

14. It should be apparent that the information an employer receives from indicators such as these will be sequential. For example, if a job candidate's résumé reflects mediocre academic performance, unrelated work experience, and a lack of mastery of the English language (spelling and grammar mistakes), it is unlikely that the candidate will have the opportunity to score well on the tests, interviews, or work simulations the company utilizes.

15. While there is always the chance that some of the material gathered during an investigation of a position and of oneself will be inaccurate, in all likelihood, a job candidate will have more accurate perceptions of the job market, his or her marketability, his or her desires, etc., than if such investigative actions are not taken.

4

How Applicants Evaluate Jobs:
An Overview

Having discussed in the last chapter how a person can find out about job opportunities (job search) and then research what a given job entails (job investigation), attention will now be given to how individuals use the information they have gathered in making job-choice decisions. In covering the job evaluation process, research addressing the job and the organizational attributes that job seekers value will be addressed first. Next, several job-choice models will be examined. These models have been suggested as capturing the process by which a job candidate actually determines whether to accept a job offer. The final section of this chapter will discuss the importance of the information presented in this and the preceding chapter to designing an effective employee recruitment strategy.

THE IMPORTANCE OF EXAMINING WHAT
ATTRIBUTES JOB CANDIDATES VALUE

Although there are a number of explanations for how an individual decides whether or not to accept a job offer, all of these job-choice models stress the fundamental role that job and organizational attributes play. Simply stated, all job-choice models predict that a job offer will be accepted if a job candidate feels that the attributes a position offers make it more attractive than some other alternative (going to graduate school, remaining in one's current job, etc.). Thus, from a recruitment perspective, it is important for an organization to be aware of what attributes prospective employees see as desirable. Given such an awareness, an employer may be able to take steps to increase the attractiveness of its open positions.

One step that an employer can take to make job openings more attractive is to modify existing job and organizational attributes. For example, to make nursing positions more attractive, hospitals have improved salaries, offered more regular work hours, and reduced the amount of nonprofessional duties (Harper, 1988).

Although certain factors may limit an organization's ability to increase the attractiveness of a job, some actions can usually be taken to make a job more appealing. In addition to modifying job and organizational attributes, in some cases the perceived attractiveness of a job can be increased simply by making sure that applicants are aware of the desirable attributes it offers. For example, studies such as that done by Taylor and Sniezek, 1984, have shown that recruiters frequently tell applicants considerably less about a job opening than the applicants would like to know. If this is so, it is likely that some recruits may assume that a job does not provide certain attributes they desire when, in fact, it does. Acting on this erroneous assumption, some people may withdraw as candidates for a position with a given employer.

Improving a job and making certain that recruits are aware of what it entails in order to increase the perceived attractiveness of the job opening requires both that an organization knows what a job offers and that it is aware of the attributes that individuals desire in a position. There is extensive literature that has addressed the various job analysis strategies an employer can use for determining the duties, skills, and so on that a job entails, so this issue will not be addressed.[1] However, because the methodologies for determining what attributes job seekers value in a position have received much less attention, these methodologies do merit some discussion.

Methodologies for Determining the Importance of Job and Organizational Attributes

Although determining what attributes individuals view as desirable or important in a job may appear to be a fairly straightforward task, this has not proven to be the case. In fact, the two most common methodologies for determining job attribute desirability have major weaknesses.[2]

The most commonly used approach for assessing the desirability of job attributes has been labeled the "direct estimate" approach (Schwab et al., 1987). This methodology involves providing individuals with a fixed list of job attributes and having them rate the desirability of each (for example, "1 = not important . . . 7 = very important"). In order to eliminate the possibility that each job attribute might receive the same importance rating from an individual, some researchers, such as Lacy, Bokemeier, and Shepard, 1983, have employed a variation of the direct estimate approach that requires respondents to rank in order the list of job attributes they are given. A third version of the direct estimate approach (see, for example, Feldman and Arnold, 1978) is to provide a fixed number of points and have each respondent distribute these points across a given set of job attributes in such a way that the number of points received by each attribute reflects its relative importance to the person.

A second approach for determining the relative importance attached to job attributes is known as "policy capturing" (Zedeck, 1977). In policy capturing research, individuals typically are provided with brief job descriptions and asked to arrive at an overall evaluation of each job. This evaluation may be a rating ("On a scale of 1 to 7, how attractive is this job?") or a more absolute decision ("Would you accept this job: yes/no?"). In creating the various job descriptions, a researcher systematically varies the level of the job attributes to be studied. For example, a set of job descriptions might vary in terms of salary and the amount of overnight travel required. By using a statistical technique such as multiple regression, a researcher is able to treat each of the manipulated job attributes as a predictor variable with the overall job evaluation judgment serving as the criterion variable. By examining the weight attached to a given job attribute, a researcher can infer the importance a person attached to that attribute in arriving at an overall evaluation of each of the job scenarios presented.

Despite the brevity of these descriptions, it should be apparent that a key difference between policy capturing and the direct estimate approach is that policy capturing does not require that an individual directly report the value he or she attaches to a job attribute. It should also be evident that both the direct estimate and the policy capturing approaches allow the researcher to control which job attributes are studied. Although in some circumstances giving this control to the researcher is desirable (if, for example, an employer wants to determine whether providing flexible hours would increase the attractiveness of a position), there is a price for such control. For example, if a researcher fails to include job attributes that a job candidate considers essential, such as not having to relocate to a new city, in the list of attributes examined, the researcher may incorrectly conclude that job attribute attractiveness is a poor predictor of job choice.

Although it would be nice if researchers who have used different methodologies had arrived at similar conclusions concerning the relative importance of job attributes, this has not been the case. For example, Rynes (1991) notes that studies based on policy capturing have tended to show extrinsic job attributes such as salary as receiving greater weight than studies that required persons to directly evaluate the importance of job attributes. Not only does one find inconsistencies in the conclusions drawn from studies that use different methodologies, one also finds inconsistencies among studies using the same methodology. For example, Jurgensen (1978) found that job security was ranked as the most important job attribute out of ten factors by his sample. In contrast, Lacy et al. (1983) found that security was ranked fourth out of five outcomes.

In order to understand the reasons for such inconsistent findings and, more important, the difficulty in measuring the relative attractiveness of job attributes, a brief review of some of the major problems that have hindered previous research studies in this area is important.

Weaknesses of Research Examining Job Attribute Attractiveness

A problem that plagues much of job attribute research is the heavy reliance on college students as a source for research data. Although some studies have used students who were seeking full-time positions (see, for example, Harris and Fink, 1987), there still ought to be concern about whether findings based on relatively young and inexperienced student samples can be generalized. For example, Jurgensen (1978) found that, in comparison to older male employees, younger males attached greater importance to pay and advancement opportunities and less importance to job security. In addition to the relative inexperience of undergraduate students in job hunting, their potential lack of seriousness in rating job attributes may also limit the generalizability of results. For example, while a serious job seeker may carefully weigh the value he or she attaches to a particular job attribute in making a job-choice decision (as in the value of job security to the chemist portrayed in Vignette 3 in the previous chapter), a student may go quickly through a list of job attributes and make attractiveness ratings with little serious reflection.

Another weakness of the methodologies traditionally used to assess the importance of job attributes is the artificiality of the situation. For example, the direct estimate approach assumes that the attractiveness ratings given to a list of job attributes in an experimental situation reflect the values attached to those attributes during an actual job search. In many cases, such an assumption seems implausible. For instance, in providing job attribute ratings in a research setting, students may be sensitive to how the researcher will react to their ratings (e.g., "If I rate starting salary as being most important will the researcher see me as selfish?"). Such so-called "social desirability" bias may lead to job attribute ratings that do not accurately reflect a person's real values (Schwab et al., 1987).

The direct estimate approach has also been criticized because typically only one level of each job attribute is rated (e.g., "opportunity to use my abilities"). Furthermore, exactly what level of the attribute is to be rated is often vague. For example, Jurgensen (1978) asked individuals to rank in order of importance such job attributes as "pay (large income during year)" and "benefits (vacation, sick pay, pension, insurance, etc.)." From the wording used, the difficulty in ranking such attributes should be obvious. One would imagine that many individuals would be uncertain about what exactly was meant by a "large income during the year" ($30,000? $75,000?) or by "benefits" (ten days of vacation? one hundred percent company-financed insurance?).

Another weakness of the direct estimate approach concerns the number of job attributes that are examined.[3] Although there are exceptions, in most studies a limited number of job attributes were rated. For example, Feldman and Arnold (1978) had six attributes evaluated, Lacy et al. (1983) had five job attributes rated, and Jurgensen (1978) had ten attributes rank ordered. Given the limited number of job attributes examined in these studies, it is quite likely that several important job attributes were overlooked. In fact, in most studies, such potentially important attributes as on-site child care, medical insurance, and the amount of travel required were not included in the list of attributes to be rated. The potential significance of not examining certain job attributes should be apparent. If a job attribute that is important to job candidates is not included in the list to be rated, the researcher will never discover that it is viewed as important.

As a way to get around some of the weaknesses of the direct estimate approach, some researchers have advocated the use of policy capturing (see Zedeck, 1977). Although policy capturing may lessen or avoid some of the problems that affect the direct estimate approach, generalizing from policy capturing studies is still a questionable practice. One major weakness of policy capturing is that it requires each research participant (generally an undergraduate student) to read and react to a large number of job scenarios. For example, in order to investigate the effects of four job attributes (starting salary, geographical location, promotion opportunity, and type of work), Rynes, Schwab, and Heneman (1983) provided each subject with 120 scenarios. These scenarios were rated in two sessions lasting sixty to ninety minutes each. Thus, on average, a subject spent less than two minutes reading and making decisions about a scenario. Given such hurried decision making, it is difficult to argue that the level of cognitive processing taking place in this policy capturing study parallels that of job candidates making decisions about real job offers. Unfortunately, given the requirements of the statistical methods used for analyzing policy capturing data, there is no way to escape the need to rate numerous scenarios. Furthermore, the number of scenarios required increases dramatically as the number of job attributes to be examined increases. Thus, policy capturing limits the number of job attribute effects that can be examined in any one study.

Another potential weakness of the policy capturing methodology is that the level of the job attributes incorporated into the job scenarios can determine whether or not a particular attribute is found to be important for predicting a person's overall evaluation of a position (Rynes, 1991). For example, consider two researchers who are interested in determining the importance to job candidates of starting salary and geographic location in choosing among jobs. Both researchers conduct their research with students attending the same university in Southern California. Researcher A describes sales positions that offer a starting salary of either $20,000 or $27,000 and an employment setting of either San Diego or Los Angeles. Researcher B describes sales positions that offer a starting salary of either $22,500 or $24,500 and employment in either San Diego or Buffalo. Researcher A finds that salary is a powerful predictor of how the sales jobs were evaluated while location had a little effect. Researcher B discovers that salary had little effect on the evaluation of the sales jobs, but that geographic location had a powerful influence. From this simple example, it should be clear that great care should be exercised in determining what level (or type) of job attributes to build into one's experimental job scenarios.

Drawing Conclusions from Research on Job Attributes

Although additional weaknesses of the direct estimate and policy capturing approaches could be presented, the need for caution in generalizing from such studies should be apparent from those already noted. However, as can be seen in the passages reproduced in Exhibit 4.1, researchers have been willing to draw a few tentative conclusions concerning the importance of certain job attributes. From these passages, it seems safe to conclude that many job candidates attach value to positions that offer good salaries, opportunities for advancement, job security, opportunities for recognition, and the chance to assume some responsibility and be creative.

EXHIBIT 4.1   Researchers' conclusions concerning common preferences for job attributes*

London and Stumpf 1982, p. 57: "The job attributes viewed to be important by individuals include opportunities for task accomplishment, opportunities for advancement, salary level, continued knowledge and skill development, possibilities for recognition, opportunities to be creative, congenial interpersonal relationships, flexible task assignments, security, and opportunities to assume responsibility. The relative importance of these attributes depends on a person's sex, age, career interests, and amount of past work experience. However, the largest differences seem to be idiosyncratic. Further, individuals who have not conducted extensive self-assessments seem to have a limited ability to state their preferences and then choose positions that fit those preferences, even when given clear lists of how specific jobs vary on the job attributes of interest."

Hall 1976, p. 65: "The following summary is based on surveys which have asked students what factors they consider important in choosing their first jobs:

Very Important Factors

1. Opportunities for advancement
2. Social status and prestige—the feeling of doing something important and the recognition of this by others
3. Responsibility
4. Opportunities to use special aptitudes and educational background
5. Challenge and adventure
6. Opportunity to be creative and original
7. High salary

Important, But Less So

1. A stable and secure future
2. A chance to exercise leadership
3. Opportunity to work with people rather than things
4. Freedom from supervision
5. Opportunity to be helpful to others"

continued

---

*References and footnotes have been removed from these passages.

EXHIBIT 4.1   *Continued*

Heneman, Schwab, Fossum, and Dyer 1989, pp. 270–271: "Not surprisingly, job attributes have been found to be major determinants of the decisions to apply for, pursue, and accept jobs. There is some, albeit only suggestive, evidence to show that a few attributes—particularly pay and nature of work offered—are important to the decisions of many types of job seekers. In addition, geographic location and promotion opportunities appear to be important among managerial and professional job seekers, as does degree of job security among many blue-collar applicants. Nature of benefits offered, working conditions, hours, and nature of supervision and co-workers appear to be relatively unimportant considerations for many. Clearly, there are many exceptions to these generalizations, and preferences may well change as job seekers consider trade-offs among attributes in different combinations or packages."

Although considerable effort has gone into documenting the importance attached to the job attributes cited in Exhibit 4.1, few employers are likely to be surprised by these findings. Most employers are cognizant of the need to improve such job attributes as salary level and job security. Instead of research that looks at general job attributes, what would be useful for an employer who is developing a recruitment strategy would be to know the value attached to more unique attributes that the employer offers or is considering offering. For example, Apple Computer offers paid sabbaticals to its managers. An obvious question for a company that is considering offering a similar benefit would be: "In comparison to other benefits of equal cost, does the opportunity for a paid sabbatical help us attract desirable job candidates?" On the other hand, Apple Computer does not have a company pension plan. It would be interesting to know what effect this has on its ability to recruit employees.

While the need for job attribute research that addresses less common job and organizational attributes is clear, the difficulty of conducting such research should also be apparent. Rather than conducting research on college undergraduates or some similarly convenient sample, it becomes important to focus on the particular group from which the employer is likely to recruit. For example, Gulf Oil used mail and telephone surveys to determine what data processing professionals valued in a job and in a company.[4] The surveys were targeted toward DP professionals living in two different geographic regions from which Gulf Oil recruits heavily. Such research can help a company determine what job attributes are important to prospective recruits and what level of a particular job attribute is seen as necessary or desirable (e.g., what is the minimum level of salary that must be offered before other job attributes enter into an applicant's job-choice decision process?).

At a minimum, researchers who are interested in assessing the value attached to various job attributes should consider allowing research participants to add job attributes to the lists of attributes they are asked to rate, if important ones are missing. By allowing individuals to do more than passively respond to research stimuli, it is likely that we will increase our understanding of how job hunters make job-choice decisions. For example, given the job attribute lists commonly used, the three job attributes (tuition reimbursement, regular work hours, and a research environment) valued most highly by Lori Springer, the nursing student portrayed in Vignette 1 in the previous chapter, are not likely to have been tapped. Thus, Lori's job-choice decision process may have appeared to be less predictable than it actually was.

JOB-CHOICE DECISION-MAKING MODELS

In order to understand how a person makes a job-choice decision, not only is it important to understand what job attributes the person values, it is also necessary to understand how the job candidate uses (e.g., combines, weights) the job attribute information available (Wanous and Colella, 1989). To date, a number of "job-choice models" have been proposed. These models differ in the assumptions they make about how job-choice decisions get made.[5]

The most commonly discussed decision-making models are "compensatory" models (Dawes, 1988). Compensatory models suggest that a job seeker makes trade-offs between various job attributes so that a favorable level of one attribute (e.g., a high salary) can make up for an unfavorable level of another attribute (e.g., a poor fringe benefit package).[6] The two most common compensatory models have come to be known as the maximum expected utility model and the expectancy theory model. Although both of these models are based on the assumption that a decision maker will simultaneously consider multiple job alternatives, they also differ in important ways.

Maximum Expected Utility Model

In 1957, Simon described a model of an "economic man" that is based on the assumption that in making decisions a person attempts to maximize the expected utility of his or her job choice. The basic tenets of Simon's conception of an "economically rational decision maker" are summarized by Taylor (1984, p. 75):

> To maximize expected utility, a decision maker must list all relevant decision alternatives, the events that may result from choosing each alternative, and the payoff for that event. Then personal probabilities are assigned to the events and utilities assigned to the payoffs. The expected utility for any action is found by multiplying the probability of an event leading to an outcome by the utility of the outcome, then adding the products for all events that would result from taking the action. Finally, the course of action yielding the largest expected utility is chosen.

While it can be argued that, in theory, an individual should attempt to maximize the expected utility of his or her job choice, most researchers have questioned the reasonableness of this model. For example, Simon (1957) noted that the limited information-processing capabilities of human beings make it unlikely that a decision maker will process the abundance of information in the manner prescribed by the maximum expected utility model: "The capacity of the human mind for formulating and solving complex problems is very small compared with the size of the problems whose solution is required for objectively rational behavior in the real world— or even for a reasonable approximation to such objective rationality" (p. 198).

Furthermore, given the nature of job-choice decision making (e.g., often a person has to decide on one job offer before he or she knows whether another one will be received; thoroughly investigating a job opening can be very time consuming), it may not be rational or even possible for a person to attempt to use a strategy designed to maximize one's expected utility. Instead, job seekers generally have to act on incomplete information about the courses of action they could take and the consequences of those actions. They typically are not able to fully explore all alternatives relating to a given decision, and they frequently are unable to attach accurate values to given outcomes of a job-choice decision (Bazerman, 1990). In summary, although the maximum expected utility model provides a good comparison standard against which to evaluate other job-choice models, the assumptions underlying this model seem untenable for most job-choice decision-making situations (Schwab, 1982).

The Expectancy Theory Model of Job Choice

Probably the most commonly studied job-choice model is the expectancy theory model (Wanous and Colella, 1989). This model addresses both how a person determines the overall attractiveness of a job with an organization and how motivated the person will be to pursue a job opportunity. According to expectancy theory, determining the overall attractiveness of a position is a function of a person's belief about the existence of job attributes and the importance he or she attaches to these attributes. For example, an individual may believe that a position with Company A means a high likelihood of job security (e.g., 90 percent) and a low probability of being promoted within the first two years (e.g., 20 percent). In comparison to Company A, the individual may believe that a job with Company B means a lower likelihood of job security (e.g., 70 percent) and a higher probability of quick advancement (e.g., 50 percent). Having estimated the probability of job security and quick advancement at the two companies, the job candidate next considers the relative importance of these attributes. If the person highly values job security and attaches little importance to rapid advancement, he or she may view a position with Company A as being more attractive than one with Company B.

Stated more formally, according to the expectancy theory model of job choice (Wanous, Keon, and Latack, 1983), the overall attractiveness of a job with a given organization reflects a mathematical computation whereby the importance attached to each job attribute a person considers (e.g., "I rate this attribute a 6 on a scale of 1 to 7 with higher scores reflecting greater importance") is multiplied by the job candidate's belief about the attribute's existence (e.g., 90 percent probable). The products of these computations (the importance of quick advancement multiplied by the likelihood of quick advancement) are then summed to arrive at an overall job attractiveness score.

However, just because an individual rates a position as being attractive does not mean the person will pursue it. Conceivably, although the job is highly valued, the person may see little or no chance of receiving a job offer. For example, a mediocre college basketball player may be highly attracted to a career in professional basketball while at the same time realizing he has no chance of being signed by a professional team. To account for this fact, in determining the probability of whether a person will pursue a position, the expectancy theory model also considers a job candidate's perception of the likelihood that he or she will receive a job offer. According to the expectancy theory model, to determine the probability that a person will pursue a given job opportunity, one needs to multiply the overall attractiveness of the position to the job candidate (its overall attractiveness score) by the candidate's estimate of his or her probability of attaining that position (job offer expectancy). By considering job offer expectancy, one can see how a candidate may be more highly motivated to pursue a job that is lower in overall attractiveness than another position.

From this abbreviated discussion of the expectancy theory model of job choice, it should be apparent that to predict an individual's job-choice decision, one must know how a job candidate views a job situation. It should also be clear that the expectancy theory model assumes that the decision maker is both motivated and able to handle a large amount of complex information in arriving at a job-choice decision. Finally, it should be apparent that a major difference between the maximum expected utility model and the expectancy theory model is that the expectancy theory model does not assume that the decision maker has complete and accurate information about all decision alternatives. Rather, the expectancy theory model assumes that the decision maker uses the information that is available to him or her about the job alternatives.

Tom's Matching Hypothesis

Although Tom's research (1971) has received little attention in the job-choice literature, it highlights a potentially important variable—job candidate self-image—and thus will be briefly discussed. Building on Super's theory of vocational choice (1957), Tom hypothesized that a job seeker makes a job-choice decision by comparing his or her own self-image against the image the person has of various organizations for which he or she might work. According to Tom, the closer the "match" between the person's self-image and the image of a potential employer, the more likely a job with that employer will be accepted.

As noted by Wanous and Colella (1989), Tom's conceptualization of the job-choice decision process is similar to the maximum expected utility and the expectancy theory models in that it is compensatory in nature and may involve simultaneous comparisons among several potential employers on several job attributes. However, Tom's orientation differs from these other two compensatory models because he believes a job candidate seeks a job that is congruent with his or her self-image, and not the "best" job.

Reynolds's Job Choice Model

In addition to the three compensatory job-choice models just discussed, two noncompensatory models have also received some attention by researchers. In contrast to compensatory models, noncompensatory job-choice models assume that a job candidate will not allow trade-offs among job attributes, that is, a lack of one attribute cannot be made up for by a high level of another one. One of the earliest and simplest explanations for job-choice decision making was offered by Reynolds (1951).[7] Based on his research, Reynolds concluded that unemployed job seekers rarely evaluate the attractiveness of alternative job offers in the complex compensatory manner suggested by the maximum expected utility model, the expectancy theory model, or Tom's matching approach. Rather, Reynolds concluded that job hunters establish minimum acceptable standards for one or two important job attributes (usually pay and type of work). According to Reynolds, the first job alternative that meets or exceeds these minimum standards is accepted. Although Reynolds's theory has not received much attention from researchers studying job choice decision making, there is some support for his position. For example, Rynes et al. (1983) feel that their results were consistent with Reynolds's basic assertion that some minimum level of compensation must be offered in order for a job to be viewed as acceptable.

Soelberg's Job Search and Job Choice Model

As noted by Power and Aldag (1985) in their review of Soelberg's research (1967), "attempts to test Soelberg's model have been rare, incomplete, and of questionable validity. To a considerable degree, researchers have tested differing interpretations of Soelberg's model, hypotheses, and arguments, probably in part because of ambiguity generated by Soelberg himself" (p. 56). Given these problems, Soelberg's model will not be presented in detail. However, it is important to present a few of its central tenets.

Soelberg's model consists of four phases. The first phase involves a person identifying an ideal occupation before beginning a job search. According to Soelberg, the choice of an ideal occupation is a function of a person's "personal values" (i.e., the outcomes one wants from a job) and one's perceived job qualifications. Having identified one or more ideal occupations (it is possible that no ideal occupation is identified), Soelberg proposes that a person next plans his or her job search. Soelberg outlines several possible planning strategies that a job candidate could use (for example, conceptualizing the ideal job and thinking of at least one entry-level position that will lead to it).

Soelberg's third phase, and the one that is most relevant for employee recruitment, involves job search and choice. According to Soelberg, most job candidates use a noncompensatory model to screen job alternatives until an "implicit favorite" is discovered. This implicit favorite must meet minimum acceptability levels on a few critical job attributes. However, unlike Reynolds's model, instead of immediately accepting the first offer that satisfies the criteria for an acceptable job, Soelberg believes that job hunters attempt to find at least one other minimally acceptable job offer for comparison purposes. If another minimally acceptable alternative is identified, the two offers are compared. According to Soelberg, in conducting this comparison there is generally a perceptual bias in favor of the implicit favorite (Schwab et al., 1987). Although Soelberg's description of the third phase of his job search process is ambiguous, it appears that he believes that job candidates may change their screening procedures (e.g., what they see as an ideal job, how they weigh different job attributes) over time.

Having made a provisional job choice (i.e., having tentatively decided to accept an offer but not having formally accepted it), Soelberg hypothesizes that a job seeker next moves into the decision confirmation and commitment phase. During this phase, an individual attempts to verify information about his or her implicit job choice, negotiate improvements in this job offer (e.g., bargain for a higher salary), and allow time to ensure that a significantly better offer is not forthcoming (Power and Aldag, 1985).

A Comparison of the Job-Choice Models

From this overview, it should be apparent that these job-choice models are based on different assumptions. For example, in explaining how a job-choice decision is made, some models presume that job candidates weigh job attributes in a compensatory fashion while other models presume a noncompensatory decision-making approach. The models also differ in terms of the assumptions they make about the complexity of the job-choice decision process. Given these differences, it is natural to ask which model best reflects how job choice decisions are made. Unfortunately, the current state of the job-choice literature does not enable one to definitively answer this question. Although there are several reasons for being unable to determine the "most correct" job-choice model (e.g., generally the models have not been tested against each other in the same study; many tests of the models are designed poorly), the conclusion to be drawn from research on job-choice decision making is still disappointing: "Unfortunately, we are left with the conclusion that the voluminous body of empirical research does little to help us choose among the various conceptualizations of job choice processes" (Schwab et al., 1987, p. 34).

BEHAVIORAL DECISION THEORY RESEARCH

Possibly due to the inability of researchers to develop a model that seems to capture how job-choice decisions are made, research on job-choice decision making per se has decreased substantially in recent years (Wanous and Colella, 1989). However, at the same time that research on job-choice decision making has been declining, research dealing with decision making in a more generic sense has been increasing. This body of research, which has come to be known as "behavioral decision theory" (Dawes, 1988), has considerable relevance for job-choice decision making and thus for employee recruitment.

Although early research in the behavioral decision theory area examined whether complex compensatory models (e.g., the maximum expected utility model, an additive difference model) reflected how humans made decisions,[8] behavioral decision theory researchers have gradually come to accept the view of March and Simon (1958): "Choice is always exercised with respect to a limited, approximate, simplified 'model' of the real situation" (p. 139). Stated differently, most behavioral decision theory researchers now assume that (1) human beings have a limited cognitive capacity for processing information and (2) when confronted by decision situations involving a multitude of information (e.g., numerous choice alternatives, each having multiple attributes), it is natural and necessary for humans to attempt to reduce the complexity of the actual situations they encounter. In addition to these two basic premises, based on research conducted in the 1970s and 1980s, most researchers also have come to believe that the same decision strategy will not and should not be used for all decision situations. Therefore, over the past several years, behavioral decision theory research has investigated numerous decision strategies that may be employed in various choice situations in order to simplify situations that would otherwise overwhelm the information processing capability of the decision maker (Hogarth, 1987).

Behavioral Decision Theory Models

Given that the basic premise of behavioral decision theory research is that humans have a limited capacity for handling information, it is not surprising that the maximum expected utility model is seen as unrealistic for most situations. In fact, many researchers have questioned the realism of the expectancy theory model (see Hogarth, 1987). Instead of such compensatory models, behavioral decision theory research has generally focused on more simplistic, noncompensatory models. For example, Simon (1957) proposed a "satisficing" model that is based on the assumption that a decision maker will accept the first alternative that exceeds some minimum level on all dimensions (e.g., job attributes) that are relevant to the decision maker. A slight variation of this satisficing model is the "conjunctive" model. According to this model, a decision maker establishes certain cut-off points on all the choice attributes. Any alternative that has even one attribute that falls below a cut-off is eliminated from consideration (Hogarth, 1987).

The "elimination-by-aspects" model developed by Tversky (1972) has drawn considerable support from research on behavioral decision making. Tversky's model presents choice as a covert elimination process. In deciding among multidimensional alternatives, a decision maker is assumed to proceed in the following way: "A dimension or aspect is selected. Then all the alternatives that do not possess that dimension or aspect are eliminated. The procedure is repeated until all but one of the alternatives is eliminated. The probability of selecting an aspect or dimension is assumed to be proportional to its weight or relative importance" (Payne, 1976, p. 368).

A Summary of Behavioral Decision Theory Findings

A consistent finding of behavioral decision theory research is that different individuals make choice decisions in different ways.[9] Complicating matters further, researchers (for example, Billings and Marcus, 1983) have found that, when facing complex decision choices, some individuals use a noncompensatory strategy to eliminate most choice alternatives and then shift to a compensatory strategy to decide among the few remaining alternatives.

In investigating what factors cause a decision maker to become overloaded with information and thus to rely on a noncompensatory approach, researchers have discovered that attributes of the choice itself (the decision task) and aspects of the decision environment are important (Dawes, 1988). Concerning the decision task, the number of alternatives (e.g., job offers) has been found to be the most important determinant of choice complexity. For example, Payne (1976) has shown that, when only two choice alternatives are involved and they are presented simultaneously, decision makers tend to use a compensatory model (i.e., an expectancy or additive difference model). In contrast, when several choice alternatives are presented simultaneously, most decision makers rely on a noncompensatory strategy.

Other decision attributes that have been shown to increase the complexity of a choice situation and thus to lead to the use of noncompensatory decision models are: (1) choice alternatives having more than one dimension to be considered, (2) lack of familiarity with the type of choice being considered, (3) sequential decision making (in contrast to having information on all choice alternatives at the same time), (4) uncertainty about the existence of certain choice attributes, and (5) difficulty in recalling information about the various choice alternatives. Generalizing these results to job-choice decision making, this research suggests that an individual is more likely to use a noncompensatory decision strategy when he or she is inexperienced in job hunting, cannot consider all job offers simultaneously, has more than two job offers that differ on several dimensions, is uncertain about the existence of certain job attributes, and/or cannot clearly recall certain information about the various job openings.

In addition to the reliance of decision makers on noncompensatory decision strategies when the amount of information they must consider becomes overwhelming, there is evidence that noncompensatory models are sometimes used even when the information environment is not overly complex (Hogarth, 1987). In particular, it appears that individuals may use a simplified decision strategy when they believe that the consequences of choosing the "wrong" decision alternative are either minimal or easily undone. While in the context of job-choice decision making it may be difficult to think of making a "bad" job choice as having few negative consequences (this could occur if all job offers are very similar), one can imagine situations in which a bad choice can be somewhat easily undone. For example, the nurse portrayed in Vignette 1 in the preceding chapter believed she could quickly find another job if the position she accepted did not live up to her expectations.

SOME ADDITIONAL DECISION-MAKING CONCEPTS

As will be shown shortly, the issues addressed in the preceding section have great importance for anyone interested in employee recruitment. However, before discussing the ramifications of these behavioral decision theory findings, two additional concepts that can affect job-choice decision making need to be introduced.[10] These findings concern general tendencies that individuals exhibit in attending to decision-relevant information, in recalling this information, and in using this information for making decisions. These tendencies are noteworthy because they generally result in a biased decision-making process.

Attending to Information

As has been noted throughout this chapter, humans have a tendency to reduce the complexity of the decisions they face. One of the ways to reduce decision complexity is by not paying attention to all of the information that is available. While it is possible to conceive of a situation in which ignoring certain information would not significantly distort the decision-making process (e.g., if redundant or trivial information were ignored), research has shown that individuals selectively attend to information in systematic ways that can dramatically distort their views of decision situations. This tendency to selectively attend to some information while ignoring other information has been labelled "selective perception." As described by Hogarth (1987), selective perception includes the tendency of individuals to (1) let what they expect to see bias what they do see, (2) seek information consistent with preconceived views, and (3) downplay or totally disregard information that conflicts with their initial impressions.

The implications of selective perception for job-choice decision making are considerable. For example, if a job candidate initially forms a positive impression of a position with an organization, that person will tend to pay attention to information that supports that impression. However, if his or her initial impression is negative, information contradicting this impression may be discounted or ignored. Given this selective perception tendency, in planning a recruitment strategy an employer should take actions that increase the likelihood that job candidates form accurate first impressions.

Recalling Decision-Relevant Information

In order to make sound job choice decisions, a job candidate not only must attend to and store decision-relevant information in an appropriate manner (e.g., if all relevant information cannot be attended to, one should attempt to process the most important information regardless of whether or not it is congruent with one's initial impressions), but also must accurately recall the stored information from memory. Given the limitations on human information processing that have been stressed throughout this chapter, it should come as no surprise that humans have a limited ability to recall information. In fact, research has shown that the way people recall information is greatly affected by a so-called "availability bias," a process that tends to significantly distort what a person remembers (Bazerman, 1990).

Availability bias refers to a tendency for certain types of information to be more easily recalled from memory than other types of information. In particular, it has been found that information is more easily remembered if it has been processed (attended to and stored) recently and/or is vivid in nature. Although the fact that more recently acquired information is easier to recall is not surprising (and therefore will not be discussed further), an example may help clarify the concept of vividness. As used by researchers (e.g., Hogarth, 1987), information is vivid if it is distinctive or unique. Thus, information about a position that offers flexible hours, the ability to work at home, and retirement at age 55 would be more vivid (that is, more available to memory) than information about a position that requires working a traditional schedule in a regular office setting with a retirement age of 65.

Making Use of the Information That Is Recalled

Bias can be introduced into the decision making process not only at the information acquisition (e.g., selective perception) and retrieval (e.g., availability bias) stages, but also at the information evaluation stage. This latter bias results from a tendency that has been referred to as the "certainty effect" (Kahneman and Tversky, 1979).[11]

More specifically, based on their research on how individuals make choices among risky alternatives, Kahneman and Tversky (1979) concluded that decision makers "exhibit several pervasive effects that are inconsistent with the basic tenets of utility theory. In particular, people underweigh outcomes that are merely probable in comparison with outcomes that are obtained with certainty. This tendency, called the certainty effect, contributes to risk aversion in choices involving sure gains and to risk seeking in choices involving sure losses" (p. 263). In essence, Kahneman and Tversky have presented both a theoretical rationale and empirical support for the old adage that "a bird in the hand is worth two in the bush." This tendency of decision makers (e.g., job candidates) to prefer a sure gain over a possible gain with a greater average expected return should not be surprising. In all probability, the reader would prefer the certainty of a $500,000 gain over a 60 percent chance of a $1,000,000 gain and a 40 percent chance of gaining nothing, even though the average expected gain for the first option is less than that of the second option.

Although this certainty effect may not be relevant in a job-choice situation where all job offers of interest have been received before a job choice has to be made (such as the nursing student in Vignette 1 in Chapter 3), its importance should be evident for a job-choice situation in which offers are received sequentially (such as the HRM major in Vignette 2).

JOB SEARCH, JOB INVESTIGATION, AND JOB EVALUATION: IMPLICATIONS FOR EMPLOYEE RECRUITMENT

In this and the previous chapter, considerable research concerning how individuals locate, investigate, and evaluate jobs has been reviewed. Given the academic nature of much of this material, the reader may question its relevance for the actual recruitment of employees. In this section, a number of practical applications of this research will be discussed. In later chapters, several other implications of the research reviewed on job search, job investigation, and job evaluation will be provided.

Uncertainty, Information Gathering, Complexity, and Simplification

In order to apply the research on job candidate behavior to designing more effective recruitment strategies, it is helpful to view a job candidate as both an information gatherer and a processor. In most cases, from the very beginning of the job search process, an individual lacks relevant information. This job candidate uncertainty is reflected in the following questions that individuals often ask themselves at various stages of the job hunting process: What do I want in a job? What is the best way to locate such a position? How many job offers can I expect? When will I hear from Company XYZ? Was I Company ABC's first choice? Now that I have accepted a job with Company ABC, am I sure I made the right choice? As reflected in the last question, a job candidate may experience uncertainty not only until a job offer is accepted or rejected but conceivably even after a job-choice decision has been made (so-called "post-decision dissonance").

In order to reduce the uncertainty experienced at various stages of the job hunting process, a job candidate typically will gather information to help him or her make a job-choice decision. However, a common result of this information acquisition process is information overload. That is, given a person's limited information processing capability, the individual finds that he or she cannot process all of the information that is available. As a way to reduce the complexity of the information available, a person will generally use one or more "heuristics" (for example, selective perception).[12] Although the use of such heuristics allows a job candidate to simplify the decision-making situation, as noted earlier, they also can introduce bias into the decision process. Such bias can result in a bad job-choice decision, which in turn can have negative consequences for both a job candidate and for the hiring organization. In summary, in designing a recruitment strategy, an organization must be sensitive to a job candidate's need for information and at the same time consider the danger of information overload.

In addition to such general problems, such as uncertainty and information overload, that an organization must consider in designing a recruitment strategy, recruitment planning is made even more difficult because of the individual differences that are involved. For example, different job candidates may rely on different types of sources for both locating and researching job openings. Adding to the complexity is the fact that not all individuals attach the same values to job attributes (Jurgensen, 1978) and that people often employ different decision-making strategies in making job-choice decisions (Payne, 1976). Furthermore, the same person may employ a different decision strategy depending on the number of job offers being considered and whether the offers are received simultaneously or sequentially.

So how can an organization that wishes to design a better recruitment program make use of this information concerning job candidate uncertainty, information overload, and the tendency of decision makers to simplify job-choice decisions? For presentation purposes, several steps that should be considered will be presented under three general headings: organizational visibility, recruitment communications, and the timing of recruitment-related actions.[13]

Organizational Visibility

Because many individuals locate jobs by applying directly to an organization (self-initiated recruitment) even though no position has been advertised, the importance of organizational visibility should be apparent. For example, Merck & Co. found that being named by *Fortune* magazine as the nation's most admired company and by *Working Mother* magazine as one of the ten best companies for working mothers was a definite asset in recruiting employees. A company spokesperson, who described Merck as "not a household name," stated that such publicity helped them attract "over 100,000 applications for jobs from New Jersey alone."[14]

The size of the geographic area in which an employer should be visible will depend on the type of candidates the employer is interested in attracting. For example, to recruit secretaries, it may only be important to be visible in the immediate area. In contrast, in recruiting faculty, a university may desire nationwide or even international visibility. It is also important to remember that the area in which an employer needs to be visible can change. For example, although hospitals used to recruit nurses from their surrounding communities, some hospitals now recruit nurses from other countries.

Although there are many ways in which an organization can be visible to potential employees, including sponsoring community events and participating in career days, not all visibility is desirable. For example, a company can gain notoriety by losing a major product liability lawsuit, being caught bribing foreign officials, or being responsible for a major oil spill. A good example of the effects of negative publicity is Hooker Chemical Company, which found it difficult to recruit employees after its name was indelibly linked to the chemical pollution problems at Love Canal in Niagara Falls, New York. A key factor in recruiting, therefore, is not simply being visible, but being viewed favorably by desirable potential recruits.

How does an organization come to be viewed as an attractive prospective employer? Although such actions as producing a high-quality product, providing first-rate service, treating employees humanely, and avoiding public scandals should provide the basis for a good organizational reputation, in terms of recruiting employees, a more proactive stance is recommended. One approach that an increasing number of organizations have utilized is "image advertising" (Garbett, 1988). Image advertising involves an employer marketing itself in ways that present it as an attractive place to work. A recent example of such image advertising is the marketing campaign conducted by Dow Chemical. The "Dow Lets You Do Great Things" campaign does not advertise a specific company product, nor does it attempt to fill a particular job opening. Rather, this series of advertisements simply portrays Dow Chemical as a humane, caring company in which college graduates (and others) can do socially important work. McDonnell-Douglas has also recently launched an image campaign ("A Company of Leaders") involving radio advertisements and *Wall Street Journal* ads.

In addition to the use of image advertising to create a positive public awareness, there are a host of other public relations activities that organizations can use to better market themselves as places of employment. To create a positive image in the minds of the general public, organizations might make donations to museums, hospitals, or other charities. In terms of creating a positive awareness among members of a particular group (human resource specialists, for example), employers can encourage staff professionals to publish papers in trade publications and give presentations at professional meetings. To increase their visibility with college and high school students, organizations can sponsor scholarships and awards and develop internship and "co-op" programs (Bowes, 1987).

Given the affirmative action obligations under which a number of employers operate, many organizations have a particular interest in creating a positive image as a place to work in the minds of women and minorities. As noted by Charlene Watler of Dow Jones and Company, Inc., a company can increase its visibility vis-à-vis members of protected groups by attending job fairs and targeting college recruitment at universities with large percentages of female and minority students.[15] It is particularly important in such recruitment efforts that some of the recruiters be women and minorities. Another approach that has been used by several large organizations to attract the attention of minorities is placing image advertisements in magazines and periodicals geared toward minority group members (e.g., *Minority MBA* magazine). No matter what approach an employer uses to promote itself, it should remember the advice of Ms. Watler. To paraphrase her comments, in terms of recruitment, visibility does not mean simply that potential recruits have heard of you. It means they think of you as a desirable place to work.

Recruitment Communications

In determining whether a given organization is a desirable place to work, individuals will draw on information from several sources (such as the media and friends). However, one of the most important sources of information about an organization is the organization itself. Given this fact, an organization should carefully consider the information it wants to transmit through its recruitment communications and how best to convey this message.[16]

In planning a strategy for the communication of recruitment information, an employer faces several complex issues. One issue concerns how much information to present. Given the human tendency to simplify complex decision situations, an organization must be wary of overwhelming a job candidate with information, especially information that the person is not likely to see as important (a recent college graduate, for instance, may not be interested in pension information). On the other hand, if an organization fails to communicate information about the existence of job attributes that a candidate values (such as the opportunity to relocate to the West Coast), the recruit may incorrectly undervalue the job and decline a job offer if one is made. A second issue an employer must be concerned with is the credibility of the information sources it uses. As noted earlier, research has shown credibility to be influenced by an information source's expertise and trustworthiness (Fisher, Ilgen, and Hoyer, 1979). Unless an organization's recruitment information is seen as credible, it is likely to be discounted. A third issue involves whether the information communicated to job candidates should describe only the positive aspects of working for the organization or try to present a more balanced picture that includes both desirable and undesirable job features.

Not surprisingly, there is no universally effective way to deal with these issues. Any approach an organization takes will have potential drawbacks. For example, as will be discussed in Chapter 6, presenting realistic information about a position may cause some desirable job candidates to decide not to pursue a position. On the other hand, if everything said about a position is very favorable, the job seeker may question the credibility of the information provided. So what actions should an organization consider?

An organization can take several steps to avoid or reduce information overload. The first action it should consider is investigating what information job seekers see as important for making job choice decisions (see the section on marketing research for recruitment purposes in Chapter 5). Once the organization knows what information most recruits view as important, it needs to decide how to effectively communicate this information. To enhance the credibility of the information it provides, an organization should strongly consider using job incumbents as an information source. Job incumbents have been shown to be a particularly credible source of information (Fisher et al., 1979). During conversations with job incumbents, an applicant can ask questions about aspects of the job that have not been covered in more formal recruitment communications. In addition, job incumbents are likely to present a realistic view of what the job in question entails (Breaugh and Billings, 1988). While such realism may result in some job candidates losing interest in the organization, it may also lead to a decline in employee turnover because realism allows individuals to self-select out of jobs that are not perceived as meeting important needs (see Chapter 6).

In order to facilitate job candidate recall, an organization should try to present the most important job attribute information in a vivid manner. For example, rather than relying on a personnel department interviewer to describe certain aspects of a job, an employer might use a professionally developed videotape, a tour of the worksite, and/or conversations with job incumbents. Another approach for aiding recall is for an employer to provide job candidates with a written document that summarizes the various features of the job under consideration, which the job candidate could review at a later time to refresh his or her memory. A candidate could also be encouraged to contact the organization in the future should additional questions arise.

In addition to being concerned about communication-related issues, an organization also must be concerned about the first impression it makes on job candidates. As was discussed earlier in this chapter, a person's initial impression can result in subsequent information being distorted or ignored (Hogarth, 1987). Because members of the personnel department are often in contact with potential job candidates, the personnel department can have a significant impact on the initial impression a job candidate forms about working for an organization. For example, a professional-looking recruitment brochure distributed by an enthusiastic company representative at a job fair may not only cause a prospect to pursue a job with the organization, but may also result in this prospect saying positive things about the company to other job candidates. In contrast, unprofessional actions by a campus recruiter (making sexist remarks, not having company literature to pass out, and so on) may negate subsequent recruitment actions by the organization, especially if the recruiter's actions are seen as a reflection of the organization as a whole.

Several other organizational actions will be discussed in later chapters. From the recruitment actions that were described, however, three important themes should be apparent. First, it is essential that an employer be aware of what it offers prospective candidates. Only by having an accurate view of the positive and negative features of a particular job will the organization be able to intelligently plan recruitment communications. Obviously, a key part of assessing what a job entails is knowing what comparable positions the organization's competitors offer ("How do our starting salaries stack up against those of similarly situated companies?"). The second theme involves the need to make trade-offs in designing a recruitment information strategy. For example, in trying to reduce applicant uncertainty about what a job involves, an organization runs the risk of inundating job applicants with information that is not necessary for a job-choice decision. The third theme concerns the importance of an organization carefully thinking through its communication strategy before beginning the recruitment process. Only by thoughtfully considering what it wants to communicate to prospective employees can an employer make rational choices concerning such varied issues as the design of recruitment literature and whether conversations with job incumbents should be part of the recruitment process.

The Timing of Recruitment-Related Actions

An issue that is related to the topic of recruitment communication but that deserves separate treatment is the timing of recruitment activities. Lewis (1985) provides a vivid example of the end result of poor recruitment timing. According to Lewis, because a particular banking organization failed to enter the recruitment process early enough, "they inherited a pool of applicants largely formed of those who had been consistently rejected by the other employers" (p. 32). Not surprisingly, the bank was not able to find a sufficient number of qualified applicants in such a mediocre pool of talent.

Although most organizations realize that proper timing is important in starting the recruitment process (e.g., placing job advertisement),[17] employers have recently become more aware of the importance of appropriate timing for other recruitment actions (e.g., scheduling follow-up interviews, making job offers). Based on the research reviewed earlier in this chapter, there are several reasons why the timing of recruitment activities can have a significant influence on an applicant's job-choice decision making.

One reason is that the job search process generates considerable anxiety for many job candidates, and to reduce this anxiety applicants may develop subconscious preferences for early job offers (Schwab et al., 1987). Thus, a job offer may be viewed more positively and therefore be more likely to be accepted by a candidate if it is received earlier in the job hunting process. As discussed by Simon (1957) and others, a second reason that an organization may be wise to make early job offers is because of the complexity of the information that is involved in making job-choice decisions. This complexity is hypothesized to cause a job candidate to use a noncompensatory decision strategy that may result in the person accepting the first job offer that meets what he or she sees as minimum acceptable levels on important decision criteria. Another factor that highlights the importance of making early job offers is the certainty effect introduced by Kahneman and Tversky (1979). According to these authors, individuals tend to "overvalue" a certain positive outcome in comparison to an uncertain outcome that "objectively" has a higher overall utility. In the context of job-choice decision making, this suggests that an individual is likely to prefer the certainty of a good job offer over the possibility or uncertainty of receiving a better job offer. Because organizations generally restrict the time a candidate has to make a decision about a job offer, the certainty effect clearly should affect applicant decision making.

The timing of a job offer may also have an influence on the decisions made by job applicants in another way. If a long period of time (as defined by an applicant) elapses between the end of the formal selection process and the receipt of a job offer, an applicant may question the employer's interest in him or her. For example, the applicant may assume that he or she was not the employer's first choice and that an offer was forthcoming only after others had rejected it. Although such an assumption may be inaccurate, a time delay may nevertheless result in an offer being viewed as less attractive than it would have been if it had been received earlier.[18]

Appropriate timing is not only significant when starting the recruitment process and in making job offers, but the timing of organizational actions may also be important at other stages during the recruitment process. For example, after going through screening interviews but before receiving a firm offer, a recruit may contact the organization for more information or to express his or her interest in a position. By promptly returning telephone calls and/or responding to mail inquiries, an employer can convey a strong interest in the candidate. In deciding between similar job offers (and job offers are frequently very similar), this perception of genuine interest on the part of a prospective employer may be a determining factor in whether that employer's job offer is accepted.

Another period during which timely organizational actions can affect the outcome of the recruitment process is after a job offer has been accepted.[19] It is not uncommon for individuals who have accepted job offers to have second thoughts about their decisions, particularly if a very attractive job offer from another organization is received after the applicant has accepted a position, which can result in a job applicant reneging on his or her job acceptance. One way in which an employer can reduce the postdecision dissonance that job hunters often experience is by keeping in regular contact with the individuals it has hired after they have accepted positions. Such contact may include periodic phone calls and letters from one's future supervisor and co-workers. The results of such actions have been shown to reduce the incidence of individuals backing out of job commitments (Ivancevich and Donnelly, 1971).

Although the preceding discussion of recruitment timing overly simplifies the factors involved (Thurow, 1975, for example, has argued that the advantage of early recruitment may be most pronounced for the most desirable employers) and was selective in its treatment of research findings (research relevant to timing issues by Arvey, Gordon, Massengill, and Mussio, 1975, will be discussed later in the text), nevertheless it highlights how important it is that an employer be sensitive to recruitment timing and scheduling issues. In particular, this discussion emphasizes the importance of an organization being sensitive to the assumptions that applicants may make when delays in the recruitment process occur. An awareness of the importance of timing issues may enable an organization to take appropriate actions to reduce the likelihood of an applicant making an incorrect assumption about the employer's interest in him or her.

From this abbreviated discussion of the organizational implications of research on job search, job investigation, and job evaluation, the importance of understanding the applicant perspective in designing an effective recruitment campaign should be evident. In future chapters, many of the organizational implications introduced in this chapter will be expanded upon.

FUTURE RESEARCH DIRECTIONS

From the information presented in this and in the previous chapter, it is apparent that there is still much we do not understand about how individuals search for, investigate, and make decisions about job opportunities. One of the reasons for this current lack of understanding is that many of the recruitment studies that have been conducted have methodological weaknesses. In this section, a few suggestions for designing studies that have more internal and external validity are offered.

A major methodological weakness of many recruitment studies is their failure to introduce the uncertainty and complexity that job candidates typically experience during the job search process. In the future, it is important that studies be designed so that research participants experience the effects of both of these important variables. For example, instead of using experimental situations in which subjects can evaluate all job opportunities simultaneously and with total confidence in the information provided as has frequently been the case, researchers should enhance uncertainty by designing situations in which persons have to decide whether to accept an offer before another one is forthcoming and to deal with information that is less than 100 percent credible.

In terms of introducing complexity, studies should be more realistic rather than simply ask people to rank in order a limited number of job attributes or to react to policy capturing scenarios in which only two or three job attributes are manipulated. For example, individuals might be asked to make trade-offs among job attributes (say, a higher starting salary versus less job security) or to deal with complex job scenarios in which several attributes are varied and information on the same attributes is not provided in each scenario. Additional complexity could be introduced if gathering information on a job involved money, time, or other costs. Unfortunately, as noted by Schwab et al. (1987), in most recruitment studies information was simply given to the research subject as if it were a free commodity.

Although the preceding suggestions may help improve the external validity of experimental recruitment research, research by Abelson (1988) and Fischoff, Slovic, and Lichtenstein (1980) raises doubts about the value of most experimental research for gaining an understanding of how job applicants make decisions. Abelson's research was stimulated by the failure of many social psychology studies to find a strong association between a person's attitudes and his or her behavior. In trying to understand the failure of attitudes to predict behavior, Abelson concluded a key factor involved the attitude measurement process: "Not infrequently, when respondents are asked about their attitudes, they may conform to the demands of the question or interview by concocting superficial attitudes on the spot. Such superficial expressions of attitudes are extremely labile over time and have come to be called 'nonattitudes'"(p. 267). In other words, Abelson suggests that "we may be devoting too much attention to attitudes that people do not care about . . ." (p. 267). However, Abelson's article is not just a critique of past research; he also points out a new direction. In a series of creative studies, he demonstrates the value of studying attitudes that are held with "conviction." Abelson's concern seems quite relevant for much of the recruitment research. One can make a strong case that researchers frequently study "nonattitudes" about recruitment issues reported by undergraduate students.

Fischoff et al. (1980) support the thrust of Abelson's concern that more attention should be paid to individuals with firmly developed attitudes and values and also raise additional methodological concerns about the traditional ways that have been used for measuring values.[20] Fischoff et al. are particularly concerned about how the values that individuals appear to attach to outcomes change depending on how they are measured. For example, these researchers report data suggesting that the particular value attached to a given event or outcome can be affected by such things as what other outcomes were rated for attractiveness prior to it, the response scale used, when the value was measured, and how the outcome was worded. Rather than present a detailed description of how these methodological factors can affect the values reported, it is more important to discuss the recommendation by Fischoff et al. for improving the measurement of values: "If one is interested in what people really feel about a value issue, there may be no substitute for an interactive, dialectical elicitation procedure, one that acknowledges the elicitor's role in helping the respondent to create and enunciate values" (p. 417).

Although there are clearly costs to such an interactive procedure—among other things, much more time will be necessary for data gathering and providing for respondent anonymity may be more difficult—these costs will likely be offset by the richness of the information that the investigator obtains. In the future, researchers should rely less on questionnaires as a measuring device. Only by using more creative approaches, such as interviews with or diaries that are kept by job hunters, can we hope to acquire greater insight into the job seeker's thought process, which in turn should help us design more effective recruitment strategies.

SUMMARY

In this and the previous chapter, the importance of an organization viewing the recruitment process from the perspective of a job candidate has been emphasized. In particular, it has been suggested that, by being aware of how job candidates search for, investigate, and evaluate potential jobs, those responsible for recruitment can make more effective decisions. Based on research relevant to job applicant decision making, numerous recruitment-related actions that an organization might take to improve the quality of its recruitment efforts were discussed. The material presented on the applicant's view of the recruitment process was designed to provide a foundation for the discussion of various recruitment topics in later chapters in this text. Thus, the coverage in this chapter was selective. However, despite this selective coverage, the reader should be aware of the crucial need for more research on applicant-related issues. Simply stated, at present there is still much we do not know about how applicants make job-related decisions.

Part of the reason for this lack of knowledge is the gap between the concerns that job candidates often experience and the concerns reflected in the typical recruitment study. For example, of the four vignettes presented in the previous chapter, only the case of Lori Springer, the nursing student, has much in common with the typical research study of job-choice decision making. As with the participants in a number of research studies, Lori had an applied major (recruitment studies have often used nursing, engineering, and accounting majors), expected to receive multiple job offers, was inexperienced in job hunting, and expected to receive job offers during roughly the same period (i.e., she was able to evaluate all offers simultaneously). In contrast to Lori's job hunting experience, the experiences of the individuals portrayed in the other vignettes differed greatly from that of the typical research subject. For example, Edith Marble, the retiree, and Jerry Katz, the chemist, were contacted by companies rather than vice versa. In addition, each of them had a paramount concern (the ability to socialize and job security, respectively) that few undergraduates would have. At the same time, unlike many undergraduate students, neither Edith Marble nor Jerry Katz appeared to attach great significance to salary level. In contrast to most subjects in recruitment studies, Mark Smith, the HRM major, had to make a job decision on his only offer without knowing whether any others would be forthcoming.

NOTES

1. For more information, see Gatewood and Feild (1990) or Levine (1983).

2. For a discussion of other approaches that have been used to determine job attribute importance, readers should refer to Rynes (1991), Schwab et al. (1987), and Zedeck (1977). More information on determining job attribute attractiveness will be presented in the section on marketing research for recruitment purposes that appears in Chapter 5.

3. See Schwab et al. (1987) and Rynes (1991) for other factors that limit the generalizability of job attribute ratings derived from the direct estimate methodology.

4. See Krett and Stright (1985).

5. As with the discussion of other topics in this chapter, the coverage of job-choice decision making is selective. Readers who are interested in more detailed treatment of the models discussed here or in other job-choice models are referred to Lord and Maher (1990), Power and Aldag (1985), Rynes, Schwab, and Heneman (1983), Schwab, Rynes, and Aldag (1987), and Wanous and Colella (1989). Although some of the decision-making models discussed here were not developed in the context of job-choice decision making, for presentation purposes each will be discussed in this context.

6. In some cases, rather than thinking in terms of the level of a job attribute (e.g., starting salary), it makes more sense to think in terms of the whether or not the attribute exists (e.g., is child care provided?).

7. Simplest in terms of the cognitive processing that the job candidate goes through. In other ways, Reynolds's theory is quite complex. For example, he suggests that in establishing a minimum level of acceptability for pay, the job candidate bases this level on his or her past wage history and the cost of living rather than on market conditions (e.g., what other companies are paying). Rynes et al. (1983) discuss how Reynolds and other economists who support his theory pay careful attention to the range of pay offers (and other job attributes) across job alternatives.

8. Tversky (1969) proposed an "additive difference model," which assumes that an intradimensional evaluation strategy is used by decision makers. This model hypothesizes that in choosing between two choice alternatives one compares them directly on each relevant dimension. For each dimension, a difference score is derived, and these difference scores are summed. Although Tversky never specified how this model would apply when there were more than two alternatives to choose from, Payne (1976) suggested that a decision maker might compare a given alternative to only the best of the preceding alternatives. If the given alternative was more desirable, it would become the new standard against which future comparisons would be made.

9. The material presented in this section draws heavily on the work of Payne (1976), Hogarth (1987), Dawes (1988), and Beach and Mitchell (1978).

10. Many of the issues discussed in this section are covered in more detail by Bazerman (1990), Dawes (1988), and Hogarth (1987).

11. Although the psychological processes underlying the certainty effect are complex, for our purposes a brief treatment of this phenomenon will suffice. Readers who are interested in greater detail should refer to Kahneman and Tversky's presentation of their "prospect theory" (1979) and Hogarth's treatment of "anchoring and adjustment bias" (1987).

12. As defined by Dawes (1988), the term *heuristic* refers to "automatic thinking processes that can be described by certain psychological rules" (p. 7). Heuristics are simplifying strategies that help an individual deal with a complex decision environment. However, the use of heuristics can be problematic in that "they systematically lead us to make poorer choices than we would by thinking in a more controlled manner about our decisions" (p. 7).

13. In this section, most examples are based on the assumption that the hiring organization is in competition with other organizations for a limited supply of high-quality job candidates. The examples of the steps an organization might consider taking are not intended to be all-inclusive, nor are they intended to reflect all of the complexity involved in taking such actions.

14. See Feinstein (1989b).

15. See Lawrence (1989).

16. In this section, the emphasis will be placed on how an organization can communicate an image through its recruitment communications to prospective job candidates. Readers who are interested in a more general treatment of communicating a corporate image should refer to Garbett (1988).

17. More will be said about appropriate timing for starting the recruitment process in later chapters. However, the reader should be aware that deciding when to start the process is not always an easy matter. For example, for some positions job advertisements need to be placed months in advance; for others a few weeks is appropriate. Such differences in lead time can be due to such factors as the type of job being filled and the type of advertising outlet being used.

18. Rynes (1991) provides a good discussion of how applicant perceptions of organizational nonresponsiveness can affect applicants' interest in an organization.

19. For purposes of this discussion, it will be assumed that the recruitment process does not end with the acceptance of a job offer, but rather continues until the job candidate actually begins work.

20. Fischoff et al. (1980) define values as ". . . evaluative judgments regarding the relative or absolute worth or desirability of possible events" (p. 398).

5

How Recruitment Information Can Improve Person–Job Fit

The first two chapters of this text were designed to provide the reader with a general introduction to the topic of employee recruitment. Among the issues examined in Chapter 1 were the way that the recruitment process affects and is affected by other human resource practices and how the scarcity of labor to fill certain jobs has stimulated the use of several innovative recruitment strategies such as employee leasing. Chapter 1 also provided a number of examples of how poorly thought out recruitment actions can result in undesirable consequences for both organizations and job applicants. Chapter 2 was intended to place the employee recruitment process in the context of strategic business planning and to provide a framework for examining specific recruitment activities in the remainder of this text. In Chapter 2, four phases of the recruitment process were delineated—planning, strategy development, carrying out recruitment activities, and the evaluation of past recruitment practices. Chapters 3 and 4 highlighted the importance of an organization viewing the recruitment process from the perspective of a job candidate. In these two chapters, different approaches that individuals use for locating, investigating, and evaluating job opportunities were examined. Based on the research on job candidate decision making that was reviewed in these chapters, several implications for the development of a recruitment strategy were discussed.

Having provided an introduction to the employee recruitment process in these first four chapters, Chapter 5 now introduces and discusses in some detail the important concept of "person–job fit," which will serve as an organizing mechanism for several of the topics that will be discussed throughout the remainder of this text.

MAXIMIZING PERSON–JOB FIT

Basic Considerations

Although several subtle factors can affect the degree of person–job fit, for the purpose of this chapter a few basic factors are all that need to be considered. In attempting to understand the interaction between a job seeker and a prospective employer during the recruitment process, it is useful to view what is going on as an exchange relationship.[1,2] In filling positions, an organization is looking for individuals who have certain attributes (abilities, academic degrees, values, personal characteristics, and so on). In order to entice individuals who possess these attributes to join it, an employer may offer a variety of incentives, such as interesting job duties, high salaries, and/or access to the most modern equipment.

Just as an organization seeks certain things from a job candidate, a job candidate also seeks certain things from an employer. In general, a person will attempt to obtain a position that can satisfy his or her particular needs and/or desires (a certain salary, a desired location, etc.). In exchange for the opportunity to satisfy such needs and/or desires, a job seeker offers a variety of attributes that an employer may be seeking. In summary, both parties to the recruitment interaction are looking for particular valued characteristics from the other, while at the same time offering certain potentially valuable attributes. In other words, the recruitment process involves ". . . a *dual* matching process between human capabilities and job requirements, and between individual needs and organizational climates" (London and Stumpf, 1982, p. 62).

Although in theory increasing person–job congruence (that is, reducing the discrepancy between the attributes an organization requires from a prospective employee and the characteristics the person offers and the discrepancy between what the person wants from the organization and the incentives the employer offers) may not seem to be a difficult objective, for a variety of reasons, improving this individual–organizational fit has proven to be a challenging task. In order to better understand why improving person–job fit has been so difficult, it is useful to consider a typical recruitment situation.

A Typical Recruitment Interaction

In viewing the recruitment process, it is important to consider the differing perspectives of an individual who is seeking a position and of an organization that is attempting to fill projected job openings. In terms of the job seeker's perspective, individuals are typically quite concerned with making themselves look very attractive to those organizations for which they are potentially interested in working. Among some of the actions that job seekers may take to enhance their attractiveness are dressing in a certain fashion for interviews, getting professional help in developing their résumés, thoroughly researching an organization, and preparing and rehearsing answers to likely interview questions. Not surprisingly, in attempting to enhance their attractiveness to potential employers, some job candidates exaggerate or even fabricate information about their academic record and work experience. [3]

During recruitment interactions, it is not only job candidates who are motivated to emphasize their desirable characteristics. In order to recruit the "best" job candidates, organizations are also interested in presenting themselves in an attractive manner. [4] For example, organizations expend considerable resources on image advertising—Dow Chemical's "Dow Lets You Do Great Things" advertising campaign and the U.S. Army's "It's a Great Place to Start" campaign are two examples—in order to develop a positive image in the eyes of potential job candidates. In addition to image advertising, other methods that organizations use to create favorable impressions are distributing impressive-looking recruitment literature, holding lavish receptions for M.B.A. students, wining and dining job candidates during on-site visits to the organization, and emphasizing the desirable features of working for them during employment interviews. In their attempts to be perceived as desirable places of employment, it should not be surprising that the information that employers share about themselves often conveys an exaggerated picture of the positions under consideration (Phillips, 1987).

As noted in Chapter 1, recruitment and selection activities generally occur simultaneously. Thus, at the same time that a job candidate is trying to appear attractive to a potential employer, the person is also trying to make decisions about whether to continue to pursue a position with that organization or, in some cases, whether to accept a job offer from it. In a similar vein, while an organization is attempting to project a positive image to prospective future employees, it is generally also trying to reduce the number of applicants it is considering by using various selection devices.

Unfortunately, the fact that these dual attraction–selection processes are occurring simultaneously creates problems both for an individual looking for a position and for an organization searching for employees. In terms of a job applicant, in order to decide with which organizations to continue to pursue positions, the person needs specific, factual information about what working for each of them would entail.[5] In theory, the responsibility for making sure that an applicant possesses such information should be jointly shared by both the potential employer and the individual. However, given an organization's motivation to project a favorable image, an applicant cannot rely on an organization to provide accurate information about a potential work situation. Consequently, if a person wants accurate information about a job opening, the person must take the initiative in gathering it.

But because job seekers also are interested in projecting a positive image, they are often hesitant to seek out information that they view as important but about which an organization may be sensitive. For example, having read an article that criticized a particular aspect of a given company (its business prospects, for example), an individual may have reservations about that company as a place of employment. However, so as not to jeopardize making a good first impression, the person may not raise these concerns during a campus interview. Since the recruit did not mention these concerns, the company recruiter may fail to present the company's rebuttal to the criticisms raised in the article. Ultimately, the recruit's failure to understand the company's position (e.g., "Although business prospects are not good for one of our subsidiaries, they are excellent for the division you are considering") may result in the person deciding not to pursue a position with the organization.

In summary, a job candidate's desire both to look attractive to and to evaluate potential employers can create conflict within the individual. The tendency of job seekers to be hesitant to ask "tough" questions in combination with an organization's conscious management of its impression frequently results in job candidates having to make job-choice decisions based on incomplete and inaccurate data about what particular positions with particular employers are like. Not surprisingly, the information that applicants end up acting on generally presents an overly attractive view of the jobs under consideration (Wanous and Colella, 1989).

However, it is not just the job seeker who must make decisions based on incomplete and inaccurate data. Given the motivation of recruits to look as attractive as possible to potential employers, organizations often have doubts about the veracity of the information supplied by job seekers. For example, in selection interviews individuals often are less than candid. A person might, for instance, state a willingness to relocate in the future even though he or she does not anticipate being willing to do so when the time for such a move arrives.

Employers are also partly responsible for the quality of the information that they have available for making selection decisions. Frequently, an organization could improve the accuracy and the completeness of the information it has on a job candidate if it were willing to take certain steps such as requiring documentation of an applicant's academic and work record. For example, Hough (1984) describes an "accomplishment record" approach for selecting professionals that requires that applicant-provided information be verified by another person who is familiar with the person's work record (the applicant supplies the names of people who can verify the information). Although such a verification procedure should improve the accuracy of the data on which an employer bases its hiring decisions, job candidates may react negatively to having a potential employer question the truthfulness of the information they have supplied. Knowing this, many organizations are hesitant to probe too deeply for information that might help them make better selection decisions.

Exhibit 5.1   The attraction–selection situation: Conflicting job candidate and employer objectives

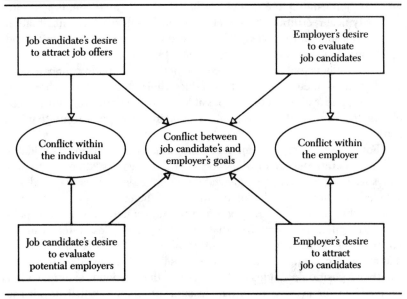

Source: Exhibit adapted from Porter, Lawler, and Hackman (1975).

In summary, just as there is conflict between a job candidate's desire to look attractive to organizations and that person's desire to evaluate potential employers, an employer faces similar conflict. Exhibit 5.1 expresses the various conflict situations (i.e., within the individual, within the employer, and between the candidate and the employer) discussed in the preceding paragraphs.

An Ideal Recruitment Interaction

From the preceding discussion of a typical recruitment situation, it should be apparent how what commonly transpires can result in a person–job mismatch. Because both the job seeker and the employer have adopted a competitive posture—the job candidate sees himself or herself in competition with other individuals for scarce job offers and the company sees itself in competition with other employers for a limited number of suitable job candidates—rather than openly share potentially important information, both parties in the recruitment interaction are concerned with managing their impressions. The end result of such impression management is likely to be a lack of a person–job fit.

Having discussed a typical recruitment situation, it is instructive to view the job candidate-employer interaction as it could (should?) occur. As in a typical recruitment interaction, in an "ideal" recruitment situation both applicants and employers have the dual concerns of attraction and selection. However, in an ideal recruitment situation, both parties recognize the conflicts that can occur because of these competing concerns. To avoid such conflicts (or at least to reduce their magnitude), rather than trying to appear as attractive as possible, both the employer and the applicant are concerned with facilitating an open exchange of accurate information.

For an employer, this means attempting to provide job candidates with an accurate picture of what working there involves.[6] In order to provide such a perspective, an organization cannot hide or downplay undesirable features of the specific job opening or of the organization in general. By providing an accurate as opposed to an exaggerated view of a job opening, an organization recognizes that some people may lose interest in the position it is trying to fill. On the other hand, the employer also realizes that an open exchange of information will allow a job candidate to decide whether a position provides certain features that the job seeker may view as important or even as essential. In sum, an employer that decides to provide accurate information about a job opening accepts the fact that it may have a smaller applicant pool from which to select. However, it does so with the expectation that those individuals who remain interested in a position after receiving accurate information will make better employees, if they are ultimately hired.[7]

In order for there to be an open exchange of information, recruits also have a responsibility. Instead of trying to maximize their attractiveness to potential employers, they should instead present accurate information about themselves and aggressively seek the information they need from employers in order to be able to intelligently evaluate job openings.[8] For example, if a law school graduate has concerns about a particular law firm's commitment to public service, the person should ask whether associates are encouraged to do pro bono work. In a similar vein, if a person does not want to have to travel extensively, the person should communicate this fact to potential employers. Although such openness may result in a person being eliminated from consideration for some jobs, it should also increase the likelihood that, if a job offer is obtained, the position will be one that is suitable for the individual. However, an applicant should not automatically assume that such honesty will diminish his or her likelihood of receiving a job offer. Some organizations may find such applicant candor refreshing. Thus, openness may actually increase the attractiveness of the candidate to some employers.

Person–Job Fit: An Overview of Key Issues

Although in principle most would agree that an open exchange of information between a job candidate and a prospective employer is desirable, in reality, it appears that such exchanges do not commonly occur (Herriot, 1984). Instead, both employers and job seekers try to maximize their attractiveness to each other.[9] While it may seem naive to hope that individuals and organizations will share information that may not reflect positively on them, there may be certain circumstances that facilitate the sharing of such information. For example, it has been suggested (see Porter, Lawler, and Hackman, 1975) that a job candidate may be less concerned with impression management when the person senses he or she will have little trouble finding a good position or when the candidate already has a good position.

In terms of an organization's willingness to present an accurate as opposed to a flattering view of itself, it seems likely that a company that anticipates having little trouble filling positions (e.g., due to a tight job market or its having a favorable reputation as an employer) would be more willing to disseminate accurate information than an employer that does not expect to be able to fill jobs easily. In addition, if an organization is experiencing considerable turnover that appears to be the result of newly hired employees possessing inaccurate job expectations, the employer is likely to consider taking steps to improve the accuracy of the information about itself that it conveys during the recruitment process.

Although the emphasis in this section on person–job congruence has been on the willingness or motivation of job candidates and organizations to communicate accurate information about themselves, their ability to do so should not be overlooked. If an individual's needs are not met by a job situation, the person will be dissatisfied. Thus, it is important for a job applicant to be able to communicate what he or she is looking for in a job. Unfortunately, unless an individual has spent considerable time reflecting on what he or she wants in a position, the person may be unable to share such information with a potential employer, even if the candidate wants to do so (Kotter, Faux, and McArthur, 1978).

In a similar vein, although organizations often spend considerable time determining the attributes they seek in new employees, employers frequently do not give much attention to the rewards that they offer to new employees. In particular, employers often are unaware of intangible factors they offer, such as friendly co-workers. Such factors are important because they can have a major effect on how job candidates react to a new job and because many candidates lack information about them (Wanous, 1980). However, if an organization is not aware of what it offers to recruits as potential inducements, it cannot communicate such information, even if it wants to do so.

The material presented so far regarding person–job fit obviously has left many questions unanswered. In the final section of this chapter, many of these questions will be addressed in detail. However, at this point, it is important to clarify one issue. Although researchers have discussed the concept of person–job fit as a desired state of affairs, in reality perfect congruence has been seen as an unattainable objective. For example, Herriot (1984) discusses the process by which organizations and individuals attempt "to achieve a workable degree of congruence" (p. 147). Similarly, Dawis and Lofquist (1984) discuss how a job seeker has a "range of tolerable discorrespondence" between what the person seeks in a job and what he or she can accept. In this text, although the term person–job fit will be used, the reader should be aware that in reality the goal of both the job candidate and the organization should be to minimize person–job incongruence.[10]

INCREASING THE ACCURACY OF RECRUITS' JOB EXPECTATIONS: THE EMPLOYER'S ROLE

From the preceding section, it should be clear that job candidates can take several steps to increase the accuracy of their job expectations and hence to improve the likelihood of person–job congruence.[11] In addition, through its selection system, an employer can try to determine the extent to which job candidates have accurate knowledge concerning a given position.[12] However, because the focus of this text is on employee recruitment, in this section attention will be given to the various recruitment actions an organization can take to increase the accuracy of a job applicant's expectations. Exhibit 5.2 is a schematic summary of the major points discussed in the remainder of this chapter.

An organization that decides to present an accurate picture of itself to job candidates must address several fundamental questions.[13] Among these are: What information should be communicated to prospective employees? What is the best way to communicate this information? When should this information be communicated? In discussing the communication of job-related information in this section, research that has focused on a recruitment mechanism known as a "realistic job preview" (RJP) will be heavily drawn on. However, the discussion that follows should not be seen as relevant only if one is interested in designing an RJP (RJPs will be discussed in detail in Chapter 7). The treatment in this chapter is more generic. The issues discussed have relevance for the design of a recruitment brochure, a job advertisement, a work sample test, a campus interview, or a job fair presentation.

In an important theoretical paper, Popovich and Wanous (1982) showed the relevance of the psychological literature on attitude formation and change in developing a recruitment program that conveys accurate information.[14] Based on their integration of research on attitudes, Popovich and Wanous argued that four factors—the source of the job-related information, the medium used to transmit it, the information content, and characteristics of the information recipients—merit particular attention if one wants to improve the accuracy of job candidate expectations. Breaugh and Billings (1988) have suggested that, although all four of Popovich and Wanous's communication-related factors are important, the most important factor an employer must be concerned with is information content (i.e., the actual message that is conveyed). Therefore, before examining issues related to the source of the information, the medium used to transmit it, and the characteristics of the information recipients, attention will first be given to key properties of the job-related information that is to be communicated.[15]

Exhibit 5.2   Increasing the accuracy of applicant job expectations: A simplified model

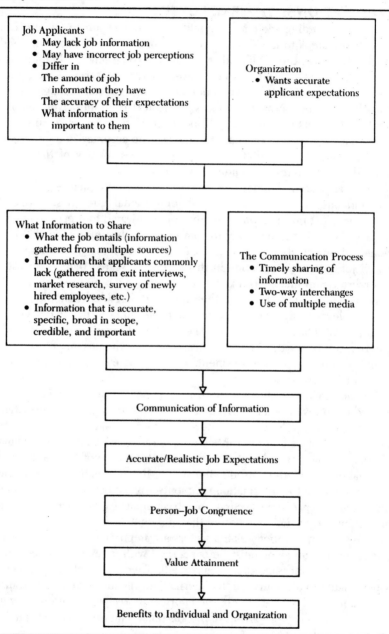

What Information to Communicate:
Five Key Properties of Information Content

If an organization truly wants to provide a prospective employee with information that will help the person determine whether there is likely to be acceptable person–job congruence, there are at least five key properties of its recruitment message with which an employer should be concerned: accuracy, specificity, breadth, credibility, and importance.

Information Accuracy

In communicating information to job candidates, an organization must obviously be concerned about the veracity of the message that it presents (Breaugh and Billings, 1988). Although designing recruitment mechanisms that provide accurate information about both the positive and the negative attributes of a position may seem to be a straightforward task, this is not always the case. For example, the top management of a corporation may be committed to a pay-for-performance philosophy, and this fact may be publicized in its recruitment literature. However, a few recalcitrant supervisors, despite corporate policy, may use seniority as their primary determinant of salary increases. Thus, if a newly hired individual ends up reporting to a supervisor who resists performance-contingent pay, the information given to this new employee did not accurately describe the person's work situation. In a similar vein, the top decision makers of an organization may be committed to a policy of equal employment opportunity and may have advertised this fact. However, a particular manager may let factors such as an employee's race, age, and/or sex inappropriately influence his or her decision making. In summary, in attempting to present accurate information about itself, an organization must be sensitive to numerous subtleties that ultimately will influence the accuracy of its recruitment information. More extensive coverage of improving the accuracy of recruitment information is provided in Chapter 7.

Information Specificity

Information provided during the recruitment process that will enable a person to make an informed decision about the degree of person–job congruence must be more than merely accurate; it must be reasonably detailed. For example, a job advertisement stating that the salary for a chef's position is competitive may be accurate, but it may not be specific enough to be of much use. In contrast, a statement that the starting salary for this position is between $39,500 and $44,500, depending on experience, may enable a potential candidate to decide that, because he is currently making a salary of $48,750, he will not to pursue the position. Similarly, a statement such as "some overnight travel required" in an advertisement is not specific enough to allow a person to determine if during an average month the job requires three, six, or nine days of travel. Conceivably, an excellent job candidate who would have no trouble coordinating three nights away would not pursue the position because he or she believes more nights are involved. If in reality only three nights are involved, the organization may have lost a desirable job candidate.

In summary, if an organization wants to communicate information that will help a job candidate determine the degree of fit between his or her needs and what a position offers/requires, the employer should convey information that is sufficiently detailed to allow such a determination. Stated in terms of information processing concepts introduced in the last chapter, specific job information is important because it is more likely to be attended to, more likely to be stored in long-term memory, and more likely to be recalled or available than more general job information (Bazerman, 1990). In other words, specific information is more effective at reducing job candidate uncertainty than is more general information.

Information That Is Broad in Scope

In attempting to provide recruits with useful information, a key issue is determining the range of topics that should be addressed. In order to make an informed decision about a position, most job candidates want accurate and specific information about a wide range of job and organizational attributes. Unfortunately, it appears that the recruitment communications of many organizations have failed to adequately address several important job attributes (Breaugh and Billings, 1988). In particular, Wanous and Colella (1989) have noted that job candidates often lack information about the more subtle (intangible) aspects of a position (e.g., What is the work group climate? Is decision making participative in nature?). Without extensive information about a position, most job applicants will have a difficult time assessing whether there is a sufficient degree of person–job fit. Thus, if an employer wants to help individuals determine whether a particular job is a good one for them, the employer should make certain that the recruitment information it conveys addresses a wide range of job–related concerns.

The Credibility of the Job-Related Information

In addition to being accurate, specific, and broad in scope, if a job seeker is to perceive information as being useful for making a job-choice decision, the information must also be viewed as credible. Stated differently, it is not sufficient for the information that an organization disseminates during the recruitment process to be accurate; the information has to be perceived as accurate by the recipient.

For example, after being recruited by three companies, a Hispanic engineer may conclude that, although Company A and Company B claimed to be committed to affirmative action, only Company C is truly committed. This perception of Company C may be based on such things as minorities being present in the photographs in company brochures, a Hispanic being part of the campus recruitment team that interviewed her, and the fact that she saw several minorities when she visited Company C. Given this perception, this engineer may decline job offers from Company A and Company B and accept an offer from Company C. What is important to focus on in this example is that this job candidate's perception may be incorrect. Conceivably, Company A may be the most committed to affirmative action. However, in making job-choice decisions, individuals' perceptions (not "objective" reality) determine what decisions are made. Thus, in planning recruitment communications, an employer should pay careful attention to the credibility of the information in the eyes of prospective job candidates. As has been frequently noted (see Rynes and Boudreau, 1986), it appears that information communicated during the recruitment process often lacks credibility.

In terms of enhancing the credibility of the information that is presented, psychological research has shown that two factors—communicator expertise and trustworthiness—are key. In terms of recruitment communications, such credibility is likely to be enhanced when the source of the information is seen as being quite familiar with the job opening under consideration as well as having no reason to distort the information being conveyed. Research in the recruitment area (see Fisher, Ilgen, and Hoyer, 1979) has shown that job incumbents are a particularly credible source of information. Although less important than expertise and trustworthiness for establishing the credibility of recruitment information, research (see Petty and Cacioppo, 1986) has also shown that the number of sources from which an individual receives information can also affect information credibility. More specifically, research suggests that when a job candidate receives consistent, noncontradictory information about a given job attribute, such as advancement opportunities, from multiple information sources (e.g., a job incumbent, a corporate recruiter, a recruitment brochure), it is more likely to be perceived as veracious.[16]

The Importance of the Information Conveyed

In designing recruitment communications, an organization must give careful consideration to the importance of the information that is provided. Although in theory one would like to be able to provide complete information about a job opening, due to various constraints (e.g., limitations in the attention span of recruits, restrictions on the length of campus interviews) this is not likely to be possible. Thus, an organization must carefully consider what is the most important information to convey in the limited space or time that is available.

For the most part, information about a position that is already known by a job candidate will not be seen as particularly important. Therefore, in planning recruitment communications, an employer generally should be concerned with transmitting information that recruits are lacking or that will correct misperceptions they have. In some cases, an organization may need to do on-site research to discover what information it should convey. In other cases, an organization may be willing to make decisions about what information is important to communicate based on published research.

For example, Dean, Ferris, and Konstans (1985) suggest that employers should supply job seekers with information concerning job content (use of various skills, autonomy), job context (compensation, supervision), and career facilitation (advancement opportunity, developmental activities) during the recruitment process. James and James (1989) point out four general areas—leader support and facilitation; work group cooperation, warmth, and friendship; job challenge and autonomy; and role stress and lack of harmony—of a job situation that have been found to be related to how positively an employee reacts to a job situation. Based on interviews with recently hired employees, Suszko and Breaugh (1986) highlight five categories of job information—physical working conditions, work hours, work duties, career opportunities, and relations with supervisors and co-workers,—that should be addressed in recruitment communications. In summary, although an organization would be wise to conduct its own research on what job and organizational attributes to address in its recruitment communications, research by Dean et al., James and James, and Suszko and Breaugh highlights several areas that should be given consideration.

Information Source, Communication Medium, and Recipient Characteristics

Having briefly discussed five key information properties that an organization should attempt to maximize in providing job-related information during recruitment interactions, it is now important to address how the other three information-related factors—the information source, the recipients of the communication, and the communication medium—highlighted by Popovich and Wanous (1982) can influence the accuracy and the usefulness of the information that is provided to recruits.

The Source(s) of the Information Presented

Given that an organization wants to communicate job-related information that is accurate, specific, comprehensive, credible, and important, a key question is how one compiles such information. In order to collect information that has these desired properties, an organization generally will need to use several information sources. For example, in garnering information for inclusion in their realistic job preview of a bank teller position, Dean and Wanous (1984) used incumbent tellers, senior bank managers, and personnel executives as information sources. Among the possible sources that an organization may need to rely on for compiling job-related information are: job incumbents, supervisors, employee handbooks/personnel manuals, written job descriptions, personnel department representatives, persons who have recently held the job (e.g., individuals who have left the organization, people who have transferred to a new position), and employees who interact regularly with those who hold the position under consideration.[17] In gathering information from these sources, an employer may need to rely on multiple data gathering procedures (e.g., individual interviews with job incumbents, group meetings with supervisors, surveys sent to those who work with people in the position being studied, and direct observations of people in the job).

Important Characteristics of the Information Recipients

In planning a campaign for sharing information about itself, an organization obviously needs to be aware of its intended audience. Although there are numerous ways one could approach this topic, it may be simplest to focus on the ability and motivation of those who comprise one's intended audience to use the information conveyed. In terms of ability, two factors are of particular importance.[18] The recipients of the information must be able to understand the terminology used in a recruitment communication and the information should be provided in such a way that recipients are not overwhelmed by it.

With regard to the use of appropriate terminology, this appears not to be a major problem. In most cases, job advertisements, recruitment brochures, campus recruiters, etc., do not use language that is inappropriate (the use of technical terminology is appropriate and may even be desirable if anyone suitable for the position should be familiar with it). However, employers do have to remain alert for situations in which recruitment materials should be translated into other languages. In terms of recruits being overwhelmed by information, this can be a more difficult issue. With regard to written information, this may not be a problem; one can assume that recipients can go at their own speed and reread information where necessary. However, when information is tranmitted orally and/or visually, an employer must take steps to allow for adequate cognitive processing by information recipients.[19] For example, if a videotape is used for recruiting, it should be pretested to make sure that information is presented at a speed at which a typical applicant can adequately process it. In a similar vein, to aid the recall of information at a later point in time, an organization should consider allowing time for candidates to take notes on the material presented. Alternatively, to save time, an organization could provide a written summary of the information that was presented.

In addition to being concerned with the ability of a job applicant to process information, an organization should also be concerned with factors that may influence a person's motivation to attend to and actively process this information. For example, with regard to printed information such as a recruitment brochure, the use of text, pictures, and graphics that are especially distinctive are likely to attract a reader's attention.[20] Given this fact, many large organizations hire advertising agencies to help them design creative recruitment materials.

A particularly important factor to consider in attempting to motivate individuals to attend to a recruitment communication is the "personal relevance" of the message to the recipient. According to Petty and Cacioppo (1986), information is more likely to be seen as having personal relevance if it addresses topics that are of particular importance to the information recipient. The personal relevance of the information provided during recruitment can be increased in several ways. For example, providing information that is both specific (e.g., detailed information that is tied to a particular job opening) and broad in scope (e.g., covering lateral relationships) should improve the likelihood that the recipient will see the information as having importance. Since information that is seen as lacking credibility is unlikely to be perceived as being important, the value of using job incumbents as an information source should be apparent.

The Medium Used to Convey the Job-Related Information

The fourth and final factor addressed by Popovich and Wanous (1982) in their paper on recruitment communications is the medium used to convey information. In theory, an organization could use a variety of different recruitment media to publicize a job opening. However, given that recruitment methods differ in several important ways, an employer should carefully consider their relative advantages and disadvantages in selecting among them. Although a detailed discussion of the specific advantages and disadvantages of the various recruitment media will be saved for Chapter 11, two potentially important media attributes should be noted: whether the communication method is one-way or two-way, and whether the medium requires, or at least encourages, the information recipient to actively process the information communicated. These two attributes are important because they can directly affect the personal relevance of the recruitment information to prospective employees.

Recruitment media can allow for either one-way or two-way communication. One-way recruitment media, such as a direct mail advertisement, only allow for the transmission of information from an employer to a job candidate. A potential deficiency of one-way recruitment media is that prospective job candidates are not able to receive immediate answers to questions they may have concerning a job opening. In contrast, other recruitment media, such as in-person interviews with job incumbents, allow for a two-way exchange of information. That is, both the organization and the candidate can request and provide information.

In addition to being aware of the distinctions between one-way and two-way recruitment media, an organization should also consider the extent to which the recruitment media it uses require or encourage the active processing of the information that is conveyed. Among the recruitment media that are likely to result in passive information processing are newspaper advertisements, direct mail ads, posted job notices, and recruitment brochures. In contrast to these media, which require little active involvement of the recipient, recruitment devices such as taking part in work simulations, tours of work sites, and/or in-person interviews generally require that the recruit play a much more active role. For example, in comparison to the relatively passive information processing activity of reading a job advertisement (the person may skim over sections that are of little interest and does not expect to be questioned about the information presented), a person taking part in a work simulation may receive a variety of distinctive visual, auditory, and tactile stimuli, and may expect to be asked about what he or she has experienced immediately after the simulation.

One reason why organizations should be concerned with facilitating the active processing of recruitment information is that active and passive information processing have different effects on attitude formation and change.[21] According to recent attitude research (see Petty and Cacioppo, 1986), it appears that the active (i.e., central) processing of information, in contrast to passive (i.e., peripheral) processing, results in both the formation of more stable attitudes as well as greater attitude change. Thus, in the context of recruitment, one would expect that, in those cases in which a job candidate lacked information about a particular job attribute, providing information via a medium that stimulates central processing should result in a recruit developing a more stable view of that attribute. Perhaps more important, central processing is more likely than peripheral processing to amend inaccurate impressions of a position that a job candidate may hold so that the job candidate's perceptions become more accurate.

Having briefly discussed several factors that should be considered by an organization as it plans its strategy for communicating job-related information, it is now important to provide some examples of how the preceding discussion should enable an employer to more effectively recruit employees.

DEVELOPING A RECRUITMENT PROGRAM FOR CONVEYING ACCURATE INFORMATION

Despite the fact that there are obvious advantages to providing information to job candidates that is accurate, specific, broad in scope, credible, and important, this is not an easily accomplished task. In many cases, an organization may want to present a complete and accurate picture of a job situation but it may be limited in the amount of information it can actually convey. For example, in most publications, the longer the job advertisement, the more expensive it is to run. Thus, cost constraints can limit the amount of information that can be disseminated. However, even if an employer were able to present a detailed picture of a job, many prospective applicants would not be willing to attend to the information provided (e.g., commit the time to read a lengthy job description or watch a forty-minute videotape at a job fair). Furthermore, even in those rare situations where the organization is able to present a detailed picture of a job and some individuals are motivated to attend to the extensive information, the prospective applicants may be overwhelmed by the amount of information and thus unable to adequately process all of it.

From the examples cited above, it should be apparent that in order to maximize the effectiveness of its recruitment communications, an employer must carefully plan its strategy. Frequently, it will need to compromise conflicting recruitment objectives (such as presenting detailed information versus minimizing advertising costs). Rather than focus on what organizations may not be able to do, it is more constructive to focus on how they can improve the ways in which they currently communicate job-related information. In the next section, it will be shown that, by carefully considering the five key properties of information content, most organizations can improve their recruitment-related communications.

Investigating a Job in Order to Plan Recruitment Communications

Assuming that an organization wants to communicate accurate information about a job opening, one of the first things the employer needs to address is the process it will use for investigating what a given position involves. Reilly, Brown, Blood, and Maletesta (1981) have suggested that the same basic process that an organization uses for establishing the content validity of a selection device is appropriate for developing an information base to use for recruitment purposes. Following Reilly et al.'s logic, an employer should gather information about a given job from multiple sources who have insight into what the job involves. Various information gathering methods, such as individual interviews, questionnaires, and direct observation, could be used for gathering information about a position.[22] Although the job analysis approaches one might use to justify a selection device and to decide on what information to communicate during the recruitment process are similar, there is one important difference: the information gathered to analyze a job for recruitment purposes is generally broader in scope than the job description that results for content validity purposes. For example, if the focus of a job analysis is on supporting the soundness of a selection device, one should generally not be concerned with such aspects of a job situation as co-worker relations, department politics, or the supervisory style of a particular manager. In contrast, information that addresses such topics as these could be particularly important for a person who is trying to determine whether there is a good person–job fit (Dean and Wanous, 1984).

In investigating what a job entails for recruitment purposes, it is important that an organization not just focus on the position itself. Although what the position involves is of major importance to most job candidates, other factors may also have a significant influence on their job-choice decisions. The effect of such contextual factors as an on-site child care facility or access to public transportation can be particularly pronounced when an individual is considering two or more job offers that are similar in terms of job content attributes. For example, in deciding between two very similar jobs with competing firms located in different geographic areas, an individual may give considerable weight to whether the communities in which the positions are located offer affordable housing or good job opportunities for a spouse.

IOMEGA, a manufacturer of cartridge disk drives located in Ogden, Utah, is a good example of an organization that has examined and attempted to publicize what it offers to prospective employees in terms of contextual factors. As described by Halcrow (1986), rather than view its location in Utah as a disadvantage in recruiting engineers from out of state, IOMEGA developed a job advertisement with the title "24 Things to Do in Ogden, Utah," which included the following text: "Ogden is a community that has safe streets, clean air and water, schools that kids can walk to, affordable housing, all the things most of us grew up taking for granted . . . and can't seem to find these days." Although the family orientation of this ad may have caused some engineering prospects to see Ogden as an undesirable location, overall it appears that the ad was very successful, so successful, in fact, that the Ogden Chamber of Commerce sought permission to use it to promote tourism.

Investigating Applicant Perceptions of a Position with an Organization

Once an organization has developed a good understanding of what it offers to and requires from job candidates, it next should consider the accuracy and the completeness of the perceptions that prospective employees have of a position with the organization.[23] There are several methods that can be used to examine applicant perceptions.

As was noted previously, recently hired individuals can be a good source of information on job-related topics that job applicants are likely to be misinformed or uninformed about. An organization can use interviews or short questionnaires to determine specific topics about which new employees held incorrect perceptions or simply lacked information. However, there are potential problems with relying exclusively on new employees as a source of information. First, they may not remember certain job attributes about which they lacked or had incorrect information. Second, they may be hesitant to admit that their perceptions were incorrect or incomplete. For example, a new employee may not want to acknowledge that he or she finds certain job duties to be more difficult than expected for fear that such an admission will reflect badly on his or her capabilities. A third problem with relying solely on recently hired individuals as a source of information is that this group may not accurately reflect how members of the general applicant population, or even the smaller applicant pool, feel about working for an organization. For example, it is possible that a sizable number of persons in the applicant population have very negative perceptions of a given organization as a place of employment. Holding such perceptions, these individuals may decide to not even submit applications for employment. While the perceptions held by this segment of the applicant population might be grossly inaccurate, if an employer relies only on the persons it has hired (who may have had more accurate job and organizational expectations) as a source of information, it may never discover that many potential recruits possess incorrect job perceptions.

One way around this problem is the use of recruitment-oriented marketing research. Although an in-depth discussion of how to conduct a marketing research study is beyond the scope of this text, an overview and an example of this approach are instructive.[24] In planning a marketing research study, an organization (frequently with the help of a consulting firm that is hired to conduct the study) must make several important decisions. It must clearly state the objective of the study (e.g., "We want to know how we are viewed by prospective employees." "What comes to mind when they think of a position with us?" "What advantages of working for us are overlooked?" "What incorrect perceptions do people have?"). In terms of getting answers to such questions, an employer must decide from what potential applicant population it seeks information (e.g., new engineering graduates). The employer must also decide what methodology it wants to use to conduct the study (e.g., one-on-one interviews, focus groups, surveys). In planning a study to assess prospective employee perceptions, an organization obviously must make trade-offs between the budget available for such a project and the quality of the data gathered. For example, with a large budget, an organization not only will be able to have a large sample but may also be able to pay study participants. By paying participants, an organization should increase the participant response rate and, thus, improve its ability to generalize with some confidence to the applicant population as a whole.

The experience of NEC Information Systems (NECIS) is a good example of the use of a recruitment-related marketing research study. As described by Albert McCarthy, its vice president of employee relations, NECIS is faced with the constant challenge of attracting and hiring the best professionals in a highly competitive job market (A. H. McCarthy 1989). Rather than continue to rely on its traditional approaches to recruiting, NECIS, with the help of a consulting firm, looked for new approaches.[25] Using focus groups, NECIS tried to determine what systems analysts and marketing specialists wanted in a job and what motivated these professionals to apply for a specific position with a particular organization. NECIS focused on these two groups because they were the most difficult and the most expensive to hire.

The first step of the NECIS study involved using focus groups to determine what systems analysts and marketing professionals considered to be the ideal workplace,[26] how NECIS was perceived as a company for which to work, how some of NECIS's competitors were perceived, and the reactions of the focus group members to the recruitment advertising then being used by NECIS and its competitors. Based on information obtained from these focus groups, NECIS concluded that it needed to provide more specific information in its job advertisements. NECIS also determined that systems analysts and marketing professionals should not be recruited in the same way. For example, marketing professionals were found to be interested in the entire company—"its image, goals, directions." They also sought professional growth and expressed a need to have an impact on the company. In contrast, systems analysts were more interested in such aspects of the specific position they would fill as good working relations with co-workers and input into product decisions.

Following the use of the focus groups, NECIS conducted 100 interviews with individuals who were considered potential targets for jobs with NECIS in high-technology positions. The interviewees first answered a battery of questions about how they would look for a new job and the type of information they wanted in a recruitment advertisement. The interviewees were then shown a rapid series of images from past newspaper advertisements that NECIS had run to determine the effectiveness of the ads. The results of the interview study suggested several ways in which NECIS could improve the way it recruits. For example, the study showed that systems analysts and marketing professionals expect and want recruitment ads to provide specific information concerning job responsibilities, necessary applicant qualifications, starting salaries, and whom to contact and how.

Although it is always difficult to evaluate the effectiveness of a recruitment campaign, NECIS was very pleased with what it found out from the research it conducted. For example, NECIS believes that the modifications it made in its recruitment ads based on their focus group and interview studies have led to fewer interviews per hire and greater administrative efficiency. In addition, NECIS estimates it saved more than $500,000 in one year because it had to use employment agencies less frequently to fill positions. In summarizing the results of its research project, A. H. McCarthy (1989) notes that NECIS no longer makes recruitment decisions "in an information vacuum in which its thoughts and expertise were the ultimate authority. The focus is now on what the *targeted* audience will respond to." Given the success of its initial marketing research study, NECIS is now using a similar approach to expand "its understanding of additional applicant groups at the non-exempt level."[27]

The Importance of First Impressions

Given the importance of the first impression a job candidate forms and the subsequent operation of selective perception, an organization cannot start too soon in attempting to provide an accurate view of what working for it is like. For example, the written job descriptions of open positions that are commonly placed on bulletin boards in the personnel office should present an accurate picture of what the positions involve. Similarly, presenters at job fairs or at college career days should be instructed as to how to characterize job opportunities accurately.

Newspaper advertisements cause many job seekers to form initial impressions of positions that are overly positive. For example, among the phrases included in advertisements published in a couple of recent issues of a leading business newspaper were: "outstanding opportunity for rapid advancement," "unique assignments that challenge your every talent," "we offer excellent compensation and benefits," "we offer a stimulating work environment," and "if you have that pioneer spirit and are looking for a company where you can develop your talents to your fullest potential. . . ." In contrast to the regularity with which such positive phrases as these occurred, companies rarely noted anything that might be considered a negative job attribute. In fact, in what was admittedly a less than scientific sampling of help-wanted advertisements, the most negative phrase was "flexibility regarding travel is required." Although some may suggest that the use of ads that glamorize or exaggerate particular job attributes is harmless because readers expect such exaggeration, it is difficult to imagine that employers pour millions of dollars into such ads if they do not have at least some impact on the job search behavior of individuals.

In a recent study, Rynes and Boudreau (1986) found that, in recruiting new college graduates, companies relied heavily on recruitment brochures to convey initial information about what jobs with them entail. Thus, in recruiting college seniors, organizations that are interested in enhancing the accuracy of recruit perceptions should make sure that the information contained in the brochures they distribute is factual. Unfortunately, research on recruitment literature (see Rynes and Boudreau, 1986) has shown that it often presents an overly positive view of what a job with an organization is like.

In summary, if an organization is interested in the formation of accurate job perceptions by recruits, it should take actions to ensure that from the very start its recruitment mechanisms (e.g., job advertisements, job fair presentations) transmit factual information.

Two-Way Interactions as a Mechanism for Maximizing Recruitment Effectiveness

Given the conflicting recruitment objectives that have been discussed, employers are often forced to make difficult choices in planning recruitment activities. For example, how can a company hope to develop a recruitment information campaign that is inexpensive, does not overwhelm job candidates with information, and yet presents an accurate and comprehensive view of the position that it needs to fill? Although not a panacea, the use of two-way recruitment mechanisms—those that allow communication back and forth between a candidate and one or more representatives of the organization—does offer particular advantages.

Two-way recruitment interactions have potential advantages in terms of the breadth, specificity, credibility, and personal relevance of the job-related information that is communicated. For example, with a recruitment communication that is one-way (e.g., a newspaper advertisement), the same information is conveyed to all prospective recruits,[28] which presents several potential problems. For example, many candidates may have little interest in some of the recruitment information (tuition reimbursement, for example). Another potential problem is that a recruitment communication may fail to address topics that are important to a particular job candidate (such as one's prospective co-workers) or may fail to address the topic in sufficient detail (as in the statement "salaries are competitive"). Such an absence of information or such superficial treatment may cause a candidate to see the recruitment information as lacking in personal relevance. Moreover, because some of the most commonly used one-way recruitment media (e. g., company brochures) are somewhat passive modes of communication, they frequently do not arouse enough interest in the message or stimulate the active processing of the information conveyed.

By using two-way recruitment communication devices, the potential disadvantages of one-way media are lessened or even eliminated. For example, if during an interview with a potential co-worker certain desired information is not presented, a job applicant has the opportunity to request it ("How are salary increases determined?"). Similarly, if the information provided during an interview was general in nature ("We all get along pretty well."), a job candidate can ask for greater specificity ("Do you socialize together after work?"). By being able to ask such questions, an applicant should be able to increase the personal relevance of the information he or she receives from the organization.

Another advantage of two-way media is that they make for the efficient use of time. For instance, instead of providing the same information to all job candidates, as is typically done, a recruiter can ask a candidate whether he or she is knowledgeable about and/or interested in certain topics and then tailor the recruitment information to the applicant's needs. Such custom-tailoring should allow a candidate to receive the maximum amount of personally relevant information during the limited time available.

With regard to customizing recruitment information, as was noted earlier in this chapter, there appear to be certain categories of job-related information that most job seekers seem to be interested in (starting salary, a description of job duties, supervision, etc.). This does not mean that an organization can address these topics in a general way, however. For example, although the top management of a company may be committed to participative decision making, affirmative action, performance-contingent pay, etc., this does not guarantee that these attributes will be found in every work group. Instead, it is likely that substantial differences will be found among supervisors and work groups. Given such work group differences, it is quite likely that, if an organization presents the same information to all job candidates, some of them may be misinformed.

Supervision is probably the most important job-related attribute that recruits need situation-specific information about. As noted by Nadler, Hackman, and Lawler (1979), "In many ways, the supervisor is the organization to a new employee. If he or she does a good job of performing key tasks, the organization is usually viewed favorably. If a supervisor is ineffective in working with the newcomer, the organization itself is seen negatively" (p. 135). Given the numerous dimensions on which supervisors can differ (delegation, providing feedback, tying rewards to performance, and so on) and the subtleties of many of these differences, it is next to impossible for an organization to present general information about supervision that would be of much use to a job candidate. In fact, by trying to describe a specific job situation by using general job information (e.g., a recruitment brochure that describes a company as committed to participative management), an employer may actually end up misleading candidates. For example, a newly hired employee may expect a supervisor who is committed to participative management only to quickly discover that his or her supervisor rarely involves subordinates in decision making.

Although additional suggestions concerning how to custom-tailor recruitment information to a specific work situation will be provided in later chapters, the value of job incumbents for communicating what things are like in their work group (including their supervisor's leadership style) should be obvious. Given their perceived expertise and trustworthiness (Fisher et al., 1979), these job incumbents maximize the credibility of the recruitment information that is conveyed. Furthermore, because of their intimate knowledge of the work environment into which a job candidate will move, they can provide detailed information about a host of important topics. A particular advantage of using "off-the-record" conversations with job incumbents is that they allow for the communication of important but sensitive information that the organization may be hesitant to include in more permanent recruitment media such as written brochures.

MAKING RATIONAL RECRUITMENT COMPROMISES

Using Research as a Foundation for Making Compromise Decisions

From the material presented in this chapter, the need to make compromises among various recruitment objectives should be evident. It should also be apparent that research can provide a good foundation for arriving at such compromises. For example, research on information source credibility (see, for example, Fisher et al., 1979) suggests the importance of having job incumbents play a major role in the recruitment process.[29] In a similar vein, Petty and Cacioppo's (1986) attitude research supports the use of two-way communication media in order to enhance the personal relevance of recruitment information to prospective employees. The NECIS study (A. H. McCarthy, 1989) provides an example of the importance of asking prospective employees what they want to know about a position with an organization and how best to present information about job openings.

Organizational Politics as a Factor in Making Recruitment Decisions

Although a consideration of recruitment-related research should have a major influence on the recruitment decisions that are made, clearly political factors within an organization can also influence these decisions. For example, in some organizations a manager who is responsible for recruitment may be instructed by a higher-level executive that his or her role is to make a position with the organization look as attractive as possible. In order to do this, the recruitment manager may feel pressured to exaggerate the attributes of a position during the recruitment process. In a less extreme case, a recruitment manager may not feel forced to exaggerate specific aspects of a vacant position but may feel pressure not to disclose the negative features of the position. Thus, while in this second case the manager may not actually exaggerate what a position entails, by failing to provide a complete picture of the position to be filled, he or she would still be responsible for presenting a somewhat distorted picture of the job opening.

In some cases, a manager with recruitment responsibilities may be limited in his or her ability to present an accurate and complete picture of a position because of resistance from the line managers for whom prospective job candidates will work. For example, a line manager may feel threatened by "off-the-record" conversations with job incumbents. Such a manager may be fearful that job incumbents will not present an accurate picture of what being a member of the work group is like or that job incumbents will present an accurate but unflattering picture of the job under consideration. In addition to resisting access to co-workers, line managers may also interfere with the presentation of accurate recruitment information in other ways. For example, when asked to supply information about a job opening for the purpose of designing a job advertisement, a manager may provide a distorted picture of the position to the recruitment manager.

Although the pressures briefly described above can create ethical dilemmas for a manager who is responsible for employee recruitment (e.g., Is it ethical to intentionally exaggerate what a position involves?), such pressures can also influence the effectiveness of a recruitment program. In the next chapter evidence will be presented that suggests that hiring candidates who have inflated job expectations can lead to several undesirable organizational outcomes, including a high turnover rate. Another important but relatively overlooked consequence of incorrect job expectations on the part of job candidates is the possibility of legal action. As has been recently noted in a number of articles in the business press (for example, Reibstein, 1987), individuals have begun to sue employers for fraud or breach of contract. Typically, such legal action involves a person who was hired by an organization and who subsequently concludes that he or she was intentionally misled during the recruitment process. Although lawsuits of this type are still relatively rare, employers should be aware that the courts have made sizable monetary awards to some plaintiffs. Furthermore, even if a damage award is small or the company wins the lawsuit, the filing of such charges can influence the public image of the organization as a place of employment and thus potentially affect the ability of the organization to recruit in the future.

SUMMARY

In this chapter, the importance of person–job fit has been stressed. As a mechanism for improving such individual–organization congruence, the need for an organization to communicate accurate and complete information about itself to potential job candidates has been emphasized. Obviously, the approach advocated in this chapter is based on the assumption that job candidates frequently do not have accurate perceptions of what a position with a given organization involves. Unfortunately for both employers and job candidates, there is considerable evidence that shows that recruits often have inflated job and organizational expectations.[30]

Some readers may question whether it is realistic to expect employers to go through the work involved in order to present accurate job information to recruits. Other readers may question whether it is naive to expect organizations to willingly communicate information about potentially undesirable aspects of jobs they are attempting to fill. In response to the first question, there are several reasons that make a commitment of such effort worthwhile. In the next chapter, a model will be presented that highlights the numerous advantages of providing job seekers with factual and relatively complete job information. In terms of the issue of naivete, it is clearly realistic to expect organizations to present information concerning both the desirable and undesirable features of job openings. In fact, several employers, including AT&T, Procter & Gamble, Data General, Prudential Insurance, A. G. Edwards, the U.S. Marine Corps, and Bell Canada, are already doing so. For example, the New York investment banking house of Morgan and Stanley encourages individuals it is considering hiring to discuss the demands of the position (e.g., new recruits sometimes work 100 hours a week) with their spouses or companions. Morgan and Stanley's managing directors and their spouses take promising job candidates and their spouses or companions out to dinner to make certain they understand what the job demands. According to Pascale (1984), the point of such interactions "is to get a person who will not be happy within Morgan's culture because of the way his family feels to eliminate himself from the consideration for a job there."

In closing, four issues should be briefly addressed. First, it is important that the reader remember that this chapter is intended only to provide an introductory treatment of several recruitment topics. In the remaining chapters, more information will be provided on several of the issues raised in this chapter (such as the use of two-way communication media, designing job advertisements). Second, it should be noted that, for presentation purposes, several of the issues in this chapter were addressed as being "black or white." For example, recruitment communications were treated as being either accurate or inaccurate and recruitment media were categorized as allowing for either one-way or two-way communication. In reality, we often have to deal with subtle distinctions in making recruitment-related decisions. In addressing various recruitment topics in later chapters, these subtle distinctions will be addressed in more detail. A third point that needs to be made concerns the fact that some experts do not support all of the suggestions put forth in this chapter. The positions of these experts will be presented throughout the remainder of this text. Finally, it should be acknowledged that for a variety of reasons some organizations simply will not be interested in presenting a more accurate and complete picture of the positions they are attempting to fill. Even these organizations should find many of the suggestions made in this chapter and in the remaining chapters to be of use. For example, such organizations may still want to use marketing research to find out how potential job candidates view them.

NOTES

1. This section draws heavily on the ideas of Herriot (1984), Lewis (1985), Porter, Lawler, and Hackman (1975), Schein (1978), and Wanous (1980).

2. In this chapter, the discussion of recruitment activities will focus largely on what transpires after an individual and an organization have been in contact (e.g., a job candidate has sent a résumé, a company has contacted a prospective employee via a direct mail campaign). Clearly, as will be emphasized in later chapters, an effective recruitment campaign also includes actions taken prior to such contact being made (e.g., image advertising).

3. For a more detailed discussion of how job candidates attempt to manage the impressions they make, the reader should refer to Fletcher (1989).

4. "Best" in the sense of being most highly sought by employers in general. As will be reiterated throughout this text, the most highly sought after job candidates may not be the "best" recruits for a given organization (e.g., they may be more likely to leave during their first year on the job).

5. In most cases, due to time and financial constraints, a job seeker will not try to pursue positions with all possible employers. Instead, a job candidate generally will try to eliminate organizations for which he or she would have difficulty imagining himself or herself working. For example, a candidate may eliminate an organization from consideration because it was not seen as affording the career opportunities the individual desires. Alternatively, a job seeker may not pursue a position with an organization because the person sees very little likelihood of the organization making him or her a job offer.

6. In order to be able to provide an accurate view of what working for an organization entails, the employer obviously must have an accurate perception of itself. For example, representatives of the organization must be able to convey information to job candidates concerning such factors as job duties, advancement possibilities, job security, future business prospects, etc. Specific methods for increasing the accuracy of applicants' job expectations will be discussed later in this chapter.

7. More detail on why possessing accurate information is thought to be associated with having better employees (e.g., higher levels of performance, less turnover) will be provided in the next chapter.

8. Chapter 3 presented an overview of some methods a job candidate could use for increasing his or her degree of self-awareness, a prerequisite for the accurate self-disclosure of information.

9. In addition to a concern with impression management, generally both the organization and the job candidate have a short-term focus in presenting information and in evaluating each other. That is, attention is generally paid to the first job that will be held while little attention is given to the individual's career with the organization (London and Stumpf, 1982).

10. Although the concepts of person–job fit and person–organization fit have been frequently used in the literature (e.g., Chatman, 1989), there is no agreed on way of measuring the degree of fit. For example, some researchers have simply asked employees to evaluate the degree of fit they have; other researchers have asked employees how much of an attribute (e.g., participation in decision making) they want and then compared this rating to some objective index of how much of that attribute the position offers. As used in this text, person–job fit generally will refer to a new employee's perception of the congruence between his or her skills and what the job demands and between his or her needs/desires and the rewards a position offers. For some job/organizational attributes, an individual may seek neither too much nor too little of an attribute (e.g., travel). For other attributes, the more the organization offers (e.g., pay), the better individual will evaluate the fit.

11. Several of these actions (e.g., researching what a position with an organization entails) were described in some detail in Chapter 3.

12. For example, an organization could quiz a job applicant concerning his or her knowledge about the position under consideration during an employment interview. Alternatively, an organization could pay careful attention to a recruit's prior employment history. If a job applicant has worked previously in a position similar to the one under consideration, the organization might assume that the individual has an accurate view of at least some of the job features working for it would involve (e.g., having worked as a bank teller in a competitor's bank may be quite similar to working as a teller for this bank).

13. Although for presentation purposes terms such as *accurate* and *inaccurate* are used in this chapter, in reality the recruitment information presented by an organization is rarely totally accurate or inaccurate. Rather, the information varies in its degree of accuracy.

14. Although Popovich and Wanous (1982) focused specifically on the use of realistic job previews as a mechanism for transmitting information, their theoretical integration of the social-psychological literature on attitudes applies equally to any recruitment approach used for communicating accurate job information to job candidates.

15. In attempting to provide a prospective employee with accurate expectations, an organization should convey information about the job under consideration as well as about the general organizational environment in which he or she will work. To save space, in this section the term *job-related information* will be used. This term is meant to encompass both job and organization-related information.

16. In terms of enhancing the credibility of the job-related information available to a job candidate, a particularly good mechanism is first-hand experience. For example, if an individual has done an internship at an organization, the person is unlikely to doubt the accuracy of the information he or she has about working for that organization.

17. From this brief discussion of information sources, the similarity of these sources and the typical sources used for a job analysis should be apparent. This similarity will be addressed in more detail later in this chapter.

18. Obviously, several other "audience" characteristics (e.g., intelligence) could be discussed. Readers who are interested in a more complete discussion of such characteristics should refer to Jablin, Putnam, Roberts, and Porter (1987) or any basic reference text on attitude formation and change.

19. Although one could consider written recruitment information as being a subset of visual information, the convention is to draw a distinction between written information and information that is presented visually but in a nonwritten mode.

20. *Recruitment Today* annually gives awards to job advertisements that it considers to be outstanding. Readers who are interested in seeing examples of distinctive ads should refer to past issues of this periodical.

21. Readers who are interested in a detailed discussion of information processing in the context of attitude formation and change should see Petty and Cacioppo (1986).

22. Because several possible sources of job-related information (e.g., job incumbents, former employees) and means of gathering information from these sources (e.g., questionnaires, interviews) were discussed earlier in this chapter, these topics will not be addressed further in this section.

23. Technically, once an organization has developed a good understanding of what it offers to prospective employees, this information should be integrated with other information (e.g., affirmative action pressures) and used as a basis for determining an applicant population at which to target recruitment communications. However, because affirmative action and other issues relating to the selection of an applicant population have not yet been covered, the selection of an applicant population will be saved for later in this text.

24. Readers who are interested in the topic of marketing research should refer to the *Journal of Marketing Research*.

25. According to McCarthy, the research that NECIS conducted was multifaceted. Among NECIS's objectives were to discover how it was perceived as a place of employment, how it could improve its recruitment advertising, and how it could cut its advertising costs.

26. In Chapter 3, the use of the direct estimate approach and policy capturing were discussed as ways of determining what prospective employees see as important attributes in a job. In using focus groups, the methodology for determining job attribute importance is generally less formal. Typically, focus group members are encouraged to nominate attributes they see as important. After job attributes have been named, other group members are asked to comment on whether they agree that the particular attribute is important. Based on the tone of the focus group discussion, the focus group coordinator makes a judgment about the relative importance attached to job attributes. In contrast to the use of focus groups, the marketing research literature also offers several complex techniques for determining the relative importance of job attributes (in the marketing literature these methodologies have been applied to a wide range of marketing topics). For example, conjoint analysis and multiattribute utility technology have been applied to various decisions in which determining individual preferences among attributes was important.

27. Readers who are interested in another example of the use of a marketing research study (in this case, by Gulf Oil) to improve recruitment activities should refer to an article by Krett and Stright (1985). In this article, the authors discuss the use of marketing research as the final step of a three-stage process. The first two steps involve market analysis (i.e., analyzing what the organization offers a prospective job candidate) and competitive analysis (i.e., determining what the competition is doing).

28. In theory, an organization could tailor recruitment messages to a particular audience (readers of a specific newspaper or a certain radio station's listening audience). However, this is rarely done.

29. Although the use of job incumbents has been stressed in this chapter, in most cases the use of multiple information sources is generally preferred. This theme will be developed in the remainder of this text.

30. The interested reader is referred to academic works by Rynes and Boudreau (1986), Herriot (1984), and Wanous (1980). Readers who are interested in a more popular treatment of recruits having unrealistic expectations should refer to articles by Carroll (1982), Harlan (1988), Reibstein (1987), and Fishman (1987).

6

Understanding the Initial Employment Period: A Model for Improving Person–Job Fit

In the previous chapter, a strong case was made for the importance of person–job fit. However, many of the factors that make such congruence important were not addressed. This chapter will examine several factors that make the existence of person–job fit during the initial employment period so crucial for both an employee and an organization. In this chapter, particular attention is given to the development of a "psychological contract" between a new employee and his or her employer and to the influence of events that occur during the recruitment process on employee perceptions of this contract. Following this discussion, a model portraying how an individual develops accurate job expectations is presented.

THE CRUCIAL INITIAL EMPLOYMENT PERIOD

Although human resource management experts do not always agree with each other, there is one topic about which there appears to be near unanimous agreement: "The very early employment period—the first year or even the first few months—is very crucial to the development of a healthy individual–organizational relationship" (Porter, Lawler, and Hackman,

1975, p. 178). One reason this initial employment period is so important is that it is during this time period that new employees and their employers begin to form stable impressions of each other. For example, if upon beginning work a person discovers that his or her job duties are far below what was promised by his or her supervisor during the recruitment process, the new employee may come to have doubts about the trustworthiness of his or her supervisor, and conceivably about others in the organization.

This initial employment period is also important because it is during this time that a new employee and his or her employer must learn to adjust to each other. During this period of adjustment, an organization tries to shape a new employee's behavior, values, and attitudes so that they are consistent with its needs. This shaping process is commonly referred to as "socialization" (Greenhaus, 1987). At the same time that an employer is attempting to influence the behavior, values, and attitudes of a new employee, the employee is also trying to influence the organization so that it treats him or her in a manner that will allow the individual to derive personal satisfaction from his or her new position. This process has been labeled "individualization" (Porter et al., 1975). Not surprisingly, the events that take place during the recruitment process can have a significant effect on how new employees react to an organization's attempts to socialize them during their first few weeks or months on the job.

Employee Socialization

Although an in-depth discussion of the employee socialization and individualization processes is beyond the scope of this text, an overview of a few basic issues is important in order to better understand the effects of recruitment activities on these important processes.[1] As used by most researchers, employee socialization refers to "the process by which employees are transformed from organization outsiders to participating and effective members" (Feldman, 1981, p. 309). The socialization process can be thought of as involving three distinct phases: prearrival (sometimes referred to as pre-entry socialization), encounter, and change and acquisition. Since only the prearrival and encounter phases of the socialization process are particularly relevant to employee recruitment, only these two phases will be discussed.

The Prearrival Phase

This phase of the employee socialization process encompasses all that an individual has learned before he or she joins an organization. Prior to beginning a job, a person has developed a set of values, attitudes, styles of behavior, and job expectations.[2] Among the factors that can influence these values, attitudes, behaviors, and job expectations are the person's educational experiences, his or her family and friends, the individual's prior work experience, and the media. For example, individuals who have attended certain types of schools, have been reared in certain types of homes, have lived in certain types of neighborhoods, or have had particular types of work experience may bring to an organization different views toward teamwork, travel, following rules, relocation, meeting deadlines, attendance, the interference of work with family life, or honesty than do persons who have had different experiences. In addition to these factors, a person's expectations about a job with a particular employer also can be affected by such things as conversations with employees of the organization and news stories about the employer (Jablin, 1987). Although individuals may vary considerably in terms of the comprehensiveness and accuracy of the perceptions they hold prior to starting a job, it is difficult to imagine a person knowing nothing about his or her employer.

Not surprisingly, their prearrival experiences may result in some new employees having values, attitudes, behavioral styles, and job expectations that are not consistent with what their employer desires. For example, a new employee may see family responsibilities as taking priority over work duties, while the person's employer may prefer the opposite ordering of priorities.

Rather than accept the fact that its employees' values, attitudes, behaviors, and job expectations may be inconsistent with what it desires, an organization generally will take several steps to end up with new employees who are somewhat attuned to the organization's value system. For example, an employer may try to recruit from a particular applicant population whose members are likely to possess the attitudes and values it desires. Alternatively, an organization may try to communicate accurate information about a job in its recruitment communications so that candidates who would not fit in well will not submit applications (the process of individuals removing themselves from consideration for a job is commonly referred to as "self-selection"). An employer may also use selection devices in order to "weed out" individuals who do not possess the characteristics that it sees as necessary in its employees (Gatewood and Feild, 1990). In addition to using recruitment and selection as mechanisms for obtaining employees who possess the appropriate attitudes, values, and behaviors, an organization will also attempt to change a newly hired individual's attitudes, values, and ways of behaving during the encounter phase of the socialization process.

The Encounter Phase

This phase of the socialization process involves the initial contact between a new employee and his or her employer once the individual begins work. During the encounter phase, an individual discovers what working for the organization is really like. In the encounter phase, a new employee is likely to experience pressure from the organization to modify his or her attitudes, values, job expectations and/or behaviors (Greenhaus, 1987). Most organizations will use both formal and informal methods to socialize their new hires. Three of the common approaches used to bring a new employee's values, attitudes, and behaviors in line with the organization's value system are reinforcement, nonreinforcement, and punishment. That is, when a new employee exhibits a desirable attitude, value, or behavior, the organization can in some way reward the individual for what he or she has done. Conversely, to try to lessen or eliminate an unwanted attitude or behavior, an employer will frequently ignore or withhold approval of what the employee has said or done. Finally, in some cases an organization may take the more direct action of punishing the employee.

In concluding this brief discussion of the socialization process, one final issue should be addressed. In attempting to socialize new employees, an organization will not see all employee attitudes, values, and behaviors as being equally important. For example, in terms of their importance for acquisition, Schein (1971) has distinguished among three types of behaviors that an employee may exhibit. "Pivotal" behaviors are those that an employer considers essential. According to Schein, if a new employee does not exhibit behaviors in this category, the person will not be considered an acceptable employee. For example, a company may see it as essential that an employee never speak disparagingly of it in public. "Relevant" behaviors are ways an employee may act that the organization sees as being desirable but not absolutely necessary. Porter, Lawler, and Hackman (1975) describe behaviors in this category as improving one's chances for success in the organization, but as not being essential for continuing with the organization. Finally, Schein distinguishes "peripheral" behaviors. These behaviors are not seen as being necessary or even important for an employee to be successful in an organization.

Although Schein (1971) focused only on employee behaviors and how organizations attach different levels of importance to their acquisition depending on whether they are seen as pivotal, relevant, or peripheral, his three categories seem equally applicable to employee attitudes and values. For example, one would expect that an organization's recruitment, selection, and socialization processes also would be geared to creating a work force of individuals who accept the employer's pivotal values. In contrast, one would anticipate that an organization would give relatively little attention to values held by individuals that its sees as being relatively inconsequential.

Individualization

Just as organizations attempt to influence the people they hire, individuals also try to influence the organizations they join. For example, although a person may accept a position knowing that it typically requires considerable out-of-town travel, the person may attempt to convince his or her employer that the job can be done successfully with a lesser amount of travel by making greater use of the telephone and a fax machine. Relatively little research has been conducted on how new employees attempt to influence their employers, so what is known about the individualization process is limited. Nevertheless, three assumptions appear reasonable.

The first assumption is that new employees will be most interested in trying to change those job attributes that conflict with their most important attitudes, values, and/or preferred ways of behaving. Conversely, new employees are likely to be willing to accept organizational influence attempts that address attitudes, values, or ways of acting that are not perceived as being of particular significance to them. The second assumption is that, all other things being equal, new employees will be more likely to try to change those job attributes that they see as being more amenable to modification. Finally, it is assumed that new employees differ somewhat in their willingness to conform to an organization's desires. In terms of their reactions to socialization, Schein (1968) has classified employees into three general categories.

Schein's (1968) first category of individualization is "conformity." Persons in this group are seen as quite willing to accept an organization's norms, values, and standards for behavior, even its most peripheral ones. At the opposite extreme on a continuum of individualization is "rebellion." This label applies to individuals who are solely concerned with fulfilling their own needs and who are unwilling to accept any of an organization's values, norms, or standards for behavior with which they disagree. Not surprisingly, if a new employee is totally resistant to an employer's socialization attempts, typically he or she will either voluntarily leave the organization or be dismissed. The third category of individualization has been labeled "creative individualism." "This type of response to socialization involves a person's acceptance of the pivotal or absolutely essential (from the organization's standpoint) norms and values, but rejection of many of the relevant or peripheral ones. This presumably would be the most successful form of individualization for both parties—the employee gains by exerting some influence on the total collective body (or some subunit of it), and the organization gains by an infusion of fresh ideas and possibly more effective modes of performance" (Porter, Lawler, and Hackman, 1975, p. 171).

Are Unmet Employee Expectations Really a Problem?

In this text, considerable emphasis has been placed on the importance of person–job fit. At this point, some readers may question whether this emphasis is really needed. That is, they may wonder whether the jobs of new employees actually fail to live up to expectations. Although the research of several individuals (see Louis, 1980) could be reviewed to demonstrate the degree to which employee expectations are unmet, a study by Dunnette, Arvey, and Banas (1973) provides a particularly good example of the inconsistency between the prehire job expectations and the subsequent job experiences of new employees.

Dunnette et al. examined the interplay between the initial job expectations and the subsequent job experiences of 1,000 college graduates who went to work for a large manufacturing company. These new employees were surveyed to determine whether their first job assignments lived up to their expectations. Specifically, these individuals were asked to rate whether fifteen attributes of their first job were better than expected, as they expected, or worse than they expected. Participants in this study also rated these job attributes in terms of how important they were to them. In presenting their results, Dunnette et al. grouped employees according to whether they were still with the company three years later (only 50 percent were).

The findings of this study can be somewhat simply summarized. In terms of the overall pattern of results, those who left the company rated fourteen of the fifteen job attributes as being worse than they expected. For those who remained, thirteen of the fifteen attributes were rated as being worse than expected. Thus, in their initial job assignments, both "leavers" and "stayers" reported experiencing several unmet job expectations. With regard to the five job attributes—pay, interesting work, opportunity to advance, use of abilities, and accomplishment—that were rated as being most important by the individuals in this study, all five were rated as worse than expected both by those who quit and by those who remained with the company. An interesting finding of this study is that for those who resigned the four attributes receiving the lowest absolute ratings (i.e., those rated as the farthest below expectations in comparison to the other attributes) were among those five most important job attributes. Thus, for those who left, their greatest disappointments involved the job attributes they saw as being most important.

Although both the stayers and the leavers in Dunnette et al.'s study rated the great majority of job attributes as below expectations, it is useful to compare these groups in terms of the degree to which they saw the fifteen job attributes as falling below expectations. For twelve of the job attributes (including four of the five rated as most important), those who left reported lower absolute ratings than those who remained. That is, even though both groups generally reported that their job expectations were not met, those who quit reported greater discrepancies between their expectations and what they actually experienced than those who remained. Of the remaining three job attributes, the groups did not differ on two of them. The only attribute that those who remained rated as falling farther below expectations than those who left was the opportunity to use their abilities.

Although one should be cautious in generalizing from Dunnette et al.'s study to other organizations,[3] as exemplified in the following two quotes there is a considerable body of literature that suggests that new employees frequently have unrealistically high expectations of what their job with an organization entails. "The findings suggest that the young manager goes through a process of adjustment and change during the early years of his career. His attitude toward the company becomes less favorable, and his optimistic expectations are toned down considerably" (Campbell, 1968, p. 11). "A number of new engineers found themselves in situations quite different from what they had expected. . . . [These] difficulties resulting from their original expectations undoubtedly reduced their development and effectiveness during this period" (Harris, 1968, p. 27).

THE PSYCHOLOGICAL CONTRACT

In order to better understand the reactions (anger, disappointment, surprise, satisfaction) of a new employee and of his or her employer during the initial employment period, it is useful to consider the idea of a "psychological contract." As noted in Chapter 5, during the recruitment process each party comes to have certain expectations of the other. More specifically, an individual forms an impression of what an organization expects from him or her and what the employer, in turn, will give to a new employee. Similarly, an organization develops expectations about what a job candidate offers and about what the candidate expects from it. In some employment relationships (professional sports is a good example), an individual and a prospective employer may actually sign a written contract in order to formalize what each expects from and will give to the other party. In the majority of cases, however, there is no written employment contract. Instead, the new employee and his or her employer enter into a so-called psychological contract.

A psychological contract is "an implicit contract between an individual and his organization which specifies what each expects to give and receive from each other in the relationship" (Kotter, 1973, p. 92). As has been noted by Kotter (1973) and others such as Schein (1978), a psychological contract generally involves expectations about hundreds or even thousands of items. Some of these items—job duties, office accommodations, etc.—may have been discussed in detail during the recruitment process, while others may have been agreed upon more implicitly. For example, a person who goes to work for a company that is known for its "no lay-off" policy may assume that he or she has job security even though the employer did not state that its no lay-off policy applied to that individual. In a similar vein, an employer may assume that a new employee knows that stealing company property is grounds for discharge even though this policy was not mentioned during recruitment interactions.

From this brief description of a psychological contract, several things should be apparent. First, it should be evident that there is a strong likelihood that each of the parties will at some time feel the other is not living up to their understanding (Kotter, 1973). For example, a new employee may have been told she would have a private office, but when she starts work she may discover that a private office is not currently available. Second, it is more likely that a disagreement over "contract" interpretation will occur when the issue involved was not explicitly discussed during the recruitment process than when the issue was specifically addressed. Third, one would expect that individuals and organizations will react more negatively to an expectation that is not being lived up to by the other party if the expectation in question is seen as important rather than if it is viewed as being relatively unimportant. Fourth, the reaction of an employer or employee to a perceived violation of the implicit contract is likely to be more negative if one party sees the other as having been intentionally misleading rather than if the violation is seen as a result of changed conditions. For example, if a company concludes that an employee intentionally deceived it during the recruitment process by stating his willingness to relocate, its reaction is likely to be different than if the organization perceives that the employee's life has changed since the psychological contract was "negotiated" because his child has recently become critically ill.

The Organization's Role in Clarifying the Psychological Contract

From this brief introduction to the concept of a psychological contract, its relevance to employee recruitment should be obvious. If an organization wants to improve person–job fit, it should take steps during the recruitment process to make sure that job candidates are aware of what it offers to them and what it expects from them. By taking appropriate recruitment actions such as providing candid information in its recruitment literature and having recruits talk to job incumbents, an employer should be able to minimize the "reality shock" that many new employees experience and, thus, the negative consequences that have been linked to it.[4]

An organization that is interested in taking steps to reduce the reality shock experienced by its new employees must address the difficult question of what specific topics should be covered in its recruitment communications.[5] Although a totally correct answer to this question might be that an employer should provide information about all job-related topics that are important to a prospective candidate (particularly those topics about which the job candidate lacks information or has unrealistic expectations), for a practitioner, this answer is little better than no answer at all. Given the almost endless number of job-related issues an employer could try to address during the recruitment process and the various constraints on an employer's recruitment efforts (limited budgets, recruit attention span, etc.), the question of what topics an organization should address becomes particularly important.

Although there is no easy answer to this question, the strategies discussed in Chapter 5 (asking new employees what information they were lacking, conducting a marketing research study, drawing inferences from what other researchers have found to be important job attributes, and so on) should help an organization make decisions about what information to communicate during the recruitment process. In most cases, the use of one or more of these strategies will result in an organization discovering that it has not been doing a good job of sharing important information with recruits. More specifically, employers will find that they should convey a greater amount of information and that they need to convey information that corrects mistaken impressions or unrealistic job and organizational expectations held by job candidates.

Although it is recommended that an organization do its own study in order to discover how it is viewed by prospective employees, what specific information they are interested in, and what inaccurate impressions they have, a lack of resources or other factors may make it impossible for an employer to conduct its own study. In such a case, generally an organization can still improve its recruitment communication strategy if it compares the type of information it conveys against the type of information that past research has shown to be important to job candidates. For example, a review of research studies that have examined what job and organizational attributes cause workers to react either positively or negatively to their jobs suggests that several topics should be addressed in recruitment communications. Among the most important aspects of a position that an employer should consider addressing in its recruitment communications are: (1) day-to-day job activities, (2) compensation and benefits, (3) career issues, (4) the general organizational culture, (5) co-workers, and (6) supervision. The importance of conveying information during the recruitment process about each of these topics will now be briefly discussed.

Day-to-Day Job Activities

In terms of day-to-day activities, it should be obvious that prospective employees want to have a good understanding of what specifically they will be doing if they receive and accept a job offer (Herriot, 1984). Although how much job candidates know about day-to-day job activities will vary based on such things as the visibility of the job to the public, even visible jobs such as security guard and high school teacher can vary considerably in terms of particular attributes. For example, some security guards patrol in motorized vehicles while others are required to walk considerable distances each day. Although this difference may appear to be somewhat trivial, for an individual with bone spurs it may determine whether or not the person is interested in the security guard position.

Compensation and Benefits

Of the six job attributes that will be discussed, employers generally do the best job of communicating information about compensation and benefits. This may be due to the relatively objective nature of compensation and benefits compared to more subjective job features such as work climate. Employee benefit information regarding maternity leave policy, free parking and so on, is frequently highlighted at an early stage of the recruitment process in order to pique the interest of potential candidates, while compensation matters are generally addressed at a later stage of the recruitment process, most commonly during an interview with the candidate's prospective supervisor.

Career Issues

In addition to being concerned about day-to-day work activities, compensation, and benefits, many prospective employees also are interested in a variety of career-related issues (see Greenhaus, 1987). Among the career-related topics that may be of interest to job candidates are whether a position provides mechanisms such as corporate training programs for developing their talents, whether a position offers considerable opportunity for advancement, and whether a position offers a reasonable level of job security. Although information about career-related issues may not be important for all job candidates, for individuals who have aspirations of career growth and/or of remaining with one organization, this type of information may help a candidate decide between two job offers that are roughly equivalent on other important job features.[6]

The Organization's Culture

In determining whether to pursue a position with a particular organization, many individuals desire information about various aspects of the organization's culture.[7] Among the aspects of an organization's culture that may influence job candidate decision making are its underlying philosophy vis-à-vis communication (e.g., open versus restricted), decision making (e.g., hierarchical versus participative), standards for making business decisions (e.g., compliance with the letter of the law versus exhibiting high ethical standards), affirmative action (e.g., equal opportunity for minorities and women versus having the minimum number of minorities and women necessary to eliminate external pressure), formality (e.g., formal versus informal dress), and status (e.g., an executive dining room and reserved parking spaces versus a company cafeteria and open parking).[8]

Co-workers

In selecting among jobs, an important factor can be the nature of one's prospective co-workers (Jablin, 1987). For example, most individuals would prefer to work in a cohesive work group rather than in one where co-workers do not get along. Job candidates may also see prospective co-workers as an important mechanism for helping them master a new position. Thus, they may be attracted to positions that offer co-workers who are technically proficient. For some job candidates, one's co-workers may also be important in terms of affording social opportunities after work hours. For example, a new college graduate who is single and will need to relocate to a new city may like the idea of working with others who have similar backgrounds and are thus more likely to offer companionship outside of work.

Supervision

One of the most important factors in determining whether a person will be satisfied with a new position is his or her supervisor (Jablin, 1987). Among the important job-related factors that a supervisor may influence are the types of tasks a new employee works on, the amount and the type of feedback the person receives, whether rewards follow good performance, the degree to which an employee has input into decisions, and the work group climate. Given the impact that one's supervisor can have on these and other potentially important aspects of a job, it is not surprising that most job candidates would like to receive considerable information about what their prospective supervisor is like before having to make a job-choice decision. Providing specific information about a recruit's prospective supervisor is particularly important because research has shown that new employees are frequently dissatisfied with their first supervisor. In fact, Hogan, Raskin, and Fazzini (1990) have recently noted that the results of numerous field studies suggest that 60 percent to 75 percent of the workers surveyed reported that the worst or the most stressful aspect of their jobs was their immediate supervisor.

From this overview, the importance of an employer communicating accurate information about key aspects of a job opening at some point during the recruitment process should be evident. However, from the preceding discussion, it should also be apparent that in most cases an employer cannot use the same recruitment mechanism to communicate different types of job information. This is due to the fact that, although certain information about benefits, corporate culture, and some career-related issues may be relevant to most or even all of the jobs within a given organization, information concerning other issues such as day-to-day activities may be unique to a given job. Further complicating the planning of recruitment communications is the fact that some information is not only unique to a given job, it may be unique to a specific job within a given work group. For example, it generally makes little sense to talk about supervision in general or co-workers in general. Job candidates want specific information about the prospective supervisors to whom they would report and about the co-workers with whom they would work.

In summary, in planning a strategy for disseminating information during the recruitment process, an organization can either do its own research or it can rely on existing research that has documented the importance attached by prospective employees to information concerning job duties, compensation and benefits, career issues, organizational culture, supervision, and co-workers. In either case, an organization is likely to determine that some of the information it should be communicating is generic to most of its jobs and thus can be conveyed to candidates for a wide range of different jobs with the employer (e.g., via a videotape shown at job fairs). However, it will also likely discover that some of the information that recruits seek is unique to a given job and thus will need to be communicated by more individualized mechanisms (e.g., a conversation with a job incumbent).

THE FORMATION OF JOB EXPECTATIONS AND THEIR INFLUENCE ON IMPORTANT EMPLOYEE ATTITUDES AND BEHAVIORS: A PROCESS MODEL

In several places in this text, the potential benefits of job candidates possessing accurate information about positions they are considering has been emphasized. However, the treatment of this important topic has been somewhat fragmented. More specifically, the process by which job candidates develop accurate job expectations has not been directly addressed and the likely consequences of such expectations have not been thoroughly discussed. Therefore, in this section a model portraying how an individual develops accurate job and organizational expectations is presented (see Exhibit 6.1)[9] This model also highlights the benefits both to an individual and to an organization of a recruit possessing accurate and extensive information about a position with the employer.

In reflecting on the various components of the model, it is important to remember that it applies to different types of job candidates. For example, some individuals may not currently be working and may be relatively inexperienced in the job search process (e.g., new college graduates). Other candidates may be employed, but dissatisfaction with their current positions may have stimulated their interest in seeing if better job opportunities exist. In some cases, a person may not even be actively looking for a job. Rather, the person's interest in a position may be the result of having been contacted by an organization. For example, as a way

Exhibit 6.1 The formation of job expectations and their influence on important employee attitudes and behaviors: A process model

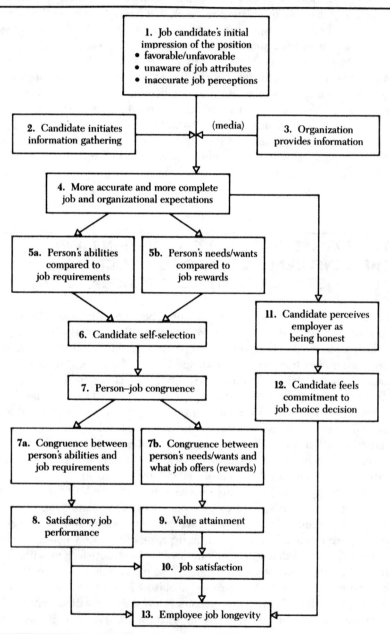

to fill vacant nursing positions, hospitals have begun to contact nurses who used to work for them (many of whom left to begin families) to inquire about their interest in returning to work. In many cases, the hospitals are willing to offer flexible or part-time work schedules in order to accommodate family responsibilities (Harper, 1988).

The starting point for this model is the point at which a job candidate initially considers the merits of a particular job with an organization and decides that the position is worth investigating further (Box 1). In considering the initial impression that a candidate has of a position, it is important to distinguish three underlying dimensions: favorability, comprehensiveness, and accuracy.

With regard to favorability, the model suggests that a person has an initial impression of a position that is either positive or negative based on information that he or she possesses prior to formally investigating the job. If a person has a reasonably favorable initial impression of a job, he or she is likely to try to gather more information about it. However, if one's initial impression is negative, the person generally will not pursue the position further.[10,11]

The information possessed by job candidates at the start of the job search process (Box 1) can differ both in terms of its comprehensiveness and its accuracy. In terms of comprehensiveness, because jobs can vary in a multitude of dimensions, the initial impression a person has of a position typically will be based on incomplete information. That is, in determining whether to remain interested in a position, a job candidate generally will be unaware of some important job attributes. In addition to being uninformed about certain job attributes, a job candidate will typically have certain beliefs about a position that are inaccurate (Dunnette, Arvey, and Banas, 1973). However, because the person believes them to be true, these beliefs will nevertheless influence the job candidate's behavior.

To recapitulate, the model in Exhibit 6.1 suggests that, once a job candidate becomes aware of a job opportunity, the person considers what he or she knows about the position and subsequently forms an overall impression of it (Box 1). If this impression is sufficiently favorable, the candidate generally will decide to gather additional information about the position being considered (Box 2). (The reason an arrow does not go directly from Box 1 to Box 2 in the model is to reflect the fact that a job candidate's first impression of a position can have a long-lasting influence on the person's ultimate perception of a position.)

There are several methods that a candidate can use to investigate a job opening (Box 2). Chapter 3 describes some of these methods. For the purpose of this chapter, it is sufficient to state that by gathering information about a job opening a person is likely to develop a more complete and a more accurate understanding of what it entails (Box 4).[12]

Although a job applicant can discover a good deal about a position with a particular organization by taking the initiative in data gathering (Stumpf and Hartman, 1984), in most recruitment situations, an organization also will take the initiative in disseminating information about a job opening (Box 3). As discussed in Chapter 5, the information provided by an employer can vary in terms of its accuracy, credibility, breadth, specificity, and importance. (The model presented in Exhibit 6.1 is based on the assumption that an organization wants to maximize these five attributes.) Among the media that an organization can use to convey information to job candidates are newspaper advertisements, employee referrals, job descriptions made available at state employment offices, videotapes shown at job fairs, presentations given by company officials at career days, recruitment brochures, direct mailings, personal interviews, work simulations, tours of a work site, radio advertisements, and actual experience doing the job (as in an internship).[13] Although the advantages and the disadvantages of using these and other media will be discussed in more detail in later chapters, by taking some of the steps discussed in Chapter 5, such as using job incumbents, presenting a consistent message, allowing for two-way communication, and using multiple media, an organization should be able to improve both the completeness and the accuracy of a candidate's job expectations (Box 4).[14]

According to the model in Exhibit 6.1, as a job candidate's initial expectations of a position (Box 1) become more complete and more realistic (Box 4), the person is better able to determine whether he or she has the necessary abilities to perform the job (Box 5a). By comparing the rewards the job offers against his or her needs/wants (Box 5b), the job candidate is also able to assess whether the position is likely to reasonably satisfy his or her needs/wants. The model predicts that, by having more complete and more accurate job expectations, an individual may have the opportunity to self-select (Box 6) out of consideration for a job that is not seen as a reasonably good fit in terms of his or her abilities (Box 5a) and/or needs (Box 5b). This prediction of self-selection is based on the assumption that a job candidate perceives a more desirable alternative (e.g., going back to school, remaining in the job he or she currently holds, remaining unemployed) than the job being considered.[15] (The situation in which a job candidate does not have a better alternative and thus may continue to pursue a position which is not viewed positively will be discussed shortly.)

Given that job candidate self-selection occurs, the model predicts that person–job congruence (Box 7) will result. That is, it is expected that, for those persons who are eventually hired, there will be a good fit between the candidates' abilities and the job requirements (Box 7a) and between their needs/wants and the rewards that the job under consideration offers (Box 7b).[16,17]

As can be observed in Exhibit 6.1, it is hypothesized that congruence between a person's abilities and the skills required by a job (Box 7a) results in a satisfactory level of job performance (Box 8), which in turn is predicted to result in job satisfaction (Box 10) and job longevity (Box 13) for the employee. The expectation that a good match between an individual's abilities and the requirements of a job will result in satisfactory job performance has received strong support in the personnel selection literature (Gatewood and Feild, 1990). The subsequent linkage between job performance and job longevity in Exhibit 6.1 is based on the assumption that employees who perform well will be less likely to lose their jobs due to layoffs or termination. The hypothesized linkage between job performance and job satisfaction is based on the assumption that persons who perform their jobs successfully will receive intrinsic and/or extrinsic rewards that they will find satisfying (Pinder, 1984). Obviously, for job situations where intrinsic and extrinsic rewards do not follow performance, no linkage between job performance and job satisfaction is predicted.[18]

With regard to the benefits of a good fit between a person's needs/wants and the attributes (rewards) a job offers (Box 7b), it is hypothesized that such symmetry ordinarily will result in a sense of value attainment (i.e., need fulfillment) for the job candidate (Box 9). This expectation is based on the logic that, if a job offers outcomes that some job candidates value and if candidates who do not value these outcomes are able to self-select out of consideration for this job, then those individuals who continue to pursue a position will, if hired, report a relatively high level of value attainment. Such value attainment is hypothesized to result in job satisfaction (Box 10), which is hypothesized to be linked to job longevity (Box 13).

In summary, the model presented in Exhibit 6.1 suggests a logical sequence of events that ideally would occur during the recruitment process. However, it should be emphasized that the flow of events presented in this model is based on a number of important assumptions that have not always been clearly stated in the job choice/recruitment literature. For example, the information provided by an organization (Box 3) during the recruitment process does not always result in a job candidate possessing more accurate and more complete job expectations (Box 4). Instead, information provided by an employer frequently leads to inflated job expectations. In a similar vein, although some researchers have suggested a direct connection between a candidate possessing realistic job expectations (Box 4) and subsequent job satisfaction (Box 10), the model in Exhibit 6.1 suggests a less direct connection. According to the model, in order for the possession of realistic job information to result in job satisfaction, the candidate must be able to remove himself or herself from consideration for a position that is not expected to be a good fit (Box 6). If, on the other hand, a candidate has an accurate and negative view of what a job involves, but has no other viable alternatives, the model does not predict subsequent job satisfaction. Instead, if no self-selection occurs, the model suggests the person will experience a lack of person–job fit (Box 7a, Box 7b) that he or she anticipated. This incongruence is predicted to result in poor job performance (Box 8) or a lack of value attainment (Box 9).

Although the flow of events discussed to this point suggests that the possession of realistic job expectations will have no positive benefits for either the individual or the organization if job candidate self-selection does not occur, this is not an entirely accurate picture. To the extent that a job candidate believes that the information he or she has about a position is accurate (Box 4) and is the result of an organization providing candid job-related data (Box 3), it is predicted that the individual will perceive the employer as having been honest and forthcoming (Box 11). This perception of employer honesty is expected regardless of whether the candidate feels he or she was able to self-select out of an unattractive job situation. Empirical data reported by Suszko and Breaugh (1986) provide tentative support for this prediction. In their study, a realistic job preview was provided by an organization to a randomly selected group of job applicants. No realistic information was given to another group of applicants. Individuals in the group who received candid job information reported that the organization was significantly more open and honest with them than the members of the other group. Interestingly, Suszko and Breaugh also found that employees who reported having had realistic job expectations (regardless of whether they received a realistic job preview) were significantly more likely to see the organization as being honest and open with them.

The immediate consequence of a job candidate believing that an employer was honest in its communications during the recruitment process is job candidate commitment to his or her job choice decision (Colarelli, 1984). That is, it is predicted that an individual who believes that an employer was honest during the recruitment process (Box 11) will be more committed to his or her job choice decision (Box 12) than will a new employee who feels an organization was intentionally misleading in its recruitment communications. This commitment to one's job choice decision (i.e., accepting a given job offer) is predicted to lead to greater job longevity (Box 13). This last prediction is based on the assumption that when an individual makes a fully informed choice the person feels an obligation to remain in the position for a reasonable period of time (Reilly et al., 1981).

EVIDENCE SUPPORTING THE MODEL

Although a study testing the entire model proposed in this chapter has yet to be carried out, a number of researchers (see Feldman, 1976, Suszko and Breaugh, 1986, and Vandenberg and Scarpello, 1990) have published studies that support the validity of pieces of the model. A review of this sizable body of research is beyond the scope of this chapter. However, a brief review of two studies is provided to give the reader a sense of the type of research that has been conducted. In addition to generally supporting the model presented in Exhibit 6.1, this selective review of research highlights the important need for future research in this area.

Greenhaus, Seidel, and Marinis (1983)

As noted previously, over the years a number of researchers have proposed a direct connection between the possession of realistic job expectations and job satisfaction. Building on the work of Locke (1976), Greenhaus and his associates argue that an important intervening variable had been overlooked. These authors propose that having realistic expectations would only result in job satisfaction if one were able to fulfill important needs on the job. Greenhaus et al. refer to such need fulfillment as value attainment. In other words, Greenhaus and his associates propose that, if a job candidate's expectations about a position are positive and they are realistic (i.e., ultimately fulfilled), then the person will experience job satisfaction. However, if an individual's job expectations are negative and fulfilled (e.g., because the person was not able to self-select out), then the person will not be able to attain important values. Thus, even though the person has accurate job expectations, job satisfaction will not result. Greenhaus et al. not only propose value attainment as an intervening variable between having realistic expectations and experiencing satisfaction, they gathered data to test this assertion.

In a field study, Greenhaus and his colleagues assessed the realism of the job expectations of 125 recent college graduates concerning fourteen important job outcomes or attributes (e.g., autonomy, cooperation among peers, ethical behavior). These outcomes were grouped into three general categories: task characteristics, interpersonal relationships, and company practices. Greenhaus et al. also assessed the degree to which these new employees reported value attainment (i.e., what an employee experienced was similar to what he or she would like to have experienced) for the fourteen job outcomes. Finally, the participants in this study were asked to rate their satisfaction vis-à-vis the fourteen outcomes. Greenhaus and his associates created value attainment scales and satisfaction facet measures that reflected the same three categories as reported for the job expectation measures.

Greenhaus et al. conducted a number of different statistical analyses. The results of these analyses were consistent. Repeatedly, there was strong evidence supporting the fact that value attainment was an important mediator of the realistic expectation–job satisfaction relationship. For example, Greenhaus et al. used regression analysis to assess the strength of the relationship between each of the three facets of satisfaction and the corresponding realistic expectation measure with the appropriate value attainment measure held constant. The partial r^2s were respectively task = .12, interpersonal relations = .05, and company practices = .04. In contrast, with the corresponding realistic expectation measures held constant, the partial r^2s between the value attainment scales and the satisfaction facets were task = .46, interpersonal relations = .46, and company practices = .52. Based on these findings and the results of their laboratory experiment, which will not be discussed here, the research by Greenhaus et al. provides considerable support for the fact that value attainment (Box 9) should mediate the relationship between realistic job expectations (Box 4) and job satisfaction (Box 10). Unfortunately, Greenhaus and his associates did not measure whether the employees in their sample felt they had the ability to self-select (Box 6) out of consideration for jobs that were not perceived as a good fit, nor did they measure employee perceptions of person–job congruence (Box 7).

Stumpf and Hartman (1984)

In a study that involved gathering data at three points in time from individuals using the placement service of a large graduate school of business, Stumpf and Hartman examined the relationships among a number of the variables included in Exhibit 6.1. For example, in terms of the influence of job candidate information gathering (Box 2) on the accuracy and the completeness of the candidate's job expectations (Box 4), these authors found that candidate information gathering was highly correlated with the amount of information that candidates reported having ($r = .52$; $p < .01$), but only modestly correlated with the reported accuracy of their job expectations ($r = .16$; $p < .10$).

Stumpf and Hartman also reported data concerning the relationship between later reports of person–job congruence and the amount of job information participants reported having ($r = .30$; $p < .01$) and between person–job congruence and the realism of job expectations ($r = .48$; $p < .01$). Thus, even though the ability of job candidates to remove themselves from consideration for potentially undesirable jobs was not considered, the results of Stumpf and Hartman's study suggest that having more accurate and more complete information about a position (Box 4) is predictive of person–job congruence (Box 7).

In terms of the relationship between person–job congruence (Box 7a) and job performance (Box 8), Stumpf and Hartman's results must be viewed with caution because they used self-ratings rather than supervisory ratings of job performance. Nevertheless, the relationship hypothesized in Exhibit 6.1 was supported ($r = .67$; $p < .01$). Although this study did not consider value attainment as an intervening variable, it did examine the relationship between person–job congruence (Box 7b) and job satisfaction (Box 10). As predicted, person–job fit was found to be highly correlated with job satisfaction ($r = .71$; $p < .01$).

Some Summary Comments on the Model

Although the model presented in Exhibit 6.1 is grounded in both theory and empirical research, more research is clearly needed before this model can be viewed as more than a tentative framework for understanding the formation of job expectations and how they influence the attitudes and behaviors of new employees. In particular, research that examines the formation of job expectations and attitudes over several time periods and that includes samples other than new college graduates would be valuable. In future studies, it is also important that attention be given to whether job candidates feel that they can realistically turn down job offers that are not perceived as providing a good person–job fit and to the number of individuals who actually do self-select out of the job search process.[19] In designing studies, researchers also need to pay more attention to whether job candidates actually had unrealistic job expectations prior to hiring and to whom (e.g., themselves or the organization) they attribute the realism or unrealism of their expectations.

Although considerably more research on the formation of job expectations and their relative influence on subsequent employee behaviors and attitudes is needed, the model introduced in this chapter should provide a useful starting point for those who are interested in understanding these processes. It should also serve as a useful framework for individuals who are responsible for planning an employee recruitment strategy. For example, the model highlights the fact that providing accurate information to job prospects can have benefits to the organization even when applicants may not be able to self-select out of jobs.

SUMMARY

As noted at the beginning of this chapter, human resource management experts generally agree that an individual's first year or even first few weeks on a job are a crucial employment period. During this period, new employees form stable impressions of their employers and are subject to socialization attempts from their organizations. Given that recruitment events can affect what new employees expect from their employers (their understanding of the psychological contract), an organization's recruitment strategy can play an important role in determining how smoothly new employees and their employers adjust to one another during this crucial initial employment period.

In order to increase the probability of person–job congruence, this and the preceding chapter have strongly advocated that organizations use recruitment devices that inform prospective employees of what a given position with an organization really entails. In the next chapter, specific methods for providing recruits with such information will be discussed. However, in order for an organization to plan a recruitment campaign for disseminating accurate information, an employer must have a thorough understanding of what it offers to job candidates. An organization must also be confident that the long-term consequences of such recruiting honesty (e.g., more satisfied and more productive employees) will outweigh the possible short-term consequences of such candor (e.g., the loss of some desirable job candidates).

The following quote by Schein (1978) succinctly sums up the spirit of this philosophy of recruitment realism. "[A] good principle for recruiting might be, 'Know as much as possible about the job, the organization, and the career paths within it, and then tell the truth as much as possible; admit uncertainty and gray areas if they exist; don't oversell, because a short-term success in getting bodies in the door does not solve the company's long-range human resource problem'" (pp. 90–91).

NOTES

1. For more information on employee socialization, the reader should refer to Porter, Lawler, and Hackman (1975), Greenhaus (1987), or Feldman (1981).

2. In this section the terms *values, attitudes, behaviors,* and *job expectations* are used repeatedly. Although it is important to distinguish these characteristics of a job candidate, typically an employer is most concerned with predicting how an individual will behave if hired. Job attitudes, employee values, and job expectations are important because of the influence each of these factors can have on the manner in which a new employee behaves. More will be said about these interrelationships later in this chapter.

3. In comparison to the turnover rate reported by Dunnette et al. (1973), Phillips (1987) reports that in some organizations the turnover rate for new college graduates can be as high as 50 percent during their first year of employment. Readers who are interested in a discussion of unrealistic recruit job expectations from an organization's perspective should refer to Schein (1964). For example, according to Schein, companies have a stereotype of a newly hired college graduate as being "overambitious and unrealistic in his expectations regarding the possibilities of advancement and increased responsibility."

4. Because the focus of this text is on recruitment, reality shock will be discussed in terms of the ways an organization can attempt to minimize it. It should be noted, however, that organizations can also experience reality shock (Louis, 1980). That is, organizations are also often surprised and disappointed by the skills, competencies, motivation, values, expectations, etc., that new employees bring to the employment relationship.

5. The reader should keep in mind that the term *recruitment communications* is being used as a general label that encompasses such recruitment devices as a job advertisement, image advertising on television, a presentation at a job fair, and one-on-one interviews with organization members.

6. In deciding whether to communicate information about these issues, an organization must carefully consider its decisions. For example, some courts have used comments made by organizations concerning job security as evidence against them in lawsuits by laid-off employees claiming an "implied contract" of a permanent employment relationship (see Schlei and Grossman, 1989).

7. The concept of organizational culture is somewhat nebulous. As used by most authors, organizational culture refers to philosophies, ideologies, values, beliefs, assumptions, expectations, attitudes, and norms that are widely shared by organizational members (see Kilmann, Saxton, and Serpa, 1985).

8. These are not the only aspects of organizational culture that may be important for a job candidate. For example, Woolfe (1990) highlights five aspects of corporate culture as being potentially important for job candidates in determining whether a potential job would be a good fit: "corporate structure," "paternalism vs. individualism," "pace and hours," "cooperation vs. competition," and "turnover and mobility patterns."

9. As with most models reflecting HRM processes, the model presented in Exhibit 6.1 is simplistic. For example, it does not include all of the variables that can influence the formation of employee job expectations. Rather, only certain key variables are considered. In addition, the model presents the formation of job expectations as if this process could be broken into discrete stages when such stages are frequently far from distinct. Although there is considerable research to support the various steps portrayed in this model, not everyone agrees with all of the hypothesized relationships between variables presented in the model.

Readers who are interested in other models that address the process described in this model should refer to Rynes (1991), Stumpf and Hartman (1984), Vandenberg and Scarpello (1990), and Wanous (1978). The model presented here has much in common with the models developed by these researchers.

10. In determining whether a position looks good enough to investigate further, different job candidates may use different comparison standards. For example, an out-of-work engineer may compare the position under consideration against his or her current state of unemployment. Alternatively, a college student may compare his or her initial impression of a position against job offers he or she anticipates receiving in the future. In most cases, a person who is currently working will use his or her current position as the standard against which a prospective position is evaluated.

11. Given that an initial negative impression may result in a job candidate eliminating a position from further consideration, it is not surprising that organizations place considerable importance on their corporate image. In fact, it appears that there is an ever-increasing number of companies that are now doing image advertising (see *Recruitment Today* for numerous examples of corporate efforts to improve their public images as places of employment).

12. Although their variables were not operationalized in a way that exactly reflects the variables portrayed in Boxes 1, 2, and 3, a study by Stumpf and Hartman (1984) is relevant to the hypothesized relationships in these boxes. In this study, environmental exploration (i.e., researching occupations, jobs, and organizations) was found to be highly correlated with the amount of job information a job candidate reported having ($r = .52; p < .01$). The relationship between environmental exploration and the realism of one's job expectations was in the predicted direction but not statistically significant.

13. As noted in Chapter 5, recruitment media differ in terms of whether they allow for one-way or two-way communication. However, they also differ in terms of which of a job candidate's senses they are directed toward. Although typically recruitment media tend to be visual (e.g., a recruitment brochure) or audio-visual (e.g., an interview) in nature, this is not always the case. For example, a radio advertisement is an audio medium. Conceivably, recruitment media could address any of the five senses. For example, during a tour of a work site, a job candidate may receive information about a job both via his or her sense of touch (e.g., high humidity) and smell (e.g., a pungent sulfur odor). Even an individual's sense of taste could be the target of job-related information (e.g., a work sample test for the job of wine taster). Receiving job-related information through multiple senses may increase the distinctiveness of the information, and, thus, whether the information is attended to, stored, and subsequently recalled.

14. Readers who believe that undue attention is being given to the inaccuracy and incompleteness of recruitment communications are referred to Rynes and Boudreau (1986). This article documents the fact that, although organizations typically believe the recruitment information they present is fairly accurate and complete, several studies have shown that recruitment communications are uninformative (see Taylor and Sniezak, 1984), unrealistically favorable (see Wanous, 1980), and noncredible (see Fisher, Ilgen, and Hoyer, 1979).

15. Although only limited research has addressed the topic of job applicant self-selection, studies by Suszko and Breaugh (1986), Mason and Belt (1986), and others support the fact that providing specific information relevant to the position under consideration can cause applicant self-selection. For example, Mason and Belt (1986) found that, in comparison to job information concerning an engineering position that provided few specifics about desired applicant characteristics, a job description that provided specific information con-

cerning desired applicant characteristics resulted in a reduced probability that unqualified engineering students would pursue the position. Thus, the study by Mason and Belt suggests that by providing specific information concerning a job opening an organization may enable unqualified applicants to self-select out of the recruitment process.

16. In addition to the process of candidate self-selection affecting person–job congruence, an organization's selection system can also have an influence on the degree of person–job fit. However, because the focus of this text is on employee recruitment, the impact of a selection system will not be discussed further. Readers who are interested in more information on how a selection system can improve person–job congruence should refer to Gatewood and Feild (1990) and, in particular, Rynes and Gerhart (1990), who examine the ability of interviewers to assess applicant–job fit.

17. As discussed in Chapter 5, in order for an individual to be able to intelligently consider whether a given position will provide a good fit, the individual must have a reasonable sense of self-awareness (Herriot, 1984). That is, the individual must be able to determine with a reasonable degree of accuracy what skills he or she possesses and what specific needs he or she has. Specific mechanisms that individuals can use for improving their self-awareness are discussed in Chapter 3. In Chapter 7, the importance of an organization attempting to assess an individual's extent of self-awareness will be briefly discussed.

18. Given the complexity of Exhibit 6.1, it was decided not to include a box reflecting the intervening variable of rewards between job performance and job satisfaction.

19. Both Rynes (1991) and Wanous and Colella (1989) have pointed out that, in the context of realistic job preview experiments, researchers have tended to operationalize the "self-selection" construct in terms of job offer acceptance rates. As Rynes and Wanous and Colella noted, the fact that persons who received realistic job previews declined job offers does not mean that the matching process hypothesized in Exhibit 6.1 actually occurred. As an alternative explanation to the matching hypothesis, Rynes suggested that in RJP experiments the most qualified job applicants may have withdrawn from the applicant pool on receiving the accurate (and generally more negative) information. The concern raised by Rynes and Wanous and Colella is an important one. In the future, researchers should investigate why job applicants withdrew from job consideration.

7

Improving the Accuracy of Job Candidate Expectations

In previous chapters, considerable research has been presented documenting the fact that job candidates frequently lack information and/or have inaccurate expectations about positions they are considering. Research linking incomplete and inaccurate job expectations to undesirable outcomes for both the individual and the employer has also been reviewed. In attempting to understand why possessing incomplete and inaccurate job information can have undesirable effects, concepts such as "person–job fit," "psychological contract," "self-selection," and "pivotal values" were introduced. In this chapter, several methods that an employer can use for improving the accuracy and completeness of a recruit's job expectations will be discussed. However, prior to this discussion, an overview of some of the reasons why job candidates have incomplete and inaccurate job expectations will be presented.

SOME OF THE CAUSES OF INCOMPLETE AND INACCURATE JOB EXPECTATIONS

Causes That Can Be Attributed to the Job Candidate

As was discussed in Chapter 3, job candidates are partly responsible for their having incomplete or inaccurate information about a job opening. For example, some applicants do not know how to research a job opening.

In other cases, job candidates know how to research job opportunities, but they are not motivated to do so.[1] In still other situations, individuals are not willing to seek important information (by, for example, asking tough questions during an interview) because they are afraid that doing so will cause potential employers to view them in a negative way. And, even if an individual knows how to research a position and is motivated to do so, limitations on human information processing and decision making (see Chapter 4) can still result in the person having incomplete and inaccurate information about a position. For example, such cognitive tendencies as selective perception and availability bias can result in applicants making job-choice decisions without considering all of the information that is potentially available to them.

Causes That Can Be Attributed to the Prospective Employer

Although job candidates may be partly responsible for their incomplete and/or inaccurate job expectations, in most cases organizations are also responsible. For example, members of an organization who are involved in recruiting, such as representatives from the personnel department, are frequently unfamiliar to some degree with important attributes of the positions they are trying to fill (Hughes, 1988). This lack of job familiarity often makes it difficult for recruiters to adequately answer some of the questions they are asked by job seekers. Because recruiters may not be able to supply job candidates with the type of information they need to make informed job-choice decisions, these decisions may end up being made based on incomplete and inaccurate information.

A second reason why job candidates may not receive important information about a job opening is because recruiters often make the mistake of assuming that applicants already possess considerable information about what a position with their organization involves. For example, in discussing recruitment interviews, Berger (1989) noted that interviewers "frequently assume that applicants know far more about the company than they actually do, particularly if the company is large or an industry leader" and that interviewers "also erroneously assume that applicants know what a job entails, especially if they are applying for a generic position, such as secretary, registered nurse, or janitor" (p. 14). According to Berger, these erroneous assumptions "lead interviewers to present extremely limited job descriptions and company overviews. The result is that applicants are left to draw their own conclusions, which often are ill-founded" (p. 14).

Another reason why job candidates often end up lacking information and having inaccurate job and organizational expectations is that they receive misleading information from a prospective employer (Breaugh, 1990). For example, a corporate recruiter may emphasize his or her company's pay-for-performance philosophy to a recruit. However, the specific manager to whom the job candidate would report may not adhere to the corporate philosophy. Thus, if the individual should receive and accept a job offer, the person would discover that the information provided by the organization concerning its reward system was misleading. In the situation just described, while there was no conscious intent on the part of the company to mislead the job candidate, the information conveyed by the recruiter was misleading because the supervisor refused to abide by corporate policy.

Although job candidates are sometimes unintentionally misled by company recruiters, probably a more frequent situation is one in which recruits end up with incomplete or inaccurate information because they were intentionally misled by an organization. For example, Feldman (1976) describes a situation in which an undesirable aspect of a job—a difficult interpersonal situation—was not typically discussed with recruits. "The employees in accounting mainly do such clerical work as billing, typing, filing, and keypunching. A very important aspect of these jobs, however, is dealing with patients and lawyers, who are often hostile and who are trying to unravel payment problems or billing errors. *This part of the job is often not mentioned to new employees.*" (p. 441, emphasis added). Feldman (1976) notes that these employees, who were not told of the unpleasant aspects of working in the accounting department, generally felt that they could have found jobs better suited for them elsewhere.

This incident cited by Feldman (1976) should not be viewed as an isolated case. Based on the results of a survey of 900 human resource professionals, Rynes (1987) suggests that many "recruiters are willing to tell applicants whatever they think applicants want to hear in order to 'sell' a vacancy." Rynes concluded that the majority of the survey respondents see recruiting as a "sales function, much like product advertising."[2] In attempting to sell a job opportunity, not only will an organization fail to communicate important job information such as in the Feldman example, sometimes an organization will actually present inaccurate information to recruits. For example, Paul Thompson, professor of management at Brigham Young University, describes a drug company that "told applicants it was growing 50% annually and promised supervisory positions in 18 months." According to Thompson, the company was actually growing slowly and employees left in droves when the supervisory positions did not materialize.[3]

In summary, it appears that job candidates frequently receive misleading information from potential employers during the recruitment process. In some cases, an organization may have consciously intended to mislead job candidates, either by failing to provide information about important aspects of a job or by exaggerating one or more features of a position. In other cases, there may have been no organizational intent to mislead.[4,5] In an ethical sense, most readers would probably view the behavior of an organization that consciously attempts to mislead job candidates as being much worse than that of an organization that unintentionally misleads recruits. However, in terms of understanding the behavior of job candidates during the recruitment process and the behavior of newly hired employees, the perception of the individual, not the organization's intention, is likely to be the more important factor. For example, if an individual believes that he or she was intentionally misled by an organization during the recruitment process, this perception, even if inaccurate, may well result in such negative consequences for the organization as a new employee not trusting the organization or a recruit telling others that the company lied to him or her.

Consider the case of Dean Witter Reynolds, Inc., brokers.[6] According to a recent *Wall Street Journal* article, a growing group of new Dean Witter brokers are "fuming over having to hawk stocks alongside socks at Sears, Roebuck & Co. stores." The brokers claim "they were never told they'd have to put in their time at the retail outlets." Not only are the brokers concerned about having to do business in a less than favorable environment like a busy department store, they also dislike having to travel long distances to Sears stores. The *Wall Street Journal* story suggests that having to work in Sears stores has led to a high level of turnover among new brokers. In some cases, the alleged lack of candor on Dean Witter's part has led to transfers and to a climate of distrust. For example, one recent transfer stated, "I wish I would have been advised up front. . . . I didn't get a thing out of the [Sears stores]." Another broker stated, "A lack of ethics begins at the entry level, and festers into other areas." In addition to complaints about not having been told about having to work in Sears stores, several brokers complained that Dean Witter misled them about the compensation they would receive: "If they had told me I would have had to go to Sears and only get a six-month draw, I never would have started there," said one former Dean Witter broker who has since gone to work for a large bank. In fairness to Dean Witter, it should be emphasized that in the *Wall Street Journal* article a company spokesperson stated that all broker trainees were told in advance that they would have to work in a Sears store. In addition, Dean Witter believes there are benefits to working in the Sears stores, not just disadvantages.

Although it is difficult to tell from a newspaper report such as the one on Dean Witter whether a company intentionally misled individuals during the recruitment process or whether their inaccurate initial job expectations were the result of an honest mix-up in communication, one thing seems clear. Many of its current and former brokers believe Dean Witter intentionally deceived them. The results of this perception, whether it is accurate or not, seem to have been turnover, distrust, and, perhaps most important, very negative publicity for Dean Witter. Given the *Wall Street Journal's* vast readership, it is difficult to imagine that this story will not affect future recruitment efforts by Dean Witter.

From this overview of some of the reasons why job candidates end up with incomplete and inaccurate job perceptions, several actions that an employer could take to improve the accuracy and the completeness of job candidate perceptions should be apparent. For example, the importance of a campus recruiter being quite knowledgeable about the jobs he or she is trying to fill should be evident. Similarly, it should be obvious that anyone involved in recruiting should be made aware that job candidates generally want more information about both the position and the organization than they usually receive. Although several other suggestions for developing a recruitment strategy could be pointed out, these recommendations will be introduced in the context of specific methods that organizations can use for improving the accuracy and completeness of the job and organizational expectations held by job seekers.

GENERAL RECOMMENDATIONS FOR IMPROVING RECRUITMENT COMMUNICATIONS

In this chapter, several ways in which job candidates can be provided with more accurate and more complete job information during the recruitment process will be presented. However, before examining specific approaches an organization could use, a number of general recommendations that cut across several of these approaches will be reviewed. Because many of these recommendations for improving recruitment communications have been described in detail in earlier chapters, they will only be briefly discussed in this section.

Chapters 5 and 6 discussed the advantages of conveying recruitment information that is accurate, specific, broad in scope, important, and likely to be seen as credible. In order to maximize each of these attributes, the need to gather information about a specific position with a given organization from multiple sources was emphasized. In particular, it was recommended that an employer seek information from sources who reflect a variety of viewpoints and are very familiar with the job opening. In terms of the specific aspects of a position that should be addressed in recruitment communications, six general content areas were highlighted: job duties, compensation and benefits, career-related issues, organizational culture, supervisors, and co-workers.

Concerning how to convey the information about a position that has been gathered, in previous chapters a strong case was made for the use of media that allow for two-way communication between the recruit and the organization, such as "off-the-record" conversations with job incumbents. The benefits of using a variety of different recruitment media (so long as the message they communicate is consistent) were also noted. The use of two-way media was recommended because such media stimulate the active processing of information (Petty and Cacioppo, 1986) and they allow the recruitment message to be somewhat custom-tailored to the unique information needs of a job candidate. The use of multiple media was encouraged because information from different information channels that communicate the same theme has been shown to enhance information credibility (Harkins and Petty, 1981).

In designing recruitment communications, it is important that the issue of timing not be overlooked (Wanous, 1989). For example, in order for accurate job information to allow an individual to self-select out of consideration for a job, the information must be received prior to accepting a job offer from the organization.[7] Presenting candid information early in the recruitment process (at a minimum, before a job offer is accepted) is also important if an organization wants to convey an impression of being open and honest with the job candidate. Another reason why the timing of a recruitment communication is important has to do with the information-processing tendencies that influence the decision-making process of job candidates. For example, if an employer presents an exaggerated view of a position early in the recruitment process, later on it may not be able to undo the inflated expectations it has created (see the discussion of selective perception and the rigidity of first impressions in Chapter 4).

From this brief review of several themes developed in earlier chapters, it should be apparent that there are a number of important principles that an organization should try to incorporate as it designs a recruitment information strategy for disseminating accurate information about a position to job candidates. As will become apparent shortly, certain recruitment methods allow for the incorporation of more of these principles than other approaches.

USING REALISTIC JOB PREVIEWS TO IMPROVE THE ACCURACY OF JOB EXPECTATIONS

As was noted in Chapter 1, in recruiting employees many organizations adopt a "flypaper" approach (Wanous, 1980). That is, they try to make their job openings look as attractive as possible. In order to do this, an organization may exaggerate attributes of the job opening and/or hide undesirable features of the position. Employers that use this flypaper approach (this approach has been so commonly used in the past that Wanous actually refers to it as the "traditional" philosophy of recruitment) appear to believe that it will allow them to hire the best job candidates and that, although the individuals who are hired may be disappointed in their jobs, they will still make good employees (that is, once hired they will "stick" to the organization and perform effectively). As has been suggested repeatedly throughout this text, an increasing number of organizations have rejected this flypaper philosophy of recruiting. Instead they have adopted a philosophy of realistic recruitment. Although this growing commitment to realism has been reflected in many different ways, it has perhaps been most clearly manifested in the increasing use of "realistic job previews" (RJPs).

The Use of Realistic Job Previews

As used by most researchers (Dilla, 1987), the term *realistic job preview* refers to a presentation of factual information about a job opening that is given to job candidates (or, in some cases, new employees) by an organization. Simply stated, the objective of providing an RJP is to improve the accuracy (realism) of the job expectations held by the RJP recipients.[8] In the past, the two most commonly used methods for presenting RJP information have been booklets and videotapes (Wanous and Colella, 1989). Although the preferred timing of an RJP is early in the recruitment process (at least prior to job offer acceptance), it appears that RJPs have more often been provided after job offer acceptance (Wanous and Colella, 1989).

Given the cost of training insurance agents and the high turnover rate for this position, it is not surprising that the insurance industry was one of the first to make extensive use of RJPs. For example, the first published report of the use of an RJP was by Weitz (1956) and involved the use of an RJP booklet produced by Life and Casualty Insurance Company of Tennessee. Shortly thereafter, Youngberg (1963) reported on the use of an RJP booklet by Prudential Insurance in which Prudential tried to correct numerous job candidate misperceptions about what it was like to be an insurance agent. For example, Prudential's RJP booklet instructed job candidates that being an agent meant working four or more nights a week, taking insurance courses to update their technical knowledge, dealing with impolite customers, canceling family plans at the last minute, driving to a prospect's home only to find no one there, losing clients because the home office was slow to process an application, etc.

In order to get a better sense of exactly what is involved in developing and implementing an RJP, two studies will be briefly reviewed. Both of these studies reflect a high standard of conceptual and methodological rigor.

Colarelli (1984)

Historically, most researchers have used either a written brochure or a videotape to provide a realistic job preview. Although both of these RJP media have been shown to have beneficial effects, Colarelli felt that a potentially more powerful RJP medium was being overlooked. Colarelli hypothesized that a face-to-face interview with a job incumbent would be a more effective RJP medium than either an RJP brochure or videotape because: (1) a personal conversation "is more likely to facilitate receiver attention and comprehension than other (especially one-way) communication processes;" (2) an applicant is more likely to acquire personally relevant information ("the two-way communication process allows the applicant to ask questions about his or her unique concerns and the relatively equal status between the applicant and the incumbent and the nonevaluative purpose of the discussion should free applicants from most of their inhibitions about asking questions"); (3) an incumbent can provide information that an organization may be hesitant to include in a brochure or a videotape; and (4) applicants are more likely to trust job incumbents and view them as a knowledgeable source of job information. In sum, Colarelli predicted that, in comparison to an RJP brochure or videotape, an RJP provided by a job incumbent in an interview was more likely to provide information that was accurate, important, specific, broad in scope, and seen as credible.

Colarelli's study involved applicants for teller positions at a large bank that had been experiencing considerable teller turnover. He used a task inventory and individual interviews to determine what information to include in his RJP. Job incumbents and other persons who were familiar with the teller position were the sources of the RJP information. Based on the information provided by these sources, Colarelli created a 1,500-word RJP brochure. Colarelli randomly assigned applicants for the teller position to one of three groups. One group read the RJP brochure. The RJP information was communicated to those in the second group in individual interviews. Persons in the third group, the control condition, received no RJP information. Individuals in the two RJP groups received the RJP information after a job offer had been made but before it was accepted or declined.

Applicants in the RJP interview group spoke with either a bank teller or a teller trainee. All of these "RJP interviewers" went through training during which they were instructed to make it clear to applicants that the purpose of the interview was solely to provide information about the job. During the training, the interviewers were given the RJP brochure and told that this was the principal information they were to provide to applicants.

In order to evaluate the effects of using different methods for communicating the RJP information, Colarelli gathered several types of information. In terms of the realism of their job expectations, Colarelli found that applicants in the two RJP conditions believed they had more realistic job expectations than those in the control group (the two RJP groups did not differ). Concerning applicant perceptions of the amount of job-related information they received, the findings were as predicted. Those in the RJP interview condition reported receiving more information about the teller position than those in the RJP brochure group, who in turn reported receiving more information than those in the control condition. This same pattern of results was also reported with regard to applicant perceptions of the personal relevance of the information they received. That is, those in the RJP interview group reported that the information they received was more personally relevant (e.g., "All of the major issues that concerned me were addressed in the information I received") than those in the RJP brochure group, who in turn reported a higher level of personal relevance than those in the control group. Colarelli found no differences between the two RJP groups in terms of subsequent job satisfaction, but found that those in the RJP interview group had less turnover than those in the other two groups.

Although based on his findings Colarelli concluded that an RJP presented by a job incumbent in a face-to-face conversation was better than the use of a "one-way, nonhuman communication medium (a brochure)," one should be cautious in generalizing from his results. A critical look at Colarelli's study shows that it was a relatively "weak" test of RJP effectiveness; thus, Colarelli may actually have underestimated the potential influence of an RJP. For example, it appears that no applicant self-selection occurred (i.e., everyone who was offered a job accepted it). Although it is conceivable that the teller position was a very attractive job opportunity, it may also have been the case that some applicants perceived no other viable job alternatives (Colarelli stated that the local unemployment rate for clerical personnel was 8.9 percent at the time the study took place). Thus, some of Colarelli's subjects may have accepted job offers they would otherwise have declined had other opportunities been available. The fact that the RJP was not tied to a specific teller position (e.g., information on one's boss and co-workers was not provided) should also have weakened the effects of the RJP.

Meglino, DeNisi, Youngblood, and Williams (1988)

Although RJPs have typically been discussed in the context of reducing inflated job expectations, in theory an RJP also could be used to increase unrealistically low expectations. This was the situation faced by Meglino et al. in a study they conducted that involved basic trainees in the U.S. Army. Based on considerable research, including interviews with command personnel and a longitudinal survey of trainees prior to and during basic training, these researchers concluded that trainees generally overestimate the difficulty of certain training activities and events, such as the type and duration of daily physical training and the standards to be met for graduation, and underestimate the difficulty of the emotional adjustment to basic training (e.g., homesickness and lack of privacy).

In order to improve the accuracy of trainee expectations, Meglino and his associates created two different videotapes. Their "enhancement" RJP video provided a twenty-seven-minute overview of basic training activities and events about which trainees typically have unrealistically low expectations. Their "reduction" RJP videotape was a twenty-four-minute presentation that covered the emotional aspects of basic training. The "reduction" videotape not only identified adjustment problems that were not likely to be anticipated by trainees, but it also presented suggestions for dealing with them.

The design of the Meglino et al. study involved three experimental groups and one control group. Of the experimental groups, one viewed the "enhancement" videotape, one watched the "reduction" videotape, and one viewed both videos. In all three experimental conditions, the videotapes were shown after trainees had entered the Army and been processed but before they had started basic training. Meglino et al. used surveys to measure several different trainee perceptions at three different points in time: prior to the RJP experience, immediately after the RJP experience, and after five weeks of basic training. Those in the control group filled out surveys at the same times. Meglino and his associates also measured voluntary separation from training prior to graduation.

Given the numerous statistical analyses reported by Meglino et al., including comparing the four groups on nine different attitudinal measures and on turnover and making group comparisons at three points in time, only a few of their results will be summarized here. In terms of the self-report data, a frequent finding was that those trainees who had received both the "enhancement" and the "reduction" previews responded more positively to basic training than those in the other groups. For example, after five weeks of training, those who had viewed both videotapes reported being more committed to the Army and a higher level of overall satisfaction than did the trainees in the other three groups. With regard to perceiving the Army as having been honest with them, those in both the "reduction" RJP group and the "reduction and enhancement" RJP group gave the Army higher ratings than those in either the "enhancement" or the control condition. In terms of trainee turnover, those individuals who had viewed both RJP videotapes were less likely to leave basic training than those in the other three groups. Individuals who had viewed only one of the RJP videotapes did not differ from those in the control group in terms of turnover.

As with Colarelli's study, Meglino et al.'s RJP study can be criticized. For example the "reduction" videotape presented not only realistic information but also techniques for coping with difficult conditions. In addition, since the RJP manipulation occurred after they had already enlisted, it is unlikely that trainees felt they had much opportunity to self-select out of job consideration.

Contributions of the Colarelli and Meglino et al. Studies

Although one can cite flaws in these studies, both of them represent contributions to the RJP literature. For example, Colarelli (1984) showed the power of using a two-way RJP media and Meglino et al. (1988) highlighted the fact that job expectations are sometimes too low and that an RJP can be used to raise such erroneous expectations. In addition, rather than looking simply at the effects of RJPs on outcome variables such as turnover, both studies investigated process variables (e.g., perceptions of organizational honesty) that have been hypothesized to underlie RJP effectiveness.

Drawing General Conclusions About the Use of RJPs

Although much research on the use of RJPs still needs to be conducted, from the research that has been carried out it seems safe to draw a few tentative conclusions about their use. Based on the results of recent meta-analyses (see Premack and Wanous, 1985), it appears that RJPs can have a beneficial influence on the accuracy of the initial job expectations held by job candidates and on subsequent employee turnover, satisfaction, and commitment. Although the estimated impact of an RJP on these variables has not been overwhelming (Premack and Wanous estimate that in a typical organization the use of an RJP will reduce voluntary turnover by 5 percent to 10 percent), an argument can be made that the potential effects of RJPs on these variables have been underestimated. For example, in many of the studies included in the meta-analyses, the RJPs were provided after job offers had been accepted, the RJPs provided no information concerning the job candidate's prospective supervisor or co-workers, the job examined was very visible to the public, and/or the job candidates appeared to have little ability to turn down job offers that were not seen as desirable.

As will become apparent from this chapter, RJPs have been used increasingly in recent years by employers. Although there is little doubt that one of the reasons for this increasing use is their documented effect on reducing employee turnover, a second reason is that, in comparison to many other human resource techniques, RJPs are relatively inexpensive to develop and implement. For example, although McEvoy and Cascio (1985) found that job enrichment programs had a more powerful effect on employee turnover than did the use of a realistic job preview, in many cases the cost of enriching a job (if it was even possible) would be much greater than providing an RJP.

LESS COMMONLY USED APPROACHES TO PROVIDING AN RJP

As was noted previously, most RJP studies have involved the use of either a short booklet or a videotape. However, as demonstrated by Colarelli

(1984), an RJP does not have to be presented by such impersonal one-way media. In order to get the maximum value from a realistic recruitment program, it is important that an employer not simply focus on the use of a specific RJP booklet, videotape, or interview. Instead, an organization must view the use of RJPs as part of a process by which it can provide recruits with a more complete understanding of what a job with it involves. If one views the use of RJPs as part of a recruiting realism process, it becomes apparent that several different mechanisms can be used to convey job-related information and that this information can be conveyed at different points during the recruitment process. It should also be evident that, in order to minimize costs, it may make sense for an organization to use relatively inexpensive RJP mechanisms such as job advertisements early in the recruitment process and use more labor-intensive ones such as elaborate work simulations later in the process.

In this section, several additional ways in which an RJP can be provided will be introduced. Given space constraints, the treatment of these alternative RJP approaches will be both brief and selective (i.e., not all possible approaches will be examined). Although many of the approaches discussed in this section have not traditionally been considered as formal RJP approaches, they clearly fall under Dilla's (1987) definition of an RJP presented earlier in this chapter.

The Use of Interviews and/or Informal Conversations

Although Colarelli's study (1984) provides a good example of the use of an interview for communicating realistic job information, the interview he used was not ideal. For example, his interviewers were not prospective co-workers of the RJP recipients. Thus, they could not supply information concerning the style of a particular teller supervisor, the group cohesiveness among tellers, or the climate of a particular branch of the bank. In addition, from Colarelli's description of his study, it appears that his interviewers were supposed to formally present the RJP information that was included in his RJP booklet. Therefore, they may have felt that they could not present additional information that was not contained in the RJP booklet.

Other examples of the use of two-way interchanges to provide people with realistic job information have been reported by Gomersall and Myers (1966) and Pascale (1984). The study by Gomersall and Myers was carried out at Texas Instruments and involved presenting RJP information after individuals had accepted job offers and reported for work. In con-

trast to the formal presentations of RJP information in the studies by Colarelli (1984) and Gomersall and Myers (1966) is Morgan and Stanley's
informal presentation of realistic job information (i.e., an informal discussion of job demands at a dinner with the job candidate and his or her
companion), which was discussed in Chapter 5.

Job Advertisements

If an employer is committed to a philosophy of recruitment realism, it
should plan its recruitment activities so that at no point during the recruitment process are job candidates misled. Because the first impression
that many individuals form about a position comes from a job advertisement, the importance of such advertisements conveying accurate information should be obvious. For example, if there are certain essential requirements for a job, they should be communicated in an advertisement.
In a similar vein, if there are certain attributes of a job about which many
job candidates lack information or have unrealistic expectations, an organization should consider including in an advertisement information that
would improve the completeness and accuracy of their expectations. Considerable material on job advertising is provided in Chapter 11, so rather
than go into detail on this topic in this section, an example of the use of
advertising as part of a recruiting realism strategy will be presented.

As with most hospitals, Los Angeles County/University of Southern
California Medical Center has an ongoing problem attracting a sufficient
number of nurses to fill its staff openings.[9] With the help of Thompson
Recruitment Advertising, LA County/USC Medical Center designed a
television commercial to attract nurses to the open houses it held as well
as to stimulate applications for employment. Rather than "glossing over
the perceived disadvantages" of working for a public facility whose beds
are filled with the indigent and with many low-income people who lack
medical insurance, the commercial addressed these "disadvantages" directly. It did this by introducing a fictional woman named Helen who was
described as old, alone, suffering from diabetes, and having been "beaten
within an inch of her life." According to the copywriter of the commercial,
the ad says to prospective candidates for nursing positions, "'Look, life
here is difficult, demanding, and complex, but it means you'll be able to
help people who need you. You won't be any doctor's handmaiden and
you'll have the chance to become the best nurse of your entire career.'"
According to the copywriter, LA County/USC Medical Center chose to
directly address the type of patients it has because it knew it could not

fool its audience: "Nurses are like engineers, they know what's going on in all different opportunities in their area." The hospital chose to use a television ad because it wanted to make contact with nurses who were not actively looking for a job.

Although the preceding example involved the use of a TV advertisement, the use of this medium is uncommon. In trying to fill positions, employers more typically rely on newspaper ads, radio ads, direct mail ads, and job notices placed in periodicals oriented toward particular professions. Although the choice of an advertising outlet places limits on the amount of information an employer can communicate, each of these outlets can be used effectively to convey accurate information to prospective employees. Thus, no matter what job advertising approach it uses (including job notices posted for the recruitment of internal candidates), an employer can attempt to improve the accuracy and completeness of prospective employees' job perceptions.

Recruitment Literature

One of the ways in which an employer can communicate information about its job openings is through the recruitment literature it distributes. For example, based on its experience recruiting law students from top schools, General Motors (GM) became convinced that students undervalued positions in its legal department.[10] As a way to address what it saw as the "incredibly inaccurate myths" that existed concerning working in a corporate job, GM developed a recruitment brochure that starts out by describing legal practice with GM as "incredibly dull and boring." The GM brochure goes on to describe its attorneys as "just a bunch of lazy, inefficient corporate types who have and want no challenges, work short hours, do low-level routine work, take endless vacations, and work for meager pay." After acknowledging these myths, the GM brochure provides information "to debunk them."

The Central Intelligence Agency (CIA) distributes a reading list to prospective employees in an attempt to give them a better understanding of what working for it involves.[11] Although the majority of the books included on this list present a favorable view of the CIA, the list also includes several books that have been highly critical of it. In explaining its decision to include such books on the reading list, a CIA spokesperson explained, "It's only logical that they should read the pros and cons. . . . We're not recommending the views, obviously, being put across by these critics, but employees should be coming in with their eyes wide open."

Observing the Work Environment

Although reading about what a position with an organization encompasses can be instructive, the adage "seeing is believing" also holds true for recruitment. Thus, in trying to convey information about a position, it may be wise for an employer to try to use a more active mode of communication than printed material. For example, information about a job could be provided by means of a videotape, a tour of the work site, or a slide show.

Wang Laboratories is an example of an organization that has relied on the use of videotape for conveying a sense of what a job with it involves.[12] According to Sue Morse, director of corporate staffing, Wang created a short videotape to show at job fairs on college campuses to encourage students to explore employment opportunities with it. Wang was not interested in presenting a public relations piece that exaggerated the benefits of working for Wang. Instead, Wang's video was designed "to give students a feel for the company philosophy, culture and environment," so that individuals could weed themselves out if they "weren't interested in a company in which shorts and tank tops are common." In order to convey a sense of what working for Wang was like, the videotape contained brief statements by Wang employees about what a job with Wang meant as well as footage of informal meetings and work settings (e.g., cubicles with computers). As described by Morse, the goal of the video was to "get students interested in talking with our campus recruiters, in visiting the company, and in reading our literature."

Although a videotape can be useful for conveying information, especially if it is shown early in the recruitment process (e.g., at a job fair), an organization should consider the use of an in-person tour of the work site when it has reduced the number of viable job candidates to a manageable number. An in-person visit can provide information that is difficult to communicate in other ways. For example, it is one thing to describe a job in a plant as being hot and noisy, but actually experiencing these conditions may add a new level of appreciation to a job candidate's perception of the job. First-hand experience of such vivid stimuli should also aid the job candidate's recall of information when a job-choice decision needs to be made.

Work Simulations

Although a person can learn a good deal about a position by reading an RJP booklet, talking to a job incumbent, viewing a videotape, or touring a work setting, actively participating in a work simulation can often provide a prospective employee with information that could not have been gotten from these other RJP approaches. Although it may be difficult for an organization to create a realistic job simulation for some jobs, such as those that require considerable training, simulations can be created for a variety of jobs. For example, Cascio and Phillips (1979) were able to develop job simulations for several city government positions. More recently, Schmitt and Ostroff (1986) developed a work simulation for the job of police department emergency telephone operator.

An interesting example of the use of a work simulation is provided by Merrill Lynch, which developed a stock broker simulation in order to provide candidates for such positions with a better understanding of what the job involved.[13] This simulation is designed both to help Merrill Lynch eliminate individuals as job candidates and to expose candidates to the demands of the job, thus facilitating self-selection. The stock broker simulation takes place after work hours, so a tape recording is played to realistically simulate such office noises as ringing telephones and typing. To convey an accurate view of the life of a stock broker, each candidate faces a full in-basket, an appointment calendar with time conflicts, and sporadic telephone calls that are designed to interrupt his or her train of thought. In addition, each job candidate, acting as a stock broker, participates in a telephone simulation with an experienced employee, who role-plays an angry customer who has just lost $97,000 of a $100,000 investment because of the "stock broker's" recommendation. Although this type of simulation can only hint at what being a broker is really like, Merrill Lynch feels its simulation helps the company to determine who is likely to make a good broker and helps candidates to decide whether they should pursue the job.

In discussing the use of realistic job previews, most authors emphasize the communication of information about what the job offers and what it demands. Providing such information, it is argued, allows an organization to help a job candidate determine whether, all things considered, the job is likely to reasonably satisfy his or her needs. A particular advantage of using a work simulation as an RJP device is that it may also help a job candidate determine whether there is a good match between his or her abilities and the competencies the job requires. For example, Downs, Farr, and Colbeck (1978) administered a work sample test to a group of job applicants, all of whom received job offers regardless of their performance on the test. Interestingly, Downs and her associates found that job candidates appeared to "self-select" out of job consideration based on their ability. For example, 91 percent of those who scored in the "A" range on the test reported for work. In contrast, of those in the "C" range, only 76 percent started work, and of those in the lowest range on the test, only 23 percent reported for work. Thus, at least for this job simulation, it appears that such an RJP device facilitated self-selection on perceived ability.

Giving Job Candidates Actual Work Experience

Although going through a work simulation should improve the accuracy of a job candidate's expectations, there is only so much information that can be conveyed in a simulation. For example, although Merrill Lynch felt that its simulation gave a good preview of the job of stock broker, it acknowledged that its simulation did not provide information about the company itself. In terms of trying to improve the accuracy and completeness of the job expectations held by prospective employees, the best approach an organization may be able to use is to give them actual job experience prior to an offer of full-time employment.

For example, both Bowes (1987) and Phillips (1987) suggest that by using internships, co-op programs, part-time work, and summer employment, an employer not only will be able to make a good assessment of an individual's strengths, but the individual will be able to acquire a good understanding of the advantages and disadvantages of working for a given organization. A prospective candidate for a full-time position will be particularly able to size up a job situation if he or she works in the same department that has the job opening. In terms of realism, the advantage of using an approach where a job candidate works for an organization in a temporary capacity prior to an offer of permanent employment is summed up well by Val Burroughs, director of special programs at Michigan Bell: "Because internship and co-op participants are already familiar with the company before accepting full-time employment, they know exactly what to expect. . . ."[14]

Although it is rarely used, another method for giving candidates for full-time positions actual job experience is a so-called "job tryout." For example, in staffing its automobile assembly plant in Smyrna, Tennessee, Nissan required job applicants to work up to 360 hours without pay.[15] Although this program was designed to enable Nissan to screen employees and do preliminary training, according to Thomas P. Groom, Nissan's manager of employment, it was also designed to make it clear to people what a job with Nissan entailed.

Although researchers have suggested that programs such as co-ops and internships should reduce the "reality shock" commonly experienced by new employees, as with any other HRM program the relative success of what Bowes (1987) has referred to as "Try Before You Buy" programs will depend on the specific circumstances of the employment situation. For example, if a job candidate had a good understanding of what a job entails prior to formally making contact with the organization, a co-op program during college may not substantially improve the accuracy of the person's expectations.

The Use of Various RJP Approaches: Summary Comments

From the preceding discussion of the ways in which an organization can try to influence the accuracy of job candidate expectations, several points should be apparent. First, an employer probably should use more than one approach to conveying information. Second, in order to minimize cost, an organization should consider using the less expensive RJP devices first and save the labor-intensive ones for near the end of the recruitment process when there are fewer viable job candidates. Third, in making decisions about which RJP approaches to use, an employer should carefully consider the credibility and other properties of each approach. Finally, even the brief descriptions of the various methods of conveying realistic job information that have been presented in this chapter should make it obvious that considerably more research on these approaches is needed. For example, very few good studies have examined the use of internships (Taylor, 1988, is an exception). Although logic suggests that the approaches to improving recruiting realism that have been discussed in this chapter should be effective, substantially more empirical evidence supporting this assertion is needed.

IMPROVING THE ACCURACY OF JOB EXPECTATIONS BY TARGETING SPECIFIC GROUPS

Although authors have typically focused on the use of RJPs in addressing the topic of recruiting realism, this perspective is too narrow. Another way in which an organization may be able to improve the accuracy of its new employees' job expectations is by targeting its recruitment efforts on particular types of job candidates such as former employees who are likely to have relatively realistic job perceptions without receiving an RJP. In most cases, an organization should not automatically eliminate from job consideration an individual who is not in one of these targeted groups. Rather, an employer might give preference to those in the groups it has targeted.

Rehires

One way for an organization to increase the likelihood that the persons it hires possess a good understanding of what a position with it involves is for the employer to give preference to former employees who performed well when they previously worked for it. Although many organizations see those who quit as disloyal and thus will not consider rehiring ex-employees, research (see, for example, Taylor and Schmidt, 1983) has shown that such rehires may have lower rates of absenteeism and turn-over than persons who are recruited via other sources.

Hewlett-Packard (HP) is a good example of an organization that has made effective use of rehires. Hewlett-Packard places great importance on hiring employees who fit into its somewhat unique organizational culture. One of the ways in which Hewlett-Packard tries to ensure a good fit between its culture and its new hires is by making job candidates aware of what its culture is like during the recruitment process. For example, in recruiting employees, prospective supervisors and co-workers, who are primarily responsible for recruiting, convey a sense of the HP personality by telling company stories (see von Werssowetz and Beer, 1982). However, another way that Hewlett-Packard increases the likelihood that the individuals it hires know what they are getting into is by encouraging the rehiring of former HP employees who have performed well in the past. Such individuals already know what it is like to work in the unstructured HP environment. Because they have been socialized into the HP way of doing things, they should have a very good understanding of what they will experience if they are rehired.

If an organization is interested in giving preference to ex-employees, it should not wait passively for them to apply for advertised positions. Many suitable former employees may not be actively looking for a new job; thus, they may never become aware that a job with their former employer is available. Furthermore, even if they know that a position is available, former employees may be hesitant to apply for it because they may incorrectly believe their former employer would not consider re-hiring them. Rather than wait for applications from former employees, an organization should consider taking the initiative in contacting ex-employees who are considered desirable candidates for open positions. Many hospitals have found this strategy to be a particularly effective way to staff difficult-to-fill nursing vacancies (Harper, 1988).

Targeting Individuals with Similar Prior Work Experience

Although an organization may be able to increase the accuracy and completeness of the job expectations held by its new employees by giving preference in hiring to former employees, it may not be able to fill its available positions with rehires for a number of reasons (e.g., there is an insufficient number of former employees available). Fortunately, the logic underlying the recruitment of ex-employees may be generalized to other potential job candidate groups. For example, frequently there are jobs in other organizations that have much in common with the position an employer is trying to fill. For instance, a job selling men's clothing at Sears may be similar (evening work, being on one's feet, dealing with impolite customers, etc.) to a job selling men's clothing at J. C. Penney. If a company is interested in hiring individuals who have a good understanding of what a new position involves, it may be able to target job candidates who have worked in the same job or a similar job in other organizations. Although working in a similar job elsewhere will not provide a complete understanding of what working for a new employer is like, such prior job experience should provide at least some understanding of what the new job involves.

Employee Referrals

In attempting to recruit persons with realistic job expectations, an organization should also consider giving preference to employee referrals. In several studies, persons who were referred by current employees have been found to make excellent employees. Although one of the explanations for this is that current employees may prescreen individuals before deciding to refer someone (Breaugh and Mann, 1984), a second explanation that has been offered is that current employees provide job candidates with a realistic picture of what a job opening entails (Breaugh, 1981).[16] Although research data are limited, studies by Quaglieri (1982) and Breaugh and Mann (1984) support the fact that individuals who are recruited by current employees of an organization possess more accurate

expectations of what their new jobs are like than those who were not referred by current employees.[17]

RJP INFORMATION
AND DIFFICULT-TO-FILL POSITIONS

Having studied a job in order to determine what it entails, an employer
may conclude that providing realistic job information will make it difficult
or impossible to fill the position and thus decide to hide the undesirable
attributes of the job. Although providing realistic job information to job
candidates will most likely cause some of them to lose interest, realistic
recruitment does not automatically mean that an organization will
struggle or be unable to fill open positions. For example, if an organization concludes that a job has several undesirable features, it may be able
to improve the job in some way or decide to recruit from an applicant
population that has fewer job opportunities, such as the handicapped or
the elderly (Rynes and Barber, 1990).

In some cases, an organization will recognize that within its traditional applicant population there is probably a segment of people who will
be attracted to the unique features a position offers. A key question then
becomes: "What is unique about the position we are trying to fill?" Lenox
Hospital and Data General are examples of organizations that focused on
the unique features of the jobs they offered to recruit effectively.

In attempting to recruit operating room nurses, Lenox Hill Hospital
in New York City "realized it was a tough hospital to work in" and it
"wanted to be realistic about that" (Koch, 1990b). However, Lenox Hill
also realized that it offered operating room nurses a somewhat unique
opportunity. At most hospitals, operating room nurses do not have a
chance to see patients until surgery or to follow up with them after surgery. In contrast, operating room nurses at Lenox Hill have considerable
contact with patients both prior to and after surgery, something that most
nurses prefer. In an advertising campaign designed with the help of Bernard Hodes Advertising, Lenox Hill used the unique nursing climate it
offered as a way to attract nurses. An advertisement that appeared in several nursing periodicals publicized the fact that Lenox Hill offered operating room nurses "the opportunity to nurse the patient, psychologically
as well as physically, and the opportunity to be more of a nurse than just a
technician." According to Mary Fenwick of Bernard Hodes Advertising,
the basic premise of the advertising campaign, which helped fill 200 open

positions, was to tell nurses something about Lenox Hill that they did not know without downplaying the challenge of being an operating room nurse. "You lose people right away if you're not honest about the work environment," Fenwick said.

Data General provides another example, as described by Tracy Kidder in his book *Soul of a New Machine* (1981). In many ways Data General seemed to face an impossible task in competing against the likes of IBM for computer engineers to build its now-famous Eclipse MV/8000 computer. It could not offer comparable salaries or benefits, its office accommodations and prestige were not as glamorous, it could not guarantee job security, and the job would require long work hours. Data General decided to emphasize what it *did* have to offer—a chance to work on the development of a state-of-the-art computer and to share in the profits it generated—but it also recognized that job candidates needed to be warned about what they were getting into. To convey a sense of what they were "signing on for," prospective employees were shown the unattractive facilities (a dingy cubicle in the basement), told about their prospective co-workers ("If we hire you, you'll be working with a bunch of cynics and egotists and it'll be hard to keep up with them"), and warned about the hours ("It's gonna be a real hard job with a lot of long hours. And I mean *long* hours"). Despite publicizing such potentially undesirable job attributes, Data General was able to fill its job openings with extremely competent individuals who, against incredible odds, built a fast, relatively inexpensive, and highly profitable computer.

ISSUES TO CONSIDER IN DEVELOPING A REALISTIC JOB PREVIEW

From the selective review of the recruitment realism literature that has been presented, several things should be apparent. For example, there is evidence that RJPs reduce turnover. Moreover, there is general agreement among researchers that, for an RJP to have maximum benefit, it must be presented before a job offer is accepted. However, while there is considerable agreement on the part of RJP researchers on these and other issues, there are also some disagreements and unsettled issues that should be mentioned.

Wanous (1989) presents a number of specific recommendations for practitioners who are interested in installing a realistic job preview, which, because they clarify some key RJP issues, will be summarized here. As will become apparent, most but not all of Wanous's recommendations are in agreement with the position taken in this chapter.[18]

In presenting his recommendations for helping practitioners make "tough choices" about the use of RJPs, Wanous addresses the content of the RJP message, the medium used to communicate it, and the message source. In terms of RJP message content, Wanous points out that the information presented can either be descriptive or judgmental (i.e., evaluative) in nature. Although most studies have involved RJPs that provide descriptive information about selected aspects of a position with an organization (starting salary, work hours, and so on), Wanous believes that there are advantages to providing judgmental information. That is, rather than simply describe what a job involves, an RJP should also relate typical reactions of job incumbents to what the job requires. For example, in addition to stating that a factory job requires "being on your feet all day," an RJP could also include that many job incumbents report that such standing can "cause sore backs and/or foot problems." Wanous suggests that including evaluative information in an RJP has the advantage of providing a job candidate with "richer" data on which to base a job-choice decision. Without such judgmental information, Wanous believes, naive job candidates may not have the ability "to interpret the meaning of purely descriptive material." However, he also notes that including judgmental information increases the risk that corporate management may resist the use of an RJP.

In addressing the content of an RJP, Wanous also addresses the issue of whether an RJP should be "extensive" or "intensive." According to Wanous, an extensive RJP tries to include "all pertinent information, so that it is not a 'deficient' view of reality." In contrast to an extensive RJP (in this text the phrase "broad in scope" was used instead of "extensive"), Wanous argues in favor of an intensive RJP. An intensive RJP focuses on a few major issues or topics that recruits see as important and about which they often have inaccurate expectations. Wanous believes that an intensive RJP has two advantages: first, information concerning major issues is not "'lost' amidst other information" and, second, information gained from an intensive RJP is more easily recalled.

Wanous also addresses the medium used to convey the RJP and the source of the message. In terms of the RJP medium, Wanous deals primarily with the relative pros and cons of using a written brochure versus using audio-visual methods. Of the two approaches, Wanous advocates the use of audio-visual methods. However, Wanous also notes that, even though little research has examined its effectiveness, an interview offers considerable potential as an RJP medium. In particular, Wanous discusses how a two-way interview is likely to result in more active processing of RJP information by job candidates, which can in turn lead to greater attitude change.

Wanous's discussion of the source of the RJP message is geared toward those who have chosen to use an audio-visual method. According to Wanous, the basic choice is between using job incumbents or using actors or other company personnel to present the RJP message. In discussing the benefits of using incumbents versus nonincumbents, Wanous believes it basically comes down to credibility versus style. All things considered, Wanous recommends the use of job incumbents because of their greater credibility.

From this brief discussion of Wanous's recommendations, it should be apparent that the author of this text agrees with most of his suggestions. For example, I agree that evaluative information should be included along with descriptive information in an RJP, so long as the judgmental information is clearly labeled as such and put in context (for example, "Three of the ten people we interviewed said they resented having to work overtime on no notice"), as Wanous himself emphasizes. As should be apparent from earlier chapters in this text, this author also agrees that interviews should be used as an RJP medium and that job incumbents make an excellent source for delivering the RJP message. The major area in which I disagree with Wanous concerns his recommendation to use an intensive rather than extensive RJP. Although I agree that one must be concerned about overwhelming a job candidate with information, I believe that with careful planning an organization can present an RJP that is both extensive and intensive. For example, if RJP information is presented in small amounts at several points during the recruitment process (possibly using different RJP media), an organization may be able to present an extensive RJP while at the same time presenting very specific RJP information.

In concluding this discussion of the use of RJPs, one final issue should be addressed. Dilla (1987) suggests that, rather than provide just descriptive information, it may be beneficial if an RJP also includes "prescriptive" information that presents solutions to problems that new employees are likely to encounter. The reader may recall that the RJP "reduction" videotape used in the Meglino et al. (1988) study included information to help Army recruits cope with job demands. Although in a technical sense the presentation of such information falls beyond the definition of an RJP, it is clearly of value to job candidates and should be presented during the recruitment process. For example, it is one thing for job candidates to discover that a job they are considering has an undesirable property; it is another thing for them to learn that, if hired, they will be taught a number of strategies that have been shown to help new employees effectively cope with the job stressor.

LIMITATIONS ON WHAT A RECRUITMENT REALISM PROGRAM CAN DO

This chapter has emphasized the benefits of an organization adopting a recruitment realism philosophy. However, no matter how well designed an employer's recruitment realism strategy is, job candidates will still have some inaccurate job expectations and will thus experience at least some level of unmet job expectations. Although some of the reasons why inaccurate job expectations can never be totally eliminated have already been noted, several other reasons have not yet been addressed. For example, sometimes a job situation changes unexpectedly, as when a new employee's supervisor unexpectedly quits. In an insightful article, Louis (1980) provides an excellent discussion of many of the reasons why unrealistic job expectations have been so difficult to eliminate. Although it is difficult to summarize the essence of Louis' article (interested readers are referred to this article), some of its major themes that are relevant to the topic of employee recruitment will be reviewed.

According to Louis, there are several reasons why newcomers to an organization experience reality shock. In order to understand the "entry experiences" of an organizational newcomer better, Louis suggests that it is useful to differentiate three key features of the entry experience: change, contrast, and surprise. According to Louis, "change" is the objective difference in one or more major features between the person's new and old environments. For example, in taking a job as a flight surgeon in the Air Force after having been a resident in a large city hospital, a physician may find he has shorter work hours, less stress, and better facilities, but a less challenging group of patients in that they are almost all in excellent physical health. Many of the changes the physician experiences in becoming a flight surgeon should be predictable, both to the physician and to the public, but a few of them may not be. To the extent that the physician's change experiences are predictable, they should be addressed by a realistic job preview.

In comparison to change experiences, "contrast" entry experiences are more personal and thus less knowable to the public and to the person before he or she begins a new job. For example, an educator who has gone from a faculty position to being an associate dean may not have been able to anticipate how much he or she would miss teaching and hate administrative politics without actually having experienced the contrast between his or her past and current positions. As defined by Louis, contrast experiences are more person-specific than change experiences (e.g., not all faculty who move into administrative positions miss teaching). That is, the specific features of a new situation that emerge as being important are partly determined by a person's unique experiences in previous work settings. This fact makes it more difficult to address contrast experiences through a realistic job preview. However, an organization may be able to improve the realism of its new hires if it targets applicant groups who have worked in similar jobs previously so that the contrast between the new and the old jobs is minimized.

The third type of entry experience that Louis introduces is "surprise." Surprise refers to the difference between a new employee's anticipations and his or her experiences in a new job. Louis defines surprise as also "encompassing one's affective reactions to any differences, including contrasts and changes." "Surprise can be positive (e.g., delight at finding that your office window overlooks a garden) and/or negative (e.g., disappointment at finding your office window cannot be opened)" (p. 237). The subject of the anticipation and, therefore, the surprise can be the job, the organization, or oneself. Louis quotes several new employees to give a sense of their surprise experiences: "'I had no idea how important windows were to me until I'd spent a week in a staff room without any.'" "'I knew I'd have to put in a lot of overtime, but I had no idea how bad I'd feel after a month of 65-hour weeks, how tired I'd be all the time.'" "'I chose this job because it offered a great deal of freedom; now I realize I really don't want so much freedom.'"

From the quotes above, it should be obvious that one approach to reducing surprise experiences is to try to give new employees a good sense of what a position involves before they accept. For example, such realism interventions as job tryouts or internships may lessen the magnitude of the surprise a new employee experiences (Phillips, 1987). An organization might also try to assess the degree of self-insight that a job candidate possesses during the recruitment process in order to determine whether the recruit really knows what is important to him or her in a job. Alternatively, an employer could target for recruitment types of job candidates such as former employees who are less likely to be surprised by what the position being filled involves.

Although other approaches that an employer could use to minimize the change, contrast, and surprise experiences of new employees could be discussed, from the brief overview provided it should be apparent that all an organization can hope to do is lessen, not eliminate, the reality shock experienced by the individuals it hires. Furthermore, the mere fact that an employer attempts to present accurate job information during the recruitment process will cause most job candidates to react favorably. Those organizations that decide to use a realistic recruitment approach should be sure to inform job candidates about what they are doing and why (see Wanous, 1989).

SUMMARY

In this chapter, the potential benefits of hiring individuals who possess relatively complete and accurate job information prior to making a job-choice decision have been emphasized. In order to increase the accuracy and completeness of job candidate expectations, several different recruiting realism approaches have been discussed. Throughout the chapter, several examples of organizations that use a recruiting realism strategy were cited. Although the advantages of a recruiting realism approach were stressed, the potential disadvantages of such an approach were also raised, including the following: (1) an organization may lose some desirable job candidates because of its candor; (2) designing and implementing a recruiting realism strategy can be time consuming; and (3) some members of the organization may feel threatened by the communication of realistic information (e.g., a supervisor may not want a prospective employee to talk with job incumbents).

From this chapter, it should be obvious that realism in recruiting is not a panacea. A "bad" job may still be difficult to fill. However, this chapter did point out some possible approaches to trying to fill even relatively "unattractive" jobs. For instance, Data General was used as an example of how, by determining what is unique about a position, an employer may be able to compete effectively against "blue chip" companies that ostensibly offer more desirable positions. To fill unattractive positions, it was also pointed out that an organization may be wise to target an applicant pool that has fewer job opportunities (Rynes and Barber, 1990).

In closing, the crucial need for more research on many of the topics introduced in this chapter must be stressed. As noted by Rynes (1991), Wanous (1989), and many others, we still know relatively little about the phenomenon of realistic recruitment.

NOTES

1. In addition to a job candidate being unwilling or unable to research a job with a given employer, the person may lack the motivation or the ability to do a self-appraisal. For example, the person may not have reflected on exactly what skills and abilities he or she brings to a job or on what rewards or outcomes he or she seeks from a job. Without such a self-appraisal, it is difficult for a job candidate to compare what a job requires and offers against what he or she offers and needs.

2. Rynes (1987) provides other evidence of the tendency of recruiters to tell applicants whatever they want to hear rather than the truth about a job.

3. See Reibstein (1987).

4. Although one could argue that an organization's recruitment behavior should only be labeled as being intentionally misleading if untrue information is given to job candidates, the author believes this is an overly restrictive view. In the author's opinion, if an organization knows that a job candidate is unfamiliar with an undesirable aspect of a position and fails to inform the candidate of the job feature, then the organization has intentionally misled the job candidate. In contrast, if a recruiter is unfamiliar with an undesirable feature of a position or if the recruiter thinks the applicant is aware of the feature, then the recruiter's failure to provide information about the job feature would clearly not be intentionally misleading behavior.

5. Although many of the examples in this chapter focus on the behavior of recruiters as being responsible for the incomplete and the inaccurate job information that job seekers typically possess, recruitment literature also plays a significant role. For example, Rynes and Boudreau (1986) cite research showing that the recruitment literature distributed by companies is frequently seen by job candidates as uninformative and unrealistically favorable. In contrast to such recruit perceptions, Rynes and Boudreau found that companies felt the information they presented was fairly accurate.

6. The facts presented about Dean Witter are based on a story by Siconolfi (1990).

7. Many organizations have provided individuals with realistic information about a job after they have accepted job offers or even after the individuals have started work (see Wanous and Colella, 1989, and Wanous, 1980).

8. A more detailed explanation of the value of providing an RJP can be found in Wanous (1978), Breaugh (1983), or in Chapter 6 of this text.

9. Readers who are interested in more information about the advertising strategy used by LA County/USC Medical Center should refer to Koch (1990a).

10. See Harlan (1990) for details.

11. See Carroll (1982) for details.

12. See Koch (1990c) for details.

13. See Rout (1979) for details.

14. See Rawlinson (1988a) for details.

15. See Buss (1985) for details. It should be noted that, unless the job opening is seen as highly desirable, most job candidates may not be willing to commit the time required by the organization for a job tryout. Readers who are interested in more detail on the use of programs such as those referred to in this section should refer to Bowes (1987), Phillips (1987), and Taylor (1988).

16. This discussion of employee referrals could have been included in the section titled "Less Commonly Used Approaches for Providing an RJP." However, because most

organizations do not specifically encourage their employees to provide an RJP, it was decided to discuss employee referrals in this section.

17. It should be noted that both of these studies have weaknesses, including small samples and the failure to include applicants who were not hired, that make drawing firm conclusions impossible (see Rynes, 1991).

18. Because only a portion of Wanous's recommendations are reviewed here, readers who are interested in the topic of RJPs are strongly encouraged to refer to his thought-provoking article (1989).

8

Major Government Regulations

If you were to ask a group of human resource executives for their reactions concerning the government regulations that affect employee recruitment, many would respond negatively. Among their concerns would be excessive paperwork, frequent new regulations, and unclear directives. These complaints notwithstanding, the fact remains that recruitment actions *are* subject to government regulation, and from the government's perspective, ignorance is no excuse for noncompliance. However, these regulations can also be viewed in a positive light: For one thing, they have forced employers to be more thoughtful in planning recruitment activities.

In covering the government regulations that affect recruitment, one is faced with the difficult task of trying to provide neither too little nor too much detail. The intent of this chapter is to provide a basic understanding of the major government regulations that affect recruitment and to offer sufficient information so that readers can research specific topics on their own. To facilitate such research, a number of particularly valuable reference works will be briefly discussed before specific regulations are addressed.

SOURCES OF INFORMATION ON GOVERNMENT REGULATIONS

For the reader who is somewhat unfamiliar with the government regulations that affect human resource practices, three books are recommended: Ledvinka and Scarpello's *Federal Regulation of Personnel and*

Human Resource Management (1991), Twomey's *A Concise Guide to Employment Law* (1990), and Sovereign's *Personnel Law* (1988). Although none of these books focuses heavily on the topic of recruitment per se, each provides a good introduction to a number of regulations that are relevant to recruitment practices. For readers who are interested in a more detailed treatment of government regulations, Schlei and Grossman's *Employment Discrimination Law* (1983) is an invaluable resource. A supplement updating this legal reference work is published periodically by the Bureau of National Affairs (BNA). In addition to these reference books, there are several professional journals such as the *Labor Law Journal*, practitioner-oriented journals such as *Recruitment Today*, and information services such as BNA's *Fair Employment Practice Series* that provide useful information.

Anyone who delves into the reference material just cited will discover that much of this literature assumes at least a basic knowledge of statistics. Although a mastery of a basic statistics book should provide an adequate statistical background for most individuals, for readers who are interested in acquiring greater expertise two more advanced texts are recommended: Baldus and Cole's *Statistical Proof of Discrimination* (1980) and Barnes and Conley's *Statistical Evidence in Litigation* (1986).[1]

In addition to the information sources cited above, an employer should also make use of several government agencies. For example, the Equal Employment Opportunity Commission (EEOC) and its state agency counterpart can provide expertise concerning the federal and the state laws that apply to recruitment. With regard to affirmative action requirements, the Office of Federal Contract Compliance Programs (OFCCP) is an important source of information for federal contractors.

MAJOR FAIR EMPLOYMENT PRACTICE STATUTES

In line with the focus of this text, this chapter emphasizes those laws that have particular relevance for the way in which recruitment should be conducted. In addition, executive orders that require particular recruitment activities will be discussed. In covering these selected laws and executive orders, an overview of the general nature of the regulations will first be provided. Chapter 9 contains a more in-depth treatment of the specific relevance of these regulations for an organization's recruitment practices.

Before examining the various regulations that affect recruiting, three important points should be noted. First, it should be emphasized that space constraints necessitate that the coverage of these regulations high-light central themes while glossing over legal subtleties. Second, it should be noted that few employment discrimination lawsuits are based solely on the way in which an employer recruited employees. Rather, it is more typical that the party bringing a lawsuit will use information concerning an employer's recruitment actions as part of its evidence supporting a claim of discrimination (an example of a court case in which recruitment information was combined with other types of data is provided in Chapter 9). Finally, the reader is cautioned that laws and executive orders can be amended or rescinded. Thus, an employer should remain alert for changes in government regulations.

Title VII of the Civil Rights Act of 1964

Title VII of the Civil Rights Act (as amended) prohibits discrimination in all employment decisions that is based on an individual's race, color, religion, sex, or national origin. Title VII regulates the actions of private employers, labor unions, employment agencies, and state and local governments. Although there are a few exemptions, in general, any employment decision made by an organization with fifteen or more employees is regulated by Title VII. Several key passages of Title VII are presented in Exhibit 8.1.

Although many of the points raised in the excerpts presented in Exhibit 8.1 are straightforward, the issues of bona fide occupational qualification and preferential treatment deserve comment. Section 703(e) states that an employer can legally justify basing an employment decision on an individual's religion, sex, or national origin when being of a particular religion, sex, or national origin is a bona fide occupational qualification (BFOQ) "reasonably necessary" for the normal operation of a business. Although specifics concerning BFOQ exceptions to Title VII will be saved for later in this chapter, the reader should note that there is *no* BFOQ justification for basing an employment decision on race or color.

Another important issue raised in Section 703 concerns giving preferential treatment to certain groups. Section 703(i) makes clear that Title VII does not prohibit a business operating on or near an Indian reservation from granting preferential treatment to Native Americans. Section 703(j) addresses preferential treatment in a more general context. Although the differences among preferential treatment, affirmative action, and reverse discrimination are often subtle, they should be considered by an employer in planning a recruitment strategy. In Chapter 9, court rulings concerning what is and is not legal preferential treatment will be reviewed.

EXHIBIT 8.1   Key excerpts from Title VII

Section 703

(a) It shall be an unlawful employment practice for an employer
   (1) to fail or refuse to hire or to discharge any individual, or otherwise to discriminate against any individual with respect to his compensation, terms, conditions, or privileges of employment, because of such individual's race, color, religion, sex, or national origin;. . . .

(e) Notwithstanding any other provision of this title, (1) it shall not be an unlawful employment practice for an employer to hire and employ employees . . . on the basis of his religion, sex, or national origin in those certain instances where religion, sex, or national origin is a bona fide occupational qualification reasonably necessary to the normal operation of that particular business or enterprise.

(i) Nothing contained in this title shall apply to any business or enterprise on or near an Indian reservation with respect to any publicly announced employment practice of such business or enterprise under which a preferential treatment is given to any individual because he is an Indian living on or near a reservation.

(j) Nothing contained in this title shall be interpreted to require any employer . . . to grant preferential treatment to any individual or to any group because of the race, color, religion, sex, or national origin of such individual or group on account of an imbalance which may exist with respect to the total number or percentage of persons of any race, color, religion, sex, or national origin employed by any employer . . . in comparison with the total number or the percentage of any persons of such race, color, religion, sex, or national origin in any community, State, section, or other area, or in the available work force in any community, State, section, or other area.

Section 704

(b) It shall be an unlawful employment practice for an employer, labor organization, employment agency, or joint labor-management committee . . . to print or publish or cause to be printed or published any notice or advertisement relating to employment by such an employer . . . indicating any preference, limitation, specification, or discrimination, based on race, color, religion, sex, or national origin, except that such a notice or advertisement may indicate a preference, limitation, specification, or discrimination based on religion, sex, or national origin when religion, sex, or national origin is a bona fide occupational qualification for employment.

In drafting Title VII, not only did Congress proscribe employment discrimination based on a person's race, color, religion, sex, or national origin, it also established the Equal Employment Opportunity Commission (EEOC) to administer the act (today the EEOC is also responsible for administering the Age Discrimination in Employment Act and the Equal Pay Act). The EEOC, which has regional offices throughout the country, has three primary duties: providing technical assistance to persons subject to Title VII, enforcement of the title, and information gathering.

In terms of technical assistance, the EEOC is responsible for developing written documents that describe what actions should be taken by an employer to comply with Title VII and for providing "to persons subject to this title such technical assistance as they may request to further their compliance with this title . . ." (Section 705(g)(3)). Such technical assistance frequently involves the EEOC answering telephone inquiries from employers concerning the soundness of various personnel practices.

With regard to the EEOC's enforcement role, three steps—investigation, conciliation, and litigation—may be involved.[2] During the investigation phase, the EEOC evaluates the validity of a complainant's accusation. Often an investigation involves interviews with company personnel and an examination of personnel records. If at the end of its investigation the EEOC concludes that there is "reasonable cause" to believe that discrimination occurred (i.e., "it is more likely than not," Schlei and Grossman, 1987, p. 216), it attempts to conciliate an agreement between the employer and the complainant. If the EEOC is unable to bring about an agreement, it can litigate the case. If the EEOC finds no reasonable cause, it must dismiss the charge. However, the case can still be pursued by a private attorney.

Concerning its information-gathering role, any private employer with 100 or more employees must annually file Form EEO-1 with the EEOC. This form reports the number of women and members of four minority groups (blacks, Asian Americans, Native Americans, and Hispanic Americans) an organization employs in nine different job categories in comparison to the number of nonminority males employed in these jobs. Similar forms must be filed by labor unions, educational institutions, and state and local governments. This information on work force composition is analyzed and "distributed to all EEOC offices and all contracting offices of federal, state, and local government agencies. The data then form the basis for statistical investigations, and can be retrieved in summary form by industry or for all reporting employers in the same immediate geographic area or state, or for the nation as a whole. This allows the comparison of an individual respondent with other respondents in the same industry drawing generally upon the same available work force" (Schlei and Grossman, 1983, pp. 936–937).

Age Discrimination in Employment Act of 1967

The Age Discrimination in Employment Act (as amended) prohibits age-based employment discrimination against any person who is forty years or older unless age is a legitimate BFOQ. An employer is covered by this act if it has twenty or more employees. With regard to employee recruitment, a key part of the ADEA is Section 4(e): "It shall be unlawful for an employer, labor organization, or employment agency to print or publish, or cause to be printed or published, any notice or advertisement relating to employment . . . indicating any preference, limitation, specification, or discrimination based on age."

Rehabilitation Act of 1973
and the Americans with Disabilities Act of 1990

Until the Rehabilitation Act was passed in 1973, employment discrimination against persons with disabilities was not illegal under federal law. The Rehabilitation Act made such discrimination illegal for companies receiving federal contracts. The Americans with Disabilities Act (ADA) extended the prohibition against discrimination against qualified individuals with a disability to most employers. These acts cover discrimination on the basis of (1) "a physical or mental impairment that substantially limits one or more major life activities," (2) a former impairment, or (3) a person's being regarded as having an impairment. Not only do the Rehabilitation Act and the ADA prohibit discrimination against qualified individuals with disabilities, they mandate that employers make "reasonable accommodations" for the disabled. Reasonable accommodations might include making facilities more accessible, acquiring special equipment, or modifying work schedules. Neither act requires accommodations that would create an "undue hardship" for an employer. In determining whether an accommodation creates an undue hardship, such things as the type of business and the cost of the accommodation are considered.

In terms of employee recruitment, the Rehabilitation Act is particularly important. Section 503, which is enforced by the Office of Federal Contract Compliance Programs (OFCCP), requires that contractors and subcontractors having contracts in excess of $2,500 with the federal government undertake affirmative action to provide employment opportunities for the disabled. Not surprisingly, a key step in providing employment opportunities for the disabled is making them aware of job opportunities—that is, recruitment.

The Immigration Reform and Control Act of 1986

The Immigration Reform and Control Act (IRCA) was intended to eliminate work opportunities that attract illegal aliens to the United States and to eliminate discrimination based on a person's national origin or citizenship status. To eliminate the hiring of illegal aliens, this act requires that employers verify the employment eligibility of everyone they hire and that job applicants supply documents that establish their identity (such as a driver's license) and their employment eligibility (such as a birth certificate). The IRCA's discrimination provision prohibits discrimination against anyone (except an unauthorized alien) in recruiting, hiring, or firing because of that individual's national origin or citizenship status. While the IRCA's national origin coverage overlaps with Title VII's, it is more encompassing (IRCA covers employers with four or more employees while Title VII only covers employers with fifteen or more workers).

Civil Service Reform Act of 1978

This act, which applies only to the federal government, states that "it is the policy of the United States . . . to provide a federal workforce reflective of the Nation's Diversity." In order to provide such a diverse workforce, every federal agency is required to implement programs that will increase the employment of all groups that are underrepresented in any of an agency's occupational categories. A key component of such programs is the vigorous recruitment of the members of underrepresented groups.

State Court Actions

Fair Employment Practice Laws

Although most employment discrimination lawsuits are brought under federal statutes, many states have laws that are similar to these federal laws and, in some cases, are even more restrictive. For example, Missouri has an employment law that closely parallels the wording of Title VII with the exception that it covers employers with as few as six employees. Individuals who are interested in researching a state's fair employment practice laws should contact the attorney general's office in that state.

Fraudulent Recruitment and Hiring

Although one generally thinks of fraud in contexts other than employment, there are an increasing number of cases in which disgruntled new employees claim that their organizations intentionally misrepresented what a position offered during the recruitment process.[3] In a case involving an allegation of fraudulent recruitment and hiring, the plaintiff must show:

- that the employer made a material representation that is false and is known to be false or made recklessly an assertion of fact without knowledge of its truth or falsity;
- that the misrepresentation was made with the intention that it would be acted on with damage;
- that the plaintiff relied on the representation and was induced to act on it; and
- that the plaintiff did not know the representation was false or could not have ascertained its falsity by the exercise of reasonable care (Gerson and Britt, 1984, p. 5).

From these four points, it is clear that an employer that intentionally exaggerates what a job offers could be vulnerable to a charge of fraud. For example, the Colorado Court of Appeals upheld a $250,000 jury award against Security Pacific Information Services for concealing information during the recruitment process (see Geyelin and Green, 1990). The court ruled that a company may not have to divulge its financial condition to every job applicant, but that full disclosure is required if a company has made statements to an applicant that would create a "false impression" about its outlook and the applicant's future employment prospects. In this case, the plaintiff was recruited by Security Pacific and moved from New Orleans to Denver to accept a job. In recruiting the plaintiff, the company presented a positive picture of itself and of the plaintiff's future with it. According to the court, Security Pacific concealed its financial losses and the "substantial, known risk" that the project the plaintiff was hired to work on might soon be abandoned and the plaintiff laid off.

Although one should not get the impression that claims of employment fraud are common or easy to prove, such cases are becoming more frequent and are being won. Furthermore, if a plaintiff is successful, not only can the damage award be sizable (one jury upheld a claim by a plaintiff that an oil company never intended to keep the promises it made to him while he was being recruited and awarded him a $10 million dollar breach-of-contract judgment), but the damage to a company's reputation from the media exposure can make recruiting employees more difficult in the future.

Negligent Hiring

The final type of state court action that merits attention is an emerging legal doctrine known as negligent hiring.[4] In this type of case, the charging party (e.g., an injured co-worker) argues that an organization is responsible for the damaging actions of its employees if it failed to conduct a reasonably thorough pre-employment background check that might have disclosed that the damaging action was likely to occur. A suit involving Avis Rent-a-Car (*Jones v. Avis Rent-a-Car*) provides a good example of a negligent hiring suit. The facts of this case were that Avis hired a person as a car washer who subsequently raped a secretary. Avis hired this person without investigating his background. During the trial, it was established that the car washer had a "known record as a rapist," a record that could easily have been discovered if Avis had conducted even a minimal background check. The court ruled that Avis had "a duty to other employees to investigate applicants selected" (Sovereign, 1984, p. 290) and awarded the secretary $750,000 in damages. Because pre-employment background checks are often a responsibility of those charged with recruiting, it is important that care be exercised in fulfilling this responsibility.

WHAT IS EMPLOYMENT DISCRIMINATION?

In the preceding section, the term *discrimination* was used repeatedly but never defined. The purpose of this section is to provide the reader with an understanding of what is meant by the term *discrimination*, particularly as it relates to recruitment activities. As will become apparent, describing what is and is not a discriminatory employment practice is not always easy, due partly to the fact that the term is not defined in Title VII (Ledvinka and Scarpello, 1991).

Disparate Treatment

According to Schlei and Grossman (1983), most employment discrimination cases may be analyzed under one of three definitions of discrimination: disparate treatment, failure to make reasonable accommodation, and disparate impact. The essence of a disparate treatment case is determining whether an employer *intentionally* treated individuals differently on the basis of a group characteristic, such as race, covered by an employment law. In some cases, disparate treatment is easy to recognize, as when a school system has a policy of refusing to hire women as principals. In other cases, it can be more difficult to determine whether discrimination was intentional. For example, is the fact that a company only recruited at Catholic colleges proof that it intended to discriminate on the basis of religion?

Most disparate treatment cases have involved the process by which employees were selected rather than the way in which they were recruited. However, the process for bringing a disparate treatment case involving recruitment actions closely parallels how one brings a disparate treatment selection case.[5] In terms of recruitment, the most likely type of disparate treatment case is one that involves the way in which an employer advertised or in some other way publicized a position. For example, Section 704(b) of Title VII and Section 4(e) of the Age Discrimination in Employment Act both make it an unlawful act to advertise for a position in such a way that indicates "any preference, limitation, specification, or discrimination" based on race, color, religion, sex, national origin, or age, unless religion, sex, national origin, or age is a bona fide occupational qualification for employment.

In a disparate treatment case, if the plaintiff can establish that an organization has recruited in a way that is likely to exclude members of a protected group, the employer will be asked to justify its recruitment strategy. Once the employer has offered a legitimate nondiscriminatory reason for the recruiting approach it used, the plaintiff is given an opportunity to show that the supposedly legitimate reason offered by the organization is, in fact, a pretext to mask intentional discrimination.

Bona Fide Occupational Qualification

In terms of recruitment, when an organization expresses a preference for members of a particular group in a job advertisement or recruits in such a way as to make it difficult for members of a protected group to become aware of a job opening, the employer generally will argue that being a member of the particular group it targeted is a bona fide occupational qualification that is necessary for the normal operation of the business. Although BFOQ exemptions to employment laws are infrequently granted, BFOQ exemptions have been accepted by the courts for certain reasons involving safety, authenticity, and privacy. In terms of safety, the courts have allowed an employer to limit its recruiting and hiring to certain types of individuals when either the safety of the public or of the employees was involved. For example, the courts have granted BFOQ exemptions to the Age Discrimination in Employment Act when it could be shown that younger people are less likely to have accidents than older individuals. In terms of authenticity, BFOQ exemptions are sometimes granted when it can be shown that being a member of a particular group is necessary for serving in a given job, such as an acting role that may require a person be a female. Finally, BFOQ exceptions have been granted for jobs that involve legitimate privacy concerns. For example, a health club seeking to fill a women's locker room attendant position could legitimately advertise for "a female locker room attendant."

Religious Exemptions to Title VII

Although it is difficult for an organization to justify considering a person's age, sex, or national origin in making an employment decision, it is easier to defend considering a person's religion because Section 702 of Title VII grants an exemption for religious activities. This exemption allows a school run by a religious denomination to hire only members of that religion as teachers if the teaching involves the propagation of certain religious beliefs. It also allows giving preferential treatment based on religion for jobs that do not involve religion-related duties. For example, in a 1987 case (*Amos v. Corporation of Presiding Bishop, Church of Jesus Christ of the Latter-Day Saints*) that involved a nonprofit enterprise run by a religious organization, the Supreme Court ruled that a religious organization had the right to employ only persons who were church members even though the job in question (building engineer) required no religious duties. Thus, it appears that religious organizations may be able to justify recruiting only job candidates who belong to that faith.

Reasonable Accommodation

Lawsuits alleging discrimination because of religion or handicap frequently involve a charge that an employer was unwilling to make reasonable accommodations as required by law. As noted earlier, in this type of lawsuit a crucial factor is the extent to which making accommodations creates an "undue hardship on the conduct of the employer's business" (Section 701(j) of Title VII). Determining the difference between "reasonable accommodation" and "undue hardship" involves a consideration of monetary costs and other factors. For example, if accommodating a person's religious observances (e.g., not scheduling a person to work on Sundays) infringed on other workers' rights (e.g., other workers are forced to work Sundays), then this may be seen as an unreasonable accommodation.

Disparate Impact

Many experts (see Schlei and Grossman, 1983) believe that when Congress passed Title VII it was only thinking of discrimination charges being brought under these first two definitions of discrimination. However, in its 1971 *Griggs v. Duke Power Company* ruling, the Supreme Court described yet another "theory" of discrimination under which a charge of employment discrimination could be brought: disparate impact. Unlike a disparate treatment case, which requires that a plaintiff establish by the majority of the evidence that an employer intended to discriminate (a difficult thing to prove), a disparate impact case does not require proving intent to discriminate. Rather, as stated in its *Griggs* opinion, the Supreme Court felt that Title VII "proscribes not only overt discrimination but also practices that are fair in form, but discriminatory in operation," that is, "an employment practice which operates to exclude Negroes" and that "cannot be shown to be related to job performance" is unlawful. (In *Wards Cove Packing Company v. Atonio,* the Supreme Court modified the requirements of a disparate impact case. This 1989 case as well as pending legislation to override its effects are discussed later in this chapter.)

Simply stated, in a disparate impact case, the plaintiff needs to present evidence that a seemingly neutral employment practice adversely affects members of a protected group (providing such evidence is referred to as making a prima facie case). Once evidence of adverse impact is presented, the defendant must demonstrate that the allegedly discriminatory practice is justified on business-related grounds.[6] The most common way to demonstrate that an employment practice has adverse impact against members of a protected group is the presentation of statistical evidence (which may also be used in a disparate treatment case). Two types of statistical evidence—pass–fail comparisons and population–work force comparisons—have frequently been introduced as evidence in disparate impact cases.

STATISTICAL EVIDENCE IN LAWSUITS

Pass–Fail Comparison Statistics

Pass–fail comparison statistics (also referred to as flow statistics) involve comparing the selection, promotion, or termination rates for different groups. For example, if a case involved a claim of racial discrimination in hiring against Hispanics, in order to establish a prima facie case (that is, show that a seemingly neutral selection device had adverse impact), the plaintiff would want to demonstrate that the hiring rate for Hispanics was significantly lower than the hiring rate for nonminorities.

Although the use of pass–fail comparison statistics may be appropriate in cases involving selection, promotion, or termination decisions, their use can be misleading in cases involving recruitment actions that are alleged to have had a discriminatory impact. For example, consider this scenario: Ninety nonminorities applied for a position and forty-five were hired; two minorities applied for the same job and one was hired. While the hiring rates for both groups are the same, the fact that so few minorities applied for jobs clearly raises suspicions. In deciding whether discrimination occurred, a key question is: "Why did so few minorities apply?" If a judge concluded the reason was because the employer consciously decided to recruit at schools that had few minority students, he or she might rule that flow statistics are not relevant. Similarly, if the judge decided that the employer had a reputation for discriminating (which discouraged minorities from applying), the court might also conclude that the use of flow statistics is inappropriate.

Although discriminatory recruitment might be one explanation for the small number of minority applicants, there could also be other explanations. Conceivably, the organization is located in an area in which few minorities live, or a job advertisement may have described job qualifications that few minorities possess. In attempting to determine whether discriminatory recruitment practices or legitimate reasons led to so few minorities applying, the effective use of population–work force comparison statistics can be crucial.[7]

Population–Work Force Comparison Statistics

In contrast to flow statistics, population–work force comparison statistics (also known as stock statistics) entail comparing "the availability of the protected group in the general population or labor market in a relevant geographic area with the percentage of that protected group in an employer's work force" (Schlei and Grossman, 1983, p. 1333). In *Teamsters v. United States* (1977), the Supreme Court ruled that the plaintiffs could show adverse impact by demonstrating a substantial statistical disparity between the number of minorities in the employer's work force and the number of minorities in the general population. A formula for computing population–work force comparison statistics and an example of their use is provided in Exhibit 8.2.

Given the importance of population–work force comparison statistics as evidence in discrimination cases involving recruitment issues, several factors that may influence whether a court accepts or rejects one's statistical analyses as demonstrating adverse impact must be discussed. As will become apparent from a consideration of these factors, anyone using stock statistics must make several choices, most of which involve the numbers incorporated into the right side of the formula presented in Exhibit 8.2.[8]

EXHIBIT 8.2   Population–work force comparison statistics: A formula and an example

Formula

Total number of minorities employed by the organization in the job		Total number of minorities in the population or work force in the relevant geographic area
———————————	*Compared to*	———————————
Total number of persons employed by the organization in the job		Total number of persons in the population or work force in the relevant geographic area

Example

20 minorities employed by the organization in the job		6,000 minorities in the work force in the relevant geographic area
———————————	*Compared to*	———————————
		40,000 individuals in the work force in the relevant geographic area
400 total employees in the job		
5% minority employment rate		15% minority work force rate

Source: Formula and example adapted from Schlei and Grossman (1983).

Types of Population Comparison Statistics

Although coming up with totals for the numerator and the denominator of the left side of this formula is not difficult, coming up with numbers to use in the right side of this formula can be. To date, parties generally have relied on three sources as input for the numerator and the denominator of the right side of this formula: general population data, general labor force data, and qualified labor force data. Each of these sources has advantages and disadvantages.[9] For example, while estimates of the number of minorities in the general population are readily available, for population–work force comparison purposes, these estimates are imprecise. "General population figures include children and persons over the normal retirement age, and because the ratio of children to adults differs substantially in different groups at different times and places, as does the ratio of older, retired people to active adults, distorted availability figures may result from the use of general population data rather than civilian labor force data" (Schlei and Grossman, 1983, p. 1353). In other words, an estimate based on general population data may overestimate or underestimate the number of persons in a particular group who are of working age. Overestimating the number of minorities in the population may lead to an incorrect inference of discrimination.

Because of the imprecision inherent in the use of general population data for computing population–work force comparison statistics, an employer would usually prefer to use general labor force data if possible. However, in some circumstances, general labor force data may also provide only a rough estimate for the numerator and the denominator of the right side of the population–work force comparison formula.[10] For example, general labor force statistics often do not provide specific information on minorities who have particular skills. Rather, most sources of general labor force statistics only break down the work force into broad occupational categories. While such broad categories may be sufficient for the needs of some employers, if an organization has a legitimate need for workers who possess specific skills, general labor force statistics clearly do not provide optimal population estimates. Furthermore, if the percentage of minorities who possess these relevant skills in the general work force is less than the percentage of nonminorities (which is frequently the case), then using general labor force data may lead to an erroneous inference of discrimination.[11]

One way in which an employer can avoid the imprecision of general labor force data when the job in question requires specific skills is to use qualified labor market data, that is, data on the number of minorities in the civilian labor force with particular skills. Unfortunately, qualified labor market information generally is not readily available (Baldus and Cole, 1987). For example, an employer may find it difficult to locate data on the number of Hispanics who are trained as occupational therapists and who live in the Detroit metropolitan area.

Sources of Population Comparison Data

Although a detailed discussion of the various sources of general population data, general labor force data, and qualified labor force data is beyond the scope of this text, an overview of a few sources is appropriate. With regard to general population data, a commonly used information source has been the U.S. Census Bureau. Because a complete census is conducted only every ten years, this information can become somewhat dated. Therefore, some employers have relied on another source of information on the general population, the Current Population Survey, which is also administered by the Census Bureau. In addition to these sources of general population data, this type of information is also frequently available from local, county, and state government offices.

In terms of acquiring general labor force data, one commonly used source is the Department of Labor's Bureau of Labor Statistics (BLS), which uses employment data gathered annually by the Census Bureau. This information is provided for large metropolitan areas, large cities, and smaller cities. In addition to the BLS data, local, county, and state agencies may also provide general labor market data.

As was previously noted, information on the qualified labor force is the most difficult type of data to get. For some occupations, this sort of information is compiled by professional associations and is made available to the general public. An employer may also get qualified labor force data by contracting with the Census Bureau. [12] In some cases, an employer may be able to get qualified labor force data (and general labor force data) from a regional office of the EEOC or the OFCCP.

Other Considerations in Using Population Comparison Data

In determining whether population comparison information is adequate for its purposes, an employer not only must be concerned with whether the right type of individuals have been targeted (e.g., those with the appropriate skill), it must also be concerned about the geographic scope of the statistical data. That is, an employer must "define the area from which applicants are likely to come absent discrimination" (Schlei and Grossman, 1983, p. 1361). In some circumstances, determining the proper geographic scope is easy. For example, if a city hospital recruited physicians nationwide, then the relevant population against which to compare the composition of the hospital's work force would be physicians in this country. If the hospital recruited nurses only from the metropolitan area, then its population comparison data base for this job should include only nurses living in the metropolitan area.

Although using population comparison data that reflect the geographic area in which an organization recruits may seem reasonable, such information is not always available. Furthermore, frequently an employer cannot state with certainty what is the precise geographic area from which it recruits. While specifying a geographic recruitment area may seem unimportant, the geographic boundaries that are specified can affect whether a judge draws an inference of discrimination from population–work force comparison data. [13]

The preceding discussion of the factors that can influence whether population–work force comparison statistics will be viewed as persuasive evidence by a judge may lead the reader to conclude that the courts have created an impossible standard to meet. In fact, in *Hazelwood School District v. United States* (1977), the U.S. Supreme Court acknowledged this concern: "Absolute precision in the analysis of market data is too much to expect." Instead of "absolute precision," the Court noted it expected "refined" population–work force comparison statistics that are sufficiently accurate to provide meaningful comparison information for determining whether employment discrimination has taken place (Schlei and Grossman, 1983). [14,15]

Nonstatistical Evidence

In a trial, once a plaintiff has made a prima facie case (by, for example, producing a job advertisement that expresses a preference for members of a particular group or showing that the number of minorities in a company's work force is much lower than one would expect based on population–work force comparison statistics), the employer is then given an opportunity to defend the employment practice that is being attacked. In some cases, an organization may argue a BFOQ exception. In other cases, an employer may try to justify the allegedly discriminatory practice on business-related grounds. Once the defendant has presented its case, the plaintiff has the opportunity to rebut it (e.g., show that an accommodation would not create an undue hardship).

Although the preceding section emphasized the importance of statistical evidence, experts agree that it is always desirable to buttress statistical evidence with nonstatistical proof. For the plaintiff, one of the most important sources of nonstatistical evidence in cases involving recruitment practices is verbal testimony from applicants and employees. Such testimony often describes differential treatment during the recruitment process, such as describing a job opening in a very negative fashion to women for the purpose of discouraging them from applying. In terms of the defendant's rebutting a prima facie case, evidence concerning the presence or absence of an affirmative action program is often weighed heavily by the court. In addition, "the courts have also considered the employer's general reputation, the frequency with which discrimination charges are filed against the employer, and clear evidence of animus" (Schlei and Grossman, 1987, p. 328).

WARDS COVE PACKING COMPANY v. ATONIO AND PENDING CIVIL RIGHTS LEGISLATION

Wards Cove Packing Company v. Atonio (1989)

In the discussion of disparate impact earlier in this chapter, the emphasis was placed on the Supreme Court's ruling in *Griggs v. Duke Power Company* (1971). In its *Wards Cove* ruling, the Court modified (some experts would say clarified) the rules for bringing a disparate impact case. Although there is some disagreement among legal scholars concerning the significance of the *Wards Cove* case, the attention it has attracted and the pending legislation it has spurred justifies its brief review.

Wards Cove Packing Company is an Alaskan cannery. Jobs at the cannery can be classified as being either unskilled positions on the cannery line or skilled positions such as machinists and engineers. For the most part, the unskilled jobs were held by Alaskan Natives and Filipinos and the skilled jobs, which pay more, were filled by white workers. The nonwhite cannery workers pointed out the numerical imbalance between the racial composition of the skilled and unskilled jobs, and charged that this racial disparity was due to the company's recruitment, hiring, and employment practices, including nepotism, a failure to promote from within, and subjective decision making. The company argued that the racial disparity resulted from a hiring agreement it had with the predominantly nonwhite union that represented the unskilled workers.

In a 5–4 decision, the U.S. Supreme Court clarified some of the standards for proving disparate impact. First, the Court ruled that merely demonstrating a statistical racial disparity between the group of skilled and unskilled employees did not constitute proof of disparate impact. Instead, the Court reiterated its long-standing view that the proper comparison was between the racial composition of those in the skilled positions and the racial composition of the persons in the relevant labor market who had the qualifications and interest in performing these jobs. Second, the Court ruled that it was not sufficient for the plaintiffs to simply allege that a company's employment practices had disparate impact. Instead, the Court said the plaintiffs must specify which employment practice had the adverse impact and then link this practice to the resulting racial imbalance (the Court felt that, given the EEOC's recordkeeping requirements, making such a link should not be too difficult for the plaintiffs). Finally, the Supreme Court addressed what an employer needs to do to rebut a charge of discrimination if the plaintiff has established that an employment practice has adverse impact. In *Griggs v. Duke Power*, the Court had ruled that an effective rebuttal would require the employer to show proof of the business necessity of the practice. However, in its *Wards Cove* decision, the Court ruled that an employer only had to show that "a challenged practice serves, in a significant way, the legitimate employment goals of the employer." The Court went on to state that, while an insubstantial justification will not suffice, there is no requirement that the challenged practice be "essential" or indispensable" to the employer's business.

Pending Civil Rights Legislation

Not surprisingly, many legal scholars and legislators were upset with the Supreme Court's ruling in the *Wards Cove* case. Many experts felt that the Court had substantially increased the difficulty of a plaintiff winning a disparate impact case. In 1990, the U.S. Congress passed what came to be known as the Civil Rights Restoration Act. Proponents of this legislation said that it would have in essence reinstituted a *Griggs* standard for bringing a disparate impact case (that is, a plaintiff would not need to pinpoint the specific discriminatory employment practice; if adverse impact was demonstrated, the employer would be required to show business necessity). President Bush vetoed this bill, and Congress was not able to override his veto. At present, both the House of Representatives and the Senate are working on civil rights legislation. Whether either of these bills or some combination thereof becomes law is uncertain at this time.[16]

AN OVERVIEW OF THE LITIGATION PROCESS

Although it is not necessary to become an expert on the flow of events during the litigation process, it is important that anyone who may be involved in making recruitment decisions have a basic understanding of this process. Although the litigation process can differ slightly depending on whether an action is brought in federal or state court, certain activities are common to both judicial systems.

The first step in the formal litigation process is the filing of a *complaint* with the relevant state or federal court. In a complaint, the plaintiff (the party filing the complaint) asks the court for legal redress for an alleged illegal act committed by an employer (the defendant). A typical complaint addresses the illegal action the defendant is alleged to have taken (including what law has been violated), the result of the alleged illegal action, and the relief sought by the plaintiff. As an example, a complaint might state that XYZ Company did not publicize openings it had for sales personnel, but rather relied solely on its current sales force to refer job candidates. Because XYZ Company does not at present have any minority sales personnel, the complaint alleges that this recruitment approach resulted in qualified minorities (including the plaintiff) not hearing about the job openings and, therefore, not applying for them. To redress this wrong, the plaintiff seeks a sales position with XYZ Company.

Once a court has processed a complaint, the defendant is notified of the lawsuit, receives a copy of the complaint, and is asked to respond. Often, the time frame for a response is twenty to thirty days. Therefore, upon receiving a complaint, an employer should contact legal counsel quickly. If a response is not received in a timely manner, the defendant runs the risk of a default judgment (a judge ruling against the employer without it having an opportunity to defend itself).

The Pretrial Discovery Process

Following the filing of a defendant's response to a complaint, the *pretrial discovery* process begins. In a lawsuit involving employee recruitment, pretrial discovery will generally focus on those persons involved in recruiting and on company records documenting recruitment actions. During the discovery process, an employer should expect to receive *interrogatories* from the plaintiff's attorney. Interrogatories are written questions that are used to obtain information relevant to the case. Some of the questions that might be asked in a lawsuit involving recruitment are: "How did the employer publicize the job opening?" "Why did it choose this approach?" "What steps were taken to bring the opening to the attention of minorities and women?" "What are the backgrounds (e.g., sex, race) of the persons involved in recruiting for the position in question?"

Following the receipt of answers to interrogatories, the attorney for the plaintiff will generally take *depositions* from company officials who were involved in recruiting. Depositions also may be taken from employees who have recently been hired and from persons who applied for jobs but were not hired. A deposition entails an individual responding to a series of questions from the opposing attorney while under oath. A word-for-word transcript of the deposition is taken by a court reporter. By taking a deposition, a lawyer can determine how a person will respond to various questions. Thus, the attorney is better able to determine whether to call the individual as a witness and, if so, what line of questioning to use.

In most discrimination cases, company documents and records are important evidence. Therefore, an employer should expect that it will be asked by the plaintiff to turn over a variety of company documents. If the employer refuses, the plaintiff's attorney may ask the trial judge to order the defendant to produce the requested documents.

Personnel Record-Keeping and Reporting Requirements

Because access to personnel records is often essential for the plaintiff in building a discrimination case, one might assume that an employer would be wise to keep minimal records of its personnel activities. However, an organization does not have a choice of what records to keep. Federal regulations require the retention of certain types of information for fixed periods of time (in its *Wards Cove* decision, the Supreme Court emphasized the importance of employers keeping the records mandated by the EEOC). While an in-depth discussion of these various record-keeping requirements is beyond the scope of this text (see *Personnel Administrator,* 1985), the complexity of record-keeping requirements and the consequences of failing to keep required records should be addressed briefly.

Record-keeping can be complex because different regulations require that different types of information be kept for different lengths of time. For example, Title VII requires few employment records to be kept but mandates that any record an employer chooses to make be kept for six months from the date of making the record or taking the personnel action, whichever is later (if a lawsuit is filed, an employer must keep all records relevant to the charge until a final disposition of the case is reached). In contrast, the Age Discrimination in Employment Act requires that certain records such as job advertisements be kept for one year while other information such as payroll records must be kept for three years.

Because different federal regulations require different information to be kept and have different retention period requirements, it is important that those responsible for record-keeping be familiar with the specific reporting requirements of each regulation. With regard to federal laws, the inability to produce required personnel records can result in a judge assuming that the information, if it could be produced, would be damaging to the defendant. In terms of executive orders (which are discussed in the next section), the failure to keep adequate records can result in the loss of government contracts and/or a prohibition against bidding on future contracts.

Pretrial Settlements and Trials

As a result of the pretrial discovery process, the attorneys for both the plaintiff and the defendant should have a reasonably clear picture of the strength of each side's case. Not surprisingly, if either side believes it has a strong case, it will not be interested in negotiating a settlement prior to trial unless the terms are very favorable. However, in most lawsuits, each side's case will have some strengths and some weaknesses; thus, both sides may be unsure of the outcome of a trial. Due to such uncertainty, both sides are often interested in arriving at a pretrial settlement (if the EEOC is involved, attempts at negotiation are mandated).[17]

If the two sides are not able to resolve their dispute through pretrial negotiations, then a trial is held. In a typical employment discrimination trial, each side will introduce a variety of different documents (such as personnel records and statistical analyses) into evidence and have factual and expert witnesses testify.[18] As should be apparent from material presented earlier in this chapter, the exact nature of a trial will vary. For example, in a case involving an allegation that an employer failed to make a reasonable accommodation for an individual's disability, the plaintiff's attorney will try to prove that the accommodation would not create an undue hardship for the business and that with this accommodation the plaintiff could successfully perform the job. In contrast, the defendant's attorney will typically try to persuade the court that the accommodation would create a business hardship and/or that even with the accommodation the plaintiff would not be able to successfully perform the job. In a disparate treatment case, the plaintiff will try to convince the court that the employer intentionally discriminated against members of a protected group. In rebuttal, in this type of case, the defendant will try to show that requiring membership in a particular group was a BFOQ or that no intentional discrimination occurred. Finally, in a disparate impact case, the plaintiff will try to prove that an employment practice had adverse impact against members of a protected group. In turn, the defendant will try to establish that there was a legitimate reason for the use of the allegedly discriminatory employment practice. Ultimately, depending on the type of case, either a judge (as in a Title VII case) or a jury (as in an Age Discrimination in Employment case) will have to determine whether the preponderance of the evidence supports the plaintiff or the defendant.[19]

FEDERAL REGULATIONS REQUIRING
AFFIRMATIVE ACTION

As commonly used, the term *equal employment opportunity* refers to a situation in which a person's race, color, sex, religion, national origin, or age has no bearing on an employment decision. *Affirmative action* entails more than providing a work environment free from discrimination. Affirmative action involves an employer taking the initiative to recruit, hire, and promote members of protected groups (Ledvinka and Scarpello, 1991). Although it is clear that an affirmative action program requires that an employer make an extra effort to recruit, hire, and promote members of protected groups, there is considerable disagreement over just what an affirmative action program should entail. In particular, there has been controversy over the point at which making an extra effort to recruit and hire minorities makes an employer vulnerable to a charge of so-called reverse discrimination. While a detailed discussion of what affirmative action measures an employer can take and still remain within the law has obvious importance for employee recruitment, before this complex topic (in Schlei and Grossman, 1983, the chapter on "Reverse Discrimination and Affirmative Action" runs ninety-five pages) is addressed, a brief review of selected federal statutes and executive orders mandating affirmative action is needed.

Unlike the federal laws that were reviewed earlier, executive orders are issued by the President without the approval of Congress. The executive orders discussed in this chapter require that a contractor or subcontractor doing business with the federal government sign a contract that includes both nondiscrimination and affirmative action clauses.[20] If a contractor does not comply with the nondiscrimination or affirmative action sections of this contract, its current contract can be canceled and it can be barred from bidding on future government contracts. The Office of Federal Contract Compliance Programs (OFCCP) is responsible for administering most of the executive orders discussed in this section.

Executive Order 11246 as Amended

In terms of employee recruitment, Executive Order 11246 (as amended) has had the most impact on organizations. Fundamentally, Executive Order 11246 prohibits a federal contractor that is subject to the order (doing more than $10,000 of business with the federal government in a twelve-month period) from considering a person's race, color, religion, sex, or national origin in making any employment decision (Executive Order 11141 covers age). In addition, Executive Order 11246 requires that larger federal contractors (those with fifty or more employees doing $50,000 or more business with the federal government) develop and implement written affirmative action plans for recruiting, hiring, and promoting women and minorities whenever these groups are "underutilized" in the employer's work force, regardless of whether there was prior discrimination. The specifics of what a formal affirmative action plan should include were delineated by the OFCCP in what has come to be known as Revised Order No. 4.

Although the specific form that an affirmative action plan should take differs somewhat depending on the nature of the business relationship (e.g., construction versus nonconstruction contractors) between the employer and the federal government, three basic steps are involved. First, a contractor conducts a utilization analysis; this involves comparing the number of women and minorities it employs with their availability in the relevant labor market. Where there is underutilization, a contractor must establish goals and timetables for eliminating it. In addition, the contractor must develop and implement specific action plans for attaining these goals within the time frame established.

Although this three-step process of conducting a utilization analysis, establishing goals and timetables, and developing action plans may appear straightforward, this is not the case. In particular, conducting the utilization analysis can be a complex process. In order for an employer to compare the composition of its current work force with that of the available labor supply, it first must conduct a "work force analysis." This involves the contractor arraying job titles from lowest-paid to highest-paid within each business unit (in some cases, job titles are grouped according to job family or discipline). Following this, for each job title, the total number of job incumbents, the total number of male and female job incumbents, and the total number of male and female incumbents within each of the following groups is computed: blacks, Spanish-surnamed Americans, Native Americans, and Orientals.

Having arrayed its current work force, a contractor looks for "underutilization" of minorities or females. As defined by Revised Order No. 4, underutilization is "having fewer minorities or women in a particular job group than would reasonably be expected by their availability." A job group refers to a group of jobs having similar content, wage rates, and opportunities. In determining the availability of minorities and women,

Revised Order No. 4 has different stipulations for construction and non-construction ("service") contractors. The process that nonconstruction contractors must undertake is more complex and will be discussed first.

In determining the availability of minorities and women, Revised Order No. 4 states that nonconstruction contractors should consider at least eight factors separately for minorities and females. For minorities these eight factors are presented in Exhibit 8.3 The factors for assessing female underutilization are very similar to the eight factors for minorities. As has been noted by Ledvinka and Scarpello (1991), deriving an availability estimate from a consideration of these eight factors is a difficult and imprecise process. Depending on the relative weights the employer attaches to these eight factors, different availability estimates can emerge. In determining whether there is underutilization, the OFCCP has generally applied an "80 percent rule." According to this rule, if a contractor's work force analysis shows that the percentage of its female (minority) work force for a given job group is at least 80 percent of that available in the relevant labor pool (e.g., those having the requisite skills to do the job in the appropriate geographic area), then no underutilization has occurred. A simplified example of a work force analysis is presented in Exhibit 8.4. In a more complete work force analysis, rather than grouping the four minority groups described above together under the heading "Minority,"

EXHIBIT 8.3 Eight factors for determining minority availability

---

(1) The minority population of the labor area surrounding the facility;

(2) The size of the minority unemployment force in the labor area surrounding the facility;

(3) The percentage of the minority work force as compared with the total work force in the immediate labor area;

(4) The general availability of minorities having the requisite skills in the immediate labor area;

(5) The availability of minorities having the requisite skills in an area in which the contractor can reasonably recruit;

(6) The availability of promotable and transferable minorities within the contractor's organization;

(7) The existence of training institutions capable of training persons in the requisite skills; and

(8) The degree of training that the contractor is reasonably able to undertake as a means of making all job classes available to minorities.

EXHIBIT 8.4   Work force analysis

	Number in Current Work Force				Utilization (%)		Availability(%)		Underutilized	
	Total	Male	Female	Minority	Female	Minority	Female	Minority	Female	Minority
Faculty	355	254	101	18	28.5	5.1	35.1	14.5	No[a]	Yes
Humanities	110	66	44	8	40.0	7.3	43.5	12.4	No	Yes
Social Sciences	77	58	19	3	24.7	3.9	41.2	13.2	Yes	Yes
Math/ Physical Sciences	75	60	15	4	20.0	5.3	26.4	16.3	Yes	Yes
Education	39	26	13	2	33.3	5.1	45.5	15.4	Yes	Yes
Business	54	44	10	1	18.5	1.9	20.0	19.5	No[a]	Yes

[a]Although the percentage of females available is greater than the percentage of females utilized, based on the 80 percent rule used by the OFCCP (see text), technically there is not underutilization.

Note: The data presented in this table represent a simplified version of a work force analysis that was part of the affirmative action plan of a public university. To save space and reduce complexity, data are only presented for minorities in total rather than by subgroup (e.g., blacks). The availability data are from the National Research Council, Office of Scientific and Engineering Personnel, Doctorate Records File.

data for each of these four groups would be presented for both their utilization and their availability.

Because the focus of this text is on recruitment, there is no need to dwell on the complexities of estimating labor force availability for affirmative action purposes. However, what is important is that one of the eight factors to be considered in determining labor force availability (see Exhibit 8.3) specifically involves external recruiting (Factor 5) and one directly involves internal recruitment (Factor 6).

For those job groups where utilization falls short of availability, a nonconstruction contractor must develop goals, timetables, and affirmative action steps to correct for this underutilization. According to Revised Order No. 4, the goals "may not be rigid and inflexible quotas, which must be met, but must be targets reasonably attainable." According to the OFCCP, a contractor's compliance will not be judged solely on whether it reaches goals. Rather, the OFCCP will examine the contents of a contractor's affirmative action plan, its adherence to the plan, and its good-faith efforts to reach the program's goals within the timetables established (Schlei and Grossman, 1983). In setting goals, the OFCCP requires both annual and "ultimate" goals. For job groups where underutilization exists, annual goals are expressed in two ways: the number of protected group members to be placed during the year and as a percentage placement rate (this must exceed the availability percentage). The ultimate goal established is parity with the availability percentage in the relevant labor market. A time frame for reaching this ultimate goal must be included in the affirmative action plan.

In completing this abbreviated coverage of setting goals and timetables, it should be emphasized that in deriving both goals and timetables, it is essential that a contractor consider such factors as whether its business is likely to expand or contract in coming years. For example, a contractor who anticipates rapid growth may be able to reach availability levels much more quickly than a contractor who expects little or no growth.

As was noted earlier, the process of determining underutilization and of establishing goals differs depending on whether one is a construction or nonconstruction contractor. The major difference involves the determination of the availability of minorities and women in the labor market. Unlike the process described above that a nonconstruction contractor must follow, construction contractors do not undertake such a labor market analysis. Rather, the OFCCP regularly conducts studies to determine the availability in the labor market of minorities and women. Based on these labor market studies, the OFCCP establishes minority and female hiring goals for contractors doing business in various geographic areas.

Whether an employer is a construction or nonconstruction contractor, its affirmative action plan must carefully describe the various steps it will take to achieve its goals within the time frame it has established or the OFCCP has set. Revised Order No. 4 goes into considerable detail on what sorts of actions are expected from a contractor. For example, Revised Order No. 4 makes clear that the affirmative action plan must have support from top management. As a sign of this support, a contractor is expected to appoint a director of the affirmative action program and to allocate staff and budget for carrying out the various actions called for in the affirmative action plan. These actions can be categorized under three major headings: recruitment, removing unnecessary obstacles to employment, and auditing the affirmative action plan.

Concerning recruitment, Revised Order No. 4 goes into great detail on specific recruitment actions that a contractor should take (such as "informing all recruiting sources verbally and in writing of company policy, stipulating that these sources actively recruit and refer minorities and women for all positions listed"). An in-depth treatment of these recommended recruitment practices is presented in the next chapter. In terms of removing unnecessary obstacles to employment, actions a contractor should take include validating any selection device that disproportionately screens out women and minorities and carefully selecting and training those involved in making employment decisions to reduce the likelihood of bias. In addition, to accommodate the needs of minorities and women, a contractor should consider such actions as offering transportation and allowing flexible work hours. With regard to auditing the affirmative action program, a contractor should monitor data on recruitment, placement, transfers, promotions, and terminations to ensure that a nondiscriminatory policy is carried out. A contractor should also require formal reports from department managers that address progress being made to meet affirmative action objectives.

Rehabilitation Act of 1973

Although in developing an affirmative action plan most employers are concerned with the requirements of Executive Order 11246, they also need to be aware that the Rehabilitation Act and the Vietnam Era Veterans Readjustment Assistance Act also contain affirmative action stipulations. For example, in addition to its prohibition of discrimination against the handicapped by federal contractors, the Rehabilitation Act requires certain affirmative action steps. For small contractors (those holding contracts between $2,500 and $50,000), the required affirmative action effort is minimal (e.g., posting notices of the contractor's affirmative action obligation to employ qualified handicapped applicants). However, for larger contractors (those with fifty or more employees and a contract of $50,000 or more), a much more formalized affirmative action effort is mandated by the Rehabilitation Act.

Larger contractors must establish and implement a written affirmative action plan. Some of the requirements of such a plan are: (1) a careful review of the physical and mental qualifications for jobs to ensure that those that might screen out the disabled are job-related, (2) making reasonable accommodations to the physical and mental limitations of an employee or applicant unless the employer can show that such accommodations would present an undue hardship, (3) an external recruitment program involving such activities as recruiting at schools that participate in the training of the handicapped or contacting social service agencies that might be able to refer disabled individuals, that demonstrates a contractor's willingness to employee the handicapped, (4) an internal dissemination of information that demonstrates an employer's commitment to the handicapped (meetings with managers to explain their responsibility, and so on), and (5) the appointment of a director of the affirmative action program, who should be given top management support and the staff necessary to implement the affirmative action program.

Vietnam Era Veterans' Readjustment Assistance Act of 1974

The Vietnam Era Veterans' Readjustment Assistance Act is also enforced by the OFCCP. This act requires all employers with government contracts of $10,000 or more to take affirmative action to employ and advance disabled veterans and qualified veterans of the Vietnam era (those on active duty between August 5, 1964, and May 7, 1975). As part of this affirmative action program, all covered employers are required to list all suitable job openings with the appropriate local office(s) of the state employment service and to file with the appropriate office periodic reports detailing the hiring record for that period. Included in such a report must be information on: (1) the number of individuals hired during that period, (2) the number of nondisabled veterans of the Vietnam era hired, (3) the number of disabled veterans of the Vietnam era hired, and (4) the total number of disabled veterans hired.

For those contractors with a contract of $50,000 or more and fifty or more employees, a written affirmative action plan is required. The specifics of such a plan closely parallel what is required under the Rehabilitation Act. For example, a contractor must make reasonable accommodations to the physical limitations of a disabled veteran. The contractor must disseminate both internally (e.g., by means of the company newsletter) and externally (e.g., by contacting veterans groups) its desire to hire veterans. Special recruitment efforts should also be undertaken, such as participating in veterans' "job fairs" or cooperating in work–study programs with the Veterans Administration's rehabilitation facilities.

SUMMARY

In this chapter, information on several government regulations that have a direct bearing on employee recruitment activities have been discussed. Failure to comply with these regulations can result in costly court judgments, loss of federal contracts, and/or damage to an organization's reputation. While the coverage in this chapter may have appeared overly legalistic to some readers, the information presented is important because it provides the foundation for Chapter 9, which more directly addresses how these federal regulations affect the way an employer recruits.

NOTES

1. The book by Baldus and Cole is updated frequently by means of a cumulative supplement. Baldus and Cole use hypothetical data sets to demonstrate the appropriate use of statistics. In addition, they discuss actual court cases in which statistical procedures were used appropriately and inappropriately. Barnes and Conley's book, although written for attorneys, is a valuable source for those in the human resources area. Although the book provides an in-depth treatment of various issues relevant to statistical proof in a court case, its major contribution is its treatment of how statistical evidence should be presented and attacked in a legal proceeding.

2. Before initiating this three-step process, the EEOC must comply with deferral restrictions placed on it by Title VII. More specifically, on becoming aware of a possible violation of Title VII (e.g., a person files a written complaint), the EEOC must refer the complaint to the state or local fair employment practices agency, if there is one, that is responsible for that geographic area.

3. Fraudulent recruitment and hiring suits can be brought under either contract or tort law. For example, a new employee may claim that he and his employer had a formal employment agreement, or contract (written or unwritten), that the employer never intended to live up to. A tort involves a claim by a person that he was harmed by a wrongful but not necessarily criminal act of another party. Tort law does not require the existence of

a contract. Thus, in a tort case a new employee would not allege that an employment contract existed. Rather, the plaintiff would charge that he was injured by an employer because of a wrongful act it committed during the recruitment process. For example, a plaintiff might charge that, by lying to her about its financial instability, a company caused her to resign from a better job. Readers who are interested in more information on the topic of fraudulent recruitment should refer to articles by Gerson and Britt (1984), Reibstein (1987), Geyelin and Green (1990), and Laabs (1991a).

4. Negligent hiring suits involve tort claims. With regard to negligent hiring, the plaintiff must show that he or she was harmed and that the employer failed to exercise reasonable care in hiring the employee who caused the harm. Readers who are interested in more information on negligent hiring should refer to articles by Connolly (1986) and Glover and King (1989).

5. According to case law, the first step in proving a disparate treatment charge of discrimination in hiring is to establish a prima facie case, that is, suggestive evidence that a violation of a statute has occurred. In *McDonnell Douglas Corp. v. Green* (1973), the Supreme Court outlined a framework for establishing a prima facie claim. This so-called McDonnell Douglas test requires that plaintiffs establish: "(1) membership in a protected group; (2) that they applied and were qualified for a job for which the employer was seeking applicants; (3) that despite their qualifications, they were rejected; and (4) that after their rejection, the position remained open and the employer continued to seek applications from persons of complainant's qualifications" (Schlei and Grossman, 1983, p. 1298). Once the plaintiffs have established a prima facie case, the defendant must offer a legitimate, nondiscriminatory reason for its actions (e.g., for not hiring the plaintiffs). Following the defendant's articulation of such a reason, the plaintiffs are given a chance to show that the supposedly legitimate reason stated by the employer is, in fact, a pretext to mask intentional discrimination. In attempting to convince a judge or a jury that it did not intentionally discriminate against members of a protected group, the lawyers for an employer will not only introduce information directly related to the specific employment decision, but will also generally introduce information that indicates the employer's commitment to fair employment practice. For example, witnesses may testify about the employer's affirmative action efforts.

6. In past disparate impact cases, the courts have allowed organizations to justify the use of an allegedly discriminatory employment practice as being necessary for business reasons in one of two ways: empirical validity and content validity. Simply stated, an empirical validity defense involves an organization demonstrating a statistically important relationship between how one scores on the allegedly discriminatory practice (e.g., a selection device) and how that individual performs on important job criteria. A content validity defense does not involve showing such an empirical relationship. Rather, a content validity defense entails an employer convincing the court (e.g., through the presentation of job analysis information and the testimony of job experts) that the allegedly discriminatory practice is justified for business-related reasons. Because of the scope of this text, this treatment of these two validation approaches is overly simplified. Readers who seek more information about these validation strategies should refer to Arvey and Faley (1988), Gatewood and Feild (1990), or the *Uniform Guidelines on Employee Selection Procedures* (1978).

7. Although it is generally the plaintiff who tries to convince a judge that population–work force comparison statistics should be used instead of applicant flow statistics in cases alleging "inadequate" recruitment, in some cases, an organization (the defendant) may argue for the merits of population–work force comparison statistics. This generally occurs when

the employer has an aggressive affirmative action program that the employer alleges has resulted in the average minority who applies being less qualified than the average nonminority who applies. Given this allegation, the employer will argue that minorities should be selected at a lower rate, and therefore a comparison of selection rates for investigating discrimination is not appropriate. In cases where the employer argues that "aggressive" recruiting efforts resulted in minority candidates being less qualified than nonminority candidates, the burden of proof will be on the organization to document that an aggressive affirmative action recruitment campaign took place and that minority candidates were actually less qualified.

8. This formula will need to be modified slightly depending on the unique circumstances of the case (e.g., whether the position requires certain job skills and/or experience).

9. Readers who are interested in a more detailed discussion of these advantages and disadvantages should refer to Chapter 36 of Schlei and Grossman (1983).

10. Because individuals in the military are considered unavailable for civilian positions, it is important that one's source of general labor force statistics not include military personnel. Fortunately, most sources of general labor force statistics do not include those in the military. It also should be noted that the use of general labor force information has been criticized because this information generally does not include persons who have become discouraged and stopped looking for employment.

11. For purposes of discussion, it is assumed that these skill requirements can be shown to be job-related. If these requirements are not job-related, the employer may be in violation of Title VII and other discrimination laws.

12. Bamberger (1983) provides an excellent discussion of how an organization can acquire reasonably precise qualified labor force data from the Census Bureau. For example, the Census EEO-1 file contains information on 503 occupations by selected demographic categories. According to Bamberger, this information is available for all SMSAs, all counties, and incorporated places of 50,000 or more inhabitants. However, getting access to the precise information an employer needs can be expensive. An employer must contract with the Census Bureau to run whatever analyses it needs.

13. In general, the geographic area will be smallest for lower-paying jobs and the broadest for executive positions, for which an applicant would be expected to relocate. As a way of determining the proper geographic scope for population comparison data, the courts have generally accepted geographic boundaries that are based on the addresses of job applicants. In contrast, the courts have not been inclined to accept the use of the employees' addresses for determining geographic boundaries because past discrimination in recruitment may have affected who was hired (Schlei and Grossman, 1987).

14. Several of the principles presented in this section were drawn from the Supreme Court decision in *Hazelwood School District v. United States* (1977). In this case, which involved claims of racial discrimination in the hiring of teachers, the Supreme Court addressed the use of population–work force comparison data in considerable detail. Specifically, the Supreme Court noted that: (1) if the job in question requires special qualifications, qualified labor market information is preferred over general population data; (2) in determining the relevant geographic area from which applicants are likely to come absent discrimination, such factors as commuting patterns, the availability of public transportation, and the geographic scope of the employer's recruiting practices should be considered; and (3) possibly discriminatory acts that occurred prior to the passage of a statute or prior to the charge filing period should not be included in statistical analyses introduced into evidence.

15. Baldus and Cole (1980, 1987) present an excellent discussion of how an organiza-

tion can develop population comparison information that is likely to be viewed as sound by the courts. In particular, Baldus and Cole discuss and provide numerous examples of the creation of "proxy" populations (i.e., population comparison data bases that are "corrected" for the effects of contaminants).

16. For the purpose of this text, the pending civil rights legislation was discussed in relation to the Court's *Wards Cove* decision. In reality, it addresses several recent Court decisions. In drafting legislation, senators such as John Danforth have attempted to reach an acceptable compromise on such issues as (1) whether damages should be allowed if intentional discrimination is proven, (2) whether the legislation is a "quota bill" (i.e., encourages/requires preferential treatment in some circumstances), (3) whether the plaintiff is required to pinpoint a specific employment practice as being discriminatory, and (4) what burden of proof for showing business necessity an employer should have to meet if adverse impact is shown. Describing this burden of proof has proven to be particularly controversial. Among the wordings that have been discussed are showing the employment practice is "essential to effective job performance," "significantly related to job performance," and "substantially and demonstrably related to effective job performance."

As this book was being edited, President Bush and the U.S. Senate agreed upon a compromise civil rights bill. However, the House of Representatives has yet to approve this bill. If the House agrees to this compromise bill, charges of disparate impact would return to a *Griggs v. Duke Power* standard of proof (i.e., if the plaintiff makes a prima facie case, the defendant has the burden of establishing the job relatedness of the challenged employment practice). The pending bill provides the option of a jury trial and allows for limited compensatory and punitive damages (up to $300,000 depending upon the size of the company) if discrimination can be shown to be intentional.

17. From a defendant's perspective, a negotiated settlement may be seen as advantageous even when the plaintiff's case is seen as weak. This is due to both public relations and cost considerations. Concerning public relations, even if an employer is vindicated in court, the publicity generated by a trial may harm its corporate image. With regard to cost, given the time involved in preparing for and participating in a trial, the legal costs incurred can make it more cost-effective for a company to settle than to win a lawsuit.

18. Readers who are interested in greater detail about the sequence of events during a trial should refer to Schlei and Grossman (1983), Sovereign (1988), or a basic law textbook.

19. This treatment of what occurs during a trial obviously simplifies a complex proceeding. For example, some cases involve charges of both disparate treatment and disparate impact. In terms of defending itself against a charge of discrimination, the exact standard of proof that a defendant will be expected to meet not only differs depending on whether the case involves a charge of disparate impact or disparate treatment, but is constantly evolving. Readers who are interested in the host of complex issues involved in negating a charge of discrimination after a plaintiff has made a prima facie case should refer to Schlei and Grossman (1983, 1987), Ledvinka and Scarpello (1991), *Wards Cove Packing v. Atonio* (1989), and other legal references cited earlier in this chapter. From these sources, the reader should begin to have an appreciation of the subtle distinction between legal defenses based on business necessity, job relatedness, offering a legitimate, nondiscriminatory business reason, a BFOQ, a religious exemption, and the creation of an undue hardship.

20. Hereafter, the term *contractor* will be used for both contractor and subcontractor.

9

The Effects of Government Regulations on Recruitment Activities

In the last chapter, several government regulations that can constrain an organization's recruitment practices were introduced. While Chapter 8 focused primarily on what these regulations proscribed and/or prescribed with regard to human resource activities in general, Chapter 9 addresses the implications of these regulations for those making recruitment decisions. However, before discussing these implications, the controversy over what is affirmative action and what is reverse discrimination must be addressed. An understanding of this topic is necessary in order to appreciate the complexities involved in administering an organization's recruitment function.

AFFIRMATIVE ACTION OR REVERSE DISCRIMINATION?

As was pointed out in Chapter 8, several federal regulations mandate affirmative action on the part of an employer. Nevertheless, this issue has a long history of controversy. Specifically, there has been disagreement about what is legitimate affirmative action versus what is illegal preferential treatment of the members of one group over those of another. Recently, several court decisions have helped to clarify matters (see Schlei and Grossman, 1983, 1989). While some of the controversial personnel actions (e.g., hiring quotas) are beyond the scope of this text, employee recruitment is a key aspect of most affirmative action programs. Therefore, in this section several issues that may determine whether an affirmative action plan can withstand a court test will be briefly examined.

As was noted in Chapter 8, Title VII makes it illegal to discriminate against anyone "because of such individual's race, color, religion, sex, or national origin" (Sec. 703(a)). Section 706(g) of Title VII allows a judge to order an affirmative action plan (including one involving quotas) if an employer is found guilty of intentional discrimination ("If the court finds that the respondent has intentionally engaged in or is intentionally engaging in an unlawful employment practice . . . , the court may . . . order such affirmative action as may be appropriate . . ."). Given the wording of Sections 703(a) and 706(g) and that of Section 703(j) ("Nothing contained in this title shall be interpreted to require any employer . . . to grant preferential treatment to any individual or group because of the race, color, religion, sex, or national origin of such individual or group on account of any imbalance which may exist with respect to the total number or percentage of persons of any race, color, religion, sex, or national origin employed by any employer"), many experts felt that the preferential treatment of the members of one group over those of another was illegal unless an employer had been found guilty of discrimination in the past. These experts were surprised by a 1979 Supreme Court ruling (*United Steelworkers v. Weber*) that upheld the legality of Kaiser Aluminum's affirmative action plan for admitting workers into a craft training program it had created at its Gramercy, Louisiana plant.

Kaiser Aluminum and the union representing the Gramercy plant's hourly workers adopted an affirmative action plan voluntarily. Although the racial composition of the plant's work force was imbalanced (prior to 1974, less than 2 percent of the plant's skilled craftworkers were minorities while minorities were 39 percent of the local labor force), Kaiser Aluminum had never been found guilty of employment discrimination. According to Kaiser Aluminum's affirmative action plan, admission into its craft training program was to be based on a combination of seniority and race such that at least 50 percent of the trainees enrolled were to be minorities. This admissions quota was to remain in effect until the percentage of minority craftworkers in the plant approximated the percentage of minorities in the local labor force. This admissions procedure resulted in minorities with less seniority being admitted before more senior nonminorities. In explaining the majority opinion in this case, Justice Brennan argued that, although Title VII does not "require" affirmative action, the statute does not prohibit it under certain conditions.

Affirmative Action Plans That Require Preferential Treatment: Assessing Legality

Since the *Weber* case, several other federal court decisions (see *Wygant v. Jackson Board of Education*, 1986) have helped delineate five factors that are important in determining whether an affirmative action plan that involves preferential treatment complies with Title VII. These factors are:

1. *Voluntary versus involuntary affirmative action.* Although given various pressures one can question whether an affirmative action plan is really voluntarily adopted, technically an employer cannot be forced to institute an affirmative action plan unless it has been found guilty of discrimination.

2. *An affirmative action plan should be remedial in nature.* If an employer has been found guilty of discrimination, it can be ordered to implement an affirmative action plan. If its work force is imbalanced, an employer probably can justify an affirmative action plan. However, if the number of minorities and women an employer has in its work force are representative of the available work force, it will have a difficult time justifying the need for affirmative action.[1]

3. *A plan should not exclude all nonminorities.* In *United Steelworkers v. Weber,* the Supreme Court emphasized that a 50 percent minority admissions quota did not create an "absolute bar" to nonminorities. While it is unclear how restrictive a quota can be, it is clear that an affirmative action plan that excludes all members of a nonprotected group likely would be illegal.

4. *An affirmative action plan should be temporary.* In several recent cases, the courts have ruled that once the established affirmative action goals have been met, the plan should be dismantled.

5. *An affirmative action plan should be formalized.* The courts have upheld actions taken pursuant to formal affirmative action plans against charges of reverse discrimination. In contrast, actions taken under "informal" affirmative action plans (such as plans that lacked formal goals or failed to describe formal actions to be taken) have been found to be discriminatory.

Based on the preceding discussion, one may question whether the affirmative action steps required by regulations such as Executive Order 11246 conflict with Title VII. Although several complex issues are involved, there appears to be no conflict, for the following reasons. Concerning the voluntary nature of affirmative action (Point 1 above), the federal government has argued that no one is required to bid on contracts. Thus, no contractor is required to establish an affirmative action program.[2] With regard to Point 2, the executive orders are designed to be remedial in nature. For example, in many industries there have been several discrimination findings against contractors. Furthermore, most contractors have work forces that are numerically imbalanced. With regard to Point 3, given that the executive orders only require goals (quotas are prohibited), members of no group are totally excluded from job consideration. Concerning the temporary nature of an affirmative action plan (Point 4), this issue has not been addressed by the courts. However, it appears to be irrelevant until a contractor's work force is in balance with the available work force. Regarding Point 5, the executive orders require formal affirmative action plans.

In summary, there are clear standards for evaluating the legality of an affirmative action plan that involves preferential treatment. However, many organizations would prefer to increase the number of minorities and women they employ without using a program that involves giving preference to members of protected groups. As will be discussed shortly, a well-designed recruitment strategy is one way in which an employer may be able to increase the number of minorities and women it employs without giving preferential treatment.

CATLETT v. MISSOURI: AN EXAMPLE OF A LAWSUIT INVOLVING EMPLOYEE RECRUITMENT

As was noted in Chapter 8 most employment discrimination cases are not based solely on the way an organization recruited employees. Instead, recruitment information generally is combined with information about other employment decisions such as selection data. Although recruitment information generally is not the only evidence used to prove discrimination, this does not mean that it is unimportant. In fact, recruitment data have frequently played a crucial role in cases made by both the plaintiff (e.g., establishing adverse impact) and the defendant (e.g., demonstrating a good-faith effort to hire minorities and women). To provide a realistic picture of how recruitment information can enter into a lawsuit, a synopsis of an actual court case (*Catlett v. MO Highway & Transportation Department*, 1987) that involved a charge of sex discrimination is instructive.[3]

Background Information

The focus of this lawsuit was the process used for filling the position of "maintenanceman" in the Highway Department of the State of Missouri. According to the Highway Department, this position is an entry-level job. The basic requirements for being hired as a maintenanceman are having at least an eighth-grade education and the ability to operate lightweight equipment such as pickup trucks and mowers. The duties of this position include mowing grass, plowing snow, filling potholes, and maintaining rest areas.

During the time period relevant to this lawsuit (January 1, 1975, through May 31, 1980),[4] the Highway Department relied almost exclusively on word-of-mouth recruitment for filling maintenanceman positions (occasionally the Missouri Division of Employment Security was informed of open positions). No job advertisements were placed in the news media. The maintenanceman work force was entirely male until December 1976, when the first woman was hired (note that no woman had ever been hired until sex discrimination charges had been filed). Between 1976 and 1980, women never comprised more than 3 percent of the maintenanceman work force.

In December 1976, Robert Hunter, the chief engineer in the Highway Department, issued a directive instructing all district engineers that the traditional method of word-of-mouth recruiting must no longer be relied on for recruiting. Instead, district engineers were instructed to advertise job openings. Despite this directive, neither Hunter nor the district engineer for District Eight, the region subject to this lawsuit, modified the way in which they recruited for the maintenanceman position.

Hiring decisions for the maintenanceman position were made on the basis of information derived from an application form, which could be obtained at any of the Highway Department's district offices located throughout the state, and from an interview. To reach the interview stage, an applicant had to be viewed as a good candidate based on the application data. According to the Highway Department, the supervisors who conducted the interviews had received no training on how to conduct an interview.

The Plaintiffs' Case

To prove that sex discrimination had occurred, the plaintiffs introduced both statistical and nonstatistical evidence. For the statistical evidence, the plaintiffs conducted two different population–work force comparison analyses: one based on a moderate definition of the relevant labor force population and one based on a conservative definition. The moderate definition, against which the plaintiffs compared the actual number of female applicants, encompassed "that group of persons who reside within the eleven counties of District Eight and who are in the civilian labor force as defined by the United States Census for 1970 and for 1980 in the job categories of sales, blue collar, farm, service, and clerical, but excluding managerial, technical, and professional workers, and who are between the ages of eighteen and seventy years and who have a driver's license and an eighth-grade education." The conservative definition of the labor force population was identical to the moderate definition with the exception that clerical employees were not included. (Because clerical employees are predominantly female, it is understandable why the plaintiffs would consider this a conservative estimate.) The available labor force population in District Eight was estimated for each year between 1975 and 1980 by adjusting the census data using a "straight-line" method.[5]

No matter which labor force population estimate was used, the results showed evidence of sex discrimination.[6] For example, statistics showed that females constituted as much as 48 percent of the relevant labor pool, yet only 10 percent of the maintenancemen hired during the relevant time period were females. During the trial, the plaintiffs argued that the use of flow statistics, such as a comparison of the hiring rates for males and females, was not appropriate in this case because discriminatory actions taken by the defendant during the recruitment process discouraged many females from filing applications.

The plaintiffs also introduced numerous types of nonstatistical evidence. They stressed the fact that District Eight did not follow the chief engineer's directive to stop relying on word-of-mouth recruitment and to start advertising openings. The application form was attacked as resulting in sex discrimination because, although it asked about relevant experience gained in jobs held with other organizations, it did not provide an applicant with the opportunity to describe relevant experience acquired through nonpaid farm experience. This was important because it was shown that many female applicants had experience with lightweight motor equipment through self-employed farm experience.

The plaintiffs also attacked the employment interview, arguing that the lack of interviewer training and interview guidelines resulted in numerous instances of discrimination. For example, it was shown that the interviewers, all of whom were males, rated the work experience of female applicants in such jobs as laborer and farming as unrelated to maintenance work, while male applicants with similar experience were rated as having job-relevant experience. Evidence was also introduced that a highly qualified female was rejected for what was said to be frequent job changes while several males with more frequent job changes were hired as maintenancemen.

Considerable information was also introduced during the trial concerning attempts by Highway Department personnel to discourage females from pursuing jobs. For example, testimony was given of an instance in which a potential female applicant was incorrectly advised that an application could only be obtained in Springfield or Jefferson City, while she actually could have obtained an application at a location that was much nearer to her home. Numerous instances were cited during the trial in which Highway Department supervisors had emphasized the negative aspects of the maintenanceman position in order to discourage females from filing applications. For example, female applicants testified that during interviews they were repeatedly told "one of the duties of the maintenanceman position was the removal of dead animals from the roads." It was also emphasized that there were no restroom facilities for females to use while on duty, and that the job required long hours and involved dangerous work and inclement weather. Male applicants did not receive such negative information. Other examples of attempts to discourage females from pursuing maintenanceman positions included suggestions to the females that they would be offended by the language used by male co-workers and statements that the Highway Department already had someone in mind for an opening and therefore the females should pursue other jobs outside the Highway Department. Perhaps the most striking single piece of evidence reflecting the hostile attitude of the Highway Department toward females involved a woman who was deemed "not one to do dirty work." At the time this woman was interviewed, she lived and worked on a farm and her background included work on a chicken ranch.

The Defendant's Case

As described in the district court's opinion, the Highway Department's case was three-fold. First, the defendant argued that much of the testimony concerning the discouragement of women applicants offered by the plaintiffs' witnesses was untrue. Second, the Highway Department argued that, even if some of these events had transpired, they represented isolated incidents and did not represent behavior of which it approved. Finally, the defendant argued that flow statistics were more appropriate than population–work force comparison statistics for determining whether sex discrimination had occurred. The defendant's flow statistics showed that between January 1, 1975, and May 31, 1980, it hired 2.6 percent of the female applicants and 2.5 percent of the male applicants for the maintenanceman position. Based on these results, the Highway Department argued that there was no statistical evidence of sex discrimination.

The Court Findings

In weighing the statistical and nonstatistical evidence presented by the two sides, the district court judge found in favor of the plaintiffs' arguments.[7] Specifically, the court was convinced that incidents in which Highway Department supervisors had discouraged women from applying for the position of maintenanceman had occurred. These incidents were so numerous that the court ruled they represented the "pattern and practice" of the Highway Department rather than isolated events. Because the trial judge felt that the defendant had in several ways discouraged females from applying for positions, he ruled that its flow statistics were seriously flawed, and thus the plaintiffs' population–work force comparison statistics were the appropriate analyses on which to rely. Given these conclusions, the judge ruled that the plaintiffs had proven that the Missouri Highway Department was guilty of sex discrimination.

The State of Missouri appealed the judge's verdict. The appellate court upheld the findings of the district court on the class action claim of sex discrimination. The reasons given by the appellate court for its decision were (1) the fact that the Highway Department ignored its own recruiting directive to advertise positions rather than rely on word-of-mouth recruitment; (2) the trial record suggested that the episodes of discouraging female applicants represented the defendant's standard operating procedure and not "isolated, insignificant, or sporadic" occurrences; and (3) given such discouragement of female applicants, the use of population–work force comparison statistics, which showed discrimination against females, is more appropriate than the use of flow statistics.

COMPLYING WITH FEDERAL REGULATIONS: RECOMMENDED RECRUITMENT PRACTICES

In this and in the preceding chapter, considerable information concerning federal regulations that affect employee recruitment has been presented.

From this discussion, it should be apparent that recruitment activities should play a key role in any affirmative action program because of their direct influence on the composition of the applicant pool. Because of the importance attached to recruitment activities by federal agencies, more detailed information concerning the recruitment practices that are necessary for establishing an affirmative action plan that is acceptable to the Office of Federal Contract Compliance Programs is now presented.

Recruitment as an Integral Part of an Affirmative Action Program

Although the specific recruitment actions that an employer may be expected to take as part of an affirmative action program can vary slightly depending on the circumstances involved,[8] the OFCCP's Revised Order No. 4, which describes affirmative action activities focused on the employment of minorities and women, provides a good framework from which to generalize to affirmative action efforts targeted at other groups such as the disabled. In terms of recruitment, Revised Order No. 4 recommends several actions for an employer to take "to improve recruitment and increase the flow of minority or female applicants."[9]

One recommended recruitment technique is for an organization to contact external sources that are likely to be able to refer minority or female applicants. For minority job candidates, the OFCCP recommends contacting such sources as the Urban League, the Job Corps, the Neighborhood Youth Corps, secondary schools and colleges with high minority enrollment, Equal Opportunity Programs, Inc., and the state employment service. To increase the number of female applicants, the OFCCP suggests contacting such sources as the National Organization for Women, the Women's Equity Action League, the Professional Women's Caucus, the Intercollegiate Association of University Women, the American Association of University Women, and Catholic, Jewish, and Protestant women's groups.

In addition to making contact with such potential sources of minority and women applicants, the OFCCP recommends that an employer demonstrate its commitment to the employment of underrepresented groups by inviting representatives from these sources to the company premises for formal briefing sessions. During these sessions, current and future job openings should be described, recruiting literature should be distributed, formal procedures for referring job candidates should be explained, and contact with minorities and women currently employed by the organization should be facilitated.

In combination with relying on the external recruitment sources described above, Revised Order No. 4 suggests that an organization actively encourage its minority and female employees to refer qualified minority and female job applicants. Some of these minority and female employees also should be made available for participation in career days, job fairs, and other types of outreach programs in the community.

Revised Order No. 4 also addresses the use of company publications such as annual reports and recruitment brochures and help wanted advertisements to increase the number of minority and female job applicants. In terms of company publications that may be distributed to potential job candidates, Revised Order No. 4 emphasizes the importance of minority and female employees being represented in any pictures of work situations. With regard to help wanted advertising, the OFCCP suggests that special efforts be made to include "minority news media and women's interest media" in the advertising outlets used. In addition, all job advertisements must include an equal employment opportunity clause stating that "all qualified applicants will receive consideration for employment without regard to race, color, religion, sex, or national origin." In order to increase the number of applications received from members of underrepresented groups, many employers include a statement encouraging applications from women and minorities in all of their recruitment literature.

Although much of the focus on recruitment in Revised Order No. 4 is geared to reaching candidates for entry-level positions, the order also deals briefly with other recruitment concerns. For example, it recommends that announcements concerning promotion opportunities be posted or publicized in other ways. Not only does the OFCCP suggest that promotion opportunities be publicized, it recommends that the employer make an inventory of current minority and woman employees to determine their qualifications. When a promotion opportunity arises, such an inventory will enable the employer to nominate minorities and women for the position or at least to encourage them to apply. Revised Order No. 4 also suggests that all personnel involved in recruitment be carefully selected and trained "to insure elimination of bias in all personnel actions."[10] It is also recommended that the members of the organization who are involved in recruiting include minorities and women.

One additional way the OFCCP suggests that employers can increase the number of minorities and women they are able to recruit for permanent positions is through the use of special transition programs that bridge the gap between temporary or part-time jobs and full-time positions. Such special programs include work–study programs geared toward minorities and women, summer jobs for underprivileged youth, and technical and nontechnical co-op programs with predominantly African American and women's colleges.

While Revised Order No. 4 addresses affirmative action that is focused on the recruitment of minorities and women, the OFCCP has also issued directives that deal with affirmative action recruiting that is focused on religion, national origin, the handicapped, and disabled and Vietnam era veterans. Although the type of recruitment actions suggested for these other groups are not identical to those for recruiting minorities and women, there is considerable overlap.[11] For example, employers are expected to enlist the assistance and support of relevant external recruitment sources (sheltered workshops, local veterans groups, religious organizations, and so on) in recruiting members of these other targeted groups. Similarly, organizations are expected to make use of media oriented toward the targeted group they are attempting to recruit.

RECRUITMENT POLICIES AND PRACTICES THAT MAY BE DISCRIMINATORY

From the preceding discussion, it should be apparent that recruitment actions taken as part of a formal affirmative action program should diversify the composition of the applicant pool as well as increase the number of job applicants for an open position. Affirmative action efforts also provide evidence of an employer's "good faith" in attempting to employ minorities and women. Such nonstatistical evidence can be important if an organization is sued for employment discrimination (see Schlei and Grossman, 1983). Therefore, even if it is under no legal obligation to have an affirmative action program, it may still be prudent for an organization to establish such a program.

Although an organization can increase the number of minorities and women who apply for a position by taking affirmative action, conversely, it can restrict the applicant pool for a job by the various recruitment decisions it makes. Since recruitment decisions that restrict the applicant pool have been the basis for several discrimination lawsuits, these decisions will be briefly addressed.[12]

Nepotism and Antinepotism Policies

Nepotism policies (i.e., employment policies that give preference to individuals who have family members working for an organization) have been closely scrutinized by both enforcement agencies and the courts because nepotism policies tend to prevent prospective candidates from protected classes from being hired and/or promoted. For example, in one case (*Bonilla v. Oakland Scavenger Co.*, 1982), the court considered whether a company could restrict the ownership of company stock to family members, all of whom were of Italian ancestry, when the ownership of such stock was necessary to be eligible for the higher-paying jobs in the organization. Although the company acknowledged that its nepotism policy had adverse impact on Blacks and Hispanics, it argued its legitimate interest in protecting family members outweighed the national interest of eliminating employment discrimination based on race and national origin. The court rejected the company's argument and ruled that the company's nepotism policy had resulted in employment discrimination.

In past nepotism cases, the courts have made clear that nepotism per se is not illegal.[13] Rather, this practice "is prohibited by Title VII where it has adverse impact on a protected class" (Schlei and Grossman, 1983, p. 573). However, given the composition of most employers' work forces, nepotism policies will generally result in adverse impact. Thus, if an organization has a nepotism policy, it had better be able to offer a strong argument supporting the need for such a policy.

Although nepotism policies frequently have resulted in discrimination findings against employers, antinepotism policies, which can have adverse impact on females, generally have been upheld by the courts.[14] As long as it is fairly applied to both females and males, case law supports an organization restricting the employment of family members. In particular, the courts have allowed the use of an "anti-spouse" rule, which restricts members of a married couple from working in the same department or prohibits one member from reporting to the other member. For example, in *Harper v. Trans World Air Lines* (1975), TWA's policy of prohibiting a husband and a wife from working in the same department was challenged. Under the policy, if two individuals working in the same department got married, TWA allowed the couple to decide which of them would continue working in that department and which one would resign or transfer to another department, if a suitable position was available. The female plaintiff in this case argued that TWA's antinepotism rule discriminated against females because women generally have lower incomes than men and thus were more likely to be the member of the couple who gave up the job. The court was not persuaded by this argument and found TWA not guilty of sex discrimination.[15]

Although nepotism and antinepotism policies can influence the composition of the applicant pool for a job opening, an organization's decision about what recruitment method or methods to use generally will have a greater impact on the types and number of people who apply for a position. In fact, there is substantial case law that addresses some of the most commonly used recruitment approaches by employers.

Word-of-Mouth Recruitment

In filling open positions, organizations have relied heavily on word-of-mouth recruitment by their employees (Bureau of National Affairs, 1988). Although the use of such employee referrals is common, this recruitment practice can also be dangerous. For example, if an employer's work force is predominantly white or predominantly male, word-of-mouth recruitment is likely to result in an applicant pool that does not reflect the composition of the relevant labor market. This recruitment outcome is due to the fact that employees "normally advise people of their own race and, to some degree, their own sex of the availability of employment in their employer's establishment" (Schlei and Grossman, 1983, p. 571). Given this consequence of using employee referrals, it is not surprising that the courts have not looked favorably on the use of employee referrals if an organization's work force is racially or sexually imbalanced. In fact, Schlei and Grossman characterize the use of word-of-mouth recruitment in such situations as having received "substantial judicial condemnation." For example, in *EEOC v. Detroit Edison Co.* (1975), "the practice of relying on referrals by a predominantly white work force rather than seeking new employees in the marketplace" was found to be discriminatory. In interpreting the court findings concerning word-of-mouth recruitment, it is important to emphasize that the use of employee referrals is not a per se violation of employment law. Rather, the courts have ruled that reliance on this recruitment method may be illegal if it results in adverse impact against members of protected groups.

Applicant-Initiated Recruitment

Another common method that individuals use to locate jobs is to apply directly to organizations for positions. That is, a job seeker takes the initiative either in person or via the mail to apply for job openings that an organization may have but has not publicized. Although there is nothing technically wrong with an employer relying on applicant-initiated recruitment for filling positions, the practice of solely or primarily relying on so-called walk-in applicants generally will be closely scrutinized by regulatory agencies and the courts if an organization's current work force is imbalanced and if this passive recruitment strategy results in a significant disparity between the composition of the group hired and the composition of the relevant labor force (Schlei and Grossman, 1983). This close scrutiny is due to the fact that regulatory agencies such as the EEOC assume that applicant-initiated recruitment is frequently the result of encouragement by current members of an organization that individuals file applications as well as advice from current employees to job candidates as to the best time to file an application, whether applications need to be refiled on a periodic basis, and how to go about filing an application to improve one's chances of landing a position.

Job Advertising

Not surprisingly, job advertisements are one of the most commonly used methods for recruiting employees. As was discussed in Chapter 8, both Title VII and the Age Discrimination in Employment Act include sections that outlaw job advertisements that "indicate any preference, limitation, specification, or discrimination" based on race, color, religion, sex, national origin, or age (exemptions may be made for religion, sex, national origin, or age where it is a bona fide occupational qualification for employment). Given that both Title VII and the Age Discrimination in Employment Act specifically address the wording of job advertisements, it should not be surprising that advertising phrases such as one indicating that an organization seeks a "young man with a college degree" for an accounting position have been found to be discriminatory (*Banks v. Heun-Norwood,* 1977).

Although today one rarely finds a job advertisement that expresses a preference for individuals of a particular race, sex, age, etc., there is one exception to this tendency. As was noted in Chapter 8, the Immigration Reform and Control Act makes it illegal for an employer to consider an individual's citizenship status if the person has a legal right to work in this country. Nevertheless, Lawrence J. Siskind, who heads a Justice Department antidiscrimination enforcement unit, found over 100 companies that advertised in newspapers for "U.S. citizens only."[16] Because such explicit wording would be expected to discourage those who are not U.S. citizens from applying for jobs, such advertisements are illegal.[17] Siskind stated that he does not believe the job advertisements seeking U.S. citizens were deliberate attempts to violate the law; rather, he believes such ads were due to employer ignorance. However, such ignorance does not exempt an organization from prosecution.

Although employers have sometimes gotten into trouble because their job advertisements express a specific preference for members of a particular group (e.g., "unusual opportunity for the man thinking of his future"), such cases are not that common.[18] Instead, advertisements are more likely to be attacked because they indirectly express a preference for members of a particular group. For example, the employment practices of an organization that uses job advertisements indicating an interest in receiving applications from such groups as "college students" or "veterans" may be closely scrutinized to determine whether discrimination against members of other groups is occurring. Stated differently, courts for the most part have ruled that the use of such "trigger words" is not discriminatory per se; rather, the effects of such phrases must be determined in a larger context (Are applications still received from older individuals? Are females hired at a reasonable rate?).[19]

The fact that the use of such advertising phrases as those noted above may not by itself be sufficient evidence to prove discrimination does not mean that an organization should include such phrases in its job advertisements. The use of such job advertisements ("recent college graduates") may be combined with other suggestive evidence of discrimination (such as the placement of job advertisements exclusively in publications geared to the youth market or the fact that only recent college graduates have ever been hired for that position) to establish a persuasive case that discrimination occurred.

Promotions from Within

Although in discussing recruitment methods the focus to this point has been on filling positions with candidates from outside the organization, recruitment also encompasses the process an employer uses for staffing positions internally. In filling positions from within, some employers use a secretive process. For example, for a newly created mid-level management position, a few higher-level managers may decide who is best for the opening. An offer is extended to this person, he or she accepts, and then an announcement of the job placement is circulated. Only with this announcement do most members of the organization become aware that there was a vacant position. In contrast to such a closed system, some employers use job posting or bidding systems in which open positions are publicized and current employees are given adequate time to express an interest in being considered for a position (Kleiman and Clark, 1984).

As with many of the recruitment methods that have been discussed, it may not be necessary for an employer to publicize job openings and allow internal candidates to apply for them if its work force is racially and sexually diverse. However, if minorities and/or women are not well-represented throughout the organizational hierarchy, "employers are well advised to either have a job posting and bidding system or to utilize a system by which current employees can indicate an interest in being considered, such as a preregistration system" (Schlei and Grossman, 1983, p. 585). Without such a system, the burden will be on the organization to defend its promotion system if it leads to minorities or women being underrepresented. For example, in *Rowe v. General Motors Corp.* (1972), an appeals court ruled that it was illegal for an employer to rely solely on foremen to recommend employees for promotion or transfer when it had been shown that a disproportionately small percentage of minority hourly workers were promoted or transferred to salaried positions and that the standards used by the foremen were subjective and there were no safeguards to ensure impartiality.

Recruitment Sources in General

In discussing the legality of particular recruitment practices, the question is often asked, "What if an organization recruits from a source that includes very few minorities and/or women but that is seen as providing high-caliber job candidates?" Surprisingly, there has been little case law that has directly addressed this issue. However, a brief review of two cases provides a sense of judicial rulings on this matter. In *EEOC v. New York Times Broadcasting Service, Inc.* (1976), the court ruled that it was illegal for a television station to recruit broadcast news personnel from only two radio stations that employed almost no women in broadcast positions. The court stated that, although radio broadcasting experience is useful in television broadcasting, the New York Times Broadcasting Service did not justify recruiting only from these two stations. In *Gavagan v. Danbury Civil Service Commission* (1983), the court prohibited a municipality that was hiring fire fighters from giving preference to individuals with voluntary fire-fighting experience. The court prevented this action because it felt that private, volunteer fire companies tend to be hostile toward the membership of minorities and women. Thus, giving preference to individuals with voluntary fire-fighting experience would severely restrict the likelihood of minorities and women being hired.

If one generalizes from these two cases, it appears that an employer will have a difficult time justifying the job relatedness of recruiting from applicant sources that have few members of protected groups. In a similar vein, if an organization places job advertisements in publication outlets that are likely to reach only members of particular groups, it may have a difficult time defending this action.

The Accuracy of Recruitment Information: Legal Claims of Fraud and Chilling

As was noted in Chapter 8, new employees have had some success in state courts in winning suits against their employers that involve charges of fraudulent recruitment and hiring. The crux of such a lawsuit is the plaintiff proving that the organization for which the person went to work intentionally misled him or her during the recruitment process and that the plaintiff acted on and suffered because of this fraudulent information. Because it appears that the courts are becoming more accepting of claims of fraudulent recruitment and hiring, those responsible for recruitment need to carefully plan and monitor the type of information being communicated to job candidates through various recruitment channels. Although a slight exaggeration of information of a general sort (such as a statement in a job advertisement that "Company XYZ is an industry leader" when it is not) is unlikely to result in a finding of fraud against an employer, the intentional distortion of important information (as when a company promises a job candidate a promotion within one year when it has no intention to fulfill that promise) may well result in a finding of fraud.[20]

In addition to being subjected to a lawsuit because it exaggerated the positive attributes of a position it offered, an organization may also open itself to legal action because it presented an overly negative view of what a job entailed. Simply stated, there is likely to be nothing legally improper about presenting an overly pessimistic view of a position if the same information is shared with all job candidates (obviously, communicating such recruitment information would make filling jobs more difficult). However, problems arise when an employer selectively communicates an overly negative view of a position. For example, in the *Catlett* case, the judge ruled that the Missouri Highway Department had presented a much more negative view of the maintenanceman position to female job applicants than to male applicants. The process by which an organization dissuades members of protected groups from pursuing job openings has been labeled "chilling" by the courts (Schlei and Grossman, 1989). If an employer can be shown to have exaggerated the negative attributes of a job for the purpose of discouraging job applications from minorities and females, it risks a discrimination finding.

RECRUITMENT MANAGEMENT STYLE IN
THE CONTEXT OF FEDERAL REGULATIONS

In Chapter 2, the difference between a reactive and a proactive management style was introduced and the general benefits of an organization being proactive were emphasized. In the context of federal regulations, the importance of being proactive can be particularly pronounced. To demonstrate this point, a reconsideration of the *Catlett v. MO Highway & Transportation Department* case is instructive.

Based on the written opinions of both the district and appellate courts, it appears that the Highway Department's management of its recruitment operation reflected a reactive style of operating (that is, because it was unaware of any major problems, the Highway Department continued to recruit for the maintenanceman position in its traditional manner). Ultimately, this reactive style resulted in a finding of sexual discrimination. However, if the Highway Department had been proactive, there is a strong possibility that sexual discrimination charges would never have been filed. Furthermore, even if charges had been filed, the discrimination verdict might have been avoided.

A proactive management style involves seeking out potential problems before they develop and manifest themselves as major concerns. If the Highway Department had been proactive and searched for potential recruitment problems, it should have discovered that (1) relevant labor market data suggested that the percentage of the females hired for the maintenanceman position was dangerously low, (2) its directive on the use of job advertisements had not been followed, (3) all its recruiters/interviewers were male, (4) these individuals were discouraging women from applying for jobs in numerous ways, and (5) female applicants who had the same job experience as male candidates were evaluated less positively.

If it had taken the initiative to discover these potential problems ("potential" in the sense that no legal charges had yet been filed), the Highway Department, assuming it was motivated to avoid a discrimination lawsuit, could have taken numerous proactive steps to address them. For example, in order to increase the number of females who heard about job vacancies, the Highway Department could have, at a minimum, made sure that vacancies were widely advertised in the media. In addition, it could have initiated special outreach programs, such as visiting junior colleges for the purpose of recruiting women students and contacting women's groups in the district. As another way to increase the number of women applicants, female employees working both inside and outside the

Highway Department could have been regularly informed of job openings and encouraged to refer qualified female applicants. In terms of the recruitment/interview process, the Highway Department could have made sure that some of the recruiters/interviewers were women (even if they came from outside the department). The Highway Department also could have trained those involved in recruiting and interviewing to make sure that male and female applicants received the same preview of what the maintenanceman position entailed and that male and female job experience was evaluated in the same way. Although there are numerous additional actions the Highway Department could have taken (including changing the name of the job to "maintenance worker") to increase its flow of female applicants, from the points raised above it should be apparent that by proactively searching for problems (conceivably such a search would have also determined that minorities were underrepresented in some jobs) the Highway Department should have become aware of potential problems at an earlier stage, before discrimination charges had been filed. Thus, it may have been able to take proactive steps to address them.

If the Missouri Highway Department had taken the proactive steps discussed above, it is likely that many more females would have applied for maintenanceman positions and been hired (assuming, of course, that the Highway Department did not consciously intend to discriminate against women) and that a sex discrimination lawsuit would not have been filed. Even if a suit had been filed, the Highway Department would have had a much stronger case than the one it actually had in the *Catlett* case. If the proposed actions had been taken, it is likely that the members of the jury, the district court judge, and the appellate court judges would have been favorably impressed by the Highway Department's good-faith attempt to increase its number of female employees. Given this sentiment, it is unlikely that either a jury or a judge would have ruled (as they did in the actual case) that the Missouri Highway Department had discriminated against women.

SUMMARY

This chapter addressed three major issues: affirmative action versus preferential treatment, recruitment actions that are part of an affirmative action plan, and recruitment practices that may be discriminatory. In order to integrate how many of the legal issues introduced in this and the preceding chapter can affect actual recruitment practice, the court case of *Catlett v. MO Highway & Transportation Department* (1987) was also discussed. Based on the material presented in this chapter, the reader should be aware of several important themes. First, it should be readily apparent that those involved in making recruitment decisions must be knowledgeable concerning the numerous federal regulations that can affect a recruitment operation.

A second important theme of this chapter is the need for an employer to formalize its recruitment practices and to recruit in a way that reflects the current state of professional practice. Although more detail concerning how to formalize recruitment practices and what is considered sound professional practice will be provided in the remaining chapters of this text, some examples would be: (1) having a formal training program for all recruiters, (2) developing a procedures manual for writing job advertisements, (3) developing outreach programs for attracting minority and female applicants, (4) conducting periodic statistical analyses that compare an organization's applicant pool against the relevant population comparison data, and (5) compiling an annual report detailing all of the organization's recruitment activities. For each job vacancy, this annual report might include such information as who was involved in recruitment, what recruitment methods were used, who responded to the job advertisements, where advertisements were placed, actual copies of job advertisements, etc.

A third theme emphasized in this chapter is the need for an employer to be proactive in its recruitment efforts. It has been argued that by seeking out potential problems, an employer will often be able to easily address them. For example, if before a job advertisement can be placed by any department its wording and where it is to be placed must be approved by someone with expertise in the human resources department, it is likely that several potentially discriminatory job advertisements would be caught before any harm was done. Although the time demands that are often placed on those involved in recruiting makes it easy to understand why a reactive rather than proactive operating style typically characterizes recruitment activities, in the chapters that follow it will be demonstrated that a proactive recruitment management style can actually save time and resources.

In conclusion, from these two chapters it should be apparent that failure to comply with government regulations can have adverse consequences for an organization. However, rather than think of these regulations as rules to be followed to avoid sanctions, it is beneficial for an organization to take a different perspective. Given the predicted labor shortages in the coming years, for most employers it will become increasingly important that they take actions to ensure they have an adequate pool of applicants from which to hire. Taking the actions required to comply with government regulations should increase the number of minorities and women who apply for positions. Stated differently, organizations that fail to take actions to increase the number of minorities and women they attract may well find themselves at a disadvantage in competing against organizations that do take such actions.

NOTES

1. In terms of who can benefit from affirmative action, the courts have made clear that one need not personally have suffered discriminatory treatment (see *Sheet Metal Workers Local 28 v. EEOC*, 1986). Rather, a person may benefit simply because he or she is a member of group that may have been discriminated against.

2. This argument for the voluntary nature of doing business with the government has been accepted by the courts (see *McLaughlin v. Great Lakes Dredge & Dock Co.*, 1980).

3. Because *Catlett v. MO Highway & Transportation Department* (1987) involved claims of sex discrimination brought under both the Civil Rights Act of 1964 and the Civil Rights Act of 1871, was brought on behalf of both four individual female plaintiffs as well as women as a class, and was appealed to the Eighth Circuit Court, it would take considerable space to fully explore all the issues involved in this case. Therefore, rather than overwhelm the reader with information, only issues particularly relevant to recruitment will be addressed. In the original trial, the class action sex discrimination claims were affirmed by both the district court judge (Title VII) and the jury (Civil Rights Act of 1871). With regard to the individuals' claims of discrimination, the judge found in favor of the individuals; the jury ruled against them. The State of Missouri appealed the rulings against it. The U.S. Court of Appeals for the Eighth Circuit affirmed the jury's findings of sex discrimination under both civil rights acts and overturned the judge's finding of discrimination against the four individual female plaintiffs. Because the claims brought by the individuals were not affirmed by the appellate court, in covering this case the emphasis will be on the class action suit.

4. The original charges of discrimination in this case were filed on July 21, 1975, with the Missouri Commission on Human Rights and on March 20, 1976, with the Equal Employment Opportunity Commission.

5. This method of adjustment involves a simple interpolation of the census data. For example, the estimate of the available applicant pool for 1979 can be derived by (1) taking the difference between the 1980 and 1970 census figures, (2) taking 90 percent of this difference, and (3) adding this figure to the 1970 census figure.

6. The percentage of women in the relevant labor pool ranged from 42 percent in 1970 to 48 percent in 1980 under the moderate definition. Using the conservative definition, the percentage ranged from 32 percent in 1970 to 37 percent in 1980.

7. As was noted earlier, because of the complexity of the *Catlett* case, this synopsis focuses only on the district court findings that were upheld on appeal. Because juries are not asked to justify their decisions in writing, this summary of the district court findings is based only on the judge's decision.

8. For example, what is required by Revised Order No. 4 may differ from what a judge orders as part of a Title VII decision.

9. As was briefly described in Chapter 8, Revised Order No. 4 also deals with several areas other than recruitment. Readers who are interested in getting a copy of Revised Order No. 4 should contact the OFCCP.

10. While the elimination of bias is a noble objective, Revised Order No. 4 unfortunately does not provide any suggestions for how to select and/or train personnel so that they are bias-free.

11. Two of these differences are worth noting. In taking affirmative action steps to recruit members of underrepresented religious groups and handicapped individuals, an employer is expected to make reasonable accommodations, such as scheduling work to allow for religious observances. Concerning affirmative action recruitment of veterans, the employer is required to list most job openings with the relevant state employment service.

12. Readers who are interested in more detail on employment discrimination cases that have involved recruitment policy decisions should refer to Chapter 16 of Schlei and Grossman's 1983 and 1989 editions.

13. If an organization's nepotism policy cannot be shown to have an adverse impact on members of a protected class, then it is unlikely that requiring family membership for employment would be seen by the courts as illegal.

14. Antinepotism policies come in several varieties. In some organizations, there are rules against two people from the same family being employed. Some employers prohibit family members from working closely together (e.g., working in the same department). In many organizations, there is a restriction against one person from a family directly reporting to another family member.

15. In this case, the plaintiff introduced evidence that in four of the five couples affected by this "anti-spouse" rule it was the woman who left her job. However, the court was not persuaded by this evidence. It rejected the plaintiff's unproven assumption that income level would be the sole or even the dominant factor in determining which member of a couple gave up a job after marriage.

16. Bradford and Smart (1988).

17. Such wording would not be illegal if U.S. citizenship was necessary for the particular job.

18. For more information concerning case law and administrative rulings on the wording of job advertisements, see Schlei and Grossman (1983, 1989).

19. As should be clear from Chapter 8, if the job qualifications listed in an advertisement (e.g., good credit rating) have an adverse impact, the employer should be able to defend their job relatedness.

20. Although certain types of exaggeration may not make an organization legally liable, the negative effects of presenting misleading information in terms of person–job fit may nevertheless result (see Chapter 5).

10

Using Research on Recruitment

From the material covered in the preceding chapters of this text, it should be obvious that this author believes that recruitment-related decisions should not be made without first considering the multitude of factors that they can both affect and be affected by. A manager who fails to consider the larger context in which recruitment activities take place may discover that a decision he or she made has resulted in a lawsuit, is at cross-purposes with other human resource activities, or interferes with the accomplishment of strategic business objectives. One obvious method for improving the quality of recruitment decision making is a careful review of the recruitment literature to see what other organizations are doing and the consequences of their actions.

Unfortunately, managers who are responsible for making recruitment decisions often are disappointed by the research on which they have to draw. For the most part, the treatment of recruitment issues in practitioner journals tends to be somewhat simplistic. Articles in these journals tend to provide narrowly focused "how to" advice with little theory or data to support the suggestions being offered. In addition, because most practitioner journals limit the length of articles, the typical article does not address how the recruitment topic being discussed can affect and be affected by other organizational decisions.

A manager with recruitment responsibilities is also likely to be disappointed with the academic recruitment literature. As noted by Rynes (1991), this literature has failed to address some of the most important questions that practitioners have concerning the recruitment of employees. Furthermore, since most academic studies have focused on the recruitment of new college graduates through college placement offices, many managers are hesitant to generalize from these studies to different recruitment contexts. Another frustration that practitioners have with academic research on recruiting is the multitude of journals in which articles appear, which makes it difficult to keep up with recruitment research. The academic literature also presents problems because some articles that have great relevance for recruitment decision making (for example, behavioral decision theory research) may not even mention the word recruitment. Thus, even a computerized search of the research literature may miss important articles.

As should be apparent from the early chapters of this text, this author believes that academic research has much to offer to practitioners who have recruitment responsibilities. This text is based on the premise that a good understanding of the theoretical and empirical research contributions in the academic literature will help managers make the important "how to" recruitment decisions with which they are faced. This belief is the reason that the primary focus of the early chapters in this text was on understanding the fundamental processes relevant to recruitment. This belief is also the reason that only a limited amount of "how to" information was presented in these early chapters.

In the remaining chapters of this text, the focus will be on applied issues. Among the topics that will be examined in these chapters are selecting an applicant population from which to recruit, the pros and cons of various recruitment methods, the selection and training of recruiters, and the evaluation of recruitment actions. In covering these topics, numerous examples of what organizations are actually doing will be provided.

FACTORS THAT SHOULD BE CONSIDERED IN MAKING RECRUITMENT DECISIONS

Space limitations make a thorough review of the information presented in the first nine chapters of this text impossible. The following review of a few central themes from these earlier chapters may be useful.

Establishing Recruitment Objectives

In order to make sound recruitment decisions, clear recruitment objectives must be established. Several possible recruitment objectives, including filling positions quickly and recruiting job candidates who will be promotable, were delineated in Chapter 1, where it was also noted that different members of an organization frequently will view different objectives as having the highest priority. Although conflict concerning the relative importance of recruitment objectives is sometimes unavoidable, it is best if it is addressed before starting the recruitment process. Otherwise, such conflict may have to be dealt with after the recruitment of employees has started, which may result in various recruitment problems.[1] Chapter 2 highlighted the need for those who establish recruitment objectives to carefully consider their organization's external labor market, its business environment, and the various government regulations with which it must comply. In this chapter, the importance of establishing recruitment objectives that are consistent with an organization's strategic business objectives and its other human resource functions was also emphasized.

Recruitment Planning and Strategy Development

Before an organization begins planning recruitment activities, it should establish its recruitment objectives and decide on a recruitment philosophy. Among the issues addressed under the rubric of recruitment philosophy were whether the employer will emphasize internal versus external recruitment and whether it will recruit to fill a given job or with a career orientation. Once an employer has integrated its recruitment objectives with its recruitment philosophy, it can begin the recruitment planning process. In Chapter 2, an overview of many of the issues that should be addressed in recruitment planning was provided. Following the recruitment planning process, an organization must develop a specific strategy for filling a given job opening. For example, an employer must decide in what geographic area it will recruit, who it will use as recruiters, and what information it will convey in its recruitment communications. Although the coverage of recruitment planning and strategy development in Chapter 2 was somewhat cursory, additional information relevant to these two topics was provided in subsequent chapters that addressed such topics as affirmative action and realistic recruitment.

Understanding the Applicant's Perspective

In order to develop an effective recruitment strategy, organizational decision makers must consider the viewpoint of the prospective employee. In Chapters 3 and 4, considerable information concerning how job seekers find out about jobs and make job-choice decisions was presented. One theme that was emphasized in these chapters was the importance of an employer being visible and having a good reputation (since many people apply directly to organizations without a job opening being publicized). It was also noted that most prospective employees lack information about jobs they are considering and often have inaccurate job expectations. Other types of job applicant uncertainty were discussed as well. For example, after interviewing with a company, a recruit may be uncertain whether a job offer will be forthcoming and, if one is, when it will be received. Upon receiving a job offer, the person may wonder whether he or she was the employer's first choice for the position. If the candidate had to wait a long time for an offer, the person may assume that other job candidates have rejected the job offer he or she received. Such an assumption (regardless of whether it is accurate) can be important because a recruit who believes that he or she was not a company's top choice may be less likely to accept a job offer. Job candidates also experience uncertainty regarding the number of job offers they are likely to receive. For example, a new college graduate may have little idea whether he or she will receive one job offer or five. This type of uncertainty can be important when a person has to decide whether to accept a particular job offer before any others have been received.

In attempting to reduce such uncertainty and verify the accuracy of the information they possess, job candidates seek out job-relevant information. They also receive unsolicited information from the organizations to which they have applied and from other sources such as people they know who are familiar with the organizations. One result of this influx of information is that the ability of an applicant to process all of it may be stressed (Miller and Jablin, 1991). In order to handle the quantity and complexity of the information available to them, candidates use a variety of simplification heuristics such as selective perception. However, as was discussed in Chapter 4, these simplification processes can result in a person forming an inaccurate perception of a job opening.

One obvious way to address such applicant uncertainty is for an employer to establish an effective recruitment communication strategy. In order to design such a strategy, an organization must consider several complex issues, including what information to communicate, how to communicate the information, and when to communicate it. For example, an employer may want to convey a large amount of information about a position, but may also realize that, given the limited information processing ability of recruits, it may overwhelm them with information. Chapters 4, 5, and 6 addressed many issues relevant to designing such a recruitment information dissemination strategy.

In order to better understand the importance of considering the job candidate's perspective, Chapter 5 introduced the concept of person–job fit. In this chapter, a strong argument was made for the benefits of there being a good match both between an applicant's skills and a job's requirements and between the applicant's needs and the attributes the job offers. As a way to improve person–job fit, it was recommended that an employer provide job applicants with candid information about the job being considered. As a mechanism for understanding the negative consequences of new employees having an inaccurate understanding of what a position involves, the concept of a psychological contract was introduced in Chapter 6. In this chapter, a model was also presented that describes how recruits develop job and organizational expectations and the consequences of their possessing accurate expectations. Central to this model was the importance of an employer doing what it can to allow a job candidate to self-select out of consideration for a position. Building on the ideas discussed in Chapters 5 and 6, several suggestions were offered in Chapter 7 concerning how an organization can improve the accuracy and completeness of the information possessed by job candidates.

In making recruitment decisions, an organization may be bound by a host of government statutes and executive orders. Chapters 8 and 9 were designed to familiarize the reader with these government regulations.

DEVELOPING AN EFFECTIVE RECRUITMENT STRATEGY

Although the earlier chapters in this text were geared toward providing the reader with a basic understanding of the multitude of factors that can affect the success of an organization's recruitment actions, these chapters also included a number of concrete suggestions for a manager with recruitment responsibilities. However, because the primary focus of these earlier chapters was on understanding rather than on application, these suggestions were not presented in a systematic fashion. Thus, it may be useful to briefly review some of these suggestions in a more organized manner and to expand upon them.

Whom to Recruit

Although some employers appear to begin the recruitment process without giving much thought to the type of people they seek, this is a mistake. The more an organization can target an applicant population that possesses the skills and abilities it needs, the more effectively it will be able to recruit. For example, by clearly describing necessary employee qualifications in a job advertisement, an organization may be able to avoid being buried in an avalanche of résumés from individuals who are not part of the applicant population from which it has decided to recruit.[2] Similarly, the more an employer can determine what a job offers in terms of rewards, the more it may be able to narrow the focus of its recruiting efforts to those who are particularly likely to be attracted to the job opening.

For example, in the late 1980s, Lockheed needed to recruit several engineers to staff positions as C-130 aircraft specialists. Not only did Lockheed face the challenge of recruiting highly skilled technical personnel, it needed to recruit persons who were willing to relocate without family members to Saudi Arabia. Based on Lockheed's past experience, it targeted ex-military personnel for recruitment. According to a Lockheed spokesperson, the reason for this was that "Military people have the mental set for that kind of job, whereas civilians may resist some of the job requirements."[3]

In his book *The Soul of a New Machine* (1981), Tracy Kidder provides another example of how a company carefully targeted a narrow segment of the labor force for recruitment. According to Kidder, the Westborough, Massachusetts, group of Data General targeted new engineering graduates instead of experienced engineers for recruitment to build a new computer because they were cheaper, they did not know what an impossible task they were being called upon to do, and they would not attract as much attention from another group at Data General with whom they were in competition.

Not only is it important for organizations that seek to fill highly skilled positions to carefully select an applicant population, it is also important for firms that seek to fill lower-level positions. A good case in point is Pizza Hut, which has been tremendously innovative in its recruitment efforts in the past few years. In attempting to staff difficult-to-fill entry-level positions, Pizza Hut has targeted an applicant population comprised of the physically and mentally "challenged." According to Pizza Hut managers, employees from this largely untapped labor resource have worked out wonderfully. For example, Laabs (1990a) reports that the turnover rate for these disabled individuals is only 20 percent of that for nondisabled employees.

Another example of the creative targeting of an atypical applicant population for filling lower-level jobs was reported by Schuler (1990). According to Schuler, Barden Corporation, a manufacturer located in Connecticut, had an opportunity to significantly increase its business during the mid-1980s. Barden's problem was how to substantially increase its hourly work force in an area with only a 2.5 percent unemployment rate. One of the ways in which Barden managed to fill the new jobs it created was by "recruiting workers whose English was very poor." Apparently, their lack of English fluency made such workers unattractive to most organizations, but these employees were able to successfully perform the jobs at Barden.

As a final example of the creative targeting of an applicant population, United Airlines presents an interesting case. According to Chauran (1989a), in the mid-1980s United was having difficulty staffing its food service jobs at Boston's Logan Airport. To address this labor shortage, United decided to target immigrants for recruitment. Because it offers free flights to its employees, United felt that this perquisite would have particular appeal to individuals who had relatives in other countries. To make contact with immigrants, United placed advertisements along mass transit routes servicing immigrant sections of Boston. According to United, the targeting of immigrants was a great success. Instead of its traditional shortage of fifty to sixty food preparers, it now reports a backlog of approximately 200 applicants.

From the preceding examples, it should be apparent that an increasing number of organizations have been successful in filling jobs by targeting members of nontraditional groups for recruitment. Although some employers may be doing this for altruistic reasons, many organizations are doing it out of business necessity.

Although the preceding examples all dealt with recruitment from an external applicant population, this is not to suggest that an employer should ignore its current work force. In many cases, an organization has an internal applicant population that can provide a sizable number of suitable job candidates (Farish, 1989). Some of these internal recruits may seek a different type of position; others may be interested in relocating to a new geographic location. In the next chapter, the use of internal recruitment mechanisms such as job posting will be discussed as a means of recruiting candidates from within the organization.

Although more will be said about targeting a particular applicant population for recruitment later in this text, several of the advantages of narrowing one's recruitment focus to a particular segment of the labor force should be obvious. Such targeting allows an employer to more intelligently determine what information to include in a recruitment communication and to decide what recruitment methods to use for publicizing a job opening. For example, if an organization is under affirmative action pressure to recruit more Hispanics, it may decide to advertise on Spanish-speaking radio stations or in Hispanic-oriented newspapers.

Where to Recruit

Once an employer has decided on the type of person it wants to attract, it must next decide on the geographic area in which it will recruit. In recruiting clerical and blue-collar workers, most organizations recruit from the surrounding area (Farish, 1989). In recruiting professional and managerial employees, organizations frequently recruit outside their immediate geographic area. Although little research has addressed how employers decide in what geographic areas to recruit, there is anecdotal evidence that suggests they frequently target locales that have high rates of unemployment. For example, during the 1970s many employers that were located in the Southwest recruited laid-off auto workers from the Midwest. However, in making decisions about where to recruit, an employer should consider more than the local unemployment rate. By doing some research on its past recruitment efforts (e.g., if newspaper ads were placed in several geographic areas, from where did most of the responses come?), an organization may gain insight into particularly beneficial areas in which to recruit.

For example, in recruiting engineers for jobs in Saudi Arabia, Lockheed discovered that more people from the Southeast and Southwest responded to its job advertisements than from other parts of the United States (Koch, 1990d). Lockheed attributed this geographic difference in interest to the fact that people who come from the southern United States are less likely to view the climate in Saudi Arabia as an unacceptable job attribute. Tannenbaum (1988) provides an example of how a consideration of geographic area helped Pizza Hut staff hourly jobs. According to Tannenbaum, Pizza Hut was unable to recruit a sufficient number of local youths to fill the jobs in its suburban New Jersey stores. Given this difficulty, Pizza Hut targeted urban areas of high youth unemployment as locales from which to recruit. To facilitate this recruitment program, Pizza Hut provided transportation to and from the urban areas.

In deciding on the geographic area(s) in which it will recruit, an organization should keep in mind the potential expense of having to relocate new hires or current employees who work at another company location. An employer should also consider the fact that for a several reasons (e.g., dual-career couples) many job seekers would prefer not to relocate. For example, in a study that encompassed over 500 companies (Lord, 1989), it was found that job applicants were much less likely to accept invitations to interview if the position required relocating than if no relocation was required.

How to Recruit Employees

Once an organization has decided on an applicant population to target and a geographic area in which to recruit, it next needs to select the methods it will use to fill positions. There are numerous recruitment methods that an employer could use, each of which offers particular advantages and disadvantages. Given the importance of the choice that an employer makes, a discussion of the various recruitment methods available to an organization will be saved for the next two chapters.

Recruitment Timing Issues

From the material presented so far in this text, the importance of the timing of recruitment activities should be apparent. As was noted earlier, if an organization is late in beginning to recruit it may discover that the most desirable candidates have committed to other organizations and that it is left with other companies' rejects (Lewis, 1985). On the other hand, if an employer recruits individuals before it really needs them, it may expend salary dollars if it hires them right away (i.e., money it would have saved if it had hired them at a later point in time) or it may need to keep them waiting for a job offer (which may result in candidates thinking the organization is not interested in them).

Not only is it important that an organization carefully consider when it begins to recruit employees, it should also be concerned about the timeliness of the actions it takes during the recruitment process. For example, there is research (Arvey, Gordon, Massengill, and Mussio, 1975; Byham, 1990) that suggests that the failure of an employer to follow up on job applications in a timely manner may result in applicants losing interest in the employer. Kotter (1988) discusses how companies that are rated as industry leaders attach great importance to timely recruitment follow-ups. Gilmore and Ferris (1986) note that many college graduates "will accept the first minimally acceptable job offer, if for no other reason than to terminate all the uncertainty generated by multiple job searches while still trying to finish their studies." Some research (Ivancevich and Donnelly, 1971) suggests that, by staying in contact with recruits after job offers have been accepted, a company can cut down on the number of persons who renege on job acceptances. Although there is insufficient data to suggest a specific time frame for recruitment follow-ups, Bergmann and

Taylor (1984) found that the college students in their sample reported that a time lag of one to three weeks between their campus interviews and some communication with the company was acceptable but that longer delays were unacceptable. However, not all research has supported the need for timely recruitment actions. For example, Taylor and Bergmann (1987) found no relationship between how long a company took to follow up on interviews and perceived company attractiveness.

Of the researchers who have addressed the timing of recruitment actions, Greer and his associates may have given it the most systematic attention. In a 1984 article, Greer pointed out that organizations tend to recruit employees when there is an upturn in the economy ("procyclical hiring") and to decrease or even eliminate hiring when there is an economic downturn. Given the fact that in many industries a company's business is linked to the general economy, such staffing practices are not surprising. However, Greer argues that the costs of such procyclical hiring are often overlooked. For example, if a company is hiring at the same time as most other organizations, it may not be able to attract as many job candidates as it would like, it may take a long time to fill job openings (thus missing business opportunities), the candidates it does attract may not be of as high a quality as it desires, and it may need to pay higher salaries than it would like in order to attract candidates. Instead of the typical practice of procyclical hiring, Greer (1984) recommends that organizations consider the benefits of "countercyclical hiring" (i.e., hiring during an economic downturn).

Among the benefits that Greer suggests may derive from such countercyclical hiring are higher quality hires, lower starting salaries, lower recruitment costs, an image as a "stable" employer, and progress toward affirmative action goals (because there is less competition for minorities and/or females). Among the potential costs of countercyclical hiring that Greer discusses are the inefficiency of an organization employing more people than are currently needed and employee dissatisfaction and turnover due to workers feeling underutilized or feeling the economy forced them to go to work for a given organization as opposed to their having made a free choice.

In concluding this overview of Greer's concept of countercyclical hiring (readers who are interested in more information should refer to Greer, 1984, and Greer and Stedham, 1989), a number of things should be noted. First, it should be stressed that Greer is not advocating countercyclical hiring as a general recruiting/staffing philosophy. Rather, he suggests it may be appropriate for employers in certain situations as a way to stockpile "a limited number of critical employees such as managers and professionals" (Greer and Stedham, 1989, p. 426). It should also be made clear that Greer does not suggest that such countercyclical hiring is descriptive of what organizations typically do. Rather, he suggests countercyclical hiring as an approach that more employers should consider. Although there is little research data to support the suggestions of Greer and his associates, their logic is certainly persuasive. A strategy of countercyclical hiring appears to offer real advantages, especially if an organization knows that in the near future it will need hire a particular type of employee who is difficult to recruit during good economic times.

What Information to Communicate and How to Communicate It

In developing a recruitment strategy, an organization can decide to recruit job candidates through numerous methods. Given the unique nature of many of these methods, each of these will be discussed individually in the next two chapters. However, there are certain generic communication principles that it makes sense to discuss prior to addressing specific recruitment methods. Most of these principles were introduced at various places in the earlier chapters in this text, so the logic underlying their importance will not be reiterated in this section.

In order to try to balance a recruit's need for information with his or her cognitive limitations, it was recommended that an organization focus its recruitment communications on those topics that job candidates see as being of the greatest importance and about which they are most likely to lack information or have inaccurate expectations. In order to discover the topics about which applicants lack information or have inaccurate data, it was recommended that an organization do some research. However, it is not enough for an organization to provide important job-related information; it also must be concerned about whether the information it communicates is perceived as accurate by the job candidate. Among the ways that were recommended for increasing the credibility of recruitment information were the use of job incumbents as an information source, the use of multiple sources of information who convey the same message, and allowing the job candidate to have first-hand knowledge of job attributes (e.g., a tour of the worksite, an internship).

Although it has been argued that information about certain job attributes will be of interest to most job candidates, it was also noted that job candidates may be interested in somewhat unique job-related information (as in the example of the immigrants who were particularly interested in the fact that United Airlines provides free transportation to employees).

In order to address this issue, it was recommended that an employer's recruitment information dissemination strategy allow for two-way interactions so that recruits are able to seek out information.

In addition to the above factors, an organization also must be concerned about an individual's ability to attend to, store, and recall the information it has provided. Among the suggestions offered for facilitating these information processing activities were providing information via different media, providing information that was distinctive, providing information at a pace and in amounts that do not overwhelm the job candidate, and encouraging recruits to call with questions they may have at a later point in time.

WHO RECRUITS: RESEARCH ON RECRUITER CHARACTERISTICS

Another key recruitment decision is who will serve as recruiters. Although it has long been assumed that the type of recruiter can influence the job-choice decisions of job candidates, it is only during the past two decades that this assumption has been tested. Beginning with a study by Alderfer and McCord (1970), several researchers (Harn and Thornton, 1985; Rynes and Miller, 1983) have examined the influence of such recruiter characteristics as gender, job title, and job knowledge on variables such as recruits' evaluations of the attractiveness of working for an employer and on their intention of accepting an offer. Most studies of recruiter characteristics have involved college students who were using their campus placement office.

The Evolution of Research on Recruiter Characteristics: Three Studies

Although it is not necessary to review all of the research on recruiter characteristics, the reader should have an understanding of how the typical study has been conducted and an appreciation of the improvement of research over time. Therefore, three studies will be briefly reviewed: Alderfer and McCord, 1970, Powell, 1984, and Taylor and Bergmann, 1987.

One of the first studies of recruiter characteristics was conducted by Alderfer and McCord (1970). In order to determine whether the type of recruiter and/or recruiter behavior had an important effect on job applicants, Alderfer and McCord had M.B.A. students evaluate the campus recruiters with whom they had interviewed. The students also were asked to rate their likelihood of receiving a job offer and their likelihood of accepting an offer if one was extended. As they predicted, Alderfer and McCord found that recruiters did influence job candidate perceptions of the quality of an interview, candidate perceptions of their probability of receiving a job offer, and their intentions of accepting an offer. For example, the students responded more positively to recruiters who were younger, showed interest in them, were willing and able to answer their questions, appeared trustworthy, and discussed career-related issues.

Although the study by Alderfer and McCord (1970) and a subsequent one by Schmitt and Coyle (1976) supported the view that recruiters influence job candidate decision making, Powell (1984) argued that to understand recruiter effects it was important to evaluate the relative influence of recruiter characteristics against that of job attributes. To do this, he distributed surveys to students when they arrived for interviews at their campus placement office. The survey asked students to rate the importance of fifteen job attributes and eleven recruitment items. Students also were asked to estimate the chances that they would accept a job offer if one was made by the interviewing company. Based on the results of factor analyses he conducted, Powell concluded that his job attribute items reflected three underlying dimensions (compensation/security, the job itself, and company/work environment) and his recruitment items reflected two dimensions (positive affect and recruiter responsiveness/knowledge).

Powell found that all five factor dimensions were significantly correlated with candidate perceptions of accepting a job offer. However, the results of a regression analysis he conducted demonstrated that, when both job attributes and recruiter characteristics were simultaneously used as predictors of job offer acceptance, only the job attributes were found to be important predictors. In summarizing his findings, Powell did not conclude that recruiter characteristics were unimportant. Rather, he suggested that recruiters are important as a source of information (or misinformation) about what a job entails. However, Powell cautioned that the importance of recruiter behavior as a direct influence on job applicant decision making has been overstated by many authors.

Although the studies by Alderfer and McCord (1970), Powell (1984), and others such as Harris and Fink (1987), Macan and Dipboye (1990), and Powell (1991) have contributed to our understanding of the effects of recruiter characteristics, these studies have generally looked at the effects of recruiters at a very early stage of the recruitment process (i.e., the campus interview). In order to determine whether the influence of recruiters becomes less important later in the recruitment process, Taylor and Bergmann (1987) designed a study that involved gathering data at several points in time, including after the campus interview, after a visit to the worksite, and following the receipt of a job offer. The individuals in this study were students from several universities all of whom had interviewed with the same large manufacturing firm.

Although their original plan was to use a longitudinal correlational design, Taylor and Bergmann were forced to rely on a cross-sectional design for most of their statistical analyses because the host organization for their study drastically curtailed its hiring. Still, the results of their study are important. For example, they found that recruitment variables were significantly associated with job applicants' reactions only at the initial campus interview stage (e.g., applicants who were interviewed by older recruiters, female recruiters, and recruiters who were affiliated with the personnel department tended to rate the company as a less attractive prospective employer). In contrast, job candidate perceptions of the attributes a position offered were significant predictors of their reactions at each stage of the recruitment process.

In summarizing their results, Taylor and Bergmann concluded that recruitment activities primarily influenced job candidate decision making through their impact on candidates' inferences about job and organizational attributes. That is, Taylor and Bergmann posited that recruitment activities provide candidates with cues about what a job entails (e.g., if a recruiter treated them with respect, this may signal how they would be treated as an employee). However, Taylor and Bergmann did not interpret their findings to mean that recruitment variables are unimportant. For example, they noted that, if recruits feel poorly treated during the early stages of the job search process, they may withdraw from job consideration before an employer has a chance to provide important job attribute information at a later point in the recruitment process.

Does the Recruiter Make a Difference? Speculation and Tentative Conclusions

Although researchers (see Powell, 1991) have cited several weaknesses, including the heavy reliance on college student samples and the lack of longitudinal data gathering, in the studies that have examined recruiter characteristics, researchers have nevertheless drawn a few tentative conclusions concerning the effects of recruiter demographics, function (personnel department versus line managers), and behavior. For example, after reviewing the research on recruiters, Rynes (1991) concluded that (1) recruiter demographics did not appear to have a major impact on applicants' job choices, (2) very little research had examined the effects of recruiter function and that what did exist was inconsistent (e.g., Harris and Fink, 1987, found no difference for recruiter function while Taylor and Bergmann, 1987, found results supporting the use of line managers), and (3) although job candidate reports of recruiter affect (e.g., warmth) and informativeness were sometimes linked to more positive ratings of the recruitment interview, these recruiter attributes had, at best, a modest relationship to actual job-choice decisions.

Given the results of studies of recruiter characteristics, it is difficult to argue with the conclusions of Rynes (1991) and others. At present, there is little empirical data that suggests that recruiter attributes have an important direct effect on the decisions made by job candidates. However, before accepting this conclusion—a conclusion that many respected companies reject—it is worthwhile to consider why, in theory, a recruiter might have an influence on job-choice decisions in certain circumstances.

The Recruiter as an Information Source

As has been stressed throughout this text, a major function of the recruitment process is providing job candidates with accurate and important information concerning various aspects of the job being filled. In order to effectively transmit such information to candidates, several recruiter characteristics are important. First, a recruiter must be knowledgeable about the position to be filled. To make sure a recruiter is familiar with a job, an organization can try to select persons who are already knowledgeable based on their own work experience, or it can rely on training as a method for providing a recruiter with information about a position (Dennis, 1984). In addition to being knowledgeable, a recruiter must be able to effectively communicate to a recruit the information he or she possesses (Phillips, 1987). For example, the recruiter should be able to speak clearly, use appropriate terminology, and efficiently use the limited time available with a job candidate (Byham, 1990). The recruiter should possess good listening skills so that he or she can respond effectively to questions a recruit may have (Harn and Thornton, 1985). However, it is not enough that a recruiter possess the necessary information about a position and is able to communicate it effectively; he or she must also be motivated to do a good job in recruiting job candidates (Dennis, 1984). Without such motivation, a recruiter may not convey a sense of enthusiasm to a recruit, prepare ahead of time for an interview, sufficiently rehearse a talk to be given at a job fair, and so on.

The Recruiter's Perceived Credibility

It is not sufficient for a recruiter to be knowledgeable about a position, able to communicate this information, and motivated to act as a recruiter; the job candidate must perceive these attributes. For example, even though a recruiter works for the human resource department, he or she may still be knowledgeable about the attributes of a given manufacturing position. However, if job candidates do not perceive the recruiter as knowledgeable, they may not be influenced by the information that he or she provides. Obviously, a key perceptual variable, then, is recruiter credibility. As was discussed previously, credibility is a function of an individual's expertise and trustworthiness. Although job incumbents generally have been thought of as the most credible recruiters, it is possible that other variables may also contribute to recruiter credibility. For example, Wyse (1972) found that African American job applicants preferred African American recruiters over white recruiters. Conceivably, minority recruiters are preferred by minority job candidates because they are seen as more knowledgeable about particular job attributes that may be of particular concern to minorities and/or because they are seen as a more trustworthy source of information. Greater perceived credibility may explain why in some studies (see Liden and Parsons, 1986) female job candidates have reacted more favorably to female recruiters.[4]

Herriot (1984), in particular, has emphasized that recruiter demographic characteristics be considered in building a team of credible recruiters. For example, in recruiting college graduates, he believes that minorities and women should be involved, especially if they attended the same university or majored in the same subject as the applicant. Herriot also believes that a team of recruiters should include young members of the organization since these individuals are more likely to be asked personal questions that are of particular interest to college graduates. To enhance the credibility of the information provided by minority and female recruiters, Herriot suggests that the location of the recruitment interview afford adequate privacy so that a candid conversation can occur. Without such privacy, a job candidate may assume that the recruiter will not disclose information that does not reflect positively on his or her employer. Furthermore, without privacy, the recruit may be hesitant to probe for important but sensitive job-related information.

The Recruiter as a Signal of Unknown Organizational Attributes

Another reason why recruiters may influence the decisions made by job candidates is because their background and/or behavior may be interpreted by recruits as a signal of unknown attributes of a position with an organization (Rynes and Miller, 1983). For example, if an applicant feels badly treated by a company representative during the recruitment process, the applicant may generalize this treatment to the way that the organization typically treats its employees. Conversely, exemplary performance by a recruiter can create a favorable organizational impression. For example, a recruit may interpret the way a company runs its booth at a job fair (e.g., well-designed recruitment literature available, knowledgeable personnel staffing the booth) as an indication that the company is very well managed.

In addition to a recruiter's behavior or background influencing a job candidate's general impression of an organization, it may also affect how the candidate views the job opening he or she is considering (i.e., the position's status within the organizational hierarchy). For example, consider the different reactions that a prospective employee might have if he or she was recruited by a low-level recruiter from an organization's personnel department versus if he or she was recruited by a high-level manager from the department the job candidate was considering joining. As was noted in Chapter 2, at companies such as General Mills and Merck top-level executives actively take part in recruiting employees (Kotter, 1988). One would anticipate that the presence of such executives would signal to a recruit that the position he or she is pursuing is viewed as quite important by the organization.

The choice of a recruiter and the recruiter's behavior may also influence a job candidate in a different way. For example, meeting an executive during a site visit may be seen by a candidate as evidence that he or she is highly sought after by the organization. In a similar vein, personalized treatment by company representatives during the recruitment process (e.g., periodic telephone calls) may signal to the job seeker that the company really wants the person to go to work for it. A timely job offer may also convey to a job candidate that he or she was an organization's first choice for a position. In contrast, if a job offer is not forthcoming in a timely manner, job candidates may lose interest in the position under consideration (Arvey, Gordon, Massengill, and Mussio, 1975).

In summary, a recruiter may not only have an influence on an individual's job-choice decision because he or she is seen as a credible source of information, the recruiter may also be influential because he or she is seen as providing cues to information that is not directly accessible to the job candidate. Given the information presented earlier in this text on how job candidates make job-choice decisions, the importance of this recruiter signalling function should not be underestimated.

Suggestions for Future Research on Recruiter Characteristics

Given the preceding discussion of how recruiters can influence the job-choice decisions of recruits, it should be apparent that this author believes a new direction is needed in this area of research. Simply stated, researchers must go beyond looking at the simple effects of such variables as recruiter age, gender, or job title. Rather, in order to understand how recruits make job-choice decisions, researchers must study more theoretically important variables. For example, instead of looking at whether a recruiter's race makes a difference, it would be interesting to know whether minority job candidates ascribe more credibility to minority recruiters or whether they perceive these recruiters as providing more useful information about job openings. In a similar vein, rather than simply looking at whether job applicants react differently to recruiters from personnel departments versus functional areas, researchers must begin examining why such background differences may have an influence on recruits (Does one type of recruiter convey more information or different types of information? possess more credibility? signal that greater importance is attached to a position?).

Only by examining such psychologically oriented variables will researchers begin to understand the importance of recruitment variables. In order to examine such variables, researchers will need to begin to use longitudinal designs such as that used by Taylor and Bergmann (1987) rather than the cross-sectional studies that have typically been employed. To more fully appreciate the effects of recruitment variables, researchers will also need to pay closer attention to contextual variables. For example, a job applicant who has talked to people who currently work in the department that he or she is considering joining or has done an internship there should be affected much less by many of the traditional recruitment variables that have been examined than the typical graduating college senior, who has been the focus of so many recruitment studies. Greater insight into how job candidates are affected by recruitment variables is also likely to come from future studies that use a greater variety of research methodologies. In particular, in-depth conversations with job seekers at several stages of their job search are likely to provide greater insight into job candidate decision making. A final suggestion concerning the design of research on recruiter effects is that studies no longer be seen as a contest between recruitment effects and job attributes. Not only has this type of study done little to advance our understanding of how to recruit employees more effectively, it has often confounded recruiter and job attribute effects (e.g., the effect of information concerning one's prospective supervisor and co-workers on job candidate decision making has been treated as job attribute information even when the recruiter was the candidate's prospective supervisor or co-worker).[5]

Selecting and Training Recruiters

Several suggestions have been made in both the academic and practitioner literature concerning how to select and train recruiters, although relatively little empirical research is available to draw on. With regard to the type of person to select as a recruiter, the practitioner-oriented literature (see Hirsch, 1989, and Lord, 1989) suggests that an increasing number of companies are concluding that it is beneficial to use either line managers such as a recruit's potential supervisor or prospective co-workers. Hough and Varma (1981) note that at Exxon engineers recruit engineers, M.B.A.s recruit M.B.A.s, etc. In terms of enhancing recruiter credibility, Herriot (1984) advocates the selection of recruiters who attended the same university as the job candidate and/or who majored in the same field. Given the implications of Revised Order No. 4, federal contractors would be wise to use minorities and women as recruiters.

The importance of communication and interpersonal skills underlies the suggestions by some researchers that a person's capability in these areas be considered in choosing recruiters (see Harn and Thornton, 1985). For example, Gilmore and Ferris (1990) stress that in identifying recruiters an employer should not only consider whether a person possesses considerable information about the open position, but also whether the person is able to communicate the information effectively. In selecting recruiters, Gilmore and Ferris also emphasize the importance of paying attention to a potential recruiter's listening skills, observation skills, and nonverbal skills.

In terms of recruiter training, as with the selection of recruiters, little hard data are available. Based on surveys of corporate practices (see Rynes and Boudreau, 1986), it appears that many recruiters receive little training. For example, research by Walters (1985) indicates that fewer than 20 percent of the recruiters in his sample were trained how to go about recruiting. In addition, where training does take place, it tends to focus on procedural issues (e.g., filling out forms), rather than substantive concerns (e.g., what information to provide about a position), that affect how applicants react to the recruitment process (see Rynes, 1991).

Although little research has been conducted, researchers have offered some advice on the training of recruiters. For example, because recruiters are often perceived as being poorly informed about the position to be filled, it is obvious that training should ensure that recruiters are familiar with the important and unique features a position offers (see Downs, 1969). Given the nature of the typical recruitment interaction, Harn and Thornton (1985) have emphasized the importance of training recruiters so as to improve their communication skills. Because job candidates may generalize from the way they are treated by a recruiter to the way the organization treats its employees, an employer should also consider providing training that addresses interpersonal skills (how to make an applicant feel comfortable asking for information). An article by Hough and Varma (1981) provides a description of how Exxon trains its recruiters. Among the topics addressed by Exxon are how to give a presentation at a job fair, how to make travel arrangements, how to plan a visit, what information to provide to candidates, what information to seek from them, and legal issues about which recruiters should be aware. Not surprisingly, Exxon's training not only involves lecture and discussion, it also involves role playing. Dennis (1984) suggests that recruiter training should ensure that recruiters are familiar with an organization's philosophy and objectives and that they be aware of any biases they have. Finally, Byham (1990) suggests that recruiters need to be trained in how to check on a job candidate's understanding of the information the person has been given during the recruitment process. Byham's recommendation is based on his finding that, although applicants for jobs with a major retailer were told that weekend work was required, exit interviews showed that many newly hired employees either had no recollection of having received the information or they did not appreciate the amount of weekend work involved.

In summary, given the existing data, the importance of recruiters should not be overstated. The perfect recruiter is unlikely to compensate for a position that has several undesirable attributes. On the other hand, it is also difficult to imagine that recruiters do not have any influence on the decisions made by job candidates.[6] Therefore, an organization should carefully consider the type of individuals it selects as recruiters and what training it provides to them.[7] In addition, an organization should never forget the need to motivate its recruiters to perform well (Phillips, 1987).

Although coming up with recruiters who can satisfy the suggestions detailed in this section may seem to be an impossible task, by being creative an organization may at least be able to improve on what it has been doing in the past. A particular approach that has been found to be beneficial is the use of a team of recruiters. For example, in recruiting engineers Hewlett-Packard brings a team of recruiters to college campuses. By using a team of recruiters, an organization may be able to divide recruitment responsibilities—a recruiter from the personnel department can discuss benefits, a potential co-worker can discuss work group cohesiveness, and a prospective supervisor can discuss projects that are anticipated in the upcoming year. If possible, an organization should try to have a minority and/or a female among its team of recruiters.

SUMMARY

The first section of this chapter highlighted the importance of several of the issues addressed in the first nine chapters of this text for those who are responsible for recruitment decision making. In covering topics such as deciding on an applicant population from which to recruit and recruitment timing issues, several examples of what actual organizations are doing were provided. Considerable attention was also paid to the importance of the recruiter. In covering this topic, the findings of the academic research literature were contrasted with actual organizational practice. In concluding this chapter, several recommendations concerning future research were discussed.

NOTES

1. For example, consider the following scenario. Because she is in a hurry to fill two vacant positions, the manager of the reservations department of a large hotel uses word-of-mouth recruitment. However, because the positions were not widely advertised, the hotel's personnel manager refuses to approve the hirings. Unable to settle this dispute, the two parties ask the hotel's general manager to intervene. In a meeting of these three parties, the reservations manager stresses the need to fill the positions quickly while the personnel manager stresses the need to increase the number of minorities the hotel employs. Trying to exercise the wisdom of Solomon, the general manager decides that the reservations manager can fill one of these openings by means of employee referral but that the other opening must be advertised.

2. As an example of how an organization can be inundated with resumes, Wein (1990) reports that the vice president of sales of a *Fortune* 200 company wanted to hire fourteen entry-level sales representatives. The vice president placed a small advertisement in a Southwestern newspaper and although the ad ran only once received 2,500 resumes!

3. See Koch (1990d).

4. It should be noted that Taylor and Bergmann (1987) found no effect for recruiter race. However, these authors did not report data concerning the number of minority job applicants or minority recruiters. Thus, it is possible that the lack of recruiter race effect is due to an insufficient number of minority applicants or recruiters in their sample. Harris and Fink (1987) found no interaction of recruiter gender and job candidate gender.

5. Rynes (1991) addresses the issue of whether potential supervisors and/or co-workers should be considered recruitment variables or job attributes. She argues that, while a case can be made for each position, given that supervisors or co-workers may act differently on the job than during a recruitment interview, they should be treated as recruitment variables (i.e., they signal what a position may entail). Although there is certainly logic in Rynes's position, it is based on the assumption that when acting as recruiters supervisors and co-workers may mislead a job candidate. The accuracy of this assumption will obviously vary by situation. For example, if, during a recruitment interview, potential co-workers are unable to answer technical questions that a recruit asks, the recruit may correctly conclude that these prospective colleagues are not at the cutting edge of their field.

6. In a recent article, Ansberry and Swasy (1989) describe how the actions of a recruiter from a prestigious Chicago law firm, which included asking a black law school graduate how she would react to being called "nigger" or a "black bitch" by adversaries or colleagues, led to the firm being suspended from recruiting at the University of Chicago Law School (one can only imagine the damage to the firm's general reputation and its ability to recruit minorities and/or women caused by the *Wall Street Journal* story).

7. Milkovich and Boudreau (1991) describe how at Eastman Kodak Company recruiters must be nominated by their managers and attend a training session. Readers who are interested in more information on the selection and training of recruiters should refer to recent issues of *Recruitment Today*. Readers who are interested in more information on planning a site visit should refer to Camuso (1984).

11

Recruitment Methods: Internal Recruitment and Job Advertising

When people think about recruitment, they frequently focus on how organizations publicize job opportunities. For example, people remember military recruiters who visited their schools and job advertisements they read in newspapers or store windows. From the material presented in this text, it should be apparent that recruiting involves much more than simply using a recruitment method. Before an organization decides on a specific recruitment method, it should carefully consider several fundamental issues.

DECIDING ON A RECRUITMENT METHOD: FACTORS TO CONSIDER

Probably the most basic question an organization should address is whether new employees are really needed. In cases such as a temporary need for increased production, an employer might be better off if it decided to use a strategy such as subcontracting or overtime rather than recruitment. Moreover, before it decides on a recruitment method, an employer also should consider how quickly a position must be filled and how much money can be expended on filling it. An organization's answers to these and other questions should have a direct bearing on the methods it uses to recruit. For example, if a position must be filled quickly, it would make no sense to advertise in a technical journal that requires several weeks' notice prior to publication. Because the myriad questions an employer should address in deciding intelligently on a recruitment method have been discussed in earlier chapters, these issues will not be reexamined in detail here. However, before discussing the various recruitment methods that are available, a brief review of a few important points may be helpful.

As was discussed in Chapter 2, one basic issue that an organization should address before selecting a recruitment method is whether it would rather try to fill jobs internally before looking for external candidates. An employer should also conduct a self-assessment to help it decide on an appropriate recruitment method. For example, a company that is visible to the public and that has a good reputation may receive many unsolicited résumés from qualified individuals. Such an employer could decide to rely on these applicant-initiated applications in filling job openings. An organization should also carefully consider the various requirements of the job it is trying to fill. For example, if a position requires specialized skills or uncommon work experience, an organization might be wise to advertise in a publication that is geared to a particular professional group rather than in a publication that is geared to the general public. In selecting a recruitment method, an employer should also consider whether suitable candidates for the position are likely to be looking for a new job. If an organization believes that the type of person it seeks may not be reached by such traditional recruitment methods as newspaper advertisements, it may need to actively target these people for recruitment via a direct mail campaign or some other mechanism.

Consideration of the issues raised in the preceding paragraphs and in earlier chapters should enable an employer to target an appropriate applicant population for its recruitment efforts. Having made this determination, the employer should then be able to intelligently decide on a recruitment method that will help it reach this population.

RECRUITMENT METHODS GEARED TOWARD INTERNAL JOB CANDIDATES

As was discussed in Chapter 2, there are several advantages to filling positions internally via promotions or transfers rather than externally. However, there are also disadvantages such as inbreeding. In those situations where an organization decides that it wants to fill a position from within, it next must decide whether it will try to widely publicize the job opening and allow employees to apply or fill the position in a somewhat secretive manner.

Job Posting

Job posting refers to the practice of an organization advertising job openings internally. Job posting can involve positions being publicized in company newsletters, on bulletin boards, or via computer systems (Moravec, 1990). Job posting is most common for blue-collar and clerical positions.[1] According to Farish (1989), job posting became more common as affirmative action pressure motivated employers to open up jobs to women and minorities. Other advantages of job posting that have been suggested are that it helps an organization discover hidden talent that might otherwise be overlooked, it allows employees to assume some responsibility for their own career development, and it helps retain good employees who dislike their current jobs and might otherwise leave for better positions elsewhere (Wallrapp, 1981). The following quotation conveys the sense of frustration that can be experienced by employees who work for organizations that do not publicize job openings:

> I have almost no idea what job openings exist or will exist outside my department. That kind of information just doesn't circulate at my level. So my capacity to get a good opportunity in some other part of the company is almost completely under the control of my bosses. Unfortunately, they don't have much incentive to want to find those opportunities for me. So I'm trapped in a narrow vertical career path, which in the long run won't be good for me. And the speed of my movement on this path is a function of strong forces I don't control. It's not a good situation. It's driving me to look for opportunities outside the company. (Kotter, 1988, p. 88)

Not surprisingly, job posting also has its drawbacks. For example, it can set off a chain reaction of personnel moves within an organization. It can result in several employees being disappointed at not having gotten a position for which they applied (Spector and Beer, 1982). Job posting can also involve considerable administrative costs (coordinating the paperwork, etc.).

Although organizations have instituted job posting systems that differ in a variety of ways, based on the experiences of several employers it is possible to offer a number of recommendations.[2] Before implementing a job posting system, an organization should carefully consider each of the guidelines enumerated in Exhibit 11.1.

Because a job posting system can involve substantial administrative costs, many organizations put limits on an employee's ability to bid for jobs. For example, Kleiman and Clark (1984) recommend that an employer require an individual to have worked for the organization for at least one year and to have been in his or her current job for at least six months before he or she is eligible to apply for a position. These authors also suggest that employees be limited to bidding on no more than three positions per year and that they not be allowed to bid on more than two jobs simultaneously. Kleiman and Clark also suggest that job bidding be restricted to employees who received at least a satisfactory overall rating on their most recent performance appraisal. If an organization decides to incorporate one or more of these suggestions, these restrictions should be communicated to all employees.

EXHIBIT 11.1   Guidelines for implementing a job posting system

1. Jobs openings should be posted/publicized in such a way that interested employees are likely to see them.
2. Job openings should be listed for a period of time that allows an interested party a reasonable amount of time to respond. The date by which a person should respond should be specified in the job notice.
3. A job notice should include a formal job title and a detailed description of the job opening. This description should address such things as job duties, equipment utilized, travel requirements, work hours, the geographic location of the position (if the position could be located in different areas), and the salary range.
4. The posted notice should describe candidate qualifications (e.g., required knowledge, skills, experience, and credentials) that must be possessed to be considered for the job (these should be legally defensible). It should also include an affirmative action statement.
5. Interested individuals should be instructed how to go about applying for a position. For example, applicants should be informed whether they should notify their supervisor prior to applying for a job.
6. A job posting system should provide applicants with notification of a decision in a timely manner. Applicants who are rejected for a position should be given feedback on why they did not get the job.

Organization-Initiated Approaches to Filling Positions Internally

Although many organizations have implemented job posting systems, for a variety of reasons (such as when the job incumbent is not aware that he or she is to be replaced), employers sometimes prefer to be more secretive in filling positions. Among the "closed" recruitment approaches that organizations have used are managerial nominations, replacement charts, and computerized job–person matching systems.

Managerial Nominations

The least formalized closed recruitment approach involves an employee simply being nominated by a manager for an open position. Managerial nominations generally involve an employee's immediate superior (or sometimes the employee's mentor) considering how the employee's characteristics match up with what a position entails. Frequently, an employee does not even know that he or she has been nominated. Because managers typically are only aware of a limited range of job openings, the use of managerial nominations often results in employees who are qualified for an opening never receiving consideration as candidates. Managerial nominations can also be influenced by a variety of biases that an employee's supervisor may hold (e.g., "A woman would not want to be a plant manager").

Replacement Charts

A more formalized closed recruitment system is the use of replacement charts. Unlike managerial nominations, replacement charts involve an organization doing succession planning before a job opening exists. Typically, their use involves managers, who hold jobs at higher levels than the job under consideration, deciding on who is in line for that job if it were to become vacant. Generally, a replacement chart will provide a rank ordered list of two or more job candidates. Frequently, these candidates have been rated in terms of their readiness for a position (e.g., "ready now," "should be ready within twelve months"). From this description, the value of replacement charts as a planning mechanism should be apparent. However, the use of replacement charts also has potential drawbacks. (e.g., rarely is there a provision for lateral moves across organizational units).[3]

Computerized Job–Person Matching Systems

A few corporations have instituted computerized information systems to help them fill positions internally (Sheibar, 1979). For example, IBM has developed the IBM Recruiting Information System, which involves employees completing a twelve-page booklet in which they describe their background and experience. This information is computerized. Thus, when a manager needs a person with certain qualifications to fill a position, the manager describes these qualifications and enters this information into the computer. The computer scans the data it has on employees and prints out a list of qualified job candidates.

In conclusion, both open and closed systems for filling positions internally offer advantages and disadvantages. What is important is that decision makers carefully consider what is best for their organization. In reality, organizations often end up combining approaches. For example, an employer may publicize jobs internally so that interested employees can apply while at the same time encouraging managers to nominate qualified subordinates.

ADVERTISING AS A METHOD FOR RECRUITING EXTERNAL JOB CANDIDATES: GENERAL ISSUES

In those situations where an organization has decided that it will recruit from external labor sources, there are a variety of methods that it can use. In the remainder of this chapter, the topic of recruitment-related advertising will be discussed.

Image Advertising

Broadly construed, recruitment advertising includes organizational activities that are intended to make an employer more visible to prospective job candidates, designed to improve an organization's image, or directed at filling a specific job opening. Advertising that is designed to make an organization more visible and to influence its reputation has been referred to as "image advertising." There are a number of books that have addressed the topic of image advertising (see, for example, Garbett, 1988), so image advertising will not be examined in detail here. However, a few examples of the recent use of image advertising is instructive. As will become apparent, image advertising can be particularly important if an organization is new, is in a highly competitive job market, and/or is trying to change its image (Magnus, 1985).

Because many job openings are filled without being publicized, the value of an organization being visible to the public should be obvious.[4] Visibility not only involves prospective job candidates recognizing an organization's name, it also entails this name being associated with what the organization does. For example, in 1984 Casa Lupita, a new chain of Mexican restaurants, had not established its identity. As a result, Casa Lupita found that its newspaper advertisements for restaurant managers were not drawing the response it needed.[5] In order to become more visible to the public and to communicate that it was a full-service restaurant and not a fast-food chain, Casa Lupita worked with Thompson Recruitment Advertising to develop a four-page "advertorial" that it ran in the *Nation's Restaurant News.* This advertorial was followed by a two-page advertisement that was designed to increase recognition of Casa Lupita as a potential employer of experienced managers. The last page of this advertisement included a coupon so that interested individuals could easily express their interest. According to Casa Lupita, this advertising campaign resulted in 450 résumés from "exceptionally qualified" managers. From this applicant pool, it hired twenty-five managers. The cost for the entire campaign was $24,800, or $992 per hire.

Although it may not be surprising that a relatively unknown company such as Casa Lupita has used image advertising, small companies are not the only ones that have felt the need to use such advertising. As a result of such things as its production of napalm during the Vietnam war (a product it stopped making in 1970, even though it still gets questions about it) and its battles over the effects of Agent Orange, Dow Chemical Company realized in the mid-1980s that its public image was lacking. In fact, its public image was so bad that, according to a Dow manager, "long-term chemists and researchers removed their company pins before boarding business flights" (Bussey, 1987, p. 1).

Dow established a task force to examine its public image. An internal report that summarized this task force's work concluded that "The current reputation of the Dow Chemical Co. with its many publics may well be at an all-time low. We are viewed as tough, arrogant, secretive, uncooperative, and insensitive" (Bussey, 1987, p. 17). Unhappy with its public image, Dow made several changes (including pulling out of South Africa). In order to communicate its new way of doing business, it began a $60 million "Dow Lets You Do Great Things" image advertising campaign, which involved both print and television advertisements. Dow also opened its plant sites for tours and publicized its philanthropic activities. Although it is difficult to gauge the success of image advertising, Bussey (1987) reported that, only a few months after it began its "Dow Lets You Do Great Things" ad campaign, a Dow Chemical study showed the public's reaction to the company had increased six percentage points.

General Dynamics is another organization that has used advertising to improve its public image. In 1988, General Dynamics began a "corporate image campaign" that had a $5 million annual budget. According to its chairman, Stanley Pace, this campaign was part of an effort to "recapture the good graces of the Pentagon and the public" (Curley, 1987, p. D1). General Dynamics's reputation had been tarnished by federal investigations of fraud and mismanagement on the part of the company,[6] and its image advertising was designed to associate the corporation in the public's mind with such "superordinate" values (i.e., values in which most people believe) as patriotism, education, and support for the handicapped. In addition to running newspaper and television advertisements, General Dynamics also tried to improve its image by sponsoring television programs on the Public Broadcasting System. At the end of each image advertisement was included the statement, "General Dynamics: A Strong Company for a Strong Country."

In summary, because an employer's public image can have a major impact on whether prospective job candidates decide to pursue jobs with the organization (Bergmann and Taylor, 1984), it is not surprising that companies such as Casa Lupita, Dow Chemical, and General Dynamics have used image advertising campaigns. Many organizations, however, already have considerable visibility and are well thought of by the public. An employer should research whether image advertising would be advantageous before deciding to use such a strategy.

Recruitment Brochures and Videotapes

In recruiting, particularly at job fairs and on college campuses, organizations frequently use brochures and/or videotapes to communicate information about themselves to prospective employees. Although in some cases recruitment brochures and videos may be developed to transmit information about a specific job opening, it is more typical that they are designed to convey more general information about the organization.[7] For example, Wang Laboratories uses a short generic videotape for recruiting at college campuses (Koch, 1990c). The goal of this video is to get students to think about Wang as a place to work and motivate them to sign up for campus interviews, as well as to provide them with a brief glimpse of the somewhat unusual work climate at Wang in order to facilitate self-selection.

Several recommendations were made in earlier chapters concerning the content of a recruitment device such as a brochure, and these suggestions will not be repeated here.[8] Rather, in this section a few major themes that are relevant to the development of recruitment brochures and videotapes will be reiterated and examples of effective and ineffective uses of recruitment brochures will be provided.[9]

As stated by Herriott (1984): "The organization's recruitment literature and job advertisements should be construed as an effort to communicate its expectations, norms, values, and image to possible applicants. They should not be treated as an effort to attract the maximum number of applicants, thereby improving the selection ratio" (p. 92). An employer must be particularly careful that its recruiting literature is not offensive. For example, as was noted earlier, in a study of graduating seniors (Feinstein, 1989a), not only was it found that students from several universities felt that the recruitment literature used by many organizations was "mundane and ineffective," but these students also found many of the recruitment brochures used by companies with whom they interviewed to be "condescending or offensive with hints of racism or sexism." In making decisions about the design of a recruitment brochure, an organization should also consider the impact of government regulations. For example, Executive Order 11246 suggests that a contractor's recruitment literature contain pictures of minorities and women. An employer should be sure that the minorities and women pictured are not all in lower-level jobs.

In order to get a better sense of the effective and ineffective use of recruitment literature, it is useful to consider the experiences of Saint John's Hospital and Health Center and PepsiCo Inc. Saint John's Hospital, which is located in Santa Monica, California, originally had intended to create a traditional recruitment brochure. However, in the initial stages of planning its brochure, Saint John's decided that a typical brochure would not do. It wanted a brochure that would "speak directly to specific candidates rather than to everyone at the same time" (Laabs, 1991b, p. 5), and it wanted a brochure that could be updated easily.[10]

Ultimately, Saint John's Hospital decided on a recruitment brochure that contained no copy whatsoever. Instead, the brochure was a simple white folder with the hospital's name on it and pockets for numerous inserts. Some of these inserts are given to all prospective employees. For example, everyone is given a welcome sheet that features a beach sunset photograph on the front and the hospital's history and objectives on the back. All applicants are also given a sheet that describes twenty-eight employee benefits the hospital offers. Other inserts provide information about particular careers at Saint John's. For example, if a person was interested in radiation therapy, there is an insert that addresses jobs in this department.

St. John's Hospital believes there are several advantages to having a recruitment brochure that makes use of such inserts. The inserts can be updated more cheaply than redoing an entire recruitment brochure. They allow the hospital to provide much more specific information about individual jobs. By carefully selecting appropriate inserts, the hospital makes it more likely that an applicant will receive important and detailed information about a job the person is interested in without being overwhelmed with information. In closing this brief discussion of Saint John's recruitment brochure, it should be noted that the hospital recognizes one of its major selling points. "In recruiting at Saint John's Hospital, I think one of the big sellers is that it's a nice community—it's a mile from the beach," said Randy Duke of Howard Advertising, who worked with Saint John's on developing its recruitment literature. "The feeling of the beach community is carried into the circular's theme with a scenic beach photo on the welcoming page and a stylized symbol of a wave on the folder's cover" (Laabs, 1991b, p. 5).

In contrast to Saint John's Hospital's well-conceived plan for developing recruitment literature is a recruitment flier distributed by PepsiCo Inc.[11] The flier, which was distributed during a recruiting trip to Northwestern University, included a "job recruitment quiz" that belittled Atlanta, Coca-Cola Company's corporate headquarters. The quiz, which was allegedly the work of a junior-level employee, asked students to compare the advantages of living in the New York City area with those of living near Atlanta. Among the comparisons listed were being close to the Metropolitan Museum of Art versus Stone Mountain Civil War Museum, having access to "any food in the world" versus "fatbacks and grits," and spending one's time yachting versus "cow tipping" (a prank in which a dozing cow is pushed over). Although the recruitment flier may not have been designed to be taken seriously, it appears many in Atlanta were not amused. For example, one Coke bottler in Atlanta reported receiving forty calls from businesses wanting to replace their Pepsi vending machines with ones dispensing Coke. In response to the controversy created by its job quiz, Pepsi took out a full-page newspaper advertisement in the *Atlanta Journal* in which it apologized to Atlanta residents. The ad was signed by Ron Tidmore, president of Pepsi-Cola South, who described himself as a native southerner who was " 'angry and embarrassed' " by the characterization of Atlanta (Associated Press, 1989, p. C14).

Job Advertising

From the preceding discussion of image advertising and recruitment brochures, the importance of these activities should be evident. However, if the amount of money spent indicates perceived importance, then organizations see a third type of recruitment advertising, job advertising that is oriented toward filling a specific position, as being of greatest importance.

For example, the Newspaper Advertising Bureau reports that in 1988 over $2 billion was spent on job advertisements in newspapers.

With such a huge expenditure of money, one might expect that employers would be very sophisticated in planning and implementing a job advertisement campaign. Unfortunately, this is not always the case. In fact, organizations regularly make mistakes in their use of job advertisements, including running advertising copy that results in allegations of employment discrimination,[12] failing to specify job qualifications, making it difficult to respond to an advertisement, and exaggerating job attributes so that newly hired employees are disappointed with their new positions. In poking fun at ineffectual job advertisements, Ray (1971) has suggested that a casual reader of the help-wanted section of a typical newspaper would conclude that (1) the "copy should start and finish with the company name," (2) "the job title should be as misleading as possible," (3) "the description of the work should be short or, better still, left out," and (4) "the conditions of employment are unimportant" (p. 20).[13]

Although job advertising is frequently thought of as a relatively simple recruitment approach, to get maximum value from an advertising campaign, an organization must consider several important questions (many of which should also be addressed if an employer uses some of the other recruitment methods discussed in the next chapter).[14] According to Hodes (1983a), the first question an organization should ask itself is, "What do I want to accomplish with my job advertisement?" In answering this question, an employer should not merely state the obvious goal of simply filling positions. It should also address (1) the qualifications a person must have to do the job successfully, (2) the number of people it wants to apply,[15] (3) its time frame for filling positions, and (4) the budget allocated for recruiting.[16]

Once an organization has established the scope of its advertising task, it next needs to decide who the people are it wants to reach. Obviously, an employer wants to reach individuals who possess the qualifications needed to be successful in the job. However, people with these qualifications may be available in different applicant populations. For example, a manufacturing facility that has a largely nonminority work force may be interested in increasing the number of Hispanics it employs. A high-tech firm may decide that the type of job candidates it needs are likely to be employed by its competitors. Once an employer has determined the type of applicant population it wants to target, it is better able to select a recruitment method for its purposes (e.g., the manufacturing facility may decide to advertise on a Spanish-speaking radio station; the high-tech firm may decide that a direct mail campaign is the best way to reach individuals who work for its competitors).

The next question that an organization needs to address is, "What information should my advertisement contain?" From earlier chapters in this text, it should be apparent that this author believes that important and accurate information about a position should be presented. In particular, an employer should consider whether it will include specific information about job duties, compensation, and the qualifications necessary to be considered for the job.[17] By including information about such important factors, an employer facilitates applicant self-selection (Mason and Belt, 1986), which in turn can lower recruitment costs and improve the quality of the people who are hired.[18] An organization also wants to be sure to communicate important information that may set it apart from other organizations. Such distinctive information (such as St. John's Hospital's proximity to the Pacific Ocean) is more likely to be recalled by job candidates as they make job-choice decisions.

In deciding what information to present in an advertisement, an employer should consider how it wants individuals to respond to its ad. If it is worried about being inundated with applications, an organization may decide to direct interested parties to send résumés to a given address.[19] For example, Edwards (1986) cites a case in which a company stated in a job advertisement: "Applicants must send resume and full salary history to be considered. No phone calls" (p. 45). In explaining its policy, the company noted that it did not want to waste time on the phone with unqualified applicants. However, as noted by Edwards, this response format makes it necessary for a person to put forth considerable effort to apply for a job. When an organization is trying to attract individuals who are highly sought after and/or are currently employed, such a policy is likely to result in relatively few applications (this was the case with the organization Edwards reported on).

In contrast to such a labor-intensive application process, some organizations allow individuals to express an interest in a job opening by telephone or by coupon. To handle phone applications, an employer must have a sufficient number of staff who can answer questions from candidates about positions and who can confirm that callers possess the minimum qualifications described in the advertisement (Hodes, 1983b). Many employers that use written job advertisements attach a coupon so that individuals can express tentative interest in a job without having to expend much effort. A typical coupon asks for basic information about a person's work and educational experience and for a telephone number and home address. The phone number allows the organization to set up an interview; the address allows the employer to send the person appropriate information such as an application blank or recruitment literature.

Once an organization has decided what information it wants to communicate in an advertisement, it next needs to decide what medium or media it will use and what outlet(s) it will use within a medium. The answers to these questions should be contingent on the answers to the earlier questions. For example, if a company decides it wants to convey a substantial amount of information about a position, a television or radio advertisement may not make sense because both of these media tend to be somewhat expensive and a viewer or listener could be overwhelmed with information (unlike a print medium, an individual cannot easily review the information presented in a television or radio commercial). In terms of choosing an outlet within a medium, if an employer wants to reach a particular applicant population (e.g., African Americans), it may not select an outlet (e.g., a radio station, a newspaper), that is oriented towards this targeted segment of the labor force.

Other factors in addition to the amount of information an organization wants to communicate and the applicant population it has targeted should influence the choice of an advertising medium. Many of these other factors will be addressed as each individual recruitment method is introduced later in this chapter.

Before discussing specific methods for recruiting individuals from outside of the organization, it is useful to review three key elements that advertising experts use to guide them in selecting an advertising medium and in deciding on the layout and content of an advertisement (Dessler, 1991).[20] Simply stated, for an advertisement to be effective it must attract attention, create interest, and motivate action.

Although it seems obvious that an advertisement must attract attention from the targeted applicant population in order to be useful, anyone who has read the help-wanted section of a newspaper is aware that many advertisements do not attract attention. There is a vast literature on attentional processes, so the numerous factors that are thought to result in people paying attention to an advertisement cannot be discussed in detail. However, as different recruitment methods are introduced in the remainder of this chapter, selective comments about their ability to attract attention (and their ability to create interest and motivate action) will be offered. Readers who are interested in more detail on the design of advertisements that attract attention, create interest, and motivate action are referred to past issues of *Recruitment Today* and to Ungersen's *Recruitment Handbook* (1983).[21]

It is not enough that a job advertisement attracts attention; it must also create interest in the job. Interest can be created by providing information about a job's attractive salary, desirable work location, flexible work hours, and/or stimulating duties. Interest in an opening can also be created by making the application process one that is not burdensome. In order to stimulate applicant interest, an organization must have a good understanding of what a position with it offers (Edwards, 1986). Once it knows what a job offers, an employer can select an appropriate segment of the labor market at which to target its advertising (recall Pizza Hut's targeting of inner-city youth as a labor market for staffing its suburban locations).

With regard to turning interest in a position into action, an employer can affect this linkage by making clear in an advertisement how an interested party should apply for the job. As was noted earlier, the easier the application process, the more likely that an interested person will file an application. As has been noted elsewhere in this text, timely organizational follow-ups on a job application and on any subsequent interviews are also important in keeping an applicant interested in a job opening.

In summary, in deciding on a specific recruitment method to use, an organization should not make a decision without considerable thought. Only by reflecting on the numerous complex issues discussed in this text will an organization likely select the "correct" recruitment method.

JOB ADVERTISING: DIFFERENT MEDIA AND DIFFERENT APPROACHES

Newspaper Advertisements

In comparison to several other recruitment methods, newspapers offer several advantages (Farish, 1989).[22] For example, newspapers allow an employer to place a job advertisement quickly. They also allow considerable flexibility in designing an advertisement. If a company is interested in targeting an audience in a given geographic area, a newspaper advertisement allows it to do this. However, the use of newspapers as a recruiting method also has potential disadvantages. Among these are that they generally only reach people who are actively looking for a job, it is difficult to make an advertisement in the classified section stand out from other job ads, and the circulation of most papers is not specialized (i.e., you pay to reach a great number of unwanted readers).[23]

Once an organization has decided to run a newspaper advertisement, it needs to select a specific newspaper as an outlet and to decide on the wording and the design of the ad. [24] It also must address the placement of the ad in the paper, how frequently to run it, and whether the advertisement will identify the name of the organization. Unfortunately, there is little research to draw on in making these decisions. Some practitioners, however, have offered some recommendations (see Ungerson, 1983).

In order to attract more attention, some organizations have started to place their ads in sections of the newspaper other than the classified section. For example, it is believed that an advertisement that appears in the sports section or the business section is likely to receive more attention than one in the help-wanted section. Such an advertisement may even motivate interest from individuals who are happily employed and do not read the classified ad section.

A key decision in placing a newspaper advertisement is whether to identify the name of the organization. The reasons why a "blind" advertisement might be considered include that there is someone currently in the position being advertised, an organization does not want to have to respond to all the individuals who submit applications, and/or an employer does not want to make known its plans for expansion to competitors (Ray, 1971). Blind ads typically generate fewer responses than if an employer's name appears (Wein, 1990). One reason suggested for this lower response rate is that currently employed individuals are afraid they might unknowingly send a résumé to the company for which they currently work (Edwards, 1986). This lower response rate may also be partly due to suspicion by job hunters, whether or not they are currently employed, about why an organization wants to hide its identity. Although a lower response rate, in and of itself, may not be seen as a disadvantage, it has been suggested that poorer quality candidates result from blind job advertisements. Unfortunately, because of a lack of research addressing this issue, we are unable at present to say with any degree of certainty whether blind ads draw responses from less-qualified individuals.

In using newspaper advertisements, an organization must also consider the frequency with which ads are placed and how many ads are running at one time. Ungerson (1983) suggests that, since most newspapers have a fairly constant readership, rerunning an ad for the same job will get many fewer replies than the original ad. Therefore, he recommends that, if a position is not filled by the initial advertisement, the organization should consider using a different recruitment method or, at a minimum, changing the style and the content of its ad. An employer should also be sensitive to the number of advertisements for different jobs it is running at one time. Dennis (1984) suggests that running numerous advertisements at the same time can create the impression that the organization has a problem keeping employees.

Magazines and Professional Periodicals

Instead of running job advertisements in general-circulation newspapers, an increasing number of organizations are using magazines and professional periodicals. One advantage of these outlets is they make it easier to target a specific audience. For example, when Bank of America was looking for a marketing professional with experience in banking, it decided to advertise in specialized trade periodicals such as *Marketing News* and *American Banker*. This decision was based on its assumption that an advertisement in a trade publication was much more likely to reach the type of person it was interested in than was an ad placed in a San Francisco newspaper (Magnus, 1985).

If an organization is considering using a magazine that cuts across industries, it should carefully research the publication. Particular attention should be given to the size and type of audience it reaches. According to Geller (1990/91), most general-circulation periodicals have their readership audited by the Business Publication Audit of Circulations or by the Audit Bureau of Circulations. Such an audit can provide valuable information concerning total circulation and circulation by job function. It should also include information concerning such things as the education level of readers and their geographic distribution. In researching a publication, an employer should also inquire about reader response to previous ads.

Recently, some general-circulation magazines have begun offering an advertising option called "split runs" that allows an organization to make decisions about the geographic or demographic distribution of their advertisements (Geller, 1990/91). A magazine that offers split runs actually creates slightly different versions of an edition. Initially, magazines created editions targeted at different geographic regions of the country. However, some periodicals now allow an advertiser to select a much more precise audience for its ad. For example, Geller discusses the possibility of an organization being able to advertise in a magazine edition that is only distributed to persons who are employed by large corporations.[25]

An interesting development in the area of magazine and periodical job advertising is the appearance in recent years of several publications such as *Black Employment & Education Journal* and *Hispanic Engineer* that are designed to bring job openings to the attention of minorities. Although the usefulness of such outlets has not been established and the cost of placing an advertisement is often very high, nevertheless, in doing recruitment planning, an organization should consider their use, particularly when the organization is required to have an affirmative action plan.

Although several other advantages (such as the longer "shelf life" of magazine ads) and disadvantages (such as the longer lead time required for placing an ad) of using magazines and periodicals could be discussed, we will conclude this section by describing a recent example of job advertising that shows remarkable creativity.[26]

As has been previously noted, a key problem with any job advertisement is getting people to pay attention to it. Another problem is conveying to prospective employees what a position entails. American Airlines faced these problems in trying to staff its flight attendant positions. After thinking about how to recruit flight attendants, American Airlines realized that it frequently had a captive audience for two or more hours with little to do but read its in-flight magazine, *American Way*, and watch its flight attendants work. Recognizing this, American decided to recruit flight attendants by placing job advertisements in its own magazine (Laabs, 1990c). Knowing that its targeted applicant population (recent high school and college graduates) was most likely to travel during the summer, American placed its first ad in the June 1988 issue of *American Way* (American estimates that each issue of *American Way* is read by 1.1 million individuals). All an interested party had to do to receive more information about being a flight attendant was circle a number on a postcard in the back of the magazine and mail it in. The ad also gave readers a phone number to call and encouraged them to refer others who might be interested. The response to its advertisement was overwhelming: over 3,000 requests for applications were received.

Encouraged by the success of its first ad, American placed a second ad that had a foreign twist in the August 1988 issue of *American Way*. This ad sought flight attendants who were fluent in German, French, Spanish, and Japanese. This advertisement generated 1,500 inquiries. More recently, American Airlines has placed ads that were aimed at recruiting minorities and at attracting persons who were fluent in other foreign languages. Given its growing international service, it is considering creating different versions of *American Way* that would be distributed in specific geographic flight areas.

Radio and Television Job Advertisements

With the exception of the U.S. Armed Forces, employers have not made extensive use of radio and television as recruitment media, but that seems to be changing. In the past few years, more traditional organizations such as Ford Motor Company have used these media increasingly for advertising job openings (Chauran, 1989b). For example, Six Flags Over Georgia recently needed to fill more than 2,000 weekend and summer jobs (Koch, 1989a). Knowing that the labor market for these positions (people aged fifteen to twenty-four) was shrinking and that teenagers and young adults tend not to read newspapers, Six Flags decided that radio advertisements made sense. Working with Bernard Hodes Advertising, Inc., Six Flags designed two ads that ran on a radio station that appeals to a teenage audience. In designing these ads, Six Flags chose to emphasize the benefits of working there (including free use of the park and after-hours concerts) rather than the salary because it felt that these benefits made a job at Six Flags distinctive from most other jobs.

In comparison to print advertisements, the use of television and radio offers several potential advantages. For example, television and radio reach individuals who are not actively looking for jobs.[27] Because few employers use these media, television and radio ads are more likely to attract the attention of viewers/listeners.[28] The use of television, particularly with the growth of cable, and radio allows an organization to select an outlet (such as a given time slot on a particular station) that reaches its intended audience. Another potential advantage of these media is that they allow for considerable creativity in designing an advertisement.

As with any recruitment method, however, the use of radio and television has limitations. For example, in order not to overwhelm a listener or viewer, generally a radio or television ad can only present a minimum amount of information. Since these advertising approaches provide information in a transitory way in that the information recipient has nothing permanent to which to refer, they may make it difficult for prospective employees to recall information. Another potential limitation on using radio and television ads is the cost of developing such advertisements. Martin (1987) notes that some thirty-second television commercials can cost $20,000 to $40,000.

Although these and other potential concerns with the use of radio and television job advertisements merit consideration, with the wider availability of cable television throughout the United States, it is likely that the use of television job advertisements will increase in future years. For example, in the late 1980s, the Financial News Network introduced "CareerLine," a half-hour program that "gives recruitment advertisers the chance to showcase employment opportunities before a national audience that boasts a potential half-million viewers per episode" (Chauran, 1989b, p. 53). "CareerLine" only devotes one-third of its time to job opportunities; the rest of the program contains "information directed at anyone interested in his or her career" (p. 53). Given the upscale demographics of the Financial News Network's audience, many employers have become convinced that it is a good investment to advertise on "CareerLine."[29]

In concluding this section on the use of television and radio as recruitment media, a couple of points should be emphasized. First, it should be obvious that old generalizations about these media (e.g., television ads are very expensive) no longer are universally true. For example, although an organization could spend millions of dollars on producing and running job advertisements on a network television station or major radio station, it does not have to. Instead, it could simply choose to have a radio announcer read the text of job advertisement or decide to rent "still screen" space on a cable television station. The second point concerns the use of a radio or television advertisement in combination with a print advertisement. As was noted earlier, using television and radio ads can produce problems that do not occur with print advertisements. For example, a person may hear a radio ad while driving to work and thus not be able to copy down the organization's phone number. In a similar vein, a person may view a television advertisement but not have a pencil and paper handy to record information about where to mail a job application. As a way to address such problems, some employers use a radio or television advertisement in combination with a printed ad. For example, a company may use a television or radio ad to draw attention to a job opening and to stimulate interest in it. At the end of its advertisement, the organization states that more information about the position and how to file an application is available in a particular publication.

The Use of Billboards, Transit Advertisements, and Similar Approaches

Although it is uncommon, some employers have begun to experiment with job advertisements placed on billboards, commuter trains, subways, buses, their products, etc. The information presented in this section is intended to give the reader a sense of the creative approaches organizations have begun to use to publicize job openings. Although the advertising approaches discussed in this section have several positive features, they share many of the weaknesses of newspaper, magazine, television, and radio job advertisements. For example, the approaches discussed in this section do not allow for two-way communication between the job candidate and the organization. In addition, they generally limit the amount of information about a position that an organization can provide.

Billboard Job Advertisements

Because most readers will be traveling in an automobile, the amount of information that can be conveyed on a billboard is limited. Another limitation of this approach is that it generally requires considerable lead time to prepare a sign. In deciding whether to use a billboard, an employer should consider the type of job to be advertised. If it is a job for which the employer is continually recruiting, it may make sense to use a billboard advertisement. Another key consideration is the choice of a location. Properly placed, a billboard advertisement may provide considerable publicity at a low cost. Conversely, if it is poorly placed (for example, if one's intended audience will not see it because they do not own cars), the use of a roadside job advertisement is a poor investment.

Transit Advertisements

Another creative approach to publicizing job opportunities is transit advertising. Transit advertising can involve placards and posters placed in subway stations and in buses and commuter trains. As with the use of billboards and many of the other nontraditional recruitment approaches discussed in this chapter, transit advertising has most commonly been used when employers have had difficulty filling positions using more traditional recruitment methods. For example, in the late 1980s, many employers in the Boston metropolitan area had difficulty filling unskilled entry-level positions (Chauran, 1989a). During the same period, the amount of job advertising in Boston's mass transit system increased from 5 percent of the system's advertising to 30 percent of the total.

Transit job advertising offers several interesting features. It is relatively inexpensive. If it is placed in a specific geographic location such as a particular subway station, it allows an organization to target its advertisement at a specific demographic group (recall United Airlines placing ads along mass transit routes in immigrant neighborhoods). If it is placed in a train car or in a public bus, a job advertisement can be seen by thousands of people per week, many of whom are a somewhat captive audience. In order to make it easy for people to respond to their advertisements, many organizations attach coupons that can be torn off, completed, and mailed.

Products as an Advertising Vehicle

Another novel method for publicizing job openings is the use of an organization's products. Consider the case of Lauriat Books, a New England chain of bookstores, which had an ongoing need for sales clerks, assistant managers, and managers. According to Paul Dexter, its director of human resources, Lauriat was unhappy with the response to its newspaper job advertisements. Working with an advertising agency, Lauriat developed the concept of using a bookmark placed in every book sold that advertised job opportunities. This concept appealed to Lauriat because it was inexpensive, it generated a steady flow of contacts, and it focused on individuals who had an interest in books (Jack, 1989). On the back of the bookmark was information about the benefits of being a Lauriat employee and a statement encouraging individuals to apply for a position. According to Dexter, the bookmark campaign was successful both in terms of generating new hires (during the first two months, forty people responded and ten of them were hired) and in minimizing costs (approximately $2,000 was spent on designing and printing the bookmarks).

Store 24, a 170-store chain of convenience markets based in New England, provides another example of how job openings can be creatively advertised (Laabs, 1991c). After trying several other advertising approaches, Store 24 decided to place job advertisements on one panel of its milk cartons. The advertising copy was written in the form of a quiz. Readers were asked questions about how much experience a job applicant needed to have, what percentage of Store 24 management started at the store level, and what a store manager can earn in a year. The carton also provided answers to the quiz (i.e., none, 85 percent, it depends on your initiative and talent). The milk carton ad also provided a phone number that connected callers with a recorded message about job opportunities and then instructed them to leave a message.

All things considered, Store 24 believes its milk carton job advertising campaign was effective. This conclusion is based on the minimal cost of producing the advertisement (less than $500), its wide circulation (Store 24 estimates the ad is on the kitchen table of 20,000 to 50,000 potential applicants each week), and the fact that Store 24 is convinced that both teenagers and adults read milk cartons when they sit at the kitchen table.

Point-of-Purchase Job Advertisements

Another approach that employers have used to fill jobs, especially lower-level ones in service industries, is point-of-purchase advertising. Point-of-purchase job advertising involves the use of materials such as signs and posters that publicize job openings and that are displayed at the location in which the opening exists. The most common type of point-of-purchase advertisement is a simple "Help Wanted" sign. However, as employers have had increasing difficulty filling positions, they have experimented with more creative approaches. For example, after becoming convinced that its clientele no longer paid attention to the "Now Hiring" signs that it always had posted, Carl's Jr. Restaurants decided to use multicolor table tents and tray liners as a way to publicize job openings (Koch, 1990e). Carl's Jr. not only wanted to stimulate interest in job openings, but it also wanted to get people to file applications. Thus, on each recruitment piece, individuals were encouraged to see the restaurant manager for an application.

Bank of America also has made use of a point-of-purchase job advertising program. Bank of America faced the problem of needing to recruit bank tellers who might be interested in working a limited number of hours during the middle of the day. Because it needed to fill part-time teller positions at over 800 branches, Bank of America used a recruitment strategy that included newspaper advertisements, job advertisements in customers' monthly statements, and a display placed in the lobby of all its branches. In order to attract attention, the display used bright colors and a catchy headline ("We're Hiring . . . Write Now"). The display included an illustration of a bright red pencil that pointed to response cards in a pocket of the display. In terms of the success of its display job advertisements, although hard data were not available, a Bank of America spokesperson considered the program a major success: "We've increased the number of hourly employees in general, and had a particularly marked increase in the number of people we are able to hire for the short-schedule-per-week program. We've also noticed a lower turnover rate in our part-time employees than with any other employment categories" (Chauran, 1988, p. 59).

Although a point-of-purchase job advertising strategy has its limitations (prospects must visit the place of business, for example) and research data are lacking, logic suggests that such a strategy makes sense for filling certain jobs. For example, in terms of the type of people its in-store advertisements would reach, Carl's Jr. felt that people who frequented a fast-food restaurant might enjoy working there. Bank of America felt that "people who were coming into our branches during the day . . . very well might be available to work during those hours. We were thinking about retired people, homemakers, maybe mothers with small children or school-age kids and college students" (Chauran, 1988, p. 59). In addition, a point-of-purchase program also generally makes it easy for interested individuals to begin the job application process (at Carl's Jr. a person could ask to speak with the manager; at Bank of America one could fill out a coupon while waiting in line for a teller).

Direct Mail Recruitment Programs

Sometimes the best candidates for a position may not be actively looking for a new job. Because many of the most commonly used recruitment methods are unlikely to reach individuals who are not in the job market, organizations have tried a variety of nontraditional recruitment approaches to make contact with these individuals. One method that has been used is a direct mail program. A direct mail program involves an employer sending a package of recruitment materials to a targeted group of prospective employees. Several factors can affect the success of a direct mail campaign, including the mailing list, the recruitment information contained in the mailing, the organization's image, and the ease with which an applicant can respond.

Of these, the mailing list may be the most important because if one's job advertisement does not reach the intended audience, it does not matter whether the employer's recruitment information is well designed or whether recipients can respond easily. There are several approaches that can be used in developing a mailing list. Some organizations have created mailing lists by purchasing the membership directories of professional associations (Bargerstock, 1989a). Allstate Insurance Company created a mailing list from its list of policyholders in the geographic area in which it needed to fill positions (Halcrow, 1989a). In trying to recruit nurses, hospitals have mailed recruitment information to former employees they think may be interested in returning to work there. In some cases, employers have contracted out the task of developing a mailing list. For example, Martin Marietta contracted with PAIRS, a Burr Ridge, Illinois, firm that specializes in developing mailing lists for companies (Stoops, 1984).

Once an organization has decided on the applicant population it wants to contact, it must next consider what information it wants to include in its mailing and how it wants individuals to respond to the mailing. For example, Northrop Defense Systems sends a packet that contains basic information on the company, the job specifications and requirements for the position it is trying to fill, and a return mail post card that requests information about the person and his or her interests.[30]

It is not possible to discuss here all of the things that an organization should consider in deciding whether to undertake a direct mail campaign, nor is it possible to address all of the issues that should be considered if it decides to go ahead with such a program (e.g., only home addresses should be utilized). Nevertheless, from this abbreviated treatment of the use of direct mail, it should be evident that this approach offers several advantages (e.g., personalized treatment) over many more commonly used recruitment methods, particularly if an employer wants to reach individuals who are unlikely to be looking for a job.

Employee Referrals

One of the most commonly used methods for bringing a job opening to the attention of prospective job candidates is referrals by current employees (Farish, 1989). Although employee referral programs can take many different forms, they are generally seen as an inexpensive method of providing quality applicants who are less likely to leave a position than individuals who are recruited by other common recruitment methods (Wanous and Colella, 1989). One explanation for why employee referrals are of high quality is that current employees do prescreening for their organization (they will only refer individuals who they think will perform well). An explanation for why persons who are recruited via employee referrals may have greater job longevity is that the employees doing the referring provide prospective employees with a realistic job preview of what working for the organization is like.[31] Another potential advantage of using employee referrals is they often bring positions to the attention of individuals who are not actively looking for a job. As was noted earlier in the text, a potential problem with using employee referrals as a recruitment method is adverse impact.

Although some employers such as Procter and Gamble do not offer rewards to their employees for referring job candidates, many organizations offer either cash or nonfinancial incentives to employees who make referrals.[32] For example, to help it staff its fashion retail stores, T. J. Maxx uses an employee referral program that gives an employee a $100 bonus for each person he or she refers who is hired and remains in the job for sixty days. Managers frequently distribute these checks at staff meetings in order to motivate other employees to refer people they know (Laabs, 1990d). Recently, University of Kentucky Hospital has implemented an employee referral program that not only offers small prizes for referring candidates for nursing positions, but also offers a grand prize. This grand prize, which is determined by a random drawing of those who have referred employees, includes round-trip airfare for two to any island in the world, deluxe hotel accommodations, five extra days of vacation, and $1,000 spending money.[33]

As with many recruitment programs, designing and implementing an employee referral program requires that organizational decision makers address several issues. Exhibit 11.2 contains some suggested rules for establishing an employee referral program in which employees are rewarded for referring job candidates. Although these rules may not make sense for every organization (e.g., a referral having to work 180 days in order for a referral award to be earned), they give a sense of the planning that should precede the establishment of a referral program. Without such planning, employees may lose faith in a program either because they do not understand it or because they do not believe it is fair.

EXHIBIT 11.2   Suggested rules for an employee referral program

---

Eligibility
- Managers with hiring authority cannot make a referral to their own department.
- The referral cannot already be employed in another position in the company.
- Employees are not allowed to refer relatives to their own department.

Program Parameters
- A referral must be fully qualified for the position.
- The referral must represent the person's first contact with the organization.
- A referral must be hired and work 180 days before a referral award is given.
- If more than one employee refers the same candidate, only the first referral received by the personnel department will qualify for a referral award.
- All information regarding the decision to hire or not hire a referral is confidential.

Procedures
- Employees must attach a referral program form to the candidate's application at the time the referral is made. The position the referral is applying for must be clearly stated.
- All awards are subject to taxes.

Note: Some of these suggested rules for establishing an employee referral program are taken from Halcrow (1988).

Job Fairs and Open Houses

In the 1980s, the use of job fairs and open houses for recruiting employees increased sharply.[34] Although these two recruitment methods have much in common in that they both allow for a two-way interchange of information between a prospective employee and a prospective employer and company representatives play a crucial role, they also differ in certain ways.

Job Fairs

Although there are different types of job fairs (some are geared to individuals with particular specialties such as engineering; in others, companies are looking to fill several different types of positions), there are certain common features. Typically, a job fair is held at a large hotel or convention center in a major metropolitan area and involves several organizations. Companies that wish to participate in a job fair are required to rent exhibition space for their booths.[35] The organization or association that is coordinating a job fair generally advertises that this event is upcoming in the local media.

There are several advantages to participating in job fairs. One of these is that an employer is able to talk with a large number of people in a short period of time (this can also be seen as a disadvantage). Another potential advantage is that job fairs often are attended by currently employed individuals who are not actively looking to change jobs. For example, an employed individual may decide to attend a job fair simply to keep informed about what the competition is doing. However, having been exposed to what another firm offers, this person may end up pursuing another job. The one-on-one contact at a job fair can also be advantageous; it may enable a company that is not widely known to stimulate interest from individuals who would not otherwise have thought of going to work for the organization.

From this brief coverage of job fairs, several things should be evident. First, it should be obvious that the individuals who represent an organization at a job fair play a crucial role. Chapter 10 presented considerable information on the selection and training of recruiters, so no more will be said about this topic in discussing job fairs or open houses. It should also be apparent that, given the nature of most job fairs, an employer will only have a limited amount of time in which to interact with a job seeker. Therefore, to get maximum benefit from their participation in a job fair, employers generally will not only rely on corporate representatives for presenting information, but also will use recruitment brochures and even videotapes.

A common occurrence at many job fairs is that the job seekers end up overwhelmed by the information they have received from the various employers with whom they have talked. Given this fact, a key question for an employer is, "How can we keep our name before the candidates?" One way to do this is to use "giveaway items" (Laabs, 1991e). For example, Owens-Corning Fiberglas Corporation frequently distributes pens bearing the company's Pink Panther logo. Other commonly used giveaway items are coffee mugs and paperweights. Given the number of people who attend job fairs, the cost of such items cannot be overlooked. However, an item such as a mug can be an ideal way to both remind a potential employee of the organization and to motivate candidates to visit its booth.

Open Houses

In contrast to a job fair, an open house typically involves only one organization. In terms of cost effectiveness, holding an open house makes the most sense when an employer has several positions to fill. Among the questions that an organization should address in planning an open house are how to publicize it, whether to offer an incentive to those who attend, and where to hold it.

For an open house to be successful, an organization must make sure that its target audience is aware that the event is going to take place. Employers have used a variety of approaches to advertise an upcoming open house, including radio announcements. In terms of motivating people to attend, many organizations have simply assumed that individuals will show up out of intrinsic interest. However, with increasing labor shortages in some career fields, organizations have begun to experiment with incentives. For example, Ingalls Memorial Hospital, a 711-bed facility in Harvey, Illinois, offered nurses a $100 bonus for coming to a four-hour open house (Laabs, 1990f). In its notices publicizing the open house, Ingalls offered to pay for child care expenses while the person interviewed. The nurses spent most of their time during the open house on the floors on which they were interested in working. At the end of their visit, candidates received a $100 bill. Overall, Ingalls viewed its open house program as very successful. Of the nursing candidates who visited, 68 percent received job offers and 61 percent of them accepted. As further evidence of Ingalls's satisfaction with the open house concept, it plans to use it to recruit pharmacists in the future.

With regard to the question of whether to hold an open house on-site or off-site, there are advantages to each (Kenney, 1982). For example, an on-site open house allows an organization to offer tours of a work site, generally makes it easier for those attending to talk with current employees, and typically costs less since no facility needs to be rented. Some of the reasons an organization may want to consider an off-site location are to minimize the distance that potential attendees would have to travel (this can be particularly important if an employer is located in a remote area), to avoid disturbing people who are working, and/or because it does not have an adequate on-site facility to hold the open house.

Although there are several other aspects of running an open house that could be discussed, such as whether candidates should be pre-screened, from the information provided the reader should have a sense of the pros and cons of using either an open house or a job fair as a recruitment method. Those who are interested in additional information should refer to the sources cited in this section.

Other Approaches to Advertising a Job Opening

Although the coverage of the various approaches that organizations have used to publicize positions is not intended to be all-inclusive, in concluding this section on job advertising, three other approaches should be briefly addressed: union hiring halls, trade association directories, and networking. In terms of the use of a union hiring hall, it suffices to say that companies frequently list certain job openings with the union that represents the bargaining unit in which the jobs exist. With regard to trade associations, many of them publish directories of job opportunities that may be of interest to their members.[36] Listing a job opening in such a directory can be an inexpensive way to make contact with hundreds or even thousands of prospective employees. Concerning networking, in the context of recruitment advertising, this term refers to informal, generally verbal efforts by organizational representatives to publicize job openings. Through telephone calls and informal conversations, an organization with high community visibility may be able to bring job opportunities to the attention of a wide and varied audience (Mondy, Noe, and Edwards, 1987).

SUMMARY

In earlier chapters in this text, it was emphasized that before an organization selects a recruitment method it first should address several basic questions. Among these questions were whether the organization wants to fill jobs internally or externally, whether it wants to provide prospective employees with realistic job information, and whether it is interested in increasing the number of minorities and women it employs. However, once an organization has decided on the applicant population it is interested in reaching and the type of recruitment information it wishes to communicate, it ultimately needs to decide on one or more recruitment methods it will use to fill its job openings. In this chapter, several different approaches to filling jobs internally were discussed. In addition, numerous approaches for advertising positions were addressed.

Although the material presented in this chapter is applied, the relevance of the theoretical concepts introduced in earlier chapters was not ignored. For example, in discussing the various recruitment advertising approaches that organizations have used, decision-making concepts such as attracting attention (advertising in the sports section), minimizing information overload (St. John's Hospital's use of a custom-tailored recruitment brochure), and aiding recall (giving out coffee mugs with the organization's name at a job fair) were mentioned.

From the material presented in this chapter, it should be apparent that some organizations have shown remarkable creativity in recruiting individuals (American Airlines' use of its in-flight magazine). In Chapter 12, several additional recruitment methods are discussed.

NOTES

1. For more information on job posting, the interested reader should refer to recent issues of *Recruitment Today*. Articles by Kleiman and Clark (1984), Spector and Beer (1982), and Wallrapp (1981) may also be of interest.

2. Milkovich and Boudreau (1991) provide a good example of how an organization can use job posting. According to these authors, every week Bank of America publishes a job opportunities bulletin that resembles the help-wanted section of a newspaper. For each job opening listed, a brief description of the work involved and the required job qualifications are provided. For each job, the bulletin also provides information concerning salary and the department, branch, or subsidiary offering the job. According to Milkovich and Boudreau, the job opportunities bulletins are placed in staff lounges, hallways, and other places frequented by employees. Each bulletin includes an application form to be filled out by interested employees and mailed to the person who coordinates the program at Bank of America.

3. For more information on the use of replacement charts and succession planning, readers should refer to articles by Friedman (1986) and Hall (1986).

4. The importance of being visible in a different context is clear from the following quote: "Do you think publicity doesn't pay? We understand there are twenty-five mountains in Colorado higher than Pike's Peak. Can you name one?" (Leibowitz, Farren, and Kaye, 1986, p. 241).

5. Readers who are interested in more information on the Casa Lupita case, as well information on the image advertising experiences of other organizations, should refer to an article by Magnus (1985). Lewis (1985) discusses the experiences of Phillips and British Petroleum with using what he called "prestige advertising" on television and in the press. Readers who are interested in an experimental study that demonstrates the influence of corporate image on the likelihood of readers responding to an advertisement should refer to Belt and Paolillo (1982).

6. McDonnell-Douglas, another large defense contractor, has also used image advertising with the theme, "A Company of Leaders."

7. In a technical sense, a recruitment brochure or videotape that is designed to make an organization more visible to job candidates could be treated as a form of image advertising. On the other hand, a brochure or videotape that is designed to fill a given position could be treated as a type of job advertisement. Because recruitment brochures and videotapes can fall into either category depending on their specific features, they are treated as a separate category of recruitment advertising.

8. From the earlier chapters in this text, it should be apparent that an organization's recruitment literature should include specific information that presents a realistic picture of a given job opening. Phillips (1987) recommends that recruitment brochures contain information about typical job opportunities, the organization (including products, services, policies, future outlook, and past performance), work locations, compensation and benefits, education and training programs, preferred degrees and majors, and the application process.

9. Readers who are interested in more information on designing recruitment brochures should refer to articles by Lubliner (1981) and Laabs (1990b, 1991b).

10. In developing a recruitment brochure, most organizations work with an advertising agency. In addition to the expense of using an outside firm, the actual production of a multicolor brochure on high-quality paper can make the development of a recruitment brochure an expensive project. For example, United Western Medical Centers (Laabs, 1990b) estimated that each recruitment brochure it distributed cost $4.50. Considering the cost and time involved in developing a traditional recruitment brochure, it is not surprising that most organizations would prefer not to produce different brochures for different jobs or brochures that will need to be updated regularly. The end result is that most recruitment brochures do not include specific information about jobs or timely information about the organization in general.

11. The material presented in this section comes from articles by A. H. McCarthy (1989) and by the Associated Press (1989).

12. See Kohl and Stephens (1989).

13. Even *Recruitment Today*, a periodical established to advise organizations on how to recruit effectively, admits to having placed a poor job advertisement. In its May–June 1989 issue, Betty Hartzell, publisher of *Recruitment Today*, criticizes an advertisement the magazine placed that produced 227 responses. "If we clearly had specified the parameters, the level of experience needed, the skills required and even the salary range, the ad would have done the job of screening candidates. Instead the ad was vague, indicating possibilities from entry level to more experienced job requirements. The result was extra work (and extra expense) in reviewing the resumes, screening the applicants and responding to the candidates" (p. 7).

14. Much of the material in this section comes from articles in *Recruitment Today* and by Palkowitz and Mueller (1987) and Hodes (1983a, 1983b).

15. As Ungerson (1983) notes, in most cases an organization wants an advertisement to produce a sufficient number of replies from qualified individuals so that it can fill its vacant position(s). At the same time, it wants to minimize the number of "wasted" replies from people who do not meet the job specifications and/or would not accept a job offer if one was extended. By analyzing its yield ratios from previous advertising campaigns, an organization may be able to come up with a rough estimate of how many applications it would like to receive.

16. Because of the complexity of the topic of job advertising, it is impossible to cover

many highly technical issues (e.g., choosing typeset, putting a job out for bid). Readers who are interested in more information on technical issues such as these should refer to Ungerson's *Recruitment Handbook* (1983), past issues of *Recruitment Today*, and the several excellent books on recruitment advertising.

17. In their study of job advertisements appearing in newspapers in Utah, Walsh, Johnson, and Sugarman (1975) found that 85 percent of the ads failed to provide information concerning wages.

18. Readers seeking additional information about the value of including specific information in a job advertisement should refer to Ungerson (1983). As an example of the phenomenon of organizations being inundated with résumés from unqualified job applicants, Lord (1989) reports on a study in which it was found that only 7 percent of the résumés received in the personnel department were seen as worth routing to hiring managers.

19. The labor market obviously will have a sizable influence on how many responses an organization receives to a job advertisement. For example, Martin (1971) reports that during a mild recession a company received 437 replies to its ad for an electronics technician who had experience with radar fire-control systems. The same company, at a time of a labor shortage, found a much larger advertisement drew only two responses.

20. Although three key elements are emphasized in this section, other writers such as Palkowitz and Mueller (1987) have made even finer distinctions such that four or even five points are distinguished.

21. Among the factors that articles in *Recruitment Today* (e.g., Lawrence, 1988) regularly consider are the use of unusual media, distinctive graphics, and intriguing headlines.

22. Because of the popularity of newspaper advertising and the fact that much of the information applicable to it is also relevant to other types of job advertising, this section will be longer than the treatment of many other recruitment methods.

23. Some newspapers in large metropolitan areas now offer "zoned classifieds" (Farish, 1989) that enable organizations to target their ads at districts in which sought after candidates are likely to reside.

24. Organizations that have chosen to address negative job features in their advertisements have used varying degrees of subtlety in their wording. For example, Lewis (1985) cites an example of a newspaper advertisement in which an unattractive feature of a job was subtly referred to in order to facilitate applicant self-selection: "On a personal level, a stable and understanding domestic situation will be necessary to meet the commitment and the significant UK travel required. . . ." (p. 125). In contrast to the tone of this advertisement is one that appeared in a London newspaper in 1900: "**Men Wanted For Hazardous Journey.** Small wages, bitter cold, long months of complete darkness, constant danger, safe return doubtful. Honor and recognition in case of success" (Tull and Kahle, 1990, p. 22).

25. Given space constraints, the section on newspapers as a method for publicizing job opportunities was necessarily simplistic. For example, the *Wall Street Journal*, although generally thought of as a newspaper, is somewhat geared to a particular audience (much like a professional periodical rather than a general-circulation newspaper) and offers several regional editions.

26. Readers who are interested in more information on the use of magazines and professional periodicals are referred to past issues of *Recruitment Today*. For example, the Summer, 1990 issue provides a planning calendar of upcoming editions of newspapers and magazines that will publish special sections geared to particular types of professionals.

27. Magnus (1988) reports that less than 15 percent of the work force reads the classified ads at any one time.

28. It has also been suggested (studies are lacking) that, in comparison to a print

advertisement, a particular advantage of a television advertisement is that the use of visual images and sound greatly enhances the vividness of the message, which in turn affects viewer attention and recall (Magnus, 1988).

29. "CareerLine" offered a number of different advertising options (e.g., five-minute segments, ninety-second spots). Cost estimates for the different advertising options ranged from $3,500 to $14,000. Readers who are interested in additional information on the use of television advertisements should refer to Magnus (1988). It should be noted that, with the bankruptcy of the Financial News Network, the future of "CareerLine" is uncertain at this writing.

30. For more details on Northrop Defense Systems's direct mail program, readers should refer to Magnus (1987).

31. An alternative explanation (see Rynes, 1991) for why those who are recruited via employee referrals frequently have higher performance ratings and greater job longevity is that employee referrals reach a different applicant population than that reached by other common recruitment methods.

32. Stoops (1983) provides a discussion of the pros and cons of using financial and nonfinancial incentives.

33. For details of this program, the reader should refer to Laabs (1991d).

34. Readers who are interested in more information about organizations' experiences with job fairs are referred to an article by Kleinfeld (1989) as well as recent issues of *Recruitment Today*. Readers who are interested in information about the use of open houses are referred to an article by Kenney (1982) and recent issues of *Recruitment Today*.

35. It is widely believed by companies that participate in job fairs that the location and design of their booth is very important. Readers who are interested in the effects of booth location and design on such factors as traffic flow and candidate impressions are referred to two articles by Weinstraub and Christman (1988, 1989) and one by Laabs (1990e). Although these articles are written for practitioners, they emphasize many of the psychological variables (e.g., attracting attention, motivating action, creating first impressions) that have been highlighted throughout this text.

36. O'Brien (1990) provides a good discussion of the advantages of using trade group directories to advertise job openings.

12

Intermediary Agencies, College Recruitment, and Other Recruitment Methods

INTERMEDIARY AGENCIES

In Chapter 11, several methods that employers can use to bring job openings to the attention of prospective job candidates were discussed. Although these job advertising approaches are commonly used and can be very effective, organizations have chosen at times to use intermediary agencies such as public employment agencies and executive search firms in staffing positions. That is, rather than the employer trying to make direct contact with prospective employees, it instead uses a third party to make such contact.

Public Employment Agencies

The public employment agencies in the United States are under the direction of the U.S. Employment Service (USES). The USES establishes national policies and oversees the operations of the state employment services, which have offices in 1,800 cities and towns.[1] The Social Security Act of 1935 requires that people who receive unemployment compensation register for work at their state's employment office. For the individuals who register with it, the state employment service gathers information about their work history, skills, education, training, and employment interest. These individuals may also be tested. Before a state employment office will refer job candidates, an organization must provide a detailed job description, its minimum job specifications, and referral instructions (such as the number of people it wants referred). In making referrals to an employer, a state employment office attempts to match the qualifications of the job candidate to those required by the employer.

Because organizations are not charged a fee for using the state employment service, this strategy is clearly an inexpensive way to recruit employees. In particular, it has been a useful source of blue-collar workers for many organizations. There are two common criticisms of the referrals made by state employment agencies: job candidates are frequently not very well matched to the job requirements and some of the individuals who are referred seem to have little interest in working. Thus, an organization can end up with new hires who make less-than-exemplary employees (Dessler, 1991).

Private Employment Agencies

In contrast to public agencies, private employment agencies generally do charge an organization a fee for referring job candidates (sometimes the candidate pays the fee). For executive positions, this fee can be as much as one-third of the position's first-year salary and benefits package. Most private agencies specialize in recruiting individuals to fill specific types of positions. Private agencies typically maintain an inventory of job candidates. Thus, they may be able to fill a position more quickly than an organization could on its own (Milkovich and Boudreau, 1991). Another advantage to using private employment agencies is that they do prescreening, which can save an employer the time and expense of weeding out unqualified individuals. This prescreening function can be particularly helpful if an organization does little hiring (i.e., it would be inefficient to maintain a recruitment/selection function). To get maximum benefit from the use of a private agency, an employer should be as specific as possible about what it is looking for in an employee (Dessler, 1991).

A somewhat unique type of private employment agency is an executive search firm.[2] Unlike most private employment agencies, executive search firms are not in the business of helping individuals who may contact them find jobs. Rather, these so-called headhunters find job candidates for organizations that are looking to fill executive-level positions. In recent years, corporations have relied heavily on executive search firms.

For example, in a *Business Week* article (Byrne, 1989), it was estimated that executive search firms represent a $2.5 billion industry. One of the reasons for this level of business according to Byrne is that today one out of every four CEOs is hired away from another company. Among the CEOs who were hired as a result of the use of executive search firms are Apple Computer's John Sculley and Pillsbury's Phillip Smith.

According to Thomas J. Neff, president of Spencer Stuart & Associates, he begins a typical executive search by getting as much information as possible from his client about the type of person it wants (Byrne, 1989). At the start of the search, the fee arrangement is also formalized.[3] Neff's next step is to identify the companies—often his client's competitors—where he is likely to find possible candidates. For a given search, Neff may contact as many as 150 sources, including executives he has placed in the past and members of corporate boards. Each contact is asked to recommend a few individuals who may be viable candidates; Neff then asks the people who were nominated for yet more names. According to Neff, the process of locating candidates ultimately comes down to networking.

As the executive search business has grown, many of the larger firms have centralized their information on job candidates on computerized databases. By doing this, a given headhunter can more easily make use of the work done by other headhunters used by the firm on earlier searches. According to Cronin (1981), some of the reasons that companies use executive search firms are that they need to fill a position quickly, they lack the time to conduct the search themselves, they feel uncomfortable approaching executives at other companies, and they believe prospective job candidates may be more comfortable with the confidentiality that dealing with an executive search firm may offer.

If an organization decides to use an executive search firm, it should conduct some research before it chooses a firm. Among the questions that Lord (1989) suggests a corporation should attempt to answer are: Does the search firm have a record of maintaining confidentiality? Is it well respected? Will the search firm understand your organization's needs? Will the search consultant present an image that is favorable to and consistent with your corporation's image? Does the search firm have sufficient time and resources to carry out the assignment?

Temporary Employees

When an organization uses an employment agency, it generally is looking for permanent staff. However, in recent years, employers have made increasing use of temporary employees for staffing positions.[4] For example, Nye (1988) reports that 95 percent of *Fortune* 500 corporations now use temporary help. Frequently, organizations have used intermediary agencies for supplying such personnel.[5] In some cases, employers use temporary workers on an "as needed" basis (for example, if a staff nurse calls in sick, a hospital may contact a "registry" for a temporary replacement). In other cases, employers contract with employee leasing firms and commit to using a given individual or group of individuals for a period of weeks or even months. As with more traditional employment agencies, most temporary help firms screen candidates before referring them to an organization.

Among the reasons why organizations have used temporary help are to meet a temporary fluctuation in workload (e.g., seasonal demand), to help out on special projects, to fill in for an employee who is on a leave of absence, to provide interim staffing for a vacant position that the organization is trying to fill permanently, and to provide increased job security for permanent employees[6] (Thrasher, 1990). Although the use of temporary help can offer an employer greater flexibility and, in some circumstances, can save it money, the use of temporary help also has potential disadvantages. For example, the compensation cost for a temporary person can be as much as 50 percent greater than for a permanent employee. The use of temporary help can make it difficult to create a cohesive work group. Staffing jobs with temporaries can also cause problems when work continuity is important. For example, some hospitals have cut back on their use of contract nurses because they feel that having different nurses interact with their patents hurts patient care (Nye, 1988). Obviously, work continuity is less of a problem if an organization has an agreement that commits the temporary help firm to supply it with the same person day after day.

According to Nye (1988), one reason that employers have increased their use of temporary help is that it allows them to use a "try before you buy" strategy. That is, an employer can evaluate an individual over a period of time while the person is considered temporary. If it is impressed by the person's performance, the organization can offer the person permanent employment. Although the agreement that an employer has with a temporary help agency may restrict its ability to convert individuals from temporary to permanent status, generally it can make a "release payment" of a specified amount to the agency in order to allow for such a conversion.[7]

Not only does the use of temporary workers help an organization determine if there is a good fit between an individual and a job, it also should help a temporary worker make such a determination. Individuals self-selecting out of job situations may explain the fact that, although approximately 50 percent of the individuals hired through temporary help agencies receive offers of permanent employment, only 20 percent accept them (Nye, 1988).

In summary, although the use of temporary help is not a panacea, this staffing strategy does offer several potential advantages. In deciding whether to use temporary workers, an organization should consider its unique circumstances.[8] For example, in deciding how to cover for a woman on maternity leave, an employer should compare the cost of using a temporary worker versus other strategies such as overtime. If, after weighing all the factors, an organization decides to use a temporary worker, it should communicate the reasons for its decision to its employees.

COLLEGE RECRUITMENT

Recruiting on college campuses is one of the most common methods used by organizations to fill professional and technical jobs and is also often used to staff managerial trainee positions. Although campus recruiting is an important source of personnel, it is not an easy recruitment strategy to use. As noted by Dessler (1991), to be done correctly, college recruiting requires careful planning regarding which campuses to visit, who to send as recruiters, and other issues. In contrast to many other recruitment approaches, recruiting at colleges can be both expensive and time consuming.[9] Considering that the first-year turnover rate for newly hired college graduates at some companies has been as high as 50 percent, it appears that at least some organizations have not implemented effective collegiate recruitment programs (Phillips, 1987).

Based on a review of the literature on college recruitment, several suggestions concerning how organizations can effectively recruit on-campus will be offered in this section.[10] Although the focus in this section will be on university-oriented recruitment, the principles outlined should also be applicable to recruitment efforts geared toward high schools or vocational schools. Because issues relevant to the choice of a recruiter and the development of recruitment literature have already been addressed, these subjects will not be reexamined as they apply to college recruitment.

How Organizations Select Colleges at Which to Recruit

In planning a college recruitment program, a key initial decision is determining which campuses organizational representatives will visit. The results of studies by Lindquest (1985) and Boudreau and Rynes (1987) provide insight into how hundreds of organizations have selected schools at which to recruit. Lindquest reported the results of a survey of 250 organizations. Representatives of these employers were asked to rate several factors in terms of their relative importance in selecting a college to visit. Among those factors rated as most important were "disciplines offered," "past success in recruiting," "reputation of faculty/program," "geographic location," and the "success of employed graduates in company." Among the factors rated as having little effect on whether a college would be selected were "solicitation by the placement office," "physical facilities of the placement office," "institutional size," and "the availability of resume books."

Boudreau and Rynes (1987) surveyed *Fortune* 1000 companies concerning several aspects of their college recruitment practices and received responses from 145 companies. In terms of the selection of schools at which to recruit, their results were similar to those of Lindquest (1985). Among the factors rated as most important by the companies in the Boudreau and Rynes sample were "reputation in critical skill areas," "general school reputation," "performance of previous hires from the school," "location," and "reputation of faculty in critical skill areas." Factors that were rated as relatively unimportant were "alma mater of CEO or other executives" and "SAT or GRE scores."

Although the results of these two studies provide information about the factors that influence the selection decisions of several organizations, this does not mean that every employer should base its selection of colleges at which to recruit on these factors.[11] For example, for a company that is not able to pay competitively, it may make sense to recruit at less-prestigious schools rather than at premier ones. In order to intelligently decide on the colleges at which it will recruit, an organization must simultaneously consider what it offers to job candidates and what it needs from them. In terms of what it wants from the students it recruits, in most cases an employer will seek students who are likely to accept a job offer (if one is extended), who will perform at least at a satisfactory level, and who will remain with the organization for a reasonable amount of time.[12]

Once it has determined what it seeks in college students and what it offers to them, an organization can then more intelligently decide at what colleges it is most likely to find the type of student it wants. Both Lockheed and PepsiCo are examples of companies that appear to have carefully considered the type of schools at which they recruit. In deciding on schools from which to recruit students who were graduating with advanced degrees in human resource management, Lockheed determined that it wanted students from programs that focused on HR management as it relates to large organizations. In selecting schools, Lockheed also reviewed its records from previous years and "narrowed its focus to include only those universities from which students typically had taken jobs in the west" (Laabs, 1991b, p. 8). Milkovich and Boudreau (1991) have described the selection strategy used by PepsiCo for choosing schools from which to recruit M.B.A. students: "rather than recruit 'hotshots' from Harvard or Stanford, PepsiCo 'shops around at second-tier business schools for people willing to get their hands dirty'" (p. 227). Phillips (1987) also provides an example of a Dallas-based bank that has carefully selected the colleges it visits. According to Phillips, based on its past recruitment experiences, this bank recruits at both local colleges and Midwestern universities because their students tend "to fit well into the bank's environment" (p. 80). The bank does not recruit at Ivy League colleges because it has found that their students do not work out as well.

In summary, a key determinant of the success of an organization's college recruitment effort is what campuses it chooses to visit. Once an employer has decided on the schools it will visit, it must next address what steps, if any, it will take to develop a presence on campus.

Establishing a Presence on Campus

As the competition for students has increased in recent years, many organizations have found it helpful, and sometimes necessary, to take actions to establish a presence on the campuses at which they recruit. Among the actions that employers have taken are (1) donating equipment, library materials, and money; (2) providing speakers; (3) funding scholarships; and (4) establishing on-going relationships with university faculty, student organizations, and the campus placement center (Farish, 1989). For example, in order to establish a better presence on those campuses at which it recruits, TRW Inc. sponsors faculty and graduate student research, has established summer employment and internship programs, provides money to purchase equipment, mails company literature to key campus contacts, and has designated a university relations officer for each college (Lehocky, 1984). These university relations officers are senior TRW managers whose duties include assessing the strengths, weaknesses, and needs of the campus they represent, making presentations to student groups, serving on campus advisory boards, and actual recruiting.

Companies believe that by taking actions such as those by TRW they will become more visible to students, improve the image students have of them as a place of employment, and receive better treatment from the campus placement office and other university departments. In sum, employers feel that by taking actions such as those described in this section they will establish a campus presence that will make it easier for them to recruit.

College Internship and Cooperative Education Programs

One of the ways in which organizations have attempted to establish a campus presence is by participating in internship and co-op programs.[13] In recent years, the use of such programs has become widespread.[14] However, co-op programs and internships offer advantages beyond establishing a campus presence. For example, Farish (1989) cites evidence that students with co-op experience generally have a lower turnover rate than those without it. Phillips (1987) found that employees with co-op experience received greater salary increases and more promotions than those without such experience. However, not all studies that have looked at the effects of pregraduation work experience have found such experience to be beneficial. For example, Taylor (1988) found only a few modest differences between students who did and did not have internship experience (among them, students with internship experience reported having a clearer perception of their vocation-related abilities and interests). However, Taylor acknowledges that several methodological weaknesses in her study (such as those in her control group reporting having as much relevant work experience as those in her internship condition) may have made her research a weak test of the advantages of an internship.

Although several explanations for the beneficial effects of internships and co-op programs have been offered, many of them relate to increased person–job fit.[15] For example, it is widely accepted that a student who has worked for an organization prior to graduation should have a better understanding of what a full-time position with the employer would entail than would a student who lacked such pregraduation work experience. Given this insight, the student with prior work experience may be able to self-select out of a work situation that he or she would not find satisfying.[16] Similarly, an employer that has had considerable exposure to a student through a co-op or internship program should have a better awareness of whether this person would make a good employee.[17]

In summary, based on the existing literature, it appears that employers who do much college recruiting should give careful consideration to the use of co-op and internship programs. In particular, Bowes (1987) has been a strong advocate of such programs because they allow an organization to adopt a "try before you buy" philosophy.

Other Recent Developments in Campus Recruitment

With computer technology becoming widely available on college campuses, it should not be surprising that this technology is increasingly being used for recruiting purposes. Recently, a few universities have created databases that list their students and alumni and have offered them to organizations for a fee. For example, Stanford University developed ProNet, a database that contains information on over 4,000 of its alumni.[18] In other cases, colleges have banded together. For example, the College Recruitment Database, which is sold to companies by the Human Resource Information Network, allows an employer to search a database of over 10,000 résumés of undergraduate and graduate students from twenty-three universities.[19]

Squibb Corporation (now Bristol-Myers Squibb Company) used computer technology in a very different way. In order to be noticed by highly sought after M.B.A. students at some of the top schools in the country, it distributed an interactive computer diskette that conveyed its recruitment message. According to Koch (1990f), several studies support the use of this medium for getting across a recruitment message: "According to studies conducted at Stanford University, people retain more information when they interact with the source, remembering 20% of what they hear, 30% of what they see and hear but 60% of what they interact with. Marketing studies also indicate that people tend to believe what they see on a computer" (p. 32).

The diskette used by Squibb presents basic information on the company, on different types of positions available within the company, and on case histories of Squibb managers. These case histories describe difficult business problems faced by recent M.B.A.s who worked for Squibb. The diskette describes each problem and then presents several possible options for solving it. Viewers are asked which solution they would choose. Subsequently, they are told which option was actually chosen. Squibb chose to use these interactive quizzes so that viewers would get involved in the recruitment information it provided. In designing the diskette,

Squibb provided a menu so that M.B.A.s could access the information they were interested in and bypass the rest. In order to try to set itself apart from other companies, Squibb also interjected humor into its "otherwise information-laden message."

To evaluate the effectiveness of its recruitment diskette, Squibb sent a follow-up questionnaire to a small group of diskette recipients. It found that "33% of them viewed the floppy diskette once, 29% viewed it twice, and 18% viewed it three times or more" (Koch, 1990f, p. 37). Although Squibb believes that its recruitment diskette was a success, this is not to suggest that Squibb could not have improved on what it did. For example, although Squibb created both 3 ½ inch and 5 ¼ inch disk formats, it sent only the latter type to Harvard M.B.A. students. Only after the fact did Squibb find out that Harvard had recently changed its computers from the larger to the smaller disk drives, which meant that many Harvard M.B.A.s were unable to view its diskette. Obviously, with minimal research, this problem could have been avoided.

From this overview of college recruitment, the importance of planning should be apparent. With the competition for talented graduates, employers who do not carefully plan their recruitment programs are likely to find themselves at an increasing disadvantage. With such planning, an employer should be able to increase its visibility on campus, improve its image, and facilitate person–job fit.

ADDITIONAL RECRUITMENT METHODS

In concluding this coverage of recruitment methods, two additional approaches will be briefly examined: applicant-initiated recruitment and the use of recruitment databases. Although it would be unusual for an employer to rely exclusively on either one of these approaches, they are frequently used in combination with other approaches.

Applicant-Initiated Recruitment

In contrast to various types of recruitment advertising, the use of an employment agency, or college recruiting, applicant-initiated recruitment does not involve an employer taking the initiative in trying to fill job openings. Instead, an organization relies on the motivation of individuals who are looking for jobs. Applicant-initiated recruitment can involve job seekers applying in person or via the mail. Key factors in determining whether an employer will receive many unsolicited applications are its visibility and its reputation.[20]

Although relying on applicant-initiated applications can be an inexpensive way to fill positions, exclusive reliance on this approach also has some disadvantages. A major drawback is that minorities frequently do not apply for jobs that have not been advertised (Scarpello and Ledvinka, 1988). If a company is a government contractor, it is unlikely that an affirmative action plan that relied on unsolicited applications for filling jobs would be acceptable. Another potential problem with this strategy is that it may create an applicant pool that does not include persons who are currently employed and not thinking about changing jobs (whether this is a problem will depend on whether an employer is interested in hiring such persons).

Before leaving the topic of applicant-initiated recruitment, it is important to address how an employer reacts to individuals who try to apply for jobs when it has no openings. Many organizations have a policy of not accepting in-person applications when they have no job openings and may discard résumés they receive through the mail if they have no open positions. In contrast to this approach, several authors (see Farish, 1989, and Ungerson, 1983) have suggested that organizations should view unsolicited applications as a way to create a "future possibles" list of prospective employees. For example, if an individual applies in person, an employer could conduct a brief screening interview to assess the person's qualifications. Based on its assessment of such job applicants, the employer could then create a list of viable job candidates should a job vacancy occur. A similar process could be used to handle résumés received through the mail. By creating such a list, an organization might be able to quickly and inexpensively fill job openings should they occur.

The Use of Recruitment Databases

A recruitment database "is a computerized collection of information on potential employment candidates" (Willis, 1990, p. 25). Such databases have been created by executive search firms, government agencies, universities, and other organizations. In recent years, the number of recruitment databases available to employers has increased dramatically. For example, according to Corporate Organizing and Research Services, in 1985 there were thirty-five firms selling résumé databases in the United States; by 1990, this number had increased to at least 159 firms (Willis, 1990).[21]

Although not all recruitment databases operate in the same way, they generally share certain features.[22] Career Placement Registry, Inc. (CPR), provides a good example of how a recruitment database works. CPR has compiled databases of both college students and recent graduates and of experienced job seekers. Among the data that CPR provides for each individual listed in its databank are the person's name, address, career goals, work experience, type of position desired, desired salary range, and educational background. A person must pay a small fee to be included in a CPR résumé database. In order to access one of CPR's databases, an organization must subscribe to DIALOG Information Services, Inc., a large computerized information network that has approximately 95,000 subscribers (Willis, 1990). Dessler (1991) reports that on average it costs an organization $20.00 to search a CPR database.

Advocates of the use of recruitment databases point out the fact that such sources can generate a list of job candidates quickly and inexpensively. Recently, a number of specialized databases have been created to access minority job candidates.[23] Even if the use of such a database does not help an employer increase the number of minorities it employs, subscribing to it shows a good-faith effort on the part of the organization. In terms of the disadvantages of using recruitment databases, two major ones have been voiced. First, it has been suggested that most employed individuals will not list themselves on a database to which the public can have access (Willis, 1990). Thus, if an organization is trying to recruit experienced personnel, the use of a recruitment database may not be the best method. Willis also has noted that some employers do not use public-access databases because they believe many of the candidates listed are "second-rate."

In concluding this discussion of recruitment databases, two facts are striking. First, there is no doubt that the use of such databases by organizations has increased considerably in the past ten years. Second, given the lack of research, it is impossible to judge the relative effectiveness of recruitment databases as a recruitment method.

AN OVERVIEW OF EMPIRICAL RESEARCH ON RECRUITMENT METHODS

Over the years, a number of studies have examined the results of using different recruitment methods (see, for example, Kirnan, Farley, and Geisinger, 1989, and Taylor and Schmidt, 1983).[24] The majority of these studies have investigated the effects of four methods—employment agencies, employee referrals, newspaper advertisements, and applicant-initiated applications—on subsequent employee turnover and, to a lesser extent, job performance (Wanous and Colella, 1989). As has been noted by Rynes (1991), it is difficult to draw conclusions from the research on recruitment methods. This is due to the fact that many of the methods discussed in this chapter (college recruitment, for example) have received little or no attention and to the inconsistent results for those recruitment methods that have been more thoroughly investigated. For example, of the nine studies reviewed by Wanous and Colella (1989) that looked at turnover, six found that informal methods (employee referrals and walk-ins) were linked to lower turnover rates than formal methods (employment agencies and newspaper ads) while three studies reported no differences. The association between recruitment methods and the subsequent performance of new employees is equally inconsistent.

In addition to investigating whether recruitment methods are associated with outcomes such as turnover, researchers have also looked at variables that may explain why different methods may be linked to certain outcomes. Among the explanations that have been offered for recruitment method effects are prescreening, differential realism, and applicant population differences. The prescreening hypothesis (see Ullman, 1966) suggests that persons recruited via certain methods such as employee referrals and scholastic recruiting in those cases where an institution screens job candidates will be of higher quality than will individuals recruited by methods that do not facilitate prescreening. The differential realism explanation for method effects (Breaugh and Mann, 1984) presumes that persons recruited via certain recruitment methods such as employee referrals and co-ops will have more accurate prehire job expectations than will persons recruited by other methods. The applicant population differences hypothesis (Schwab, 1982) is based on the assumption that different recruitment methods may reach different applicant populations. For example, running a job advertisement on a radio station that is geared toward African Americans is likely to bring a job opening to the attention of a different audience than would placing a job notice in the student newspaper of an affluent private high school. To the extent that the applicant populations reached by different recruitment methods differ in important ways, then the use of different methods may be linked to important work outcomes.[25]

Although a few studies have tried to determine which of these three explanations for recruitment method effects is most plausible, most of them have methodological weaknesses that make it difficult to conclude that any one of the explanations is correct (Rynes, 1991, Wanous and Colella, 1989). Among the weaknesses that have made it difficult to draw conclusions from recruitment method studies are (1) the use of retrospection for determining if prehire expectations were accurate, (2) the failure to measure applicant quality in a systematic way, (3) using new employees as research subjects rather than new hires and job candidates who rejected or did not receive job offers, (4) the failure to examine many of the recruitment methods used by organizations, (5) the failure to look at recruitment method effects with hypothesized mediating variables (such as realism) controlled for, and (6) the general focus of studies on lower-level positions such as telephone operators.

In summary, although a number of studies have examined recruitment method effects, with a few exceptions, most of them have had major flaws. Given these weaknesses, it is difficult to generalize from their results and to make recommendations to practitioners.

RECRUITMENT METHODS: ADVICE FOR PRACTITIONERS

Given the numerous recruitment methods available (and all of the information that has been presented on them in this chapter and in other sources), a practitioner may ask, "All things considered, which methods should my organization use?" In order to intelligently answer this question, an organization's recruitment objectives first must be stated. Is the organization interested in filling positions quickly? Minimizing recruitment costs? Recruiting women and minorities? Does the organization want to hire individuals who will perform exceptionally well? Be promotable? Not resign during their first year? Be satisfied with their jobs? However, to make recommendations about the best recruitment methods for an employer to use, it is not sufficient to know its recruitment objectives; one must also understand their relative importance to the organization (for example, is it more or less important to fill a job quickly than to hire someone who will not quit within the first year?).

Stated more directly, it is naive to think that there is a universally "best" recruitment method or methods. Rather, in determining which recruitment methods to use, an employer must consider its own unique circumstances, including the job it is trying to fill, its public image, its recruitment budget, labor market conditions, and how quickly the position must be filled. In order to answer some of these questions, an organization may need to examine data it has available on its past recruiting experiences (for example, what has been the cost per hire of using a private employment agency? Have certain colleges yielded better performers than other colleges?). An employer might also need to gather new information (Will a vocational school prescreen students based on their attendance record? How do students from New England colleges feel about moving to Alabama to work?).

Once an organization has answered questions such as these, it can weigh the various advantages and disadvantages of the numerous recruitment methods that are available to it. Based on such an analysis, it may decide that a traditional approach such as a job advertisement placed in the classified section of a newspaper makes the most sense. Alternatively, the organization may determine that a creative approach such as a milk carton advertisement, a co-op program, using temporary help, or a direct mail campaign aimed at former employees is the most intelligent method for it to use in filling open positions.

SUMMARY

In staffing positions, an organization has a variety of recruitment methods available to it. Chapter 11 focused on various methods that are available for recruiting employees from within the organization and also presented information on various job advertising approaches that can be used to recruit external job candidates. In Chapter 12, information was presented on four additional approaches to filling open positions: the use of intermediary agencies, college recruiting, the use of databases, and relying on applicant-initiated recruitment. Although the treatment of many of these recruitment methods was abbreviated and the relative strengths and weaknesses of each recruitment method were not discussed as thoroughly as they could have been had space been available, from the material presented in earlier chapters on such topics as communication principles, applicant decision making, and affirmative action, the reader should be able to adequately appraise the merits of each recruitment approach. Chapter 12 also provided a brief critique of previous research on recruitment methods, suggested ways to improve future research, and offered some advice to practitioners.

NOTES

1. Readers who are interested in more information on the USES should refer to Chapter 3 of *Fairness in Employment Testing* (National Research Council, 1989).

2. For a more detailed discussion of the differences between executive search firms and private employment agencies that fill lower-level positions, the reader should refer to Lord (1989).

3. Some firms work on a contingency fee arrangement and others work on a retainer. The pros and cons of these different fee arrangements are beyond the scope of this text. Readers who are interested in specifics concerning these different fee arrangements should refer to articles by Cronin (1981) and VanMaldegiam (1988).

4. Technically speaking, it is incorrect to refer to independent contractors, leased "employees," or other types of temporary help such as a Kelly Girl as employees. If an organization is considering staffing positions with temporary personnel, it should make sure that it is familiar with the legal regulations that determine whether an individual is an employee. Otherwise, it may discover that a person it was treating as an independent contractor is viewed by the federal government (e.g., the Internal Revenue Service) as an employee. Nye (1988), Schnapp (1989), and Thrasher (1990) all discuss the factors that have been used by the government for determining whether or not a person is an employee. Some of these factors are: Where is the work performed (at the employer's place of business or at a place determined by the person performing the work)? Who furnishes the equipment used for the work? How closely is the person supervised? Who pays for the person's work-related expenses? Are there employees doing the same work as the temporary help? What is the length of the employment relationship?

5. Although some authors have made distinctions among leased employees, independent contractors, and other types of temporary help, these differences are unimportant for our purposes. Readers who are interested in more information on the use of temporary help service firms and employee leasing firms should refer to Nye (1988).

6. That is, if there is a drop in business, the organization will eliminate temporary help before it lays off permanent employees. Among the companies that Nye (1988) reports as using temporaries as protection against layoffs are such well-respected organizations as Johnson & Johnson Products and Apple Computer.

7. Messmer (1990) discusses several criteria for selecting a temporary help agency. If an organization is considering converting temporary workers to permanent status, it should consider the "release payment" terms of various agencies in choosing a firm to contract with.

8. Jefferson (1989) describes a fascinating agreement between Boeing Company and Lockheed Corporation. This agreement, which involved Lockheed making a loan of over 600 employees to Boeing, was spurred by Boeing's immediate need for skilled and experienced personnel and Lockheed's temporary need to reduce personnel costs.

9. Phillips (1987) provides a detailed discussion of the many factors (e.g., the recruiter's transportation, lodging, meals, and salary) that should be considered in determining the overall cost of college recruitment to an organization.

10. Given the vast literature on college recruiting, the coverage in this chapter is selective. Readers who seek more information on college recruitment should refer to Bergmann and Taylor (1984), Boudreau and Rynes (1987), Lawrence (1988), Phillips (1987), and past volumes of the *Journal of Career Planning and Employment*.

11. In considering the results of the Boudreau and Rynes study, it is important to remember that their sample was comprised of huge corporations. For example, the typical organization in their sample recruited at an average of forty-seven campuses per year.

12. As has been discussed at several places in this text, an organization may have additional recruitment objectives (e.g., to increase the number of minorities and women it employs).

13. This discussion of internship and cooperative education programs is intended only to introduce the topic. Readers who are interested in more information about such programs should refer to Phillips (1987), who provides considerable detail concerning how an organi-

zation should develop internships and co-op programs so that they are of maximum benefit to both the organization and the student. Bowes (1987) and Taylor (1988) also have addressed such programs in detail. Rawlinson (1988a) provides several examples of organizations (e.g., Michigan Bell) that have used internship and co-op programs both to increase their campus visibility and to provide students with realistic job and organizational expectations. Particularly interesting is her discussion of the national INROADS program that provides talented minorities with business experiences while they are in school.

14. For example, Bowes (1987) reports that in the mid-1980s there were approximately 200,000 college interns at more than 1,000 companies.

15. Many of the advantages of using internships and co-op programs also apply to hiring students for summer employment or part-time jobs.

16. As with any organizational action that can increase the realism of a job candidate's expectations, the effects of an internship or a co-op program will be enhanced if the individual feels able to withdraw from consideration for a job that is not seen as a good fit. The ability of individuals to make intelligent self-selection decisions should also be increased if the interns or co-op students work in positions that involve similar duties to those of a full-time position they may be hired into and if they report to the same supervisor they would report to if they accepted a permanent position after graduation.

17. If a company intends to make use of an internship or co-op program to help it prescreen students for full-time employment, it should not accept students into such a program if it cannot foresee hiring them once they graduate.

18. In a later section of this chapter the use of recruitment databases will be discussed in detail. Readers who are interested in more information on ProNet should refer to Farish (1989) or Fritz (1988).

19. For more information on this database, readers should refer to an article by Lee (1989). This article also discusses how organizations are making use of computer technology to place on-line job advertisements that students can access via computer terminals.

20. Although image advertising can influence the number of applications an employer receives, as was discussed earlier, several other factors (e.g., the nature of a company's business) can also influence an organization's visibility.

21. Readers who are interested in more information on the different recruitment databases that exist should refer to Willis (1990). This article discusses five different types of recruitment databases (e.g., corporate job banks, university alumni groups) and provides addresses and phone numbers so that an organization can further investigate whether the use of a recruitment database may serve its purposes.

22. In covering recruitment databases, the focus is on those that are directly available to organizations, as opposed to those that are created for internal use by a private employment agency or by an organization. Public-access databases can differ in terms of whether they require job candidates to pay a fee to be listed and whether a candidate's entire résumé is accessible or only key information (e.g., education, current job, present salary) is included in a computer file. Readers who are interested in examples of organizations (e.g., IBM, The Travelers Corporation) that have created computerized databases (so-called job banks) of personnel who are willing to work on a temporary basis should refer to Willis (1990).

23. For example, Executive Telecom System, Inc., of Indianapolis has developed the Minority Graduate Database. This on-line service can link an organization with a databank of 12,000 minority college graduates (Messmer, 1990). Koch (1990g) reports that Hispanic Business, Inc., has developed HispanData, a computerized database of 5,000 résumés of Hispanic college graduates (some with advanced degrees and considerable work

experience). Candidates pay only a $5 fee to be included in HispanData's list. Companies pay a $7,000 corporate membership that enables them to have unlimited access to résumés. Among the corporations that Hispanic Business, Inc., reports have made use of its résumé database are Apple Computer, McDonald's Corporation, Mobil Oil, and MCI.

24. Much of the information presented in this section is drawn from excellent book chapters by Rynes (1991) and Wanous and Colella (1989). Readers who are interested in more detailed coverage of the research on recruitment methods should refer to these two sources, to articles cited in this section, and to Breaugh (1981), Caldwell and Spivey (1983), Decker and Cornelius (1979), Gannon (1971), Hill (1970), and Quaglieri (1982).

25. The logic for why prescreening, increased realism, and making contact with different applicant populations may be associated with the subsequent performance, satisfaction, job longevity, etc., of new employees is more fully explained in Rynes (1991) and Wanous and Colella (1989).

13

Managing
the Recruitment Function

From the preceding chapters, it should be apparent that recruiting employees is a complex human resource activity. If it is managed well, the recruitment function can help an organization reach its strategic business objectives. If it is managed poorly, recruitment actions can lead to a high turnover rate for new employees, lawsuits, the loss of government contracts, embarrassing newspaper stories, and the inability to fill job openings with qualified individuals. In this text, several examples of effective and ineffective recruitment actions have been described. Academic research on employee recruitment has also been discussed. The goals of this chapter are to tie up some "loose ends" and to offer some additional recommendations concerning the management of the recruitment function.

DRAWING CONCLUSIONS FROM
THE RECRUITMENT LITERATURE:
THE NEED FOR CAUTION

Despite the substantial increase in the number of articles on employee recruitment in recent years, things are not necessarily any easier for managers who are responsible for making recruitment decisions. For example, reports in practitioner-oriented publications make it appear that almost every action taken by an organization has had numerous beneficial effects.[1] In those few articles in which employers have acknowledged difficulties in recruiting, they often blame others rather than admit to their own mistakes. In contrast to the reports of recruiting successes that have appeared in practitioner journals, in several articles that have recently appeared in academic journals researchers have questioned whether recruitment activities are of any real importance.[2]

With the increasing number of studies on recruitment issues and the seemingly contradictory conclusions being reported in the practitioner and academic literatures, it is important that anyone who is responsible for making recruitment decisions be sophisticated in evaluating the published literature (Is the author objective? Is the methodology appropriate?). For example, if a manager is interested in how to recruit M.B.A. students, rather than rely solely on reports from other companies on how they recruited effectively, the manager also should be concerned about the perspective of M.B.A. students themselves (see Exhibit 13.1). Similarly, before accepting the conclusions of a research study, the manager should be confident that the study represents an adequate test of the recruitment phenomenon under investigation.[3] For example, a few researchers (see Taylor and Bergmann, 1987, Wanous and Colella, 1989) have criticized the way that many recruitment studies have been designed (such as the reliance on cross-sectional designs in which all data are gathered by questionnaires), and hence the conclusions that can be drawn from them.

EXHIBIT 13.1   An M.B.A. student looks at how organizations recruit

As an example of how organizations should be able to learn from their and from others' mistakes, an essay written by Bob Luck, an M.B.A. student at the Massachusetts Institute of Technology is instructive. Mr. Luck describes how he went from being interested in a job with an industrial company to being interested in one with a consulting firm as a result of the recruitment actions of the industrial companies. In describing his change of career interest, Mr. Luck suggests that industrial companies have been their own worst enemies as they recruit against investment banks and consulting firms for M.B.A. students. He states that the common excuse given by recruiters from manufacturing companies for their ineffectiveness in hiring M.B.A. students from the top-rated schools is that they cannot pay as well as investment banks and consulting firms, which he argues is "a dangerous simplification that ignores other problems industrial companies have in hiring talented managers."

Instead of salary being the major impediment to their recruiting the most talented M.B.A. students, Mr. Luck suggests that most manufacturing firms are being badly out-recruited by "service companies." His article describes several recruitment mistakes that manufacturers make. For example, he criticizes manufacturers for scheduling recruitment activities for the lunch hour, which is an inconvenient time of day for most students (it also limits the amount of time available for conversations between recruits and recruiters). Mr. Luck faults in-

EXHIBIT 13.1 *Continued*

---

dustrial companies for using personnel department staffers ("who weren't much use in describing the work I would actually be doing") or junior-level managers as recruiters. He also criticizes them for typically posting notices of company receptions rather than personalizing recruitment invitations, for not providing summer internship opportunities, and for failing to stay in contact with students during the year.

In contrast to his experience with manufacturing firms, Mr. Luck found that most consulting firms and investment banks personalize invitations to their recruitment functions, which are typically held in the late afternoon or evening and are scheduled for a longer block of time than the typical lunch-hour session with a manufacturer (time that allows for the exchange of more information). In contrast to the cold sandwiches and soda that many industrial companies supply at their functions, Mr. Luck reports that investment banks and consulting firms generally provide cocktails and/or dinner. Mr. Luck was also impressed by the fact that these banks and consulting firms tend to use senior managers as recruiters, provide summer internships, and make an effort to stay in touch with students after their visit to campus.

In summarizing his job-hunting experiences, Mr. Luck emphasizes how, in contrast to the manufacturing firms with which he had contact, he was impressed with the personal interest the nonmanufacturing firms took in him, which made him feel that he would be a valuable addition to their organizations. He also felt that he had much more information about what working with a service-type firm entailed; thus, he was better able to determine if there was a good match between the firm's needs and his interests.

Note: The information presented is based on an article by Luck (1986).

The current state of the recruitment literature being what it is, with inconsistent results, heavy reliance on student samples, and other deficiencies, one should be cautious in making recommendations to practitioners. Fortunately, as this chapter was being prepared, Rynes, Bretz, and Gerhart (1991) published a study that allows one to be more confident in offering advice to those with recruitment responsibilities. The Rynes et al. study will be discussed in some detail both because of its unique methodology and because many of its results contradict those reported in other studies while supporting the recruitment practices of a number of widely respected organizations (Kotter, 1988).

The Rynes, Bretz, and Gerhart (1991) Study of Recruitment

In introducing their study, Rynes and her colleagues point out that, "although recent academic research has tended to conclude that little variance in applicants' decisions is accounted for by recruitment practices, early academic research and the practitioner literature suggest that recruitment experiences can be very important in job choice" (p. 488). Rynes and her associates hypothesize that one reason for the lack of recruitment effects being reported in recent studies may be their use of simplistic research designs that do not allow recruitment variables to manifest themselves. For example, they note that in several recent studies, researchers simply gave questionnaires to college students who had just gone through an initial screening interview at their campus placement office (see Chapter 10 for more information about the typical study of recruiter effects).

In contrast to such a simplistic research design, Rynes et al. used a longitudinal design in which structured, open-ended interviews were conducted with job seekers (forty-one graduating students from a major university) at two points in time eight to ten weeks apart. These researchers went to considerable lengths to get diversity on variables that they thought might underlie recruitment effects. The first wave of interviews focused mainly on how applicants formed initial impressions of their "fit" with various organizations.[4] During their first interview, subjects were asked to nominate three companies they thought would produce the best fit and three companies they thought would produce the worst fit. The second series of interviews focused primarily on later phases of the job search process, such as site visits and job choices, and on general impressions that the students formed of specific recruitment practices. Rynes and her colleagues felt that by gathering information from job seekers both early and late in the recruitment process they would be better able to assess the influence of such variables as the timing of recruitment actions and recruiter behavior on the job-choice decisions made by the students in their sample.

From their first series of interviews, Rynes et al. report that several job and organizational characteristics had an important effect on the initial impressions their subjects formed of their fit with an organization.[5] Among the characteristics commonly cited as being important were a company's general reputation, the perceived status of the candidate's functional area within the company, training and advancement opportunities, and geographic location. Rynes et al. report that press coverage of an employer played an important role in the initial impressions formed by the students.

With regard to the impact of recruiters and recruitment experiences on the initial impressions formed by their subjects, Rynes et al. found that these factors were more likely to be seen as contributing to the formation of a negative rather than positive impression of an organization. For example, only twelve their forty-one subjects specifically mentioned their initial contact with a recruiter as favorably influencing their first impression of a company. In contrast, twenty-three of their subjects cited recruitment experiences as causing them to form negative initial impressions of fit. In terms of students changing their impressions, Rynes et al. report that sixteen of thirty-one subjects who said they had changed their initial impression of an organization mentioned recruiters or recruitment experiences as being a factor. Some of the recruitment experiences that were cited as leading to a negative impression were recruiters with poor presentation skills, rude treatment by recruiters, the failure to put at least one woman on a female recruit's schedule, and chauvinistic comments by male recruiters ("the guy at the interview made a joke about how nice my nails were"). Among the recruitment experiences that were cited as leading to positive impressions of person–job fit were liking the recruiter, the use of female recruiters, and seeing women managers during a site visit.

Rynes et al.'s second series of interviews provided information about the number of campus interviews and site visits students had and about the number of job offers they received.[6] Information concerning how and why students had changed their impressions since their first interview was also collected. Rynes and her associates found that a majority of their subjects were open to a substantial amount of influence during the job search process. Of those students whose initial impressions of an employer became more positive, 83 percent cited new information about the job or the organization as having had an effect; 61 percent mentioned recruitment-related variables as having played a role.

Among the recruitment experiences that were mentioned as having had a positive influence on recruit perceptions of an employer were the status of the people the person met during recruitment, the extent to which the recruit felt "specially" treated, the extent to which an employer was flexible in scheduling a visit, and an employer's professionalism during a site visit. The results of this second interview for those who became less favorable toward employers are particularly interesting. Of the thirty-five students who said they had lost interest in one or more of their initial favorites, twenty cited the influence of new information about job and organizational characteristics and twenty mentioned the influence of their recruitment experiences. Three of the important recruitment-related reasons provided by subjects for losing interest were their treatment during site visits, the recruiters with whom they interacted, and delays in the recruitment process.

In terms of whether their treatment during site visits contributed to a negative impression of the organization, the students in Rynes et al.'s study cited such things as a disorganized schedule (such as interviews running late) and logistical problems (such as transportation difficulties). Concerning the impact of recruiters, based on their content analysis of job candidate comments, Rynes et al. concluded that in general their influence "seemed to depend entirely on the extent to which recruiters were seen as reliable signals of what it would be like to work for the company" (p. 504). In terms of the signalling function that a recruiter can have, Rynes et al. perceived it as being less important if subjects had considerable information about an organization and/or if the recruiter was not from the applicant's functional area. These authors also reported that several students were suspicious about the motives of campus recruiters, while others questioned the extent to which recruiters understood what the job entailed.

Concerning the effect of recruitment delays, Rynes et al. reported that many of their subjects interpreted delays as indicating they were not going to get a job offer or that they were not the organization's first choice for the position. However, not everyone made such personal attributions. Some recruits attributed delays to such organizational characteristics as red tape. However, in most of these cases, the delays still caused the recruit to have a bad impression of an employer. For example, one student said a delay showed the organization was "administratively inept." Of particular significance is Rynes et al.'s finding that almost half of their sample said that recruitment delays had affected their willingness to take a job or that follow-up activity by the employer had come too late to matter.

From this synopsis of the study by Rynes, Bretz, and Gerhart (1991), it is not surprising that these authors conclude that what goes on during the recruitment process can have an important effect on the job-choice decisions made by job candidates. Given their findings, Rynes et al. offer several recommendations concerning how recruitment activities should be conducted. For the most part, their recommendations support the suggestions made in Chapter 10 concerning the selection and training of recruiters and the timing of recruitment activities. For example, the comments by the students in Rynes et al.'s study support the recommendation that recruiters be knowledgeable about the job opening, be skilled in communicating this information, and be perceived as trustworthy.

MANAGING THE RECRUITMENT FUNCTION: ADDITIONAL RECOMMENDATIONS

In earlier chapters of this text, suggestions have been made concerning (1) the type of people to use as recruiters; (2) the content of the recruitment message; (3) the timing of recruitment activities; (4) the choice of an applicant population; (5) the methods used to fill job openings; (6) the importance of an organization's image; and (7) ways to recruit so as to reduce the chance of a lawsuit. These topics will not be addressed further in this chapter. However, four topics that are important for managing the recruitment function have not received sufficient attention thus far: the site visit, recruiting nontraditional employees, recruitment information systems, and the evaluation of recruitment activities.

Managing the Site Visit

Once an employer decides that it is interested in extending an invitation for a site visit to a job candidate, it should take steps to increase the likelihood that the invitation will be accepted and that the visit will go well.[7] To increase the probability that an invitation will be accepted, an organization should think about what it can do to increase a recruit's ability and motivation to visit. One of the best ways that an employer can influence a job candidate's ability to visit is by being flexible in scheduling a trip (Reynes, 1989). By allowing a recruit to select among several possible dates, an employer may enable the person to schedule around other commitments that might otherwise preclude the person from visiting the organization.

In terms of a recruit's motivation to visit a company, both job offer expectancy (that is, the person's perception of the probability that he or she will receive a job offer) and job offer instrumentality (the relative attractiveness of receiving a job offer) are likely to be important. In other words, if a recruit sees little likelihood of his or her ultimately being offered a job or does not see working for the organization as a particularly attractive option, the recruit is not likely to accept the interview invitation.[8] An organization may be able to influence a recruit's motivation to accept a site visit invitation by making sure that the person is aware of the desirable attributes a job with it offers before the invitation is extended and by providing realistic information concerning the recruit's job chances, assuming the person has a reasonable chance of receiving a job offer. Although it is rarely discussed, an additional factor that may influence a person's willingness to accept an interview invitation is the confidentiality with which the visit can be conducted. For example, an employed individual may only be willing to visit another company if he or she is confident that his or her current employer will not find out about the trip. To ensure such confidentiality, a company may need to limit the number of people who know about a visit.

Concerning the site visit itself, there are numerous actions that an organization can take to increase its chance of successfully recruiting a job candidate. Some of these actions are important because they help a recruit get a better grasp of what a job with the organization would entail; others are important because they may be interpreted by a job candidate as signals of unknown organizational attributes. In terms of providing information to a job candidate, it is recommended that a recruit's schedule allow for in-depth conversations with both his or her prospective supervisor and co-workers. In most cases, a job candidate should also meet with a representative from the personnel department to discuss various employee benefits and other such matters. During a site visit, a recruit should be shown the immediate setting in which he or she would work. An employer should also consider providing a tour of its facility as well as of the surrounding geographic area.

No matter what information it communicates, there are certain aspects of working for an organization that are for the most part "unknowable" until after a person starts work. Such intangible aspects of working for an organization are frequently seen as being very important by recruits. As has been noted by Rynes (1991) and others, job candidates often use what they know about an employer as "signals" of unknowable organizational characteristics. Although little is known about what job and organizational features are used as signals by recruits, this does not mean that an employer should ignore the signalling that can go on during a site visit. For example, if a high-level manager cancels a scheduled interview with a job candidate, the recruit may interpret this as a sign that the manager either does not view the job opening as important or, if the interview was scheduled for late in day, as a sign that the candidate's interviews earlier in the day have not gone well. In a similar vein, a female candidate for a managerial position may interpret the fact that she did not interview with any female managers as a sign that the organization has few, if any, female managers. From these two examples, two things should be apparent. First, it is quite likely that job candidates interpret what they see as signals of what they don't see. Second, recruits may make incorrect inferences from organizational actions.

From the preceding discussion, the importance of planning a recruit's visit should be clear. During a site visit, an employer wants to do what it can to make sure a candidate receives accurate information about what a job with it offers. It also wants to be sensitive to the unintentional signals it may be sending. Because an interviewing trip is often an anxiety provoking experience, a company should also consider what actions it can take to reduce the stress a recruit experiences (Byham, 1990). Among the suggestions that have been offered for making a site visit less stressful are: (1) assigning a host who is responsible for coordinating events, (2) scheduling substitute interviewers in case anyone has to cancel at the last minute, (3) making sure that hotel accommodations are comfortable, (4) providing recruits with office space during a visit, and (5) providing an agenda for the visit ahead of time.

In summary, a site visit is an important stage of the recruitment process. If the visit goes poorly, it can cause a job candidate (and others the person talks with) to lose interest in the organization. If it is done well, it can increase the likelihood that a recruit will accept a job offer.

Recruiting Nontraditional Employees

As has been stated previously, it is predicted that in the future it will become increasingly difficult for organizations to recruit a sufficient number of traditional employees to fill their job openings. In order to be able to compete effectively, employers will have to recruit "nontraditional" workers such as the elderly and foreign nationals. In several earlier chapters, information relevant to the recruitment of nontraditional employees has been presented. For example, in discussing affirmative action (Chapter 9), several recommendations were made for recruiting minorities, women, and the disabled. Among the suggestions offered in Executive Order 11246 were including women and minorities in recruitment teams. Material relevant to recruiting nontraditional individuals was also presented in discussing the influence of recruiters (see Chapter 10). For example, it was suggested that for several reasons, minority job candidates may want to have contact with a minority who works for the prospective employer at some point during the recruitment process. A similar suggestion was made for the use of female recruiters in recruiting female job candidates. Rather than repeat the information on the recruitment of nontraditional employees that was presented in earlier chapters, in this section only a few issues that have not been adequately covered will be introduced.

In order to effectively recruit nontraditional workers, an organization must not only make these individuals aware of job opportunities, it must also interest them in going to work there. Although several of the things that were said about provoking interest in the general population also hold true for nontraditional job candidates, an organization must be sensitive to the special needs of nontraditional recruits. For example, Laabs

(1991f) describes how in recruiting minorities employers must make an extra effort to make them feel wanted as valued employees rather than as minority employees. Some of Rynes, Bretz, and Gerhart's findings (1991) suggest that organizations also need to be sensitive to making female recruits feel welcome. Although some employers already take steps to make nontraditional applicants feel welcome by having them meet with current employees who are of similar backgrounds or selecting and training recruiters so that nontraditional recruits are treated with respect, many organizations need to give more attention to the way in which they recruit such applicants. For example, Rynes et al. (1991) relate that 50 percent of their female subjects reported that at least one negative gender-related experience occurred while they were interviewing with companies.

In terms of recruiting disabled individuals, the government has provided both a carrot and a stick. Concerning the incentive, organizations who hire disabled persons may be eligible for a federal tax credit and state support. For example, Peters (1989) notes that the Tax Reform Act of 1986 provides up to a $35,000 tax credit annually for site improvements that make privately owned, publicly used businesses more accessible to the disabled. Laabs (1991g) describes how some McDonald's restaurants in Missouri receive $800 for each disabled person trained under McDonald's McJobs program. The government has not just used incentives to motivate the recruitment of disabled persons; it has also passed legislation such as Americans with Disabilities Act, which mandates that employers make reasonable accommodations for the mentally and physically challenged. Such actions could include making physical changes to the work place, redesigning jobs, and offering flexible work schedules.

In summary, recruiting nontraditional employees is a complex activity that requires familiarity with federal regulations such as immigration laws as they relate to the recruitment of foreign nationals, knowledge of how best to reach such recruits, and sensitivity concerning how best to treat such nontraditional employees during the recruitment process. However, based on company reports of their experiences, it appears that in many cases recruiting nontraditional individuals makes good business sense. For example, Laabs (1990a) reports that the annual turnover rate for Pizza Hut's disabled workers is 28 percent while the turnover rate for its nondisabled employees usually ranges from 150 percent to 250 percent. Days Inn of America, the hotel chain, has been pleased with its recruitment of senior citizens. It reports that its older workers have almost no absenteeism or tardiness and that their turnover rate of 1 percent is incredible when compared to the 40 percent rate of its younger employees.[9]

Recruitment Information Systems

In order to effectively manage the recruitment function, an organization must compile, maintain, and use a variety of different recruitment data. For example, executive orders require that government contractors document the composition of their current work force and the recruitment actions they have taken to address any underutilization of protected groups (see Chapter 9). Several federal statutes also require recruitment-related recordkeeping (see Chapter 8). In most cases, an organization should compile recruitment information that goes beyond that which is required by the government. For example, in order to be able to evaluate the relative yield of different advertising outlets or different recruiters, an organization will need to be able to determine how newly hired employees were recruited.

Although it is possible to maintain accurate, up-to-date employment records manually, companies are making increasing use of computerized systems for human resource information purposes (Kavanagh, Geutal, and Tannenbaum, 1990). In terms of recruitment, the use of a computerized "applicant tracking system" (ATS) can enable an organization to make more intelligent and more timely decisions (Witkin, 1988). For example, NCR reports that its ATS allows it to manage its decentralized college recruitment program more effectively (see Exhibit 13.2). Although space constraints preclude an in-depth discussion of computerized recruitment information systems, a few key issues merit attention.[10]

Once an organization determines that it wants to have a computerized ATS, it must decide how sophisticated a system it needs (for example, one that basically keeps track of names and addresses versus one that will track requisitions, generate reports, draft correspondence, etc.), whether it wants to buy or develop a system, how quickly it wants its system to be functional, and how much it is willing to spend.[11] With the exception of a few large companies, most organizations purchase an ATS. In evaluating any of the computerized recruitment information systems that are marketed, an employer should consider: (1) the purchase price, (2) maintenance costs such as software updates, (3) storage capabilities including size and flexibility, (4) ease of use, and (5) the level of security a system offers to protect the confidentiality of its data base.

In general, an organization will want an ATS that allows for information retrieval based on job candidate characteristics, recruitment methods, recruitment stages, and recruiter characteristics (Witkin, 1988). Concerning job candidate information, at a minimum a system should allow for data retrieval based on a person's name, social security number, and

EXHIBIT 13.2   NCR's applicant tracking system

Although NCR recognizes the value of a decentralized college recruitment program involving local managers visiting local campuses, in the early 1980s it became convinced that a centralized applicant tracking system (ATS) would enable it to improve its college recruitment operation. NCR's ATS operates on a minicomputer that is located at its Dayton headquarters and can be accessed by any of its thirty-five U.S. facilities. NCR's ATS contains two types of recruitment data: on schools and on job candidates. The information it keeps on schools allows NCR personnel to quickly determine such things as the quality of a given school, the names and phone numbers of placement officials, if it has made any donations to the campus, the nearest airport, and whether it has recently hired anyone from the campus. The information it keeps on recruits includes data on their majors, GPAs, degrees, geographic preferences, recruiter impressions, etc. As individuals are brought in for site visits, additional information such as interview ratings is added to a recruit's file.

According to NCR, centralizing its recruitment information allows each of its departments to have quick access to information on students who have been interviewed throughout the company (e.g., by other departments). This has enabled NCR to reduce the number of college visits its makes. NCR's ATS also allows it to quickly produce "personalized" letters that enable it to communicate with recruits in a timely manner. Another attractive feature of NCR's ATS is its reporting capability, which can quickly produce reports geared to a specific geographic region (e.g., listing students by name, major, and GPA who have expressed an interest in working in a particular region) or to such bottom-line criteria as the relative cost of hiring from various universities.

Source: From J. E. Lubbock, "A Look at Centralized College Recruiting" (1983).

employee identification number (for internal candidates). For some purposes, such as affirmative action reports, a firm may also want to be able to retrieve information based on such demographic characteristics as race. With regard to recruitment methods, an ATS should enable an employer to retrieve information that allows it to compare different methods it has used on various outcome measures. In terms of recruitment stage information, to help it make better decisions an organization will want access to data concerning the date that a recruitment event occurred, the time that elapsed between different stages in the recruitment process, and the number of people who have passed from one step of the recruitment process to the next. Finally, an employer's ATS should allow it to evaluate the performance of various recruiters it has used. In some cases, a firm may want to evaluate the performance of an individual recruiter (for example, how many of the students recommended by a given recruiter were also viewed favorably by line managers with job openings?). Other times, an organization may want to compare the performance of different types of recruiters (such as line versus staff).

In summary, an applicant tracking system should enable an organization to more effectively manage its recruitment operation. By examining such things as time lapse data, yield ratios, and recruitment outcome measures, a company should be able to determine what elements of its recruitment operation are running smoothly and what elements should be modified in future recruitment campaigns.

EVALUATING A RECRUITMENT CAMPAIGN

In order for an organization to make intelligent recruitment planning decisions, it needs to have accurate information about its past recruitment experiences (both its successes and its mistakes). Because an evaluation of past recruitment experiences is so important for recruitment planning, one might expect that most employers are very conscientious in evaluating their recruitment actions. Unfortunately, such an assumption appears to be erroneous. For example, in their study of college recruitment programs, Rynes and Boudreau (1986) found that (1) only 7 percent of the companies in their sample attempted to track the performance of employees recruited through different sources, (2) less than 15 percent kept track of turnover data on new employees, (3) only 40 percent of their sample kept track of advertising costs, (4) only 25 percent broke down recruiting expenses by college, and (5) only 46 percent said they tried to determine why applicants accepted or rejected job offers. Although these percentages are disappointingly low, they probably reflect an inflated picture of what an "average" U.S. company actually does. For example, Rynes and Boudreau's sample was comprised of *Fortune* 1000 companies. In all likelihood, these companies are more rigorous in their evaluation of recruitment actions than are smaller, less sophisticated companies (see Kotter, 1988). In fact, the data reported by Rynes and Boudreau may present an exaggerated picture of the recruitment evaluation efforts of even *Fortune* 1000 companies.[12]

Although most employers do not systematically evaluate their recruitment activities, they should. While the evaluation process will require careful planning and the systematic collection and storage of appropriate data, the payoff from such evaluation efforts can be considerable in avoiding discrimination charges, hiring better employees, and more cost-effective use of recruitment resources. Before discussing specific factors that an organization should consider in evaluating its recruitment actions, consider the experiences of Mattel Toys and Lockheed Missiles and Space Corporation. [13]

According to Mona Strehler, supervisor of staffing at Mattel Toys, one of the ways in which Mattel recruits employees is by placing job advertisements in a variety of different media outlets. Rather than simply assuming that these advertisements are effective, Ms. Strehler keeps a notebook with a section dedicated to each one. Each section includes a copy of the advertisement and information concerning (1) the outlet in which it appeared, (2) the date it appeared, (3) the size and cost of the advertisement, (4) where it appeared on the page, (5) where the advertisement appeared within the publication, (6) the number of responses for each position listed, (7) the number of respondents who passed on to the second and final stages of the recruitment process, and (8) the number of job offers made. According to Edwards (1986), by analyzing this information, Ms. Strehler is able to make better decisions concerning the future use of job advertisements.

Lockheed Missiles and Space Corporation has also attempted to evaluate the success of its new employee referral program that gave financial rewards to employees for successful referrals. Lockheed found that during the course of its referral program it received 3,173 referrals, which resulted in 1,889 applications (a 60 percent yield ratio), which led to 390 job offers being made (a 21 percent yield ratio), which resulted in 356 job offer acceptances (a 91 percent yield ratio). According to Lockheed, it spent $34,500 on referral rewards. Thus, its cost per hire was $96.91 and the cumulative yield ratio for its referral program was 11.2 percent.

From these brief summaries of the evaluation efforts of Mattel and Lockheed, it should be apparent that each of these organizations has gathered data that should help it make intelligent recruitment decisions in the future. However, from the information provided, it appears likely that these organizations could have improved on the evaluations they conducted. For example, Ms. Strehler of Mattel could have gathered information about such things as whether certain types of media outlets were more effective at reaching minorities or at reaching individuals who were inclined to accept job offers.

As the reader is no doubt aware, evaluating the success of any human resource activity is a complex undertaking. Given this fact, it is not possible to cover all of the issues that should be considered in designing and conducting an evaluation of a recruitment activity. [14] Instead, the treatment of this important topic must be selective. The intent of this section is to provide the reader with a basic understanding of the evaluation process.

Basic Issues in Evaluating Recruitment Activities

The fundamental question that should be addressed at the start of the evaluation process is what the organization wants to determine. For example, is it interested in discovering whether it needs to improve its image on college campuses, whether it should continue to advertise jobs in the *Wall Street Journal*, or whether job candidates have a realistic view of what a job with it involves? Unless an organization can clearly state its objective(s), it will have difficulty in answering the other questions that must be addressed in planning an evaluation study. Some of the most common objectives of an evaluation study are to assess the relative effectiveness of (1) the overall recruitment operation, (2) different recruitment methods, (3) different types of recruiters, (4) individual recruiters, (5) different applicant sources, and (6) different advertising approaches.

The need for an employer to be as specific as possible in stating an evaluation objective cannot be overemphasized. For example, consider the following objective: "We want to determine whether we are getting maximum value out of the resources we invest in our college recruitment program." In its current form, this would be a very difficult question to answer. For example, what is meant by maximum value: diversifying one's work force, hiring people who are promotable, attracting candidates who perform well their first year on the job? What activities are considered to be part of the college recruitment program: sponsoring PBS television shows, giving equipment to a campus? In contrast to this vaguely worded objective, consider the following evaluation goal: "We want to determine if the employees that we hire from Ivy League colleges perform better during their first year on the job than those we recruit from state schools." Clearly, this latter objective is much more easily addressed.

In most cases, in order to clearly specify an overall objective for an evaluation study, an organization will have to be able to describe its view of the causal relationships among recruitment variables. For example, an employer may think that the size of the job advertisement it places affects the amount of interest in the position that is generated. Or, an organization may believe that the more distinctive the information in a videotape it shows at job fairs the more likely attendees are to remember the video's message. In both of these cases, one variable such as the size of the ad is thought to influence a second variable such as interest generated. In standard research terminology, the causal variable is referred to as the independent variable and the affected variable is referred to as the dependent variable.[15]

Once an organization has specified the independent and dependent variables it is interested in studying, it needs to determine how it will "operationalize," or measure, these concepts. In some cases, this is a fairly straightforward process. For example, ad size could simply be operationalized as the area in square inches of the ad placed, and the amount of interest generated could be operationalized as the number of job applications received. However, operationalizing variables is not always so easy. For example, how would the reader operationalize the distinctiveness of the information in a videotape?

Because there are numerous criterion (dependent) variables that could be examined (Exhibit 13.3 presents just a few of them), in planning an evaluation study, a researcher must be sure that the ones chosen are relevant to the objective of the evaluation study.[16] In deciding on criterion variables, a researcher should be very concerned about possible criterion contamination (the influence of extraneous variables on the criterion variable).[17] For example, if an organization asks its campus recruiters to evaluate how prepared they were for interviews, it may get very different results than if it asks the students who were interviewed.

In planning an evaluation study, an organization should keep in mind the adage that "knowledge is knowledge of differences." Therefore, in designing a study, the organization must be sure that an appropriate comparison standard is available. For example, consider the case of a company that is interested in evaluating whether campus interviews conducted by executives result in a higher recruit job acceptance rate than interviews carried out by staff personnel. In order to make such a determination, the company designs a study in which it randomly assigns job candidates to interview with either an executive or a staff recruiter and then measures the acceptance rate for the recruits who receive job offers. The design described should make it fairly easy to determine whether it makes a difference whether executives are used as recruiters. In comparison to the preceding study, consider the following case. A company provides all of its new hires with a realistic job preview. It is interested in determining whether this RJP resulted in a lower first-year turnover rate for its new employees. How could it tell? If the company had only given some of its new hires an RJP, it could compare its RJP recipients against those who were not given an RJP. However, it did not do this; thus, no such comparison group exists. Conceivably, this organization could compare the turnover rate of its RJP recipients to the turnover rate of employees it hired in the year prior to its use of an RJP. However, any differences discovered could be due to something other than the RJP (such as a change in the local unemployment rate or a change in the company's compensation package).

EXHIBIT 13.3   Some sample criteria for evaluating recruitment activities

---

Global Criterion Measures
Number and/or percentage of
• jobs filled
• jobs filled in timely fashion
• jobs filled inexpensively (cost per hire)
• jobs filled with above-average performers
• jobs filled by members of underutilized groups
• jobs filled with people who remain at least one year
• jobs filled with people who are satisfied with their new positions

Recruiter-Oriented Criterion Measures
• Number of interviews conducted
• Quality of interviews as rated by interviewees
• Number and rated quality of career day presentations
• Percentage of people recommended who are hired
• Percentage of people recommended who are hired and perform well
• Number of minorities and women recruited
• Cost per interview

Recruitment Method-Oriented Criterion Measures
• Number of applications generated
• Number of qualified applications generated
• Number of applications generated from minorities and women
• Cost per application generated
• Time required to generate applicants
• Cost per hire
• Quality of employee hired (performance, turnover, attendance, etc.)

Another key decision point that may arise in designing an evaluation study is whether the study will involve the gathering of new information or whether existing data will be used. In many cases, there will be no choice; existing information will not be adequate to address the objective of the evaluation study. However, it has been this author's experience that, even when data relevant to a study's objective may already exist, gathering new data generally results in a stronger, more rigorous evaluation effort. With a new study, the researcher can carefully consider what data he or she needs to gather, from what individuals this information should be acquired, when data gathering should take place, etc. In contrast, when existing data are analyzed, a researcher generally has no control over such key aspects of a study.

The timing of the measurement of a criterion variable is another key issue to consider in designing an evaluation study. Precisely when a criterion variable should be assessed should be determined by the underlying relationship that is presumed to exist between this variable and the causal recruitment variable. For example, if a company believes that providing a realistic job preview will facilitate an employee's transition to a new job, it would make little sense to measure new employee job adjustment after two hours or two years in the position. Rather, in order to allow the employee to experience the transition process but not forget it, an organization might measure adjustment after one or two months of employment. A problem with many of the recruitment studies that have been conducted is that they have measured the criterion variable at a point far removed from its presumed cause. Thus, when an author reports little or no effect for the hypothesized causal variable, one does not know whether the researcher's hypothesis was incorrect or whether the effects of the hypothesized causal variable have dissipated.[18]

Of no less importance than the preceding issues is the question of who will comprise the sample for the evaluation study. Traditionally, studies that have evaluated various recruitment actions have used recently hired employees as their sample. Although for certain situations the use of new employees is appropriate, in many cases an evaluation study should incorporate information from other sources. For example, if an organization is interested in studying the effects of using different types of recruiters, it should gather information from all job applicants, not just those who were hired. In some cases, rather than focusing on applicants, an organization might be particularly interested in investigating why individuals who heard about a job opening did not apply for it. If an organization is interested in the impact of an image advertising campaign it ran, it might need to survey the general public.

In summary, in designing a study to evaluate a recruitment activity, a researcher has to carefully consider a variety of important design issues. Failure to consider these design issues will likely result in a poorly designed study. The results of such a study could lead to an organization ceasing to use a recruitment strategy that is, in fact, effective or continuing to use a strategy that does not have the effects assumed.[19]

SPECULATION ON WHY ORGANIZATIONS RECRUIT AS THEY DO

In this text, the recruitment actions of several organizations have been described. Although the actions of some of these organizations do not appear to have been carefully planned, the actions of other employers appear to be the result of a carefully developed recruitment strategy (see Exhibit 13.4). For example, in response to its increasing difficulty in recruiting teen-agers to staff its restaurants, Hardee's Food Systems, Inc., decided to recruit from underutilized segments of the labor force, including homemakers and older workers. Merck & Co. has also changed the way it recruits, even though it has experienced an increase in the number of job applications it receives.[20] As part of its new strategic plan for human resources, Merck has adopted a philosophy of promotion from within. In order to recruit staff with the talent necessary for advancement, Merck now fills most of its entry-level job openings from a carefully selected group of colleges (in the past it relied heavily on employment agencies and job advertisements). In order to sell itself as a career opportunity, Merck has modified its recruitment brochures and has shifted recruiting responsibilities from its human resources department to the company's line managers. To help it attract more female employees, Merck offers on-site child care at some of its facilities.

EXHIBIT 13.4 Compaq Computer Corp. takes Texas on the road

Although Compaq Computer has been successful since its start-up in 1982, it has constantly had a problem filling the new jobs its success has created. To address this problem, Compaq investigated what was special and distinctive about working there and what was special and distinctive about the high-tech workers it wanted to recruit. Based on its research, Compaq concluded that it had to address the negative stereotype that many non-Texans held of Texas as being arid desert country filled with sand lizards and sagebrush. In contrast to this stereotype, Compaq believes its campus-style setting in the middle of a pine forest not far from Houston is an ideal location that offers the advantages of being near a city without the disadvantages of working downtown. Compaq also studied how best to tell its story to recruits.

Based on its research, Compaq decided that it needed to develop a personalized recruiting campaign that would "place Compaq in the forefront of prospective candidates' minds" while correcting the inaccurate impressions that many of them hold. To do this, Compaq decided to stage an event it calls "Compaq, Texas" in several U.S. cities. One goal of this recruiting event was to convey Compaq's

EXHIBIT 13.4 *Continued*

park-like environment to recruits. To do this, it uses a mural depicting the entrance to the company's headquarters, props such as park benches and street lamps, videotape, and printed material.

In addition to giving prospective employees a sense of its physical environment, Compaq believes it is important to convey a sense of what working for it is like. To do this, the company believes it is essential for recruits to converse with Compaq employees. Thus, at its events, Compaq employees with various specialties are in attendance in order to demonstrate new products and answer questions that may concern technical matters or the climate at Compaq. To publicize an upcoming staging of "Compaq, Texas," the company uses display advertisements, radio and television announcements, and direct mail invitations that are sent to members of relevant professional organizations.

A typical visit to "Compaq, Texas" begins with a person being greeted in the hotel lobby by a Compaq employee. After filling out a registration form, the attendee is assigned to a recruiter who escorts the person into a ballroom where the person views an assortment of Compaq products. System engineers are present to answer technical questions, and literature concerning a variety of company attributes is also available. Attendees are also shown a video that "is made up of everyday Compaq employees explaining the company and why they feel it's special." Later in their visit, attendees go through a series of interviews. Some of these interviews are designed to provide information, such as a meeting in which Houston-area housing, tax structure, school systems, and cultural events are discussed. Other interviews are geared toward screening out individuals.

Although the cost of each staging of "Compaq, Texas" is substantial (approximately $100,000), Compaq believes it is money well spent. According to the company, some of the advantages of "Compaq, Texas" are (1) it allows the company to screen out job candidates without flying them to Houston (only about one out of ten attendees is invited to corporate headquarters for further screening), (2) it allows prospective employees to self-select out of job consideration based on the information they have received concerning the company and its culture, and (3) it gives Compaq considerable name recognition in the cities in which events are held. This name recognition is seen as helping Compaq recruit in the future as well as sell its products.

Source: Based on an article by Chauran (1989d).

Given the variety of different approaches that organizations have used for recruiting (targeting different applicant populations, using different recruitment methods, presenting realistic versus flattering recruitment messages, using line versus staff recruiters, and so on), an interesting question is why do different organizations adopt different approaches? Although little empirical research has directly addressed this question, recently a few writers have drawn on anecdotal evidence and tangentially related research to help explain differences in organizational recruitment strategies.

The Effect of an Organization's Strategic Orientation on the Way It Recruits

Olian and Rynes (1984) adopted Miles and Snow's (1978) typology of the strategic orientation of organizations ("defenders" versus "prospectors") to explain why employers use different recruitment approaches. Olian and Rynes' fundamental premise was that different types of organizations require different types of people (especially at the managerial and executive levels) and that different recruitment practices attract different types of individuals. In their article, Olian and Rynes addressed (1) the type of recruitment philosophy an employer is likely to adopt (to move quickly into new businesses, prospectors often fill jobs from outside), (2) the type of people an organization is likely to recruit (given their stable markets, the top jobs with defenders tend to be held by financial and production experts), (3) the type of recruitment information that is likely to be communicated (defenders emphasize well-defined job functions and career development; prospectors emphasize innovation and uncertainty), (4) the type of recruiter who is likely to be used (firms with change-oriented strategies are more likely to use line managers because they are better able to stay abreast of changes than staff recruiters), and (5) the type of media an organization is likely to use for publicizing job openings (given the stability of their environment, defenders are likely to use recruitment brochures or videotapes rather than informal presentations).[21]

The Rynes and Barber (1990) Model of the Applicant Attraction Process

In this author's opinion, Rynes and Barber (1990) have provided the most insightful discussion of the factors that influence the recruitment-related decisions made by organizations. Drawing on research from several disciplines, these authors developed a model of the "applicant attraction process" used by employers. In particular, Rynes and Barber discuss three strategies that an employer can adopt for doing a better job of attracting job candidates. One strategy is to alter the way it recruits. For example, an organization may change the type of people it uses as recruiters, it may modify the nature of its recruitment communications, and/or it may try to be more timely in its recruitment efforts. Improving employment inducements is a second strategy for improving an organization's ability to attract applicants. For example, an organization could increase the salaries it offers, begin providing child care, implement flextime, and/or redesign jobs to reduce unattractive job duties. According to Rynes and Barber, "A third way to increase the ability to attract labor is to direct recruitment efforts toward individuals who are, for one reason or another, less marketable than either traditional applicants or the applicants sought by competitors" (p. 295). In some cases, such relatively untapped segments of the labor force may be as qualified as members of traditional applicant populations. In other cases, those in a nontraditional applicant population may be less qualified but still able to adequately fill the open positions. [22,23]

According to Rynes and Barber, an employer's choice of an applicant attraction strategy is affected by such contingency variables as legal considerations, labor market conditions, job characteristics, and organizational characteristics. Since the choice of an applicant attraction strategy will affect and be affected by other human resource practices, Rynes and Barber note that, in order to understand which applicant attraction strategy an organization will adopt, these other HR practices must also be considered.

From even this cursory treatment of these three applicant attraction strategies, it should be apparent that they differ greatly. For example, Rynes and Barber suggest that, relatively speaking, making changes in recruitment practices is a relatively low-cost and low-risk strategy for an organization. However, according to these authors, the impact of such changes is also likely to be limited, especially if there is a tight labor market. In contrast to altering recruitment practices, changing the inducements it offers or the applicant population it targets are likely to have a greater impact on an employer's ability to attract applicants. However, Rynes and Barber believe these latter two strategies will also generally entail greater costs and risks. For example, improving starting salaries may have a spillover effect, such that a firm may also have to raise the salaries of current employees.

Based on their review of the literature, Rynes and Barber offer several predictions about the circumstances under which an organization is likely to use a particular applicant attraction strategy. Because they offer twenty-four propositions (hypotheses), an in-depth examination of each will not be provided. Instead, some of the more important ones for understanding how organizations decide on a recruitment strategy will be briefly discussed.

In terms of labor market conditions affecting applicant attraction strategy, Rynes and Barber predict that, all else being equal, in the initial stages of a labor shortage altering recruitment practices will be tried before turning to employee inducement or applicant population strategies because of the lower cost and risk associated with the former approach. With regard to the influence of job characteristics on the selection of a strategy, Rynes and Barber predict that, in contrast to filling lower-level jobs, in filling higher-level jobs organizations are most likely to use an inducement strategy, given the higher potential payoff from filling such jobs with the best people. Not surprisingly, these authors also predict that the more attractive the job opening, the more likely an organization is to present realistic information in its recruitment communications. In terms of organizational characteristics, Rynes and Barber predict that "organizations that have a low ability to pay are more likely to (or may be forced to) seek nontraditional applicants or applicants with lower productivity signalling characteristics" (p. 299).

Rynes and Barber also offer several propositions concerning the interrelationships among the three applicant attraction strategies. For example, they predict that "Decisions to target nontraditional applicants will be accompanied by shifts in recruitment sources. In particular, walk-ins and employee referrals are less likely to be used because these sources are most likely to produce applicants who are similar to current employees" (pp. 301–302). In attempting to attract nontraditional applicants, Rynes and Barber also predict that employers will use recruiters who are demographically similar to those in the targeted groups and will change their recruitment messages such that they emphasize inducements that are likely to be valued by the new targeted audience.

In concluding this discussion of Rynes and Barber's article, it should be emphasized that these authors acknowledge the speculative nature of many of their predictions and that they stress the need for research on many of the hypotheses they offer. Nevertheless, Rynes and Barber have provided a framework for better understanding why organizations may adopt the applicant attraction strategy they do.[24]

UNDERSTANDING THE RECRUITMENT PROCESS: SUGGESTIONS FOR FUTURE RESEARCH

Throughout this text, the importance of the employee recruitment process has been emphasized.[25] It has also been noted that during the past decade the amount of research on recruitment-related topics has increased dramatically. In this section, a few suggestions for designing future research studies will be offered. However, before making these recommendations, a brief statement about the current state of recruitment research is helpful.

To date, the majority of recruitment studies can be classified as being investigations of recruiter effects, recruitment method effects, or realistic job preview effects (Rynes, 1991). Typically, studies of recruiter effects have asked college students for their reactions to recruiters immediately after completing a campus interview. Studies that have focused on the effects of recruitment methods or RJPs generally have used a sample of recently hired workers and have examined such dependent variables as job satisfaction and turnover rate. In all three types of studies, dependent measures are generally assessed at one point in time and attitudes and perceptions are measured by questionnaires.

Although the types of studies described above have contributed to our understanding of the recruitment process, our ability to generalize from these types of studies is clearly limited. For example, in terms of recruiter effects, researchers have not looked at the differences between using executives and nonexecutives. In terms of recruitment methods, most studies have focused on employment agencies, walk-ins, and newspaper advertisements while ignoring other recruitment methods such as job posting systems. Rather than belabor the deficiencies of past recruitment studies, it seems safe to conclude that in the future researchers must be both more creative and more rigorous in the recruitment research they conduct.[26] Although there are an almost endless number of recommendations for improving research that could be offered, in this section only a few general themes will be emphasized.

The first recommendation is that researchers begin to view recruitment as a process rather than as a series of independent events. Although researchers have generally treated such recruitment events as the choice of recruiters and the decision to provide an RJP as though they were unrelated, organizational reports of their recruitment decisions suggest that events are interrelated. For example, a company that is having trouble staffing positions may decide to target new applicant populations, to use new recruitment methods, to be more timely in responding to job applications, and to provide realistic job information during the recruitment process (so that those who are hired are likely to remain). In this author's opinion, if we are to begin to appreciate the complexity of the recruitment process, researchers must begin to consider the interaction among the various activities that compromise recruitment. In order to investigate the recruitment process, we will therefore have to gather data over time and look at the interrelationships among various aspects of the recruitment process.

If one accepts the recommendation that we need to view recruitment as a process, this leads to the observation that we need to assess a greater range of viewpoints in order to better understand this process. Too often, researchers have felt comfortable simply using job applicants or newly hired employees as their data source. Rather than relying on one or two vantage points, researchers need to consider gathering data from a variety of viewpoints. For example, job advertisements placed in newspapers or magazines are one of the most common recruitment methods. In trying to understand the effects of a job advertisement, a researcher would clearly be interested in the perspective of an individual who responds to the ad. However, what about the viewpoint of a person who is looking for a job, reads the job advertisement, but does not respond? What about the perspective of job incumbents who read the advertisement and feel it distorts what the job entails, or the perspective of the advertising firm account executive who wrote the job notice? If the company is a government contractor, should it be concerned about how its compliance officer perceives the advertisement? By assessing the different reactions that people with different perspectives may have, researchers should gain new insight into what goes on during recruitment.

A third recommendation is that in the future researchers conduct more basic research on the applicant decision-making process and on the decision process of managers who make recruitment decisions. For example, Rynes, Bretz, and Gerhart (1991) suggest that job applicants interpret certain things that occur during the recruitment process as signals of unknown job and organizational characteristics. We need to know more about this hypothesized signalling process (e.g., what type of information is likely to be viewed as a signal by recruits?). In trying to understand how job candidates make job-choice decisions, a researcher is likely to find both relevant theory and empirical findings in behavioral decision theory research, cognitive psychology research, social psychology research, and the marketing research literature. For example, the marketing literature is filled with studies that have addressed how to design an advertisement to attract attention, facilitate recall, and motivate action. Although this research literature generally has dealt with advertisements for consumer goods rather than job opportunities, many of the findings are likely to generalize to a job advertising context. By keeping abreast of these and other research literatures, an investigator may also discover methodological innovations that are useful for studying the job candidate decision-making process.

In order to improve our understanding of the recruitment process, basic research on how managers with recruitment responsibilities make decisions is also important. For example, why do some organizations adhere to a promotion-from-within philosophy while others readily hire from outside? Why do some organizations make extensive use of internships while others do not? Although Rynes and Barber (1990) have provided several testable propositions concerning why organizations make certain recruitment decisions, to date, little empirical research has been conducted. In fact, recruitment managers are rarely asked to explain why they make the decisions they do.

In order to investigate how job candidates and recruitment managers make decisions, it is unlikely that researchers will be able to rely as heavily on questionnaires as they have in the past. Instead, it is likely that they will need to make greater use of diaries, interviews, and other data-gathering tools such as process tracing. In terms of research design, aside from the suggestions made in the preceding section on recruitment evaluation, it is important that researchers make greater use of experiments. For example, laboratory experiments could be used for investigating some of the basic information processing issues discussed in Chapter 4 (such as what makes information distinctive). Field experiments could be used for such things as investigating the effects of different types of job advertisements. For example, an organization could experiment with different types of ads (for example, blind ads versus ones in which the organization is identified) or different placements (the sports section versus the classifieds). In conducting such experiments, it is important that the research investigate why the independent variable had the effect it did.

In summary, although the number of recruitment studies has increased dramatically in the past few years, we still know relatively little about the employee recruitment process. In designing new studies, researchers face both the challenge and the opportunity of contributing to our understanding of this important human resource function.

SUMMARY

In order to intelligently plan how it will recruit in the future, an organization needs to be able to evaluate the results of its past recruitment activities. In this chapter, considerable attention was given to the evaluation of recruitment activities. In addition to several key design issues, including having a comparison group and clearly specifying the objective of the evaluation effort, the importance of a computerized recruitment information record-keeping system was addressed.

Although an evaluation of one's own organization's recruitment activities is important for making future recruitment decisions, a recruitment manager can also learn from the experiences of other organizations. Therefore, in this chapter considerable attention was given to the results of a very important study by Rynes, Bretz, and Gerhart (1991) and to the need for future recruitment research.

However, this chapter was not totally dedicated to research-related issues. Two pragmatic issues—managing a site visit and recruiting nontraditional employees—were also addressed in some detail.

CONCLUDING REMARKS

To quote Schneider (1987), "The people make the place." So how can an organization recruit the type of people it wants as employees? From the material presented in this text, the reader should appreciate the complexity of this question. And, if experts are correct in their predictions, it will become increasingly difficult to fill job openings with qualified individuals.

In writing this text, I have tried to provide the reader with a realistic view of the employee recruitment process. In order to understand the recruitment process, one needs to understand the job candidate's perspective (anxiety over finding a job, uncertainty about what a position entails, inaccurate job expectations, limitations on his or her information processing abilities, an unwillingness to be totally honest for fear of alienating a prospective employer) and the organization's perspective (worry about losing good candidates if it is totally honest, a limited budget for filling jobs, job candidates who make unreasonable demands, constraints that other HR functions place on the way employees can be recruited). One also has to be aware of government constraints (fair employment practice statues, affirmative action regulations). In addressing various recruitment topics, considerable academic research has been discussed and numerous practitioner reports of organizational successes and failures have been reported. A consistent theme of this text has been the need for an organization to be proactive, that is, to be constantly looking for new ways in which it can improve its recruitment operations.

In concluding this text, it is appropriate to return to the definition of recruitment that was offered in Chapter 1: "Recruitment involves those organizational activities that (1) influence the number and/or types of applicants who apply for a position, and/or (2) affect whether a job offer is accepted." From the material covered in this text, it is clear that we know a good deal about how to recruit effectively. It is also clear that there is much we do not know. Given this crucial need for research, this text not only stressed what we know about how to recruit employees, it also emphasized the research process by which we can increase our knowledge.

NOTES

1. This fact should not be surprising. Most of the articles that appear in practitioner-oriented publications are written by company representatives or are based on interviews with these individuals. In most cases, these individuals have a vested interested in making both their organizations and themselves look good.

2. Rynes, Bretz, and Gerhart (1991) provide an excellent review of the academic literature that has questioned the importance of such recruitment variables as the type of recruiter, the timing of recruitment actions, and the importance of the recruitment message.

3. Johns (1991) has provided an excellent analysis of how researchers have frequently inadequately tested the phenomenon in which they were interested. One of the issues on which Johns focuses considerable attention is insufficient variability (e.g., due to technological constraints, poor sampling) in the variable being investigated.

4. Rynes, Bretz, and Gerhart (1991) note that one of the reasons they focused heavily on person–job fit was because it had been their experience and the experience of two placement officials involved in this study that both recruiters and applicants regularly "mentioned the importance of 'fit' in their decisions."

5. Because of the complexity of the Rynes et al. (1991) study, only a few of their major findings are reviewed in this section. To really appreciate the significance of this study, readers should refer to their paper.

6. On average, the participants in the Rynes et al. study attended eighteen campus interviews, had seven site visits, and received three job offers.

7. With the exception of studies by Rynes, Bretz, and Gerhart (1991) and Taylor and Bergmann (1987), to date, little empirical research has addressed how the site visit can influence the perceptions held by recruits. Readers who are interested in practitioner-oriented articles that have addressed the topic of managing the site visit should refer to Byham (1990), Camuso (1984), Pitts and Swails (1982), and Reynes (1989).

8. As was discussed in Chapter 4, an individual may pursue a job that he or she is unlikely to get if it is seen as particularly attractive. Alternatively, a person with few job opportunities may pursue a job in which most people would not be interested.

9. Readers who are interested in more information concerning Days Inn's recruitment of senior citizens should refer to an article by Koch (1989b). Days Inn has also started a program that targets the homeless for recruitment (see Halcrow, 1989b). Although this program is small, relatively new, and has required some special considerations such as arranging housing, an indication of Days Inn's satisfaction with its recruitment of homeless individuals is that it plans to substantially increase its hiring of homeless persons in the near future.

10. Readers who are interested in a thorough discussion of the use of computers for human resource information purposes are referred to Kavanagh, Geutal, and Tannenbaum

(1990). Readers who are interested in specific information concerning computerized recruitment information systems (such as the advantages of using personal computers versus a mainframe computer and software packages that are available) should refer to recent issues of *Personnel, Human Resource Magazine, Personnel Journal,* and *Recruitment Today.*

11. Much of the material presented in this section on a computerized applicant tracking system is garnered from an article by Witkin (1988). Readers who are interested in more information on such topics as the various uses of an ATS and important factors to consider in purchasing or designing an ATS are encouraged to refer to Witkin's article.

12. Only 21 percent of the companies contacted by Rynes and Boudreau (1986) responded to their survey. Those companies that did respond did a larger volume of business than the average *Fortune* 1000 company. As noted by Rynes and Boudreau, it is possible that these larger organizations were more likely to respond to the survey because they were more likely to keep the information that was requested. In other words, responding to the survey was a less burdensome task because these larger companies were more conscientious in evaluating their recruitment programs. Another reason to suspect that the data reported by the companies in Rynes and Boudreau's sample may exaggerate the extent to which the evaluation of recruitment activities actually takes place is that the data were all self-report and could not be verified by other means.

13. For more information on Mattel Toys, the reader should refer to an article by Edwards (1986). For more information on Lockheed, the reader should refer to Chapter 9 of Heneman, Schwab, Fossum, and Dyer (1989).

14. Readers who are interested in more information on research design issues and statistical analysis procedures relevant to the evaluation of recruitment activities are referred to Cook and Campbell (1979), Schmitt and Klimoski (1991), and Trochim (1984). Readers who are interested in information on how to estimate the cost and the financial payoff of different recruitment approaches should refer to Boudreau and Rynes (1985).

15. Readers who are interested in information regarding the philosophy of science as it relates to research design and inferences of causality should refer to Runkel and McGrath (1972) and Cook and Campbell (1979).

16. For example, Dennis (1985) describes the inappropriateness of an organization evaluating a recruiter's performance simply in terms of the number of positions he or she has filled. Instead, Dennis suggests that an organization needs to consider the relative difficulty of the jobs that have been filled. Dennis provides a "position point factor analysis" system that he believes takes into consideration the relative difficulty of filling different types of positions. Among the factors his system considers are was the job advertised, does it require relocation, how quickly did it need to be filled, and how high a level position is it.

17. Harris and Fink (1991) have discussed some of the ways that extraneous variables can affect the evaluation of a recruiter.

18. Although this strategy is not without its drawbacks, one way around the issue of having to determine the best time to measure a criterion is to measure at several points in time.

19. For the most part, the research designs discussed in this section have been simplistic. In reality, an organization may want to use a more complex design. For example, it may make sense to measure different dependent variables at different times. Similarly, although the examples in this section only dealt with examining the effects of one "causal" recruitment variable at a time, in general an evaluation study should investigate possible interactions among causal variables. For example, by looking at the interaction between the

content of a recruitment message, the message source, and the timing of the message, an organization might discover that the best combination is a realistic message provided by a job incumbent prior to a job offer being accepted.

20. For more information on Hardee's, see Wagel (1989). For more information on Merck, see Lawrence (1989).

21. More recently, Sonnenfeld and Peiperl (1988) have offered a four-cell typology ("academies," "clubs," "baseball teams," and "fortresses") for discussing staffing policies within organizations. Their article addresses the "supply flow" (i.e., the degree to which an organization staffs itself from external sources) and the "assignment flow" (i.e., the criteria by which assignments and promotion decisions are made) of personnel. According to Sonnenfeld and Peiperl, their typology "reflects, in a human resources context, the different choices firms make in managing their overall strategy" (p. 588). Although this article emphasizes issues related to understanding career-oriented issues in organizations (e.g., executive tenure, training), it also has relevance for the area of employee recruitment.

22. In discussing applicant attraction strategies, Rynes and Barber (1990) make a distinction between attraction and recruitment. These authors see recruitment as only one of three major approaches an organization can use for attracting applicants. This author agrees with Rynes and Barber that recruitment per se and attraction are not synonymous. For example, although an organization may decide to make a job more attractive (e.g., improve the starting salary) so that it can recruit better employees, most researchers would agree with Rynes and Barber that such actions fall outside the typical definition of recruitment. However, many experts would disagree with Rynes and Barber's decision to treat the selection of an applicant population as not being a recruitment decision.

23. Rynes and Barber (1990) do an excellent job of specifying the boundaries of their treatment of the applicant attraction process. For example, they make clear that their paper only applies to the attraction of external job applicants and that it does not address ways in which an organization can deal with labor shortages other than through applicant attraction (e.g., automation). They also clearly state the assumptions on which their treatment of applicant attraction strategies is based. For example, they assume that most organizations (1) are interested in filling vacancies with at least minimally qualified people at minimum cost, (2) are concerned with filling jobs as opposed to hiring for a career, and (3) tend to rely on the methods they have used in the past for attracting candidates unless these methods are no longer working. Rynes and Barber also make clear that their model of applicant attraction is descriptive rather than prescriptive.

24. In a recent book chapter, Rynes (1989) provides additional information on how attributes of the job to be filled and labor market conditions can influence the way in which an organization recruits. For example, Rynes hypotheses that when applicants are scarce organizations are more likely to use more expensive recruitment methods, lower job specifications, recruit earlier, and give more attention to the selection and training of recruiters.

25. Many of the ideas in this section have been drawn from the seminal writings of Alison Barber, John Boudreau, Adriene Colella, Mike Harris, Judy Olian, Gary Powell, Sara Rynes, Don Schwab, Susan Taylor, John Wanous, and other researchers.

26. Obviously, many of the issues (e.g., comparison groups, longitudinal data gathering) discussed in the preceding section on the evaluation of a recruitment program are also relevant to the design of future studies. The suggestions offered in the preceding section will not be reiterated in discussing future research.

References

ABELSON, R. P. 1988. "Conviction." *American Psychologist* 43, pp. 267–275.

ACUFF, H. A. 1982. "Improving the Employment Function." *Personnel Journal* 61, pp. 407–408.

ALDERFER, C. P., and C. G. MCCORD. 1970. "Personal and Situational Factors in the Recruitment Interview." *Journal of Applied Psychology* 54, pp. 377–385.

Amos v. Corporation of Presiding Bishop, Church of Jesus Christ of the Latter-Day Saints, 483 U.S. 327, 44 FEP 20 (1987).

ANSBERRY, C., and A. SWASY. 1989. "Minority Job Applicants Say Slurs Often Surface." *Wall Street Journal* (February 10), p. B1.

ARVEY, R. D., and R. H. FALEY. 1988. *Fairness in Selecting Employees*, Reading, MA: Addison-Wesley.

ARVEY, R. D., M. GORDON, D. MASSENGILL, and S. MUSSIO. 1975. "Differential Dropout Rates of Minorities and Majority Candidates Due to 'Time Lags' Between Selection Procedures." *Personnel Psychology* 28, pp. 175–180.

ASSOCIATED PRESS 1989. "Pepsi Quiz Had Atlantans Burning." *St. Louis Post-Dispatch* (November 25), p. C14.

BACAS, V. 1988. "Desperately Seeking Workers." *Nation's Business* (February), pp. 16–17, 20–23.

BALDUS, D. C., and J. W. COLE. 1980. *Statistical Proof of Discrimination.* Colorado Springs, CO: Shepard's/McGraw-Hill.

———. 1987. *Statistical Proof of Discrimination: Cumulative Supplement.* Colorado Springs, CO: Shepard's/McGraw-Hill.

BAMBERGER, W. 1983. "Understanding and Applying Demographic Information and Techniques." *Personnel Journal* 62 (January), pp. 65–70.

BANDURA, A. 1986. *Social Foundations of Thought and Action.* Englewood Cliffs, NJ: Prentice-Hall.

Banks v. Heun-Norwood, 566 F.2d 1023, 15 FEP 1571 (8th Cir., 1977).

BARGERSTOCK, A. S. 1989a. "Establish a Direct Mail Recruitment Campaign." *Recruitment Today* 3 (Summer), pp. 52–55.

BARGERSTOCK, A. S. 1989b. "Recruitment Options That Work." *Personnel Administrator* 34 (March), pp. 53–55.

BARNES, D. W., and J. W. CONLEY. 1986. *Statistical Evidence in Litigation.* Boston: Little, Brown and Company.

BARRON, J., and D. W. GILLEY. 1979. "The Effect of Unemployment Insurance on the Search Process." *Industrial and Labor Relations Review* 32, pp. 363–366.

BARRON, J. and W. MELLOW. 1981. "Changes in Labor Force Status Among the Unemployed." *Journal of Human Resources* 16, pp. 427–441.

BAZERMAN, M. H. 1990. *Managerial Decision Making.* New York: John Wiley and Sons.

BEACH, L. R., and T. R. MITCHELL. 1978. "A Contingency Model for the Selection of Decision Strategies." *Academy of Management Review* 3, pp. 439–449.

BEER, M., B. SPECTOR, P. R. LAWRENCE, D. Q. MILLS, and R. E. WALTON. 1985. *Human Resource Management: A General Manager's Perspective.* New York: The Free Press.

BELT, J. A., and J. G. PAOLILLO. 1982. "The Influence of Corporate Image and Specificity of Candidate Qualifications on Response to Recruitment Advertisement." *Journal of Management* 8, pp. 105–112.

BENNETT, A. 1989a. "Aetna Schools New Hires in Basic Skills." *Wall Street Journal* (June 10), p. B1.

———. 1989b. "Company School." *Wall Street Journal* (May 8), p. A1.

———. 1990. "Caught in the Middle." *Wall Street Journal* (April 18), p. R9.

BERGMANN, T., and M. S. TAYLOR. 1984. "College Recruitment: What Attracts Students to Organizations." *Personnel* (May–June), pp. 34–46.

BERGER, L. 1989. "What Applicants Should Be Told." *Recruitment Today* 2, pp. 14–19.

BILLINGS, R. S., and S. MARCUS. 1983. "Compensatory and Noncompensatory Models of Decision Behavior." *Organizational Behavior and Human Performance* 31, pp. 331–352.

BLOCKLYN, P. L. 1988. "Employer Recruitment Practices." *Personnel* 65 (May), pp. 63–65.

Bonilla v. Oakland Scavenger Co., 697 F.2d 1297, 30 FEP 225 and FEP 50 (9th Cir., 1982).

BOUDREAU, J. W., and S. L. RYNES. 1985. "Role of Recruitment in Staffing Utility Analysis." *Journal of Applied Psychology* 70, pp. 354–366.

BOUDREAU, J. W., and S. L. RYNES. 1987. "Giving It the Old College Try." *Personnel Administrator* 32 (March), pp. 78–85.

BOWES, L. 1987. *No One Need Apply*. Boston, MA: Harvard Business School Press.

BRADFORD, H., and T. SMART. 1988. "Business Becomes an Enforcer." *Business Week* (May 16), pp. 36–37.

BRAHAM, J. 1988. "Hiring Mr. Wrong." *Industry Week* (March 7), pp. 31–34.

BREAUGH, J. A. 1981. "Relationships Between Recruiting Sources and Employee Performance, Absenteeism, and Work Attitudes." *Academy of Management Journal* 24, pp. 142–147.

———. 1983. "Realistic Job Previews: A Critical Appraisal and Future Research Directions." *Academy of Management Review* 8, pp. 612–619.

———. 1990. "Realistic Job Previews." In J. J. Jones, B. Steffy, and D. Bray, eds. *Applying Psychology in Business*. Lexington, MA: Lexington Books.

BREAUGH, J. A., and R. S. BILLINGS. 1988. "The Realistic Job Preview: Five Key Elements and Their Importance for Research and Practice." *Journal of Business and Psychology* 2, pp. 291–305.

BREAUGH, J. A., and R. B. MANN. 1984. "Recruiting Source Effects: A Test of Two Alternative Explanations." *Journal of Occupational Psychology* 57, pp. 261–267.

BUREAU OF NATIONAL AFFAIRS. 1984. *Bulletin to Management* (July 19), p. 3.

———. 1988. "Recruiting and Selection Procedures." *Personnel Policies Forum*, Survey No. 146 (May). Washington, D.C.

BUSS, D. D. 1985. "Job Tryouts Without Pay Get More Testing in U.S. Auto Plants." *Wall Street Journal* (January 10), p. 29.

BUSSEY, J. 1987. "Dow Chemical Tries to Shed Tough Image and Court the Public." *Wall Street Journal* (November 20), pp. 1, 17.

BUTLER, J., G. FERRIS, and N. NAPIER. 1991. *Strategy and Human Resource Management*. Cincinnati: Southwestern.

BYHAM, W. C. 1990. "Keeping Job Candidates from Becoming Lost Hires." *HR Magazine* (December), pp. 52–54.

BYRNE, J. A. 1989. "The New Headhunters." *Business Week* (February 6), pp. 64–71.

CALDWELL, D. F., and W. A. SPIVEY. 1983. "The Relationship Between Recruiting Source and Employee Success: An Analysis by Race." *Personnel Psychology* 36, pp. 67–72.

CAMPBELL, J. P., M. D. DUNNETTE, E. E. LAWLER, and K. E. WEICK. 1970. *Managerial Behavior, Performance, and Effectiveness.* New York: McGraw-Hill.

CAMPBELL, R. J. 1968. "Career Development: The Young Business Manager." Paper presented at the 76th Annual Meeting of the American Psychological Association, San Francisco.

CAMUSO, M. A. 1984. "The Recruitment Trip: Before, During, and After." *Personnel Journal* 63, pp. 66–72.

CARROLL, P. B. 1982. "Changes at the CIA: What Once Was Censored Is Now Suggested." *Wall Street Journal* (April 2), p. 25.

CASCIO, W. F. 1991. *Costing Human Resources: The Financial Impact of Behavior in Organizations,* 3rd ed. Boston: PWS-KENT Publishing Company.

CASCIO, W. F., and N. F. PHILLIPS. 1979. "Performance Testing: A Rose Among the Thorns." *Personnel Psychology* 32, pp. 751–766.

Catlett v. Mo Highway & Transportation Department, 45 FEP 1627 (8th Cir., 1987).

CHATMAN, J. A. 1989. "Improving Interactional Organizational Research: A Model of Person–Organization Fit." *Academy of Management Review* 14, pp. 333–349.

CHAURAN, T. 1988. "A Point-of-Purchase Program with Punch." *Recruitment Today* 1 (November–December), pp. 56–59.

———. 1989a. "Get High Mileage from Your Advertising Dollar." *Recruitment Today* 2 (February–March), pp. 48–51.

———. 1989b. "Prime Time for Televised Recruitment." *Recruitment Today* 2 (May–June), pp. 53–54.

———. 1989c. "The Nightmare of Negligent Hiring." *Recruitment Today* 2 (February–March), pp. 33–37.

———. 1989d. "Taking Texas on the Road." *Recruitment Today* 2 (May–June), pp. 48–53.

COHEN, L. P. 1988. "Use of Legal Temps Is on Rise but Practice Faces Bar Challenges." *Wall Street Journal* (May 12), p. 25.

COLARELLI, S. M. 1984. "Methods of Communication and Mediating Processes in Realistic Job Previews." *Journal of Applied Psychology* 69, pp. 633–642.

CONNOLLY, W. 1986. "How to Navigate the River of Legal Liability when Hiring." *Personnel Journal* 65 (March), pp. 32–42.

COOK, T. D., and D. T. CAMPBELL. 1979. *Quasi-Experimentation: Design and Analysis Issues for Field Studies.* Chicago: Rand-McNally Publishing.

CRONIN, R. J. 1981. "Executive Recruiters: Are They Necessary?" *Personnel Administrator* 26 (February), pp. 31–34.

CURLEY, J. 1987. "General Dynamics." *St. Louis Post-Dispatch* (November 29), pp. D1, D6.

DAWES, R. M. 1988. *Rational Choice in an Uncertain World.* San Diego: Harcourt Brace Jovanovich.

DAWIS, R. V., and L. H. LOFQUIST. 1984. *A Psychological Theory of Work Adjustment*. Minneapolis: University of Minnesota Press.

DEAN, R. A., K. R. FERRIS, and C. KONSTANS. 1985. "Reality Shock: Reducing the Organizational Commitment of Professionals." *Personnel Administrator* 30 (June), pp. 139–148.

DEAN, R. A., and J. P. WANOUS. 1984. "The Effects of Realistic Job Previews on Hiring Bank Tellers." *Journal of Applied Psychology* 69, pp. 61–68.

DECKER, P. J., and E. T. CORNELIUS. 1979. "A Note on Recruiting Sources and Job Survival Rates." *Journal of Applied Psychology* 64, pp. 463–464.

DENNIS, D. L. 1984. "Are Recruitment Efforts Designed to Fail?" *Personnel Journal* 63 (September), pp. 60–67.

―――. 1985. "Evaluating Corporate Recruitment Efforts." *Personnel Administrator* 30 (January), pp. 21–26.

DESSLER, G. 1991. *Personnel/Human Resource Management*. Englewood Cliffs, NJ: Prentice-Hall.

DILLA, B. L. 1987. "Descriptive versus Prescriptive Information in a Realistic Job Preview." *Journal of Vocational Behavior* 30, pp. 33–48.

DOWNS, C. W. 1969. "Perceptions of the Selection Interview." *Personnel Administration* 32, pp. 8–23.

DOWNS, S., R. M. FARR, and L. COLBECK. 1978. "Self-Appraisal: A Convergence of Selection and Guidance." *Journal of Occupational Psychology* 51, pp. 271–278.

DUNHAM, R. B., and J. L. PIERCE. 1989. *Management*. Glenview, IL: Scott, Foresman, and Company.

DUNNETTE, M. D. 1976, 1991. *Handbook of Industrial and Organizational Psychology*. Chicago: Rand-McNally.

DUNNETTE, M. D., R. D. ARVEY, and P. A. BANAS. 1973. "Why Do They Leave?" *Personnel* 50 (May–June), pp. 25–39.

DYER, L. D. 1973. "Job Search Success of Middle-Aged Managers and Engineers." *Industrial and Labor Relations Review* 26, pp. 969–979.

DZUBOW, S. R. 1985. "Entering the Job Market." *Journal of College Placement* (Spring), pp. 49–54.

EDWARDS, C. 1986. "Aggressive Recruitment: The Lessons of High-Tech Hiring." *Personnel Journal* 65 (January), pp. 40–48.

ELLIS, R. A., and M. S. TAYLOR. 1983. "Role of Self-Esteem Within the Job Search Process." *Journal of Applied Psychology* 68, pp. 632–640.

EEOC v. Detroit Edison Co., 515 F.2d 301, 10 FEP 239 (6th Cir., 1975).

EEOC v. New York Times Broadcasting Service Inc., 542 F.2d 356, 13 FEP 813 (6th Cir., 1976).

FALVEY, J. 1987. "Best Corporate Culture Is a Melting Pot." *Wall Street Journal* (April 16), p. 18.

FARISH, P. 1989. "Recruitment Sources." In W. F. Cascio, ed. *Human Resource Planning, Employment and Placement.* Washington, D.C.: Bureau of National Affairs.

FEINSTEIN, S. 1987a. "The Checkoff." *Wall Street Journal* (June 9), p. 1.

———. 1987b. "Employee Leasing." *Wall Street Journal* (November 3), p. 1.

———. 1988. "Labor Letter." *Wall Street Journal* (February 16), p. 1.

———. 1989a. "Recruiting 101: Companies Alienate Students They Try to Hire." *Wall Street Journal* (July 18), p. A1.

———. 1989b. "Being the Best." *Wall Street Journal* (October 10), p. A1.

FELDMAN, D. 1976. "A Contingency Theory of Socialization." *Administrative Science Quarterly* 21, pp. 433–452.

———. 1981. "The Multiple Socialization of Organization Members." *Academy of Management Review* 6, pp. 309–318.

FELDMAN, D. C., and H. J. ARNOLD. 1978. "Position Choice: Comparing the Importance of Organizational and Job Factors." *Journal of Applied Psychology* 63, pp. 706–710.

FISHER, C. D., D. R. ILGEN, and W. D. HOYER. 1979. "Source Credibility, Information Favorability, and Job Offer Acceptance." *Academy of Management Journal* 22, pp. 94–103.

FISCHOFF, B., P. SLOVIC, and S. LICHTENSTEIN. 1980. "Knowing What You Want: Measuring Labile Values." In T. Wallsten, ed. *Cognitive Processes in Choice and Decision Behavior,* pp. 117–141. Hillsdale, NJ: Erlbaum.

FISHMAN, A. 1987. "Are Your Employment Ads Misleading?" *St. Louis Post-Dispatch* (May 11), p. B3.

FLETCHER, C. 1989. "Impression Management in the Selection Interview." In R. A. Giacolone and P. Rosenfeld, eds. *Impression Management in the Organization,* Hillsdale, NJ: Erlbaum.

FOMBRUM, C. J., N. M. TICHY, and M. A. DEVANNA. 1984. *Strategic Human Resource Management.* New York: John Wiley & Sons, Inc.

FRIEDMAN, S. D. 1986. "Succession Systems in Large Corporations." *Human Resource Management* 25, pp. 191–213.

FRITZ, N. R. 1988. "New Older Workers." *Personnel* 65 (July), pp. 8–12.

GANNON, M. J. 1971. "Source of Referral and Employee Turnover." *Journal of Applied Psychology* 55, pp. 226–228.

GARBETT, T. 1988. *How to Build a Corporation's Identity and Project Its Image.* Lexington, MA: Lexington Books.

GATEWOOD, R. S., and H. S. FEILD. 1990. *Human Resource Selection.* Chicago: Dryden.

Gavagan v. Danbury Civil Service Commission, 32 EDP 33, 674 (D. Conn., 1983).

GELLER, L. 1990/91. "Evaluating a Publication for Your Recruitment Advertising." *Recruitment Today* 3, Sourcebook, pp. 6–10.

GERSON, H. E., and L. P. BRITT.1984. "Hiring: The Danger of Promising Too Much." *Personnel Administrator* 29 (March), pp. 5–8.

GEYELIN, M., and W. GREEN. 1990. "Companies Must Disclose Shaky Finances to Some Applicants." *Wall Street Journal* (April 20), p. B8.

GILMORE, D. C., and G. R. FERRIS. 1986. "The Recruitment Interview." In K. Rowland and G. Ferris, eds. *Current Issues in Personnel Management.* Boston: Allyn and Bacon, Inc.

GLOVER, J., and R. KING. 1989. "Traps for the Unwary Employer." *Personnel Administrator* 34 (July), pp. 52–54.

GOMERSALL, E. R., and M. S. MYERS. 1966. "Breakthrough in On-the-Job Training." *Harvard Business Review* (July–August), pp. 62–72.

GREENHAUS, J. H. 1987. *Career Management.* Chicago: Dryden Press.

GREENHAUS, J. H., C. SEIDEL, and M. MARINIS. 1983. "The Impact of Expectations and Values on Job Attitudes." *Organizational Behavior and Human Performance* 31, pp. 394–417.

GREER, C. 1984. "Countercyclical Hiring as a Staffing Strategy for Managerial and Professional Personnel: Some Considerations and Some Issues." *Academy of Management Review* 9, pp. 324–330.

GREER, C., and Y. STEDHAM. 1989. "Countercyclical Hiring as a Staffing Strategy for Managerial and Professional Personnel: An Empirical Investigation." *Journal of Management* 15, pp. 425–440.

Griggs v. Duke Power Co., 401 U.S. 424 (1971).

GUPTA, U. and J. A. TANNENBAUM. 1989. "Labor Shortages Force Changes at Small Firms." *Wall Street Journal* (May 22), pp. D2–D3.

HALCROW, A. 1986. "Anatomy of a Recruitment Ad." *Personnel Journal* 65 (August), p. 65.

———. 1988. "Employees Are Your Best Recruiters." *Personnel Journal* 67 (November), pp. 42–49.

———. 1989a. "You're in Good Hands with Direct Mail." *Recruitment Today* 2 (February–March), pp. 21–23.

———. 1989b. "Days Inn Reserves a Spot for the Homeless." *Recruitment Today* 2 (May–June), pp. 19–21.

HALL, D. T. 1976. *Careers in Organizations.* Pacific Palisades, CA: Goodyear Publishing Company.

———. 1986. "Dilemmas in Linking Succession Planning to Individual Executive Learning." *Human Resource Management* 25, pp. 235–265.

HARKINS, S. G., and R. E. PETTY.1981. "The Multiple Source Effect in Persuasion." *Personality and Social Psychological Bulletin* 7, pp. 627–635.

HARLAN, C. 1988. "Why Were the Lawyers Nodding When They Started Reading This?" *Wall Street Journal* (October 17), p. B1.

HARN, T. J., and G. C. THORNTON. 1985. "Recruiter Counselling and Applicant Impressions." *Journal of Occupational Psychology* 58, pp. 57–65.

HARPER, D. C. 1988. "An Rx for the RN Shortage." *Recruitment Today* 1 (November–December), pp. 18–26.

Harper v. Trans World Air Lines, Inc., 525 F.2d 409, 11 FEP 1074 (8th Cir., 1975).

HARRIS, D. H. 1968. "The Assimilation of Recent College Graduates into Engineering Organizations." Technical Report T8–1276/501, Autonetics Division of North American Rockwell Corp., Anaheim, CA.

HARRIS, M. M., and L. S. FINK. 1987. "A Field Study of Applicant Reactions to Employment Opportunities: Does the Recruiter Make a Difference?" *Personnel Psychology* 40, pp. 765–784.

———. 1991. "Identifying Successful Recruiters." In J. J. Jones, B. D. Steffy, and D. W. Bray, eds. *Applying Psychology in Business*. Lexington, MA: Lexington Books.

HARTZELL, B. 1989. "A Dream Job or a Bad Ad?" *Recruitment Today* 1 (May–June), p. 7.

HAWK, R. H. 1967. *The Recruitment Function*. New York: American Management Association.

Hazelwood School District v. United States, 433 U.S. 299, 15 FEP 1 (1977).

HENEMAN, H. G., D. P. SCHWAB, J. A. FOSSUM, and L. D. DYER. 1989. *Personnel/ Human Resource Management*. Homewood, IL: Richard D. Irwin, Inc.

HERRIOT, P. 1984. *Down from the Ivory Tower: Graduates and Their Jobs*. Chichester, England: John Wiley & Sons.

HILL, R. E. 1970. "A New Look at Employee Referrals." *Personnel Journal* 49, pp. 144–148.

HIRSH, J. S. 1989. "Scrambling to the Forefront: Companies Try Bolder Tactics to Win MBAs." *Wall Street Journal* (November 29), p. B1.

HODES, B. S. 1983a. "Planning for Recruitment Advertising: Part I." *Personnel Journal* 62, pp. 380–384.

———. 1983b. "Planning for Recruitment Advertising: Part II." *Personnel Journal* 62 (June), pp. 492–501.

HOGAN, R., R. RASKIN, and D. FAZZINI. 1990. "The Dark Side of Charisma." In K. E. Clark and M. B. Clark, eds. *Measures of Leadership*. West Orange, NJ: Leadership Library of America.

HOGARTH, R. 1987. *Judgement and Choice*. Chichester, England: John Wiley & Sons.

HOUGH, L. M. 1984. "Development and Evaluation of the 'Accomplishment Record' Method of Selecting and Promoting Professionals." *Journal of Applied Psychology* 69, pp. 135–146.

HOUGH, S. M., and G. H. VARMA. 1981. "Teaming Up for Recruiter Training." *Journal of College Placement* (Fall), pp. 40–42.

HUGHES, J. F. 1988. "What Employment Managers Must Know." *Recruitment Today* 1 (August), pp. 6–12.

IVANCEVICH, J. M., and J. H. DONNELLY. 1971. "Job Offer Acceptance Behavior and Reinforcement." *Journal of Applied Psychology* 55, pp. 119–122.

JABLIN, F. M. 1987. "Organizational Entry, Assimilation, and Exit." In F. M. Jablin, L. L. Putnam, K. H. Roberts, and L. W. Porter, eds. *Handbook of Organizational Communication.* Newbury Park, CA: Sage Publications.

JABLIN, F. M., L. L. PUTNAM, K. H. ROBERTS, and L. W. PORTER. 1987. *Handbook of Organizational Communication.* Newbury Park, CA: Sage Publications.

JACK, R. 1989. "Lauriat Wins with Bookmark Campaign." *Recruitment Today* 2 (Summer), pp. 57–59.

JAMES, L. A., and L. R. JAMES. 1989. "Integrating Work Environment Perceptions: Explorations into the Measurement of Meaning." *Journal of Applied Psychology* 74, pp. 739–751.

JEFFERSON, D. J. 1989. "Boeing, Facing Delays in 747 Deliveries, Turns to Lockheed for Loan of Workers." *Wall Street Journal* (March 8), p. A3.

JOHN, D. G. 1987. "Staffing with Temporary Help." *Personnel Administrator* 32 (January), pp. 96–99.

JOHNS, G. 1991. "Substantive and Methodological Constraints on Behavior and Attitudes in Organizational Research." *Organizational Behavior and Human Decision Processes* 49, pp. 80–104.

Jones v. Avis Rent-a-Car (Ind. D.C., 1981).

JURGENSEN, C. 1978. "Job Preference (What Makes a Job Good or Bad?)." *Journal of Applied Psychology* 63, pp. 267–276.

KAHNEMAN, D., and A. TVERSKY. 1979. "Prospect Theory: An Analysis of Decision Under Risk." *Econometrica* 47, pp. 263–291.

KANFER, R., and C. L. HULIN. 1985. "Individual Differences in Successful Job Searches Following Lay-Off." *Personnel Psychology* 38, pp. 835–847.

KAVANAGH, M. J., H. G. GEUTAL, and S. I. TANNENBAUM. 1990. *Human Resource Information Systems.* Boston: PWS-KENT Publishing.

KENNEY, R. M. 1982. "Open House Complements Recruitment Strategies." *Personnel Administrator* 27 (March), pp. 27–32.

KIDDER, T. 1981. *The Soul of a New Machine.* New York: Little, Brown and Company.

KILMANN, R. H., M. J. SAXTON, and R. SERPA. 1985. *Gaining Control of Corporate Culture.* San Francisco: Jossey-Bass.

KIRNAN, J. P., J. A. FARLEY, and K. F. GEISINGER. 1989. "The Relationship Between Recruiting Source, Applicant Quality, and Hire Performance: An Analysis by Sex, Ethnicity, and Age." *Personnel Psychology* 42, pp. 293–308.

KLEIMAN, L. S., and K. J. CLARK. 1984. "An Effective Job Posting System." *Personnel Journal* 63, pp. 20–25.

KLEINFELD, N. R. 1989. "Working the Floor at a Job Fair." *New York Times* (May 18), sec. 3, pp. 1, 6, 7.

KOCH, J. 1989a. "Applicants Tune in to Radio." *Recruitment Today* 2 (Fall), pp. 7–11.

———. 1989b. "Prime Time Redefined at Days Inn." *Recruitment Today* 2 (Fall), pp. 36–38.

———. 1990a. "Open Houses: TV Ads Tell the Story." *Recruitment Today* 3 (Winter), pp. 6–15.

———. 1990b. "Strong Medicine for Health Care Recruiters." *Recruitment Today* 3 (Spring), pp. 18–28.

———. 1990c. "Why Video?" *Recruitment Today* 3 (Spring), pp. 30–34.

———. 1990d. "Beyond Nuts and Bolts." *Personnel Journal* 64 (February), pp. 70–77.

———. 1990e. "Carl's Jr. Orders Tabletop Ads." *Recruitment Today* 3 (Winter), pp. 38–39.

———. 1990f. "Desktop Recruiting." *Recruitment Today* 3 (Winter), pp. 32–37.

———. 1990g. "Finding Qualified Hispanic Candidates." *Recruitment Today* 3 (Spring), p. 35.

KOHL, J. P., and D. B. STEPHENS. 1989. "Wanted: Recruitment Advertising That Doesn't Discriminate." *Personnel* (February), pp. 18–26.

KOTTER, J. P. 1973. "The Psychological Contract: Managing the Joining-Up Process." *California Management Review* 15, pp. 91–99.

———. 1988. *The Leadership Factor*. New York: The Free Press.

KOTTER, J. P., V. P. FAUX, and C. C. MCARTHUR. 1978. *Self-Assessment and Career Development*. Englewood Cliffs, NJ: Prentice-Hall, Inc.

KRETT, K., and J. F. STRIGHT. 1985. "Using Market Research as a Recruitment Strategy." *Personnel* 62 (November), pp. 32–36.

LAABS, J. L. 1990a. "Pizza Hut's New Labor Pool." *Recruitment Today* 3 (Summer), p. 41.

———. 1990b. "Brochures Say It All." *Recruitment Today* 3 (Summer), pp. 24–29.

———. 1990c. "The Captive Audience Advantage." *Recruitment Today* 3 (Summer), pp. 18–22.

———. 1990d. "The Pizza Party Incentive." *Recruitment Today* 3 (Summer), pp. 48–49.

————. 1990e. "Booth Design Enhances Image." *Recruitment Today* 3 (Fall), pp. 6–10.

————. 1990f. "$100 for Showing Up." *Recruitment Today* 3 (Fall), pp. 11–14.

————. 1991a. "Dangers of a Hard Sell." *Recruitment Today* 4 (January–February), pp. 18–21.

————. 1991b. "Tailor-Made Recruitment Brochures." *Recruitment Today* 4 (January–February), pp. 5–8.

————. 1991c. "Is Breakfast Your Best Bet?" *Recruitment Today* 4 (January–February), pp. 9–11.

————. 1991d. "A Prize Referral Program." *Personnel Journal* 70 (May), pp. 95–97.

————. 1991e. "Job Fair Freebies." *Recruitment Today* 4 (January–February), pp. 24–26.

————. 1991f. "Affirmative Outreach." *Personnel Journal* 70 (May), pp. 86–93.

————. 1991g. "The Golden Arches Provide Golden Opportunities." *Personnel Journal* 70 (July), pp. 52–56.

LACY, W. B., J. L. BOKEMEIER, and J. M. SHEPARD. 1983. "Job Attribute Preferences and Work Commitment of Men and Women in the United States." *Personnel Psychology* 36, pp. 315–329.

LAWRENCE, P. R., and D. DYER. 1983. *Renewing American Industry*. New York: Free Press.

LAWRENCE, S. 1988. "College Recruitment: The Best Get the Brightest." *Recruitment Today* 1 (August), pp. 33–40.

————. 1989. "Voices of HR Experience." *Personnel Journal* 68 (April), pp. 64–75.

LEDVINKA, J., and V. G. SCARPELLO. 1991. *Federal Regulation of Personnel and Human Resource Management*. Boston: PWS-KENT Publishing.

LEE, T. 1989. "After Shaky Start, Computerized Search Services Gain Popularity as They Sweep College Campuses." *National Business Employment Weekly* (Winter/Spring), pp. 19–20.

LEHOCKY, G. J. 1984. "University Relations: An Aid to Recruiting." *Journal of College Placement* (Winter), pp. 28–32.

LEIBOWITZ, Z. B., C. FARREN, and B. L. KAYE. 1986. *Designing Career Development Systems*. San Francisco: Jossey-Bass.

LEVERING, R. A., M. MOSKOWITZ, and M. KATZ. 1984. *The 100 Best Companies to Work for in America*. Reading, MA: Addison-Wesley.

LEVINE, E. L. 1983. *Everything You Always Wanted to Know About Job Analysis*. Tampa, FL: Mariner.

LEWIS, C. 1985. *Employee Selection*. London: Hutchinson Publishing Group.

LIDEN, R. C., and C. K. PARSONS. 1986. "A Field Study of Job Applicant Interview

Perceptions, Alternative Opportunities, and Demographic Characteristics." *Personnel Psychology* 39, pp. 109–122.

LINDQUEST, V. R. 1985. "Northwestern Endicott Report." Evanston, IL: The Placement Center, Northwestern University.

LOCKE, E. A. 1976. "The Nature and Causes of Job Satisfaction." In M. D. Dunnette, ed. *Handbook of Industrial and Organizational Psychology.* Chicago: Rand-McNally.

LONDON, M., and S. A. STUMPF. 1982. *Managing Careers.* Reading, MA: Addison-Wesley Publishing.

LORD, J. S. 1989. "External and Internal Recruitment." In W. F. Cascio, ed. *Human Resource Planning, Employment and Placement.* Washington, D.C.: Bureau of National Affairs, Inc.

LORD, R. G., and K. J. MAHER. 1990. "Alternative Information-Processing Models and Their Implications for Theory, Research, and Practice." *Academy of Management Review* 15, pp. 9–28.

LOUIS, M. R. 1980. "Surprise and Sense Making: What Newcomers Experience in Entering Unfamiliar Organizational Environments." *Administrative Science Quarterly* 25, pp. 226–251.

LUBBOCK, J. E. 1983. "A Look at Centralized College Recruiting." *Personnel Administrator* 28 (April), pp. 81–84.

LUBLINER, M. J. 1981. "Developing Recruiting Literature that Pays Off." *Personnel Administrator* 26 (February), pp. 51–54.

LUCK, B. 1986. "How Industrial Recruiters Sell Themselves Short." *Wall Street Journal* (September 26), p. 22.

MACAN, T. H., and R. L. DIPBOYE. 1990. "The Relationship of Interviewers' Preinterview Impressions to Selection and Recruitment Outcomes." *Personnel Psychology* 43, pp. 745–768.

MAGNUS, M. 1982. "Recruitment and Job Search: The Recruitment Tactics of Employers." *Personnel Administrator* 27, (June), pp. 96–104.

———. 1985. "Recruitment Ads at Work." *Personnel Journal* 64 (August), pp. 42–63.

———. 1987. "Is Your Recruitment All It Can Be?" *Personnel Journal* 66 (February), pp. 54–63.

———. 1988. "TV Channels Recruitment Efforts." *Recruitment Today* 1 (August), pp. 56–57.

MARCH, J. G., and H. A. SIMON. 1958. *Organizations.* New York: John Wiley & Sons.

MARTIN, B. 1971. "Employment Advertising: Hard Sell, Soft Sell, or What?" *Personnel* (May–June), pp. 33–40.

———. 1987. "Recruitment Ad Ventures." *Personnel Journal* 66 (August), pp. 46–63.

MASON, N. A., and J. A. BELT. 1986. "Effectiveness of Specificity in Recruitment Advertising." *Journal of Management* 12, pp. 425–432.

MCCARTHY, A. H. 1989. "Research Provides Advertising Focus." *Personnel Journal* 68 (August), pp. 82–87.

MCCARTHY, M. J. 1988a. "Employee Leasing Lives, Despite Predictions." *Wall Street Journal* (June 1), p. 27.

———. 1988b. "Managers Face Dilemma with 'Temps.'" *Wall Street Journal* (April 5), p. 33.

———. 1989. "What's More, Can You Really Call the Staten Island Ferry a Yacht?" *Wall Street Journal* (November 22), p. B1.

McDonnell-Douglas Corp. v. Green, 411 U.S. 792, 5 FEP 965 (1973).

MCEVOY, G. M., and W. C. CASCIO. 1985. "Strategies for Reducing Employee Turnover: A Meta-Analysis." *Journal of Applied Psychology* 70, pp. 342–353.

McLaughlin v. Great Lakes Dredge & Dock Co., 23 FEP 1292 (N.D. Ohio, 1980).

MEGLINO, B. M., A. S. DENISI, S. A. YOUNGBLOOD, and K. J. WILLIAMS. 1988. "Effects of Realistic Job Previews: A Comparison of Using an 'Enhancement' and a 'Reduction' Preview." *Journal of Applied Psychology* 73, pp. 259–266.

MESSMER, M. 1990. "Corporate Accountant for the Day (or Week)." *Recruitment Today* 3 (Summer), pp. 36–40.

MILES, R., and C. SNOW. 1978. *Organizational Strategy, Structure, and Process.* New York: McGraw-Hill.

MILKOVICH, G. T., and J. W. BOUDREAU. 1991. *Human Resource Management.* Homewood, IL: Irwin.

MILLER, V. D., and F. M. JABLIN. 1991. "Information Seeking During Organizational Entry: Influences, Tactics, and a Model of the Process." *Academy of Management Review* 16, pp. 92–120.

MINER, M. G. 1979. *Recruiting Policies and Practices.* Washington, D.C.: Bureau of National Affairs.

MOBLEY, W. 1982. *Employee Turnover: Causes, Consequences, and Control.* Reading, MA: Addison-Wesley.

MONDY, R., M. NOE, and R. EDWARDS. 1987. "Successful Recruitment: Matching Sources and Methods." *Personnel* 64 (September), pp. 42–46.

MORAVEC, M. 1990. "How to Avoid Poaching While Hunting for Recruits." *Wall Street Journal* (October 22), p. A14.

NADLER, D. A., J. R. HACKMAN, and E. E. LAWLER. 1979. *Managing Organizational Behavior.* Boston: Little, Brown & Company.

NATIONAL RESEARCH COUNCIL. 1989. *Fairness in Employment Testing.* Washington, D.C.: National Academy Press.

NYE, D. 1988. *Alternative Staffing Strategies.* Washington, D.C.: Bureau of National Affairs.

O'BRIEN, J. 1990. "Tactics for Tapping Trade Group Networks." *National Business Employment Weekly* (Fall), p. 30.

OLIAN, J., and S. L. RYNES. 1984. "Organizational Staffing: Integrating Practice with Strategy." *Industrial Relations* 23, pp. 170–183.

PALKOWITZ, E. S., and M. M. MUELLER. 1987. "Agencies Foresee Change in Advertising's Future." *Personnel Journal* 66 (May), pp. 124–126.

PASCALE, R. 1984. "Fitting New Employees into the Company Culture." *Fortune* (May 28), pp. 24–40.

PAYNE, J. W. 1976. "Task Complexity and Contingent Processing in Decision Making: An Information Search and Protocol Analysis." *Organizational Behavior and Human Performance* 16, pp. 366–387.

Personnel Administrator. 1985. "Record-Keeping and Reporting Requirements." Vol. 30 (December), pp. 84–98.

PETERS, J. 1989. "How to Bridge the Hiring Gap." *Personnel Administrator* 34 (October), pp. 76–85.

PETERSON, D. J., and D. MASSENGILL. 1988. "Childcare Programs Benefit Employers, Too." *Personnel* 65 (May), pp. 58–62.

PETTY, R. E., and J. T. CACIOPPO. 1986. "The Elaboration Likelihood Model of Persuasion." In L. Berkowitz, ed. *Advances in Experimental Social Psychology* 19, pp. 123–205.

PHILLIPS, J. J. 1987. *Recruiting, Training, and Retaining New Employees.* San Francisco: Jossey-Bass Publishers.

PINDER, C. C. 1984. *Work Motivation.* Glenview, IL: Scott, Foresman and Company.

PITTS, R. A. and R. B. SWAILS. 1982. "College Recruiting: After the Campus Interview." *Journal of College Placement* (Summer), pp. 50–53.

POPOVICH, P., and J. P. WANOUS. 1982. "The Realistic Job Preview as a Persuasive Communication." *Academy of Management Review* 7, pp. 570–578.

PORTER, L. W., E. E. LAWLER, and J. R. HACKMAN. 1975. *Behavior in Organizations.* New York: McGraw-Hill.

POWELL, G. N. 1984. "Effects of Job Attributes and Recruiting Practices on Applicant Decisions: A Comparison." *Personnel Psychology* 37, pp. 721–732.

———. 1991. "Applicant Reactions to the Initial Employment Interview: Exploring Theoretical and Methodological Issues." *Personnel Psychology* 44, pp. 67–83.

POWER, D. J., and R. J. ALDAG. 1985. "Soelberg's Job Search and Choice Model: A Clarification, Review, and Critique." *Academy of Management Review* 10, pp. 48–58.

PREMACK, S. L., and J. P. WANOUS. 1985. "A Meta-Analysis of Realistic Job Preview Experiments." *Journal of Applied Psychology* 70, pp. 706–719.

QUAGLIERI, P. L. 1982. "A Note on Variations in Recruiting Information Obtained

Through Different Sources." *Journal of Occupational Psychology* 55, pp. 53–55.

RAWLINSON, H. 1988a. "Scholarships Recruit Future Employees Now." *Recruitment Today* 1 (August), pp. 14–22.

RAY, M. E. 1971. *Recruitment Advertising*. London: Business Books Limited.

REIBSTEIN, L. 1985. "More Companies Use Free-Lancers to Avoid Cost, Trauma of Layoffs." *Wall Street Journal* (April 18), p. B1.

———. 1987. "Crushed Hopes: When a New Job Proves to Be Something Different." *Wall Street Journal* (June 10), p. 25.

REILLY, R. R., B. BROWN, M. BLOOD, and C. MALETESTA. 1981. "The Effects of Realistic Job Previews: A Study and Discussion of the Literature." *Personnel Psychology* 34, pp. 823–834.

REYNES, T. 1989. "Romancing the Candidate." *Recruitment Today* 3 (Fall), pp. 20–21.

REYNOLDS, L. G. 1951. *The Structure of Labor Markets*. New York: Harper and Brothers.

ROTHWELL, W. J., and H. C. KAZANAS. 1989. *Strategic Human Resource Development*. Englewood Cliffs, NJ: Prentice-Hall, Inc.

ROUT, L. 1979. "Going for Broker: Our Man Takes Part in a Stock Selling Test." *Wall Street Journal* (April 4), p. 1.

Rowe v. General Motors Corp., 457 F.2d 348, 4 FEP 445 (5th Cir., 1972).

RUNKEL, P., and J. MCGRATH. 1972. *Research on Human Behavior*. New York: Holt, Rhinehart and Winston.

RYNES, S. L. 1987. "Compensation Strategies for Recruitment." *Topics in Total Compensation* 2, no. 2. A panel publication.

———. 1989. "The Employment Interview as a Recruitment Device." In R. W. Eder and G. R. Ferris, eds. *The Employment Interview*. Newbury Park, CA: Sage.

———. 1991. "Recruitment, Job Choice, and Post-Hire Consequences." In M. D. Dunnette and L. M. Hough, eds. *Handbook of Industrial and Organizational Psychology*. Palo Alto, CA: Consulting Psychologists Press.

RYNES, S. L., and A. E. BARBER. 1990. "Applicant Attraction Strategies: An Organizational Perspective." *Academy of Management Review* 15, pp. 286–310.

RYNES, S. L., and J. W. BOUDREAU. 1986. "College Recruiting in Large Organizations: Practice, Evaluation, and Research Implications." *Personnel Psychology* 39, pp. 729–757.

RYNES, S. L., R. BRETZ, and B. GERHART. 1991. "The Importance of Recruitment in Job Choice: A Different Way of Looking." *Personnel Psychology* 44, pp. 487–522.

RYNES, S. L., and B. GERHART. 1990. "Interviewer Assessments of Applicant Fit." *Personnel Psychology* 43, pp. 13–35.

RYNES, S. L., and H. E. MILLER. 1983. "Recruiter and Job Influences on Candidates for Employment." *Journal of Applied Psychology* 68, pp. 147–154.

RYNES, S. L., D. P. SCHWAB, and H. HENEMAN. 1983. "The Role of Pay and Market Pay Variability in Job Application Decisions." *Organizational Behavior and Human Performance* 31, pp. 353–364.

SADDLER, J. 1988. "Mentor Programs Now Are Used to Attract Quality Young Managers." *Wall Street Journal* (February 23), p. 1.

SCARPELLO, V. G., and J. LEDVINKA. 1988. *Personnel/Human Resource Management*. Boston: PWS-KENT Publishing Company.

SCHEIN, E. H. 1964. "How to Break in the College Graduate." *Harvard Business Review* 42, pp. 68–76.

———. 1968. "Organizational Socialization and the Profession of Management." *Industrial Management Review* 9, pp. 1–16.

———. 1971. "The Individual, the Organization, and the Career: A Conceptual Scheme." *Journal of Applied Behavioral Science* 7, pp. 401–426.

———. 1978. *Career Dynamics: Matching Individual and Organizational Needs*. Reading, MA: Addison-Wesley.

SCHLEI, B. L., and P. GROSSMAN. 1983. *Employment Discrimination Law*. Washington, D.C.: The Bureau of National Affairs.

———. 1987. *Employment Discrimination Law: 1983–1985 Cumulative Supplement*. Washington, D.C.: The Bureau of National Affairs.

———. 1989. *Employment Discrimination Law: Five-Year Cumulative Supplement*. Washington, D.C.: The Bureau of National Affairs.

SCHMITT, N., and B. W. COYLE. 1976. "Applicant Decisions in the Employment Interview." *Journal of Applied Psychology* 61, pp. 184–192.

SCHMITT, N., and R. J. KLIMOSKI. 1991. *Research Methods in Human Resource Management*. Cincinnati: Southwestern Publishing.

SCHMITT, N., and C. OSTROFF. 1986. "Operationalizing the 'Behavioral Consistency' Approach: Selection Test Development Based on a Content-Oriented Strategy." *Personnel Psychology* 39, pp. 91–108.

SCHNAPP, R. H. 1989. "Differentiate Between Employees or Independent Contractors?" *Recruitment Today* 2 (Fall), pp. 25–27.

SCHNEIDER, B. 1987. "The People Make the Place." *Personnel Psychology* 40, pp. 437–453.

SCHULER, R. S. 1990. "Repositioning the Human Resource Function: Transformation or Demise?" *Academy of Management Executive* 4, pp. 49–60.

SCHULER, R. S., and S. E. JACKSON 1987. "Linking Competitive Strategies with Human Resource Management Practices." *Academy of Management Executive* 1, pp. 207–220.

SCHWAB, D. P. 1982. "Recruiting and Organizational Participation." In K. Rowland and G. Ferris, eds. *Personnel Management*. Boston: Allyn and Bacon.

SCHWAB, D. P., S. L. RYNES, and R. J. ALDAG. 1987. "Theories and Research on Job Search and Choice." In K. M. Rowland and G. R. Ferris, eds. *Research in Personnel and Human Resource Management*, 5th ed. Greenwich, CT: JAI Press.

Sheet Metal Workers Local 28 v. EEOC, 478 U.S. 421, 41 FEP 107 (1986).

SHEIBAR, P. 1979. "A Simple Selection System Called 'Jobmatch'." *Personnel Journal* 58, pp. 26–29.

SICONOLFI, M. 1990. "At Dean Witter, Complaints Grow over Sears Work." *Wall Street Journal* (April 17), p. C1.

SIMON, H. A. 1957. *Administrative Behavior*. New York: The Free Press.

SOELBERG, P. O. 1967. "Unprogrammed Decision Making." *Industrial Management Review* 8, pp. 19–29.

SONNENFELD, J. A., and M. A. PEIPERL. 1988. "Staffing Policy as a Strategic Response: A Typology of Career Systems." *Academy of Management Review*, 13, pp. 588–600.

SONNENFELD, J. A., M. A. PEIPERL, and J. P. KOTTER. 1988. "Strategic Determinants of Managerial Labor Markets: A Career Systems View." *Human Resource Management* 27, pp. 369–388.

SOVEREIGN, K. L. 1984. *Personnel Law*. Reston, VA: Reston Publishing Co.

———. 1988. *Personnel Law*, 2d ed. Reston, VA: Reston Publishing Co.

SPECTOR, B. A., and M. BEER. 1982. "Note on Job Posting." Harvard Business School Case 9-482-104.

STANTIAL, L., and ASSOCIATES. 1979. "Recruitment Literature: Is It Adequate?" *Journal of College Placement* (Summer), pp. 56–60.

STOOPS, R. F. 1983. "Managing Recruitment Costs." *Personnel Journal* 62, pp. 612–613.

———. 1984. "Direct Mail: Luring the Isolated Professionals." *Personnel Journal* 63 (June), pp. 34–36.

STUMPF, S. A., E. J. AUSTIN, and K. HARTMAN. 1984. "The Impact of Career Exploration and Interview Readiness on Interview Performance and Outcomes." *Journal of Vocational Behavior* 24, pp. 221–235.

STUMPF, S. A., and K. HARTMAN. 1984 ."Individual Exploration to Organizational Commitment or Withdrawal." *Academy of Management Journal* 27, pp. 308–329.

SUPER, D. 1957. *The Psychology of Careers*. New York: Harper & Row.

SUSZKO, M. K., and J. A. BREAUGH. 1986. "The Effects of Realistic Job Previews on Applicant Self-Selection and Employee Turnover, Satisfaction, and Coping Ability." *Journal of Management* 12, pp. 513–523.

SWAROFF, P. G., L. A. BARCLAY, and A. R. BASS. 1985. "Recruiting Sources: Another Look." *Journal of Applied Psychology* 70, pp. 720–728.

TANNENBAUM, J. A. 1988. "Firms Try Busing to Ease Labor Shortage." *Wall Street Journal* (December 30), p. B2.

TAYLOR, M. S. 1988. "Effects of College Internships on Individual Participants." *Journal of Applied Psychology* 73, pp. 393–401.

TAYLOR, M. S., and T. J. BERGMANN. 1987. "Organizational Recruitment Activities and Applicants' Reactions at Different Stages of the Recruitment Process." *Personnel Psychology* 40, pp. 261–285.

TAYLOR, M. S., and D. W. SCHMIDT. 1983. "A Process-Oriented Investigation of Recruitment Source Effectiveness." *Personnel Psychology* 36, pp. 343–354.

TAYLOR, M. S., and J. A. SNIEZAK. 1984. "The College Recruitment Interview: Topical Content and Applicant Reactions." *Journal of Occupational Psychology* 57, pp. 157–168.

TAYLOR, R. N. 1984. *Behavioral Decision Making.* Glenview, IL: Scott, Foresman and Company.

Teamsters v. United States, 431 U.S. 324, 14, FEP 1514 (1977).

THRASHER, J. 1990. "Build Flexibility into the Work Force with Independent Contractors." *Recruitment Today* 3 (Spring), pp. 36–39.

THUROW, L. 1975. *Generating Inequality.* New York: Basic Books.

TOM, V. R. 1971. "The Role of Personality and Organizational Images in the Recruiting Process." *Organizational Behavior and Human Performance* 6, pp. 573–592.

TROCHIM, W. K. 1984. *Research Design for Program Evaluation.* Beverly Hills, CA: Sage Publishing.

TROST, C. 1987a. "Labor Letter." *Wall Street Journal* (January 27), p. 1.

———. 1987b. "Best Employers for Women and Parents." *Wall Street Journal* (November 30), p. B1.

TULL, D. S., and L. R. KAHLE. 1990. *Marketing Management.* New York: Macmillan Publishing Company.

TVERSKY, A. 1969. "Intransitivity of Preferences." *Psychological Review* 76, pp. 31–48.

———. 1972. "Elimination by Aspects: A Theory of Choice." *Psychological Review* 79, pp. 281–299.

TWOMEY, D. P. 1990. *A Concise Guide to Employment Law.* Cincinnati: South-Western Publishing.

ULLMAN, J. C. 1966. "Employee Referrals: Prime Tool for Recruiting Workers." *Personnel* 43, pp. 30–35.

UNGERSON, B. 1983. *Recruitment Handbook.* Aldershot, England: Gower Publishing Company.

Uniform Guidelines on Employee Selection Procedures. 1978. 29 CFR 1607.2(c).

United Steelworkers v. Weber, 443 U.S. 193, 20 FEP 1 (1979).

VANDENBERG, R. J., and V. SCARPELLO. 1990. "The Matching Model: An Examination of the Processes Underlying Realistic Job Previews." *Journal of Applied Psychology* 75, pp. 60–67.

VANMALDEGIAM, N. E. 1988. "Executive Pursuit." *Personnel Administrator* 33 (September), pp. 95–97.

VON WERSSOWETZ, R. O., and M. BEER. 1982. "Human Resources at Hewlett-Packard." Harvard Business School Case 9-482-125.

WAGEL, W. H. 1989. "Hardee's: One Step Ahead in the Race for Employees." *Personnel* 66, pp. 20–24.

WALLRAPP, G. G. 1981. "Job Posting for Nonexempt Employees: A Sample Program." *Personnel Journal* 60, pp. 796–798.

WALSH, J., M. JOHNSON, and M. SUGARMAN. 1975. *Help-Wanted: Case Studies of Classified Ads*. Salt Lake City: Olympus Publishing Co.

WALTERS, R. W. 1985. "It's Time We Become Pros." *Journal of College Placement* (Summer), pp. 30–33.

WANOUS, J. P. 1977. "Organizational Entry: Newcomers Moving from Outside to Inside." *Psychological Bulletin*, 84, pp. 601–618.

———. 1978. "Realistic Job Previews: Can a Procedure to Reduce Turnover Also Influence the Relationship Between Abilities and Performance?" *Personnel Psychology* 31, pp. 249–258.

———. 1980. *Organizational Entry: Recruitment, Selection, and Socialization of Newcomers*. Reading, MA: Addison-Wesley.

———. 1989. "Installing a Realistic Job Preview: Ten Tough Choices." *Personnel Psychology* 42, pp. 117–133.

WANOUS, J. P., and A. COLELLA. 1989. "Organizational Entry Research: Current Status and Future Research Directions." In K. Rowland and G. Ferris, eds. *Research in Personnel and Human Resources*. Greenwich, CT: JAI Press.

WANOUS, J. P., T. L. KEON, and J. C. LATACK. 1983. "Expectancy Theory and Occupational/Organizational Choices: A Review and Test." *Organizational Behavior and Human Performance* 32, pp. 66–86.

Wards Cove Packing v. Atonio, U.S. 190, S.Ct. 3115 (1989).

WEIN, J. L. 1990. "The Right Way to Read a Resume." *Recruitment Today* 3 (Spring), pp. 8–10.

WEINSTRAUB, D. K., and C. CHRISTMAN. 1988. "Choose the Best Booth Location." *Recruitment Today* 1 (November–December), pp. 47–51.

———. 1989. "Booth Location Affects Performance." *Recruitment Today* 2 (February–March), pp. 14–19.

WEITZ, J. 1956. "Job Expectancy and Survival." *Journal of Applied Psychology* 40, pp. 245–247.

WILLIS, R. 1990. "Recruitment: Playing the Database Game." *Personnel* 67 (May), pp. 25–29.

WILKINS, C. 1988. "Back to the Library." *National Business Employment Weekly* (Fall), pp. 30–31, 48.

WITKIN, E. 1988. "Track Applicants, Not Paperwork." *Recruitment Today* 1 (November–December), pp. 28–41.

WOOLFE, J. 1990. "How Well Do You Fit in?" *National Business Employment Weekly* (Spring), pp. 18–19.

Wygant v. Jackson Board of Education, 476 U.S. 267, 40 FEP 1321 (1986).

WYSE, R. E. 1972. "Attitudes of Selected Black and White College Business Administration Seniors Toward Recruiters and the Recruitment Process." Ph.D. dissertation. Columbus, OH: Ohio State University. *Dissertation Abstracts* 33, 1269–1270A.

YOUNGBERG, C. F. 1963. "An Experimental Study of Job Satisfaction and Turnover in Relation to Job Expectations and Self-Expectations." Unpublished doctoral dissertation. New York: New York University.

ZEDECK, S. 1977. "An Information Processing Model and Approach to the Study of Motivation." *Organizational Behavior and Human Performance* 18, pp. 47–77.

ZEITZ, B., and L. DUSKY. 1988. *The Best Companies for Women.* New York: Simon and Schuster.

Name Index

Subject Index